# Marketization in Local Government

"During the past forty years, Public Administration has been colored by marketization. It is doubtful if any other reform strategy has been of greater importance. Marketization has been loved and hated during the aforementioned forty years. Many have changed their mind about marketization—in both ways. This book explains how marketing has been handled and changed in different countries over time. Anyone who wants to understand the branding has the benefit of this book."

—Rolf Solli, *Professor of Management, University of Gothenburg, Sweden*

"This book presents a welcome and sobering analyses of marketization in local government in a comparative perspective. Different models of marketization in England and Scandinavia are described and analyzed and interesting similarities and differences are revealed. It gives new insights in how marketizations evolves over time in relation to different reform trajectories."

—Per Lægreid, *Professor emeritus, University of Bergen, Norway*

"This book gives a necessary and highly inspiring contribution to the international public administration literature. It provides new and important insight into the different trajectories of marketization in municipal service provision in UK and Scandinavia, of great value to both scholars, students and practitioners. The book definitely deserves a prominent place on curriculums of public administration and local government programmes!"

—Harald Torsteinsen, *Professor in Political Science, University of Tromsø—The Arctic University of Norway*

"Through in-depth studies of marketization in four countries, the authors provide important insights in how marketization has evolved, what logics that have been dominating in the different periods, and how the process has varied between countries. The book is an important read for anyone wanting a deeper understanding of how central NPM reforms are adopted, translated, and implemented in different contexts."

—Dag Ingvar Jacobsen, *Professor, University of Agder, Norway*

"This book makes a key contribution to understanding the changing forms of marketization. It provides new insights into the conditions for the diffusion of marketization reforms and offers a much-needed analysis of the implications of marketization for management, organization and governance—something that has been missing in previous research. A must-read for everybody looking for an updated account of the evolution of marketization."

—Jacob Torfing, *Professor in Politics and Institutions, Roskilde University, Denmark*

"This book offers essential reading for those involved in, or impacted by public sector reforms and marketization. Municipal green space management and other parts of the public sector have experienced major changes during recent years, and this book discusses many of the 'whys' and 'hows'. I especially appreciate its international perspective and thorough evidence base."

—Cecil Konijnendijk, *Professor of Urban Forestry, The University of British Columbia, Canada*

"This book adopts a rare approach to public administration research. Marketization is studied over thirty years in four countries and encompasses two local services. This ambitious research design allows an unusually tight grip on the research question and leads to a fascinating blend of cross-time, cross-country, cross-service and cross-municipal analyses."

—Jens Blom-Hansen, *Professor, Department of Political Science, Aarhus University, Denmark*

"This book makes a valuable contribution to our understanding of the continuing marketization of the public sector. Focusing on the Scandinavian countries and the UK, the contributors investigate the development of marketization as reform strategy and the degree to which this reform is sensitive to different national political and institutional features."

—Jon Pierre, *Professor, University of Gothenburg, Sweden*

"This book is an important step forward to extend our knowledge about the re-organisation of service delivery at the local level of government. Marketization is not only studied empirically in different fields of service provision. It is also addressed from a theoretical, conceptual and methodological perspective—a combination that has not been applied in public administration so far. By adopting a cross-countries, over time and cross-sectoral comparative perspective, the book explores the national and local contexts as well as implementation strategies and effects of marketization in Scandinavia and England. The volume is a must-read for scholars and practitioners interested in the comparative study of public sector modernization, management and local government reform."

—Sabine Kuhlmann, *Professor of Public Administration and Organization, University of Potsdam, Germany*

Andrej Christian Lindholst ·
Morten Balle Hansen
Editors

# Marketization in Local Government

## Diffusion and Evolution in Scandinavia and England

palgrave
macmillan

*Editors*
Andrej Christian Lindholst
Department of Politics and Society
Aalborg University
Aalborg, Denmark

Morten Balle Hansen
Department of Politics and Society
Aalborg University
Aalborg, Denmark

ISBN 978-3-030-32480-3 ISBN 978-3-030-32478-0 (eBook)
https://doi.org/10.1007/978-3-030-32478-0



Cover illustration: National Geographic Image Collection/Alamy Stock Photo

This Palgrave Macmillan imprint is published by the registered company Springer Nature Switzerland AG
The registered company address is: Gewerbestrasse 11, 6330 Cham, Switzerland

# Preface

This book is about the diffusion and evolution of marketization—one of the most powerful and persistent cluster of ideas and models for reform and organizational change in the public sector in the last four decades. The book provides a comparative examination of four decades of marketization within two local public services—parks and roads—across municipalities in England and the three Scandinavian countries of Sweden, Denmark and Norway. Local park and road services are of special interest for a study as they have been among the first to be marketized, are representative of a broader class of services viewed as well-suited for marketization and are a common responsibility for municipalities in most countries. In turn, the four countries represent very different contexts for marketization at the local level in terms of national policies, territorial structure and municipal size and autonomy. The comparison of developments within two services embedding comprehensive experiences with marketization across four countries representing different contexts opens up for a much needed empirically grounded outlook on our understanding of shared ideas and models of contemporary marketization.

The book is a continuation and development of work and networks established within a collaborative research project carried out in the UK and Scandinavia in the years 2014–2016. The research project had the title: *Innovations in the organization of public-private collaboration in an international perspective with focus on technical maintenance services* which was abbreviated to the handier acronym 'INOPS'.[1] The INOPS project addressed a set of questions related to change and innovation in the marketization of municipal park and road services in the UK and Scandinavia. The INOPS project was financially supported by Hedeselskabet, a large Danish commercial foundation working with environmental and green services, and Department of Political Science, Aalborg University, Denmark.

The INOPS project was led by Andrej Christian Lindholst and Morten Balle Hansen, Aalborg University, Denmark. Participating researchers were: Ylva Norén Bretzner and Johanna Selin, School of Public Administration, Gothenburg, Sweden, Bengt Persson and Thomas Barfoed Randrup, Swedish Agricultural University in Alnarp, Merethe Dotterud Leiren, Norwegian Centre for Transport Research, Ingjerd Solfjeld, Norwegian University of Life Sciences, Nicola Dempsey and Mel Burton, University of Sheffield, UK, Ole Helby Petersen, Roskilde University, Denmark and Kurt Houlberg, VIVE—The Danish Center for Social Science Research.

Without the help and contributions from a number of other people it would not have been possible to carry out the INOPS project and provide the foundation for this book. We would especially thank the public and private managers in the UK and Scandinavia that devoted some of their scarce time to participate in research interviews and surveys. We also thank colleagues that provided feedback and intellectual inspiration for our research. We are in particular grateful to our colleagues at Center for Organization, Management and Administration (COMA), Aalborg University for comments and thoughts on early ideas and works. Finally, we are thankful for the co-finance and practical support provided by Hedeselskabet including the willingness to share thoughts and insights. We are here thankful to Jesper Bavngaard, John Iskov, Søren Bo Johansen, Lisbeth Sevel and Rasmus Willumsen.

Parts of the research from the INOPS project were published in series of country-based articles under the theme 'marketization revisited' in a special issue of *International Journal of Public Sector Management* in 2016 (volume 29, issue 5). The themed issue allowed us to elaborate

[1]The original Danish title of the research project is: *'Innovationer i organiseringen af det offentlige-private samspil i et internationalt perspektiv med fokus på kommunaltekniske driftsopgaver'* with the abbreviated title *'innovationer i det offentlige private samspil'*. The Danish acronym for the title is: 'INOPS'.

individual analysis of selected aspects of marketization within each of our four countries and reflect upon the broader characteristics and diversity of marketization. In addition, the work with the themed issue inspired us to rework our materials, thinking and collaborative efforts into a more wide-ranging comparative endeavour to address the diffusion and evolution of marketization across four decades and four countries. A book format seemed suitable for such endeavour. The book was written from 2017 to 2019 in a collaborative effort between 18 contributing authors. It is our hope that the result of our endeavour, this book, will assist scholars, policymakers and public managers to renew ingrained ways of thinking about marketization in the public sector.

Aalborg, Denmark
May 2019

Andrej Christian Lindholst
Morten Balle Hansen

# Contents

# Notes on Contributors

**Ylva Norén Bretzer (Ph.D.)** is Senior Lecturer in Public Administration at School of Public Administration, University of Gothenburg, Sweden. Over the last fifteen years she has investigated relationships between citizens, institutions and policies; specifically within sectors of social insurances, energy efficiency and housing. Her work elaborates institutional trust applied to national, regional or municipal agencies. Her research includes articles in Public Administration journals including *International Journal of Public sector Management* and in Politics and Governance. Her current work focuses on trust in administrative national and local bureaucracies; the implementation of the sustainable development goals, SDGs, and sustainable institutions for urban, suburban and municipal transformations.

**Mel Burton (B.Sc., M.A.)** with degrees in Ecology and Landscape Architecture, Mel worked for many years as a Chartered Landscape Architect in public and private practice before returning to academia. She is a Senior University Teacher and Director of Learning and Teaching in the Department of Landscape leading on modules in Ecological Design and Management, Professional Practice and Landscape Planning. She combines this with research focused on embedding landscape practice in teaching, place-keeping and landscape design and management in practice.

**Nicola Dempsey (Ph.D.)** is Senior Lecturer, in the Department of Landscape Architecture at the University of Sheffield, England. Her research focuses on place-keeping which conceptualizes the design, planning and management of places as an ongoing and dynamic process. This applies to a wide range of urban contexts and Nicola's recent research focuses on identifying green space interventions to boost the health and wellbeing of urban residents. She has co-published doctoral research into the acceptability and feasibility of different landscape management practices in urban parks with Dr. Jinvo Nam. Her place-keeping research is underpinned by long-term 'post-occupancy evaluation' of everyday landscapes in our towns and cities as places change over time. Her work has been recently published in a variety of books (*Staging Urban Landscapes* and *Public Space Design and Social Cohesion*) and journals including *Sustainability*, *Landscape Research* and the *International Journal of Public Sector Management*.

**Carsten Greve (Ph.D.)** is Professor of Public Management and Governance at the Department of Organization, Copenhagen Business School. His research interests are the governance of public–private partnerships and public management reform in an international perspective. He is the author of many books and articles in these fields, including *The Logic of Public-Private Partnerships* (2019, with Graeme Hodge), *Public Governance Paradigms* (2019, with Lotte Bøgh Andersen, Jacob Torfing and Kurt Klaudi Klausen), and *Nordic Administrative Reforms* (2016, edited with Per Lægreid and Lise H. Rykkja).

**Morten Balle Hansen (Ph.D.)** is Professor in Public Policy and Management at the Centre for Organization, Management, and Administration, Department of Political Science, Aalborg University, Denmark. His work focuses on management, evaluation, administrative reform and innovation in the public sector. Since the early 1990s, he has done research in public policy and management, and combined research in managerial behaviour in public organizations with research into policy processes with particular emphasis on evaluation, performance management and innovation. His research has been published in well-established journals within the field of public administration including *American Journal of Evaluation*, *International Journal of Public Sector Management*, *International Review of the Administrative Sciences*, *Public Administration*, Public *Administration Review*, *Public Management Review*, *International Public Management Journal*, *Public Performance & Management Review* and *Scandinavian Journal of Public Administration*.

**Kurt Houlberg (Ph.D.)** is Professor (mso) in local government finance at VIVE, the Danish Center for Social Science Research. His main research fields are local government finance, local government reform, public policy, public administration and contracting out. The main research interest is the influence of scale, fiscal environment and political factors on local government policy, financial management, make-or-buy decisions and effectiveness. In recent years, a particular interest has been dedicated to studies of the economic and democratic consequences of the Danish local government reform in 2007, financial management in times of fiscal austerity and the economic effects of contracting out. His research has been published in journals such as *Public Administration Review*, *Local Government Studies*, *Scandinavian Political Studies*, *American Political Science Review*, and *American Journal of Political Science*.

**Thomas Haase Jensen (cand.scient.pol)** is a consultant at the research and insight management solutions company Epinion and a former student assistant at Department of Political Science, Aalborg University and VIVE, The Danish Center for Social Science Research. As a student assistant, his work consisted of gathering, structuring and analysing data for projects in the fields of marketization and public economics. His current work focuses primarily on evaluating the effects of public programmes, resource allocation based on socioeconomic factors and user experience research.

**Troels Høgfeldt Kjems (cand.scient.pol)** is a consultant at Rambøll Management Consulting and a former student assistant at Department of Political Science, Aalborg University. His work at Aalborg University was focused on marketization and collaboration in the Danish public sector. The work had an empirical focus, with both gathering and analysing quantitative and qualitative data. His current work consists of public policy evaluation and measuring citizen, parent and student satisfaction with government-supplied services.

**Anders Kristoffersson (Ph.D.)** is Senior Lecturer at the department of Landscape architecture, Planning and Management, Swedish University of Agricultural Sciences (SLU). He has worked with research and development projects focusing on construction and management of outdoor environment at SLU for more than 20 years. He teaches in procurement of maintenance and construction of outdoor environments. He has been responsible for projects such as innovative procurement of outdoor environments and development of new forms for follow-up and monitoring of outdoor environment maintenance contracted out or delivered in-house. His research has been published in *Environment and Planning C: Politics and Space* and *Urban Forestry & Urban Greening*.

**Julie Runde Krogstad (M.A. in Political Science)** is advisor at the transport department in Agder County and former Senior Researcher at TØI—Institute of Transport Economics, Norway. Her research at TØI addresses dilemmas related to decentralization of transport policies and discretion of sub-national authorities, marketization and agencification in public transport, multi-level governance in urban transport and political anchorage of networks. Her current work focuses primarily on transport safety, cycling and mobility.

**Merethe Dotterud Leiren (Ph.D).** is Senior Researcher and Political Scientist at CICERO—Center for International Climate Research, Norway. When she joined the INOPS project, from which this book is a result, she was Senior Researcher at the Institute of Transport Economics, Norway. She has been a Research Fellow at the Public Administration programme, University of Agder, and Guest Researcher at the Humboldt University Berlin. She is particularly interested in dilemmas related to the balance between climate/environmental policy, social policy and economic efficiency in multi-level governance systems, where regulations at one political level create new challenges at other political levels. Her publications address transport, energy and climate policies at local level (in journals like *Local Government Studies* and *Journal of Environment Planning and Management*), national level (in journals like *Energy Research & Social Science*) and the EU level (in journals like *European Journal of Political Research* and *Journal of Common Market Studies*).

**Andrej Christian Lindholst (cand.scient.adm., Ph.D.)** is Associate Professor at Centre for Organization, Management, and Administration, Department of Political Science, Aalborg University, Denmark. Over the last fifteen years he has done extensive research on the organization, management and outcomes of contracting services within park and road services in comparative and national perspectives. A subtheme in his research has addressed how ideas of quality are conceptualized and operationalized within municipal park services in Scandinavia. His research has appeared in Public Administration and Planning journals including: *Local Government Studies*, *Public Administration*, *Environment and Planning C: Politics and Space*, and *Urban Forestry & Urban Greening*. His current research focuses on organizational change and the broader impacts from the marketization of the public sector including learning effects, the role of public entrepreneurship for re-municipalizations, and the wider public support for marketization.

**Claudia Leticia Martínez Velarde (Architect, Ph.D.)** was a teaching and research associate at the Department of Landscape in the University of Sheffield, UK and is currently working in private practice. Her research has focused on the way landscape regeneration and management is made in private and public areas and the potential contribution towards social and ecological sustainability, as well as the associated meaning to users. Research projects have included medium-rise housing, with an emphasis on social housing, parks and rivers considering an international perspective from Sweden, Germany, Mexico, UK and India. Her research has been presented at conferences and seminars in UK, USA and India. Her current research includes meaning and sustainability of front gardens in low- and medium-rise housing.

**Bengt Persson (Landscape Architect, Ph.D.)** is Senior Lecturer and Extension Specialist at Department of Landscape Architecture, Planning and Management, Swedish University of Agricultural Sciences at the Alnarp campus. He works with applied R&D projects, primarily concerning management and maintenance of urban open spaces. He is author of the Swedish Maintenance Manuals (1989 and 1998), and has together with Anders Kristoffersson recently performed a study on monitoring and control of maintenance contracts. He has edited several books, among others *Sustainable City of Tomorrow* (2005) and *Western Harbour—Experiences and Lessons Learned* (2013) on Malmö's transformation from an industrial based city to a European leader in sustainable urban development.

**Ole Helby Petersen (Ph.D.)** is Professor (mso) at the Department of Social Science and Business, Roskilde University, Denmark, and Director of the Center for Research on Public-Private Collaboration. His research interests include contracting out, procurement, public–private partnerships, and free choice systems. Recent papers appear in journals such as

*Public Administration Review*, *Transport Reviews*, *Local Government Studies*, *Project Management Journal*, *Social Policy and Administration*, and *Review of Public Personnel Administration*. He is currently working on research projects on transaction costs in government contracting and the impact of centralized versus decentralized public procurement on government purchasing prices.

**Thomas Barfoed Randrup (Landscape Architect, Ph.D.)** is Professor in Urban Open Space Management at the Department of Landscape Architecture, Planning and Management, Swedish University of Agricultural Sciences. Here, he leads the Research Group on Landscape Governance & Management, while studying the processes, roles and use of urban open spaces that keep them relevant and valued. He has a special interest in the concepts of Governance, Management and Nature-based Solutions. He has published more than 350 academic publications, and has previously held full professorships at both the Norwegian University of Life Sciences and at University of Copenhagen, Denmark.

**Johanna Selin (M.Sc. of Public Administration)** is a Ph.D. candidate in public administration at the School of Public Administration, University of Gothenburg, Sweden. Her research is focused on how complex issues in society, commonly referred to as 'wicked problems', are organized within public sector organizations at the local level. From a perspective influenced by actor–network theory, her research deals with the concept of social sustainability and the process by which it is made into something manageable and governable. She is expected to present her Ph.D. thesis during the spring of 2020.

**Ingjerd Solfjeld (M.A. in horticulture and Dr. scient in plant science)** is Associate Professor and head of education in the Faculty of Landscape and Society, at the Norwegian University of Life Sciences. She is also affiliated to the Norwegian Public Roads Administration, where she worked previously on the management of vegetation along roads and streets. Her current research and teaching focus on urban green space management, and examines management and strategic planning, site and soil quality, ecosystem benefits of trees, and conservation of the urban forest. Her work is published in research—and professional reports and journals, including *International Journal of Public Sector Management*. She is committed to strengthening the knowledge-base and implementing research-based knowledge into public landscape management and governance.

# List of Figures

# List of Tables

PART I

# Questions, Theory and Methods

CHAPTER 1

# Introduction: Comparing Contemporary Marketization in the Light of the Past

*Andrej Christian Lindholst and Morten Balle Hansen*

## Revisiting Marketization in the Public Sector

The integration of a variety of market-based institutions and mechanisms in public service delivery, or what with a shorthand-term can be referred to as 'marketization', represent one of the most profound doctrines in the global reform waves reshaping the public sector since the 1980s (Christensen and Lægreid 2011; Pollitt and Bouckaert 2011). Marketization has in particular become known by a set of institutionalized arrangements or mechanisms grounded in ideas of choice and competition in combination with private sector involvement for reshaping, respectively, the demand and supply sides in public service delivery (Le Grand 2007). Well-known mechanisms include, among others, competitive tendering, contracting out, user choice and purchaser–provider models.

A. C. Lindholst (✉) · M. B. Hansen
Department of Politics and Society, Aalborg University, Aalborg, Denmark
e-mail: acl@dps.aau.dk

M. B. Hansen
e-mail: mbh@dps.aau.dk



A. C. Lindholst and M. B. Hansen (eds.),
*Marketization in Local Government*,
https://doi.org/10.1007/978-3-030-32478-0_1

The broader subject of this book is the diffusion and evolution of marketization in the public sector since the early 1980s and until the mid-2010s and its implications for management, organization and performance of public service delivery. In the book we deliver a comparative exploratory analysis of marketization based on a series of cross-sectional and longitudinal-historical analyses at the level of local governments in England and the three Scandinavian countries within park and road services—two spearhead services in marketization efforts from the late 1980s and until the mid-2010s. The book provides unique and novel insights into how key mechanisms and institutions of marketization, such as contracts and competition, have evolved and diffused within and across our four countries as well as implications for management, organization and performance in public service delivery. While the primary focus is at local government, the book adopts a multilevel strategy and integrates three perspectives on marketization as (1) a globally supported approach to governance; (2) a nationally framed reform strategy and (3) locally evolving practices of marketization characterized by learning and evolution.

With point of departure in our specific research setting, the book contributes to our understanding of the impacts on public service delivery from globally promoted ideas and models for reforms through a concerted effort to evaluate the legacy of the last four decades of marketization at the level of local governments. In perspective, the book asks us to reconsider what and how we think about marketization, as a set of ideas and models for organizing public service delivery, by illuminating how marketization has changed public service delivery ***and*** illuminating how marketization itself has been changed during its implementation.

### *First Impressions, Second Thoughts*

Our book's principal research aim is to examine whether our inherited theoretical and conceptual landscape for getting to terms with marketization fits with the contemporary use of marketization in public service delivery at the municipal level of local governments. In other words, our book questions whether we can rely safely on the conventional ideas, models, concepts and the wider understanding of marketization established in the heydays of the new public management (NPM) reform wave which introduced marketization as a reform doctrine in the 1980s and 1990s or whether we need to revise our thinking and understanding in concordance with later and more recent developments in reforms and practices.

Traditionally most of the literature on marketization situates it as an integrated part of the NPM—a marriage of several reform doctrines originating in disparate theories and ideas on how to improve the public sector (Hood 1991). We suggest that the key organizing principles in the NPM version of marketization can be characterized by a combination of moves toward, respectively, (1) a strategic focus on economic objectives (e.g. cost-reductions and cost-effectiveness), (2) structural devolution of responsibilities with emphasis on horizontal and vertical specialization within and across organizations (e.g. single-purpose organizations, internal and external contracting models such as purchaser–provider models and contracting out), and (3) market-based coordination of activities based on ideas of price-based competition and choice mechanisms (e.g. benchmarking, competitive tendering and free choice of service provider).

In a global context, the initial introduction of marketization as a reform doctrine belonged to a historical epoch where neoliberalism (and its neoconservative sibling) and its re-orientation of society toward the individual, markets, competition and private ownership, was forceful in its intellectual vitality and critique of the consensus on the importance of the welfare state and Neo-Keynesian economic policies established in Western Europe in the post WWII era. Political leaders, such as Margaret Thatcher in the UK, could lead and implement major reform agendas based on neoliberal and neoconservative thoughts with strong popular support (Evans 2013; McAllister and Studlar 1989). Given the novelty of the NPM reform agenda it was also largely unfettered from any past experience and evidence which could stain its bright promises or guide its implementation. Four decades of experience have changed this situation and provided an evidence base for systematic evaluations of the merits and perils of the NPM (Hood and Dixon 2015).

A prominent account in the academic literature on the marketization of the public sector takes point of departure in marketization as a set of uniform institutional arrangements, such as contracting out or user choice, that through successive reform waves have been disseminated in various degrees across different groups of countries—or what Pollitt and Bouckaert (2011) describes as 'houses of reform'. In this account, marketization formed a key part of the NPM reforms firstly implemented through radical and wide-ranging approaches from the early 1980s and onward in a group of early 'core' reform countries notably made up by Anglo-Saxon countries. The reforms were at this stage legitimized and pursued at the backdrop of the global economic crisis of the 1970s, increasing problems with financing and managing the expanding system of services provided by the welfare state, and emerging neoliberal critiques of the welfare state and state–society relations more generally. Following the core reform countries, marketization also became a part of public sector reforms implemented through more incremental and limited approaches within different groups of countries at the European continent.

Much has happened since the heydays of NPM and neoliberal reform politics and in a critical view it can be argued that conventional ideas and models of marketization increasingly are becoming obsolete as contemporary reform doctrines and principles for organizing public service delivery. With the diffusion and widespread use of marketization across the OECD countries since the 1980s it can be argued that contemporary issues have become less about the marketization of the public sector and more about how to make reforms within an already marketized public sector. Together with the NPM, marketization can be said to have entered an age of surprises, paradoxes, the unexpected and discontinuity (Hood and Peters 2004). With a shift in focus from marketization as a path for reform of the public sector to reform within an already marketized public sector, the idea of marketization as a reform path can be argued to have become increasingly outdated.

These first impressions could lead to the overall conclusion that the main story of marketization as a path for reform is already written and relatively little new can be added. History is merely repeating itself in countries where marketization is introduced while the merits and perils of marketization have by now been explored in leading reform countries while newer reform waves are delivering the ideas and models for reshaping the public sector.

*First* it can be argued that the conventional reform models of marketization inherent in the NPM increasingly have 'got rusty', as noted by Bel and Costas (2006), and from an evidence point of view lost their contemporary appeal for further reform and improvement of public service delivery. Notably, reviews and meta-analysis of available empirical research have questioned the potential of different models of marketization for delivering the promised economic gains over time, e.g. cost reductions (Bel et al. 2010; Hodge 2000; Petersen et al. 2018). On this backdrop, some scholars have directed research interests toward alternative organizational forms, such as municipal or inter-municipal owned corporations (MOCs), and asked whether these are better means for achieving cost-effectiveness in public service delivery under certain circumstances (Bel et al. 2018; Voorn et al. 2017). Others again, have questioned the ability of market-based solutions to deliver on the broader range of public values inherent in the provision of many public services (Bozeman 2002; Clifton et al. 2016; Lindholst et al. 2018; Marie 2016). Finally, some scholars have found that municipalities in substantial degrees take back—re-municipalize—services due to failing performance and high managerial costs of private service delivery (Warner and Hefetz 2012).

*Second*, severe austerity and economic crisis from the late 2000s and onward have called for intensification and innovation of local public sector reforms (Kuhlmann and Bouckaert 2016). In turn, it can be argued that conventional ideas and models of marketization have become incapable to deal with the contemporary policy issues due to the magnitude of financial and economic challenges in times of severe austerity. The economic challenges which have arisen in the aftermath of the international financial crisis in 2007 have urged national and local governments, even in well-developed OECD countries such as the UK, to consider and engage in outright service shedding and downsizing rather than looking into the toolbox with well-established market-based reform doctrines for (marginal) improvements in the cost-effectiveness of service delivery. Thus, though post-NPM trends were clearly on the rise before, they may have been strengthened by the financial crisis in 2007.

*Third*, it can be argued that conventional ideas and models of marketization, similar to NPM more generally, have been caught up in problems with self-inflicted coordination problems and fragmentation of service delivery systems. In particular, the devolution of responsibilities has been observed to result in 'siloization' or 'pillarization' within the public sector (Christensen and Lægreid 2011). In consequence, these coordination problems, alongside the critique of the failing performance of marketization and the rise of new policy challenges, have given impetus to the rise of a broad set of newer post-NPM reform doctrines emphasizing new integrative and hierarchical coordination mechanisms for organizing public service delivery (Klenk and Reiter 2019). The marketization agenda of the NPM in the 1980s and 1990s has here been challenged or widened at the global level by the availability of a more heterogeneous mix of arrangements for organizing the relations between the public and the private in public service delivery (Hodge et al. 2012)

*Fourth*, in extension of foregoing arguments, it can be argued that the scope of newer post-NPM reforms increasingly is well beyond the challenges of addressing and fixing problems and failures in the NPM. Reforms in the post-NPM era, such as those based on the possibilities in new information and communication technologies (ICT) (Dunleavy et al. 2006) and the reorganization and redistribution of responsibilities into cross-sectorial networks (Osborne 2006), are offering new visions and setting new directions for the future organization and development of the public sector. These reforms have, among others, brought attention to the role of social enterprises, co-production, collaboration, partnerships, governance networks and digitalization and technology in public service delivery. In consequence, marketization, and its realization in what can be viewed as 'marketized service delivery systems', has now become the target—and not a vision—for reform. The content of reform waves following the NPM reforms of the 1980s has pitched the marketization agenda against a wider set of alternatives and combinations as well as infused initial models for marketization with new transformative potentials (Christensen and Lægreid 2007).

It is an open question, however, whether newer reform ideas and content drive back, reinforce or reinvent the core institutional arrangements and mechanisms in the initial marketization agenda across different country contexts. In turn, it can be asked how 'early' marketization compares to 'contemporary' marketization. Is contemporary marketization characterized by ideas or models inherited from the core-NPM era or has marketization evolved in the era of post-NPM reforms? In a further reflection on these first impressions, it can also be argued that outright dismissal of the role and reform potential of various forms for marketization is premature and unwarranted. From the perspective of neo-institutionalist thinking in its various versions, including historical (Thelen 1999), economic (Williamson 2000) and sociological (Scott 2001), it is a premise that institutions—the building blocks of complex social systems—do not emerge 'out of the blue' as value-infused and ready-made arrangements defining available paths for purposive, meaningful and coordinated behavior: they evolve and devolve in historical and time-consuming processes, they are shaped by and shaping the particular context wherein they come into being and fade away, they form part of processes of diffusion and evolution. In other words, to grasp the merits and perils of marketization as well as the phenomenon of marketization itself it is necessary to take institutional developments into account as well as the particular historical and contextual circumstances under which marketization is shaped and is given life. Differences in institutional contexts and historical circumstances are likely to produce different implications for management, organization and performance of public service delivery. In this perspective, the diffusion and evolution of marketization can be expected to diverge rather than converge within and across different country contexts and produce a degree of uniqueness in the experiences with marketization within each country context. In this case it is of interest to address the degree in which certain country contexts represent more rewarding and fruitful experiences or represents more unproductive and futile experiences. Evidence from various service sector contexts and countries already points out that marketization—even for presumably suitable services such as garbage collection (Bel et al. 2010) or in 'vanguard' countries such as the UK (Hood and Dixon 2015)—apparently haven't 'swept the board' and resulted in a rather mixed bag of experiences as well as these experiences have produced shifts in reform content. In some instances, marketization has even been 'rolled back' due to scandals and poor experiences (Larsen and Breidahl 2015), which in turn makes a thought-provoking contrast to the initial neoliberal reform ideas about 'rolling back the state' (Hood et al. 1988). Marketization has also imposed a new set of governance challenges, needs to learn as well as potential management failures (Kettl 2010). However, still some country and service contexts—such as the service contexts examined in this book—appear to have produced highly marketized and relatively uncontested systems of service delivery through incremental historical change (Lindholst et al. 2016). In perspective, the diffusion and evolution of marketization seems to include both rougher and trickier pathways as well as smoother and more straightforward pathways for public sector reforms. In this perspective, we offer the idea that the movement toward marketization in the NPM has not necessarily been made obsolete by later reforms but also been able to revitalize itself and revise the models of marketization into a set of post-NPM models by incorporating newer reform ideas and contents. In turn, it can be asked whether the ideas and models of marketization are stable over time or whether marketization is a more dynamic phenomenon where ideas and models are altered through its implementation. To address these arguments and guide the overall perspective of the book, we first ask the following research question:

*RQ1*: Are contemporary models of marketization in local service delivery in the 2010s a) similar or dissimilar to earlier models found in the NPM reform wave from the 1980s and 1990s, and b) are marketization in local service delivery converging or diverging across national contexts?

Second, we link the descriptive comparative analysis inherent in our first research question with a discussion of likely explanatory contextual factors for any observed dynamics (or stability) and divergence (or convergence). For this purpose, we ask the following second research question:

*RQ2*: How can we understand the observed patterns of divergence and/or convergence in the historical development of marketization in local service delivery across different national contexts?

## A Comparative Approach

The phenomenon of marketization and its various mechanisms lacks no attention in the literature and a vast amount of research has been published in books and journal articles over the years. The abundance is particularly evident in the availability of published literature reviews and meta-analyses on the outcomes from marketization where private providers are involved (Boyne 1998; Hodge 2000; Hodge and Greve 2007; Lindholst 2017; Petersen et al. 2018). Still, we find a scarcity of research emphasizing comparative analysis based on systematic research designs. The comparative character of our research strategy locates and distinguishes our contributions within a handful of strategies for contextualizing the phenomenon of marketization. In the marketization literature we find four major strategies. *First*, a group of studies focuses on experiences within a single country. One example is Kettl's (1993) case-based study of experiences with the use of private markets and competition in the US. Other examples are the collection of evidence on the impact from marketization on Swedish welfare found in the anthology edited by Hartmann (2011) and Hansen's (2011) analysis of the diffusion of NPM into local governments in Denmark. *Second*, a group of studies looks beyond individual country contexts to take a global outlook on marketization, such as Simmons and Elkins' (2004) study of the diffusion of marketization across nations as part of a global neoliberal movement (see also Hansen and Lauridsen 2004). *Third*, a group of studies embeds marketization as part of more general research interests in public sector reforms. Greve (2006), for example, provides an overview of public management reform in Denmark including an assessment of the relative emphasis on marketization. Pollitt and Bouckaert's (2011) contribution is another and prominent example, where marketization is positioned as part of the historical content in public management reforms in a comparative analysis of public reforms in the OECD countries. Finally, the *fourth* group of studies connects or integrates analysis of experiences with marketization across two or more countries. One example is Greer et al.'s (2017) comparison of the different ways public employment services have been re-organized by adoption of market-based coordination mechanisms in three European countries. Another example is Alonso et al.'s (2017) study which uses statistics from several European countries for a general evaluation of whether greater private involvement has led to reduced expenditures in services provided by central governments. A key difference between these two studies is the attention to the importance of national context and extensive use of qualitative data in former while the latter calls upon quantitative data for an overall evaluation of financial performance across several countries in a highly generalized way. The empirical content and details of the four highlighted research strategies are further diversified by, for example, number and type of government or service sector(s), type of data sources and materials, and applied analytical methods. Amid the wealth of research on the phenomena of marketization, however, we find that cross-national comparative analyzes of reforms and organizational developments including marketization, at the local government level combined with attention to historical-institutional contexts are scarce. Among exceptions we find books by Wollmann and Marcou (2010) and Kuhlmann and Bouckhaert (2016) which provide comparative analysis of marketization in local governments as part of more general research interests in public sector reforms.

### *Country Context: The UK and Scandinavia*

In our book, we study the phenomena of marketization with point(s) of departure in the four-country contexts of the UK/England and the three Scandinavian countries of Sweden, Denmark and Norway. In comparison, the UK is long regarded as leader in the diffusion and evolution of public sector reforms. This role has been referred to by scholars in different ways. Barzelay (2001), for example, wrote about the UK as an international 'benchmark' in the implementation of (new) public management reforms while Hood and Dixon (2015) similarly referred to the UK as a 'vanguard' and 'poster child' for NPM. Key characteristic of the reforms in the UK are their early launch from the late 1970s and onward, a predominant emphasis on 'marketize' and 'minimize' strategies and a radical implementation within a majoritarian democratic system fueled by a strong and enduring ideological re-orientation toward neoliberalism and neo-conservatism. The Scandinavian countries, on the other hand, have often been portrayed as belonging to a group of 'later' or 'reluctant' reform countries. Key characteristics of reforms in Scandinavia and the wider Nordic context are the later pick up of reforms from the 1980s (or later) and onward, a predominant emphasis on 'modernize' strategies focused on improvement of internal bureaucratic structures and processes, an incremental and pragmatic approach to implementation within consensual democratic systems and a more modest influx of neoliberal and neoconservative thinking (Pollitt and Summa 1997; Premfors 1998). More broadly, the reforms in the Scandinavian (and the wider Nordic) country group have been viewed as embodying a Neo-Weberian State (NWS) model (Greve et al. 2016; Pollitt and Bouckaert 2011). However, most of these reform comparisons have been done at the national level and one of the contributions of this book is to examine this traditional picture at the local level in two public services where the implementation of marketization commonly is perceived as relatively straightforward.

The broader context for reform also differs substantially between the countries. The three Scandinavian countries are commonly found to belong to country groups with respectively large 'Universal' welfare states (Rothstein 1998) and a 'Northern European' organization of the local government system with higher degrees of delegation of powers and responsibilities to the local level. In contrast, the UK belongs to groups of countries with 'Liberal' welfare states and an Anglo-American local government system with less degrees of autonomy for local governments (Ladner et al. 2016; Sellers and Lidström 2007). However, the characteristics of our three Scandinavian countries also differ in important respects. The municipal structure regarding size and politico-administrative capacity differs significantly—characteristics which again differ in comparison with England. Norway, for example, has municipalities with relatively small populations on the average whereas municipalities in the UK, on average, are the largest in Europe. These broader characteristics can, as it will be later argued (see Chapter 4), be assumed to hold a bearing on the scope for marketization.

In the remainder of our book, we present the order of countries according to their size (measured by population). Placing England first in this order also emphasizes the importance of this country context as a 'benchmark' or 'trailblazer' in the last four decades of marketization and wider implementation of NPM reforms.

### *Service Context: Local Parks and Road Services as Two Spearhead Services*

Municipal park and road services are used as service context(s) for our study of marketization. In comparison, the two services can be argued to represent a 'critical' context for a study of marketization. In particular, the implementation of marketization models is commonly regarded as relatively straightforward within the two services and has been initiated at early reform stages in most countries. In the UK and Denmark, for example, parks and roads where among the first services where marketization was systematically implemented as part of national initiatives for reform of service delivery within local governments (see Chapters 5 and 7). Thus, it can be argued that the two services have been 'spearheads' in the implementation of marketization. However, selecting local park and road services as context for a study of marketization involves also a focus on some marketization models over others. User choice models, for example, have not been associated with local park and road services and can theoretically be argued to be difficult to establish. In particular, local park and road services resemble 'public goods' for which it will be difficult (or very radical) to exclude local residents or visitors to use or benefit from these services and where the use by one user to a certain extent is non-rival for the use by other users. Given these characteristics, marketization of municipal park and road services should be expected to take place on the supply (production) side rather than the demand (consumer) side (see Chapters 2 and 4).

The two services furthermore represent a group of 'core services', which are common responsibilities across most municipalities in the OECD countries (as well as outside these countries). The organization of the provision of other public services varies to a greater extent across nations. In Scandinavia, most local governments (municipalities) are multipurpose organizations with responsibility for the provision of numerous 'soft' and 'hard' services. In comparison, municipalities in the US, for example, have a more limited role in the provision of soft services. The context of park and road services makes an excellent case for global comparisons and policy learning. Organization wise and operationally, the two services are furthermore closely associated. The expertise for providing maintenance services are often organized within the same department and share physical facilities. Formal planning and regulation requirements differ, however, for the two services. Economically, park and road services take up only small part of public budgets in all four countries. However, the two services provide critical infrastructures of greater economic, social and environmental value in urban communities (see Chapter 4).

### *Data Materials*

Throughout the book, we address the scarcity of comparative research on the level of local governments by calling upon an extensive and unique comparative data material based on comparable national surveys, case studies, secondary data sources and background analysis collected and carried out in the period 2014–2019. The data materials were initially collected as part of a larger international project (INOPS) conducted in collaboration with a network of researchers from England, Sweden, Denmark and Norway. Some materials, such as national statistics, have been updated in the book. Throughout our book's 16 chapters, the data materials are utilized in a set of longitudinal and cross-sectional analyses within and across England and the three Scandinavian countries.

## Content and Outline

The book is organized into three main parts followed by one concluding chapter. All chapters are organized and written as stand-alone analyses and guided by its own research question(s). The chapters can therefore be read individually and not necessarily in the order presented in the book.

Overall, the book explores the diffusion and evolution of ideas and models of marketization and its impact on management, organization and performance. The exploration takes place within the research setting defined by four countries and two local services. Two main research questions (RQ1 and RQ2) were laid out in this chapter to guide and integrate the contributions throughout the book. Recall, that our main research interest is in how we should come to terms with ideas and models of marketization within the contemporary landscape of public service delivery in local governments.

In addition, subsets of empirical and theoretical research questions are addressed in the various chapters throughout the book by which we get the pieces to get hold of the grander puzzle in the book. Each chapter explicates and addresses these 'contributing' or 'intermediate' research questions.

### *Part I*

The first part of our book is made up of four chapters, including this introduction (this chapter). This part of our book provides a general conceptual and theoretical framework for the book, the research design including the research strategy and data materials, and a detailed overview of the four countries and two services as context for analysis. Chapter 2 revisits the ideas and models for organizing marketization and provides also a framework for understanding the diffusion and evolution of marketization. Chapter 3 presents the research design and methodological matters in terms of our comparative strategy and the key data materials underpinning analysis in the various chapters throughout the book. Chapter 4 is devoted to illuminating and comparing the characteristics of each of our four countries and our two services as context(s) included in our study. The chapter addresses a range of salient characteristics of each country and discusses the importance of these for the evolution and diffusion of marketization across the UK/England and the three Scandinavian countries of Sweden, Denmark and Norway.

### *Part II*

Part II of our book is made up of altogether six chapters. Chapters 5–8 deal with the general marketization trajectories and its impact within municipal park and road services in each of our four countries from the early 1980s and until the mid-2010s. Each chapter explores how marketization has been introduced and evolved at the level of local governments in historical perspectives. The statistics in Chapters 5–8 are mainly descriptive and mainly based on INOPS survey data.

The last two chapters in Part II provide direct comparative analysis based on advanced statistical analysis. Chapter 9 compares cost effects in outcomes from competitive tendering across the three Scandinavian countries and discusses the importance of differences in institutional and structural determinants across the countries. Chapter 10 compares the characteristics of marketization as highlighted in Chapters 5–8 against our conceptual framework in Chapter 2 and extents on the analysis by providing a comparative statistical analysis of differences and similarities in contemporary models of marketization across our four countries.

### *Part III*

Part III of our book is made up of five Chapters. Chapters 11–14 provide altogether four single case studies of the practicalities of working with marketization at the level of local governments. Each of our four case studies has been selected to illustrate the forefront in the development of marketization within the context of local governments in each country. This study of the 'forefront' includes three case studies (Chapters 11–13) of lengthy, strategically and collaboratively focused contracts, which represent a break away from classical short-term and cost-oriented NPM-style of contracts and one case study (Chapter 14) provide insights into the failure of an attempt to establish a MOC within a competitive environment. Part III's last Chapter 15 is devoted to selected discussions of implications for theory and policy from the local organization and practices of marketization as illustrated by each of our four cases.

### *Conclusions*

In our concluding Chapter 16, we summarize key findings on the legacy of marketization and draw up perspectives for the future of marketization. In the chapter, we return to our two main research questions. Based on the findings from our book we ask readers to reconsider what and how we think about contemporary marketization in local governments and the characteristics and background for the reform paths followed by different groups of countries.

## References

Alonso, J. M., Clifton, J., & Díaz-Fuentes, D. (2017). The Impact of Government Outsourcing on Public Spending: Evidence from European Union Countries. *Journal of Policy Modeling, 39*(2), 333–348.

Barzelay, M. (2001). *The New Public Management: Improving Research and Policy Dialogue*. Berkeley: University of California Press.

Bel, G., & Costas, A. (2006). Do Public Sector Reforms Get Rusty? Local Privatization in Spain. *Journal of Policy Reform, 9*(1), 1–24.

Bel, G., Fageda, X., & Warner, M. E. (2010). Is Private Production of Public Services Cheaper Than Public Production? A Meta-Regression Analysis of Solid Waste and Water Services. *Journal of Policy Analysis and Management, 29*(3), 553–577.

Bel, G., Hebdon, R., & Warner, M. (2018). Beyond Privatisation and Cost Savings: Alternatives for Local Government Reform. *Local Government Studies, 44*(2), 173–182.

Boyne, G. A. (1998). Competitive Tendering in Local Government: A Review of Theory and Evidence. *Public Administration, 76*(4), 695–712.

Bozeman, B. (2002). Public-Value Failure: When Efficient Markets May Not Do. *Public Administration Review, 62*(2), 145–161.

Christensen, T., & Lægreid, P. (2007). *Transcending New Public Management: The Transformation of Public Sector Reforms*. Burlington: Ashgate.

Christensen, T., & Lægreid, P. (2011). *The Ashgate Research Companion to New Public Management*. Farnham: Routledge.

Clifton, J., Fuentes, D. D., & Warner, M. (2016, June). The Loss of Public Values When Public Shareholders Go Abroad. *Utilities Policy, 40*, 134–143.

Dunleavy, P., Margetts, H., Bastow, S., & Tinkler, J. (2006). New Public Management Is Dead—Long Live Digital-Era Governance. *Journal of Public Administration Research and Theory, 16*(3), 467–494.

Evans, E. J. (2013). *Thatcher and Thatcherism*. London and New York: Routledge.

Greer, I., Breidahl, K. N., Knuth, M., & Larsen, F. (2017). *The Marketization of Employment Services: The Dilemmas of Europe's Work-First Welfare States*. Oxford: Oxford University Press.

Greve, C. (2006). Public Management Reform in Denmark. *Public Management Review, 8*(1), 161–169.

Greve, C., Lægreid, P., & Rykkja, L. H. (2016). *Nordic Administrative Reforms: Lessons for Public Management*. London: Palgrave Macmillian.

Hansen, M. B. (2011). Antecedents of Organizational Innovation: The Diffusion of New Public Management Into Danish Local Government. *Public Administration, 89*(2), 285–306.

Hansen, M. B., & Lauridsen, J. (2004). The Institutional Context of Market Ideology: A Comparative Analysis of the Values and Perceptions of Local Government CEOs in 14 OECD Countries. *Public Administration, 82*(2), 491–524.

Hartmann L. (2011). *Konkurrensens konsekvenser: Vad händer med svensk välfärd?* Stockholm: SNS Förlag.

Hodge, G. A. (2000). *Privatization: An International Review of Performance.* Oxford and Boulder: Westview Press.

Hodge, G. A., & Greve, C. (2007). Public-Private Partnerships: An International Performance Review. *Public Administration Review, 67*(3), 545–558.

Hodge, G. A., Greve, C., & Boardman, A. E. (2012). *International Handbook on Public-Private Partnerships.* Cheltenham: Edward Edgar.

Hood, C. (1991). A Public Management for All Seasons? *Public Administration, 69*(1), 3–19.

Hood, C., & Dixon, R. (2015). *A Government That Worked Better and Cost Less? Evaluating Three Decades of Reform and Change in UK Central Government.* Oxford: Oxford University Press.

Hood, C., Dunsire, A., & Thompson, L. (1988). Rolling Back the State: Thatcherism, Fraserism and Bureaucracy. *Governance, 1*(3), 243–270.

Hood, C., & Peters, G. (2004). The Middle Aging of New Public Management: Into the Age of Paradox? *Journal of Public Administration Research and Theory, 14*(3), 267–282.

Kettl, D. F. (1993). *Sharing Power: Public Governance and Private Markets.* Washington: The Brookings Institution.

Kettl, D. F. (2010). Governance, Contract Management and Public Management. In S. P. Osborne (Ed.), *New Public Governance?* (pp. 239–254). Oxon: Routledge.

Klenk, T., & Reiter, R. (2019). Post-New Public Management: Reform Ideas and Their Application in the Field of Social Services. *International Review of Administrative Sciences, 85*(1), 3–10.

Kuhlmann, S., & Bouckaert, G. (Eds.). (2016). *Local Public Sector Reforms in Times of Crisis: National Trajectories and International Comparison.* London: Palgrave Macmillan.

Ladner, A., Keuffer, N., & Baldersheim, H. (2016). Measuring Local Autonomy in 39 Countries (1990–2014). *Regional and Federal Studies, 26*(3), 321–357.

Larsen, F., & Breidahl, K. (2015). Udfordringer og dilemmaer i det offentlige-private samspil på beskæftigelsesområdet: Markedsgørelse i flere versioner. *Politica, 47*(4), 503–521.

Le Grand, J. (2007). *The Other Invisible Hand: Delivering Public Services Through Choice and Competition.* Woodstock: Princeton University Press.

Lindholst, A. C. (2017). A Review of the Outcomes from Contracting Out Urban Green Space Maintenance: What We Know, Don't Know and Should Know. *Urban Forestry and Urban Greening, 27*(October), 50–58.

Lindholst, A. C., Hansen, M. B., & Petersen, O. H. (2016). Marketization Trajectories in the Danish Road and Park Sectors: A Story of Incremental Institutional Change. *International Journal of Public Sector Management, 29*(5), 457–473.

Lindholst, A. C., Hansen, M. B., Randrup, T. B., Persson, B., & Kristoffersson, A. (2018). The Many Outcomes from Contracting Out: The Voice of Public Managers. *Environment and Planning C: Politics and Space, 36*(6), 1046–1067.
Marie, T. T. (2016). Public Values as Essential Criteria for Public Entrepreneurship: Water Management in France. *Utilities Policy, 40*, 162–169.
McAllister, I., & Studlar, D. T. (1989). Popular Versus Elite Views of Privatization: The Case of Britain. *Journal of Public Policy, 9*(2), 157–178.
Osborne, S. P. (2006). The New Public Governance? *Public Management Review, 8*(3), 377–387.
Petersen, O. H., Hjelmar, U., & Vrangbæk, K. (2018). Is Contracting Out of Public Services Still the Great Panacea? A Systematic Review of Studies on Economic and Quality Effects from 2000 to 2014. *Social Policy & Administration, 52*(1), 130–157.
Pollitt, C., & Bouckaert, G. (2011). *Public Management Reform: Comparative Analysis of New Public Management, Governance and the Neo-Weberian State.* Oxford: Oxford University Press.
Pollitt, C., & Summa, H. (1997). Trajectories of Reform: Public Management Change in Four Countries. *Public Money & Management, 17*(1), 7–18.
Premfors, R. (1998). Reshaping the Democratic State: Swedish Experiences in a Comparative Perspective. *Public Administration, 76*(1), 141–159.
Rothstein, B. (1998). *Just Institutions Matter: The Moral and Political Logic of the Universal Welfare State.* Cambridge: Cambridge University Press.
Scott, W. R. (2001). *Institutions and Organizations* (2nd ed.). London: Sage.
Sellers, J. M., & Lidström, A. (2007). Decentralization, Local Government, and the Welfare State. *Governance, 20*(4), 609–632.
Simmons, B., & Elkins, Z. (2004). The Globalization of Liberalization: Policy Diffusion in the International Political Economy. *The American Political Science Review, 98*(1), 171–189.
Thelen, K. (1999). Historical Institutionalism in Comparative Politics. *Annual Review of Political Science, 2*(1), 369–404.
Voorn, B., van Genugten, M. L., & van Thiel, S. (2017). The Efficiency and Effectiveness of Municipally Owned Corporations: A Systematic Review. *Local Government Studies, 43*(5), 820–841.
Warner, M. E., & Hefetz, A. (2012). Insourcing and Outsourcing. *Journal of the American Planning Association, 78*(3), 313–327.
Williamson, O. E. (2000, September). The New Institutional Economics: Taking Stock, Looking Ahead. *Journal of Economic Literature*, XXXVIII, 595–613.
Wollmann, H., & Marcou, G. (Eds.). (2010). *The Provision of Public Services in Europe Between State, Local Government and Market.* Cheltenham: Edward Elgar.

CHAPTER 2

# Organizing Marketization

*Morten Balle Hansen, Andrej Christian Lindholst and Carsten Greve*

## Introduction

> *The costumer who, dissatisfied with the product of one firm, shifts to that of another, uses the market to improve his welfare or to improve his position; and he also sets in motion market forces which may induce recovery on the part of the firm that has declined in comparative performance.* (Hirschman 1970: 15)

As outlined in Chapter 1, in a narrow perspective this book is about marketization in the public sector in four North-European countries (England, Sweden, Denmark and Norway) in the two related local

M. B. Hansen (✉) · A. C. Lindholst
Department of Politics and Society, Aalborg University, Aalborg, Denmark
e-mail: mbh@dps.aau.dk

A. C. Lindholst
e-mail: acl@dps.aau.dk

C. Greve
Department of Organization, Copenhagen Business School,
Frederiksberg, Denmark
e-mail: cagr.ioa@cbs.dk



A. C. Lindholst and M. B. Hansen (eds.),
*Marketization in Local Government*,
https://doi.org/10.1007/978-3-030-32478-0_2

public services of parks and roads from the end of the 1970s to the end of the 2010s. From a broader perspective, the book has an ambition of enhancing a broader reaching understanding of public sector marketization, its diffusion, evolution, and drivers and how it relates to other important international trends in Public Management reforms. In Chapter 1, we advanced two overarching research questions to guide these ambitions throughout the book.

The purpose of this chapter is to (1) conceptualize and delimit the phenomenon of marketization as we use it in this book and (2) to review the main theories relevant to understand the logic of marketization and the reasons why it has been perhaps the most important reform trend in Public Management Reforms in recent decades.

It is important to understand the international public sector reform waves of the past four decades against the backdrop of the global expansion of the public sector throughout the twentieth century (Ortiz-Ospina and Roser 2018; Tanzi and Schuknecht 2000). Around 1900, the public sector in most countries was very small compared to present-day standards. For the four countries in our study IMF estimates government expenditures share of national GDP to be between approximately 6% for Denmark (lowest) and 12% for the UK (highest) in 1900 (Ortiz-Ospina and Roser 2018). The history of the twentieth century is many things, but it is also a history of public sector growth—both in absolute and in relative terms. Especially in the decades after the Second World War public sector growth was high and related to the idea of a welfare state with high degrees of social protection (Marshall 1950). UK for instance experienced an increase in government spending from around 34.5% of GDP in 1955 to approximately 53% of GDP in 1975 (Ortiz-Ospina and Roser 2018) when critics of increased public spending gained momentum and the Nordic countries experienced similar patterns of public sector expansion. This expansion of the public sector with new tasks and an expanding public workforce, especially within education and health care, was a significant driver of organizational change in the 1970s since old ways of organizing public administration increasingly was seen as insufficient and problematic.

The expansion itself triggered criticism and a reaction that was facilitated by the financial crises in the world economy during the 1970s. Some of the reformers in the late 1970s and early 1980s—most famously Margaret Thatcher in the UK and Ronald Reagan in the US—wanted to roll back the state while other reformers with less radical approaches intended to stop or diminish the growth of the public sector. Since the 1970s the public sector share of GDP has varied over time and between countries (OECD 2017), but the global long-term trend towards a larger public sector especially in wealthy countries was never reversed (Tanzi and Schuknecht 2000). Among the four countries analysed in this book, the government expenditure's share of GDP was estimated to be 54% for Denmark, 51% for Norway, 50% for Sweden and 42% for the UK in 2016 (OECD 2017: 74–75). A number of factors and arguments has been suggested to explain the long-term public sector growth trend, for instance varying potential productivity gains systematically disfavouring public sector activities (Baumol 1993), but in this book we focus on the reforms intending to enhance the efficiency of this expanding public sector by means of marketization.

The expansion of the state in the twentieth century indicates a mix of state and market governance in modern capitalist economies, with varying emphasis on the state and market side of societal governance in different epochs and countries (Hall and Soskice 2001; Kocka 2016; Shonfield 1968). This is also the case for the twenty-first-century capitalism (Iversen and Soskice 2019).

Advanced capitalist economies are characterized by a state managing a relatively large public sector (OECD average 40.9% of GDP in 2015) providing public services, regulations and transfers (OECD 2017). Governments have the authority to sanction citizens within their national borders in order to ensure compliance with formal legislation. In liberal democracies, government is furthermore characterized by voice options—citizens can influence governmental decisions through free elections, freedom of speech and a free press, if for instance they find public services inadequate. Markets are in principle voluntary—customers can use the exit option and choose another supplier, and thus sending a signal that they prefer one service to another. Thus, from a public sector marketization perspective the dynamics between exit and voice mechanisms are very important (Hirschman 1970, see section below). How do these mechanisms interact in sending signals concerning good and bad practice to public sector decision-makers? And how are these signals translated into practice? Both pros and cons in terms of theories of market and state failure and theories concerning why public management reforms ought to include marketization and privatization strategies have been elaborated in the literature.

It is in the context outlined above that the reform waves that introduced marketization and other changes in public management should be understood. From the late 1970s, marketization and privatization became some of the most important policy tools to reform the public sector while the broader reform movement later famously was labelled New Public Management (NPM) (Hood 1991). Notions of marketization and privatization was accepted to varying extent in wealthy liberal democracies, but was especially strong in the Anglo-Saxon countries, while the Nordic countries tended to be more reluctant reformers in terms of marketization (see, for example, Greve et al. 2016). In the late 2010s, Marketization and privatization have been on the agenda in public management reforms for around four decades and the analyses of this book revisit how the theory and practice of these tools of government have evolved over these forty years.

One of the basic notions in our book as also highlighted in Chapter 1 is that the phenomena of marketization and privatization is likely to have changed substantially since the first wave of NPM reforms in the 1980s. We envision that more or less pragmatic processes of problem-solving and evolutionary learning in many countries gradually have resulted in revised and perhaps improved models of marketization and privatization (Ansell 2011). Our aim has been to examine to what extent and in what ways the now classical marketization models from the early NPM era (Knudsen and Rothstein 1994; Pollitt and Bouckaert 2011; Premfors 1998) have been replaced or supplemented by other models.

In the remainder of the chapter, we first clarify how the concepts of marketization and privatization are related and used in this book (section "Marketization and Privatization"). Second, a section on marketization and economic theory is given which explains the main arguments supporting marketization but also indicates some of the problems related to marketization. Third, we show how institutional perspectives on marketization can help to understand the national and local patterns of the diffusion, evolution and path dependencies of marketization. Fourth, we explain the eight main models for organizing marketization. Fifth, marketization is related to NPM and various other models for Public Management Reform. Sixth, and finally we conclude with a brief discussion of the main points of the chapter.

**Textbox 2.1: Definitions of marketization**

"The exposure of an industry or service to market forces... ... The conversion of a national economy from a planned to a market economy." (Oxford Dictionary 2019)

"Marketization refers to the integration of competition and price mechanisms into public services." (Bevir 2009: 127)

"In its broadest usage, the term marketization refers to the process of transforming an entire economy away from a planned economic system and toward greater market-based organization... ...In narrower terms, marketization refers to changes within the public sector where market mechanisms and incentives are introduced within public or publicly regulated organizations." (Gingrich 2007: 547)

"The term 'marketization' refers both to market ideologies and market-oriented reforms. A market ideology reflects the belief that markets are of superior efficiency for the allocation of goods and resources. In its most extreme form, this belief is associated with the commodification of nearly all spheres of human life. Market oriented reforms are those policies fostering the emergence and development of markets and weakening, in parallel, alternative institutional arrangements." (Djelic 2006)

"Economic liberalism... ...refers to policies that reduce government constraints on economic behaviour and thereby promote economic exchange: 'Marketization'." (Simmons et al. 2006: 783–784)

"Marketization of the state ...to employ market criteria for allocating public resources and also to measure the efficiency of public service producers and suppliers according to market criteria... ... includes allowance for individuals choose in a market-like fashion between different service suppliers." (Pierre 1995, p. 56)

"Marketization of welfare ...the penetration of essentially market-type relationships into the social welfare arena." (Salamon 1993: 17)

"Marketization... ...refers to a change in the way that public authorities fund the services of external providers, i.e. through competitive transactions." (Greer et al. 2017)

## Marketization and Privatization

The literature has defined marketization in different ways (see Textbox 2.1). As indicated in the introduction in this book, we use the term marketization to refer to managerial arrangements—or packages of policy tools (Donahue and Zeckhauser 2006; Entwistle and Martin 2005; Hodge et al. 2010; McGuire 2006; Warner and Hefetz 2008)—that integrate Market-Type-Mechanisms (MTMs) into public services (Salamon 2002). We take competition and the exit option to be at the core of MTMs, while public services refer to "services that are of fundamental importance to the public …" (Le Grand et al. 2007: 4).

Marketization resembles, but is different from, the concept of privatization, which is the general concept most often used in the public administration literature (besides more specific tool-labels such as public procurement, contracting out, agencification, purchaser–provider split, etc.). While the scientific literature has defined privatization in numerous ways (Feigenbaum et al. 1998; Hodge 2000; Lundqvist 1988), all definitions emphasize the distinction between a public and a private sector and the transfer of activities and/or responsibilities from the public to the private sector. Marketization on the other hand, as we use the term here, emphasizes the introduction of various MTMs—especially provider competition and free user choice based on transparency and exit options—in the delivery of public services (Hirschman 1970; Le Grand et al. 2007) while downplaying somewhat the importance of sectors.

Although the privatization and marketization concepts are related and often combined, that is not always the case (Hartley and Parker 1991). The transfer of tasks to a private company, or the selling of shares in a State-Owned Enterprise (privatization) does often, but certainly not always, lead to better exit options for users and/or increased competition between providers of public services (marketization). Though competition and exit options have traditionally been weak within the public sector, they have been strengthened in many countries in recent decades as a result of deliberate attempts to enhance these mechanisms (internal marketization) through the introduction of vouchers and free choice for users. Thus, the relation between the two concepts/phenomena is probably best understood through a Venn diagram (see Fig. 2.1).

In some cases, privatization and marketization overlap; in some cases, we see privatization without marketization; and in some cases, we see marketization without privatization (e.g. internal marketization)

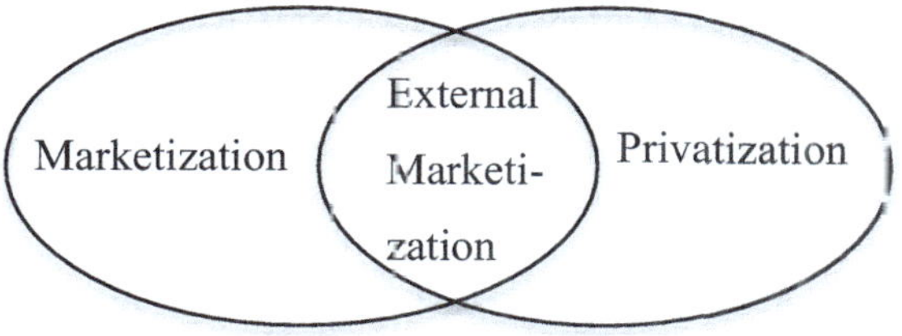


**Fig. 2.1** Marketization and privatization (*Note* Adapted from Hansen and Lindholst [2016])

(Hansen and Lindholst 2016). The basic strategy of marketization, whether deliberate or not, is thus to strengthen governance by competition—often through some combination of provider competition and free user choice. This may be done through external marketization, in which privatization—the transfer of tasks to the private sector—is used to enhance provider competition and free choice based on exit options for users. In its most drastic form, privatization may mean that state or local government-owned enterprises are transferred entirely to the private sector, and the public sector refrains from interfering in this task area. Thus, the task is no longer considered a public service and privatization moves beyond marketization as we delimit it here. Less drastic forms of privatization include outsourcing, contracting out, public procurement or public–private partnerships. Market-type mechanisms may also be enhanced within the public sector through internal marketization, such as management by contract, agencification, free choice for users, vouchers, purchaser–provider split models and other attempts to organize quasi-markets around public services. We will treat the most important management concepts related to marketization in section "Sociological and Historical Institutionalism: Diffusion and Path Dependencies". Often internal and external marketization are combined as in the case of contracting out, which is facilitated by the presence of several competing providers and a public sector organized by management by contract and purchaser–provider split models. In some contexts, marketization may be accomplished by competition between a mixture of private and public providers. As we shall see later in the book—in the policy fields of park- and road maintenance, this strategy has been especially pronounced in Denmark and Sweden.

## Marketization and Economic Theory

The concept of marketization envisions the metaphor of the market which is at the core of economics and obviously various types of economic theory have delivered influential theorizing concerning marketization and privatization. It is impossible to cover and pay justice to this vast important body of academic theorizing in the space available here, so we will settle with a few basic concepts and models that is particularly important in order to understand and discuss the basic issues of public sector marketization and privatization that we analyse in this book.

In this section, we briefly discuss public choice theory (Boyne 1998; Downs 1967; Dunleavy 1991; Niskanen 1971; Tullock 1965), Principal–Agent (PA) theory (Miller and Whitford 2007; Vickers and Yarrow 1991; Waterman and Meier 1998), New Institutional Economics (NIE) and transaction costs (Williamson 1975, 1985, 1998a, b, 2000), since they have been particularly influential in elaborating and applying economic theories to the public sector. We furthermore include brief discussions of Hirschman's exit, voice and loyalty framework (Hirschman 1970), Baumol's concept of contestable markets (Baumol 1982) and of important distinctions between different types of goods elaborated within economic theory (Ostrom 1990, 2009; Samuelson 1954).

Some initial remarks however seem important. One of the difficulties of economic theorizing is that it has both delivered scientific theorizing essential to understand marketization and arguments that have functioned as a normative ideology favouring marketization and especially privatization. More than is usually the case in social science, the theories presented here have both been integrated into a system of arguments that may be labelled the Neoliberal ideology of economic theorizing and theories that have been subject to empirical testing and analysis concerning to what extent the theory holds in practice. Perhaps most clearly exemplified in the writings of Friedrich Hayek (Hayek 1945, 2014) and the formation of the Mont Pelerin Society in 1947, parts of economic theorizing became a market ideology reflecting the belief that almost by definition "markets are of superior efficiency for the allocation of goods and resources" (Djelic 2006). While certainly influenced by these arguments, the way, however, marketization has entered public management reforms has in many countries been somewhat different. Perhaps especially in the Nordic countries marketization has entered as a mechanism envisioned to enhance efficiency and adaptation to the needs of the citizens without necessarily diminishing the role of the public sector as a public service provider. This perspective sees marketization as a means to ensure that: "… organizations do receive one sort of signal when they do something right and another sort of signal when they do something wrong, so that they in the long run will do more right things than wrong" (paraphrasing Rothstein 1998: 201). This learning perspective on marketization is also preeminent in Hirschman's seminal book on exit, voice and loyalty: "The costumer who, dissatisfied with the product of one firm, shifts to that of another, uses the market to improve his welfare or to improve his position; and he also sets in motion market forces which may induce recovery on the part of the firm that has declined in comparative performance" (Hirschman 1970: 15). This learning perspective, has been preeminent in much theorizing in the public administration literature on privatization and marketization (see, for instance, Boyne 1998; Hefetz and Warner 2004). Christopher Hood discussed the learning perspective from Hirschman in his book on "Explaining Economic Policy Reversals" (Hood 1994). Later on, Hood (1998) used the theoretical lens of cultural theory in the style of Mary Douglas to discuss how one governance form superseded another governance form.

### *Public Choice Theory and Marketization*

In recent decades a number of social scientists have utilized concepts and methods derived from economics to explain political and administrative phenomena. This approach has been called public choice theory or rational choice theory (Boyne 1998; Dunleavy 1991). A number of models concerning public sector organizing has been derived from assumptions of rational egoistic utility-maximizing (REM) actors with clear logically ordered preferences. From a governance perspective, the basic theme has been how to design formal institutions that provide incentives for rational self-interested actors to act in ways beneficial to the larger society. Public Choice theory suggests "… that the replacement of monopoly by competition is an 'institutional transformation' with beneficial effects on public services" (Boyne 1998: 7). From an explanatory perspective, the issue has been to what extent such models could explain the behaviour of actors such as voters, top-bureaucrats, street-level bureaucrats and politicians. While the explanatory models such as Tiebouts voting by the feet model (Tiebout 1956), Downs work on political parties (Downs 1957) and bureaucracies (Downs 1967) and Niskanen's budget-maximizing bureaucrats (Niskanen 1971) has been very influential they are less relevant to the type of marketization we analyse in this study. The core message of their intervention theory (Hansen and Vedung 2010) is basically that "competition from private sector organizations can significantly improve the performance of public agencies" (Boyne 1998: 102). The public monopolies characterizing much public service production in the "old public administration" up until the late 1970s needed the signals from competition to enhance efficiency.

### *The Principal–Agent Model and Marketization*

Principal–Agent relations are abundant in modern societies and at the heart of many policy problems, where some actors (agents) make decisions on behalf of some other actors (principals). In a representative democracy the elected politicians may be seen as the agents of the electorate, the government as the agent of the elected politicians, the state/municipal administration the agent of the government/municipal board, the public service producing agencies the agents of the state/municipal administration, etc. (Olsen 1978; Schumpeter 1942). From a user perspective, the service producing public agencies may be seen as agents of the users conceptualized as the principals. But Principal–Agent relations get a very specific meaning in the Principal–Agent (PA) model of economic theory (Eisenhardt 1989; Jensen and Meckling 1976; Miller 2005; Mitnick 2015; Moe 1984; Pierre and Peters 2017; Ross 1973), which focus on the basic question: How do we increase the likelihood that agents act in ways the principals want them to act? Most versions of the principal–agent model share the assumptions of rational egoistic utility-maximizing (REM) actors with the public choice models mentioned above. It may be considered a more general formulation of at least some of these models since relations between the electorate and politicians and between politicians and bureaucrats can be formulated as principal–agent relations. It then adds a few further assumptions concerning frequent characteristics of these PA-relations: (a) Different PA utility functions, (b) Asymmetrical information, (c) Adverse selection, (d) Moral hazard, and (e) Risk aversion.

The different *utility functions* (goals) of the principal and the agent (a) is at the core of the model. If they had exactly the same utility function the PA model would be less relevant.

*Asymmetrical information* is assumed. Very often the agent has much better and more precise information than the principal concerning relevant activities, outputs and outcomes. *Adverse selection* means that the agent has relevant information, which is not or only partially given to the principal. *Moral hazard* means that it is difficult or impossible for the principal to verify the activities, outputs and outcomes of the efforts of agent. *Risk aversion* means that agents will try to minimize their risks. Based on these assumptions the PA model suggests a few solutions to its basic problem—to make the agents act as the principals want them to. One solution is to design the recruitment process of agents in a way that diminish the gap between the goals of the agents and the goals of the principals. A second solution is to design better surveillance systems. A third solution is to design incentive systems, which make it in the interests of the agents to act in the ways the principals want them to. The PA line of reasoning, if not the exact model, has had a huge impact on public sector organizing in recent decades. Firstly, the internal organization of the public sector has increasingly been characterized by one type of organizational unit defined as principals (purchasers), another type of unit defined as agents (providers) and their relations regulated by negotiated contracts. Secondly, the competitive mechanism in marketization is intended to provide incentives for a more efficient public service production. The market test provides a kind of surveillance, since it, if marketization works as intended, unveils the relative efficiency of competing providers. Thus, in the PA model, marketization represents possible solutions to the problems represented by point b, c and d above. If it works marketization can reduce the problems of asymmetrical information, adverse selection and moral hazard.

### *The New Institutional Economics, Transaction Costs and Marketization*

New Institutional Economics (NIE) is a family of theoretical approaches that attempts to extend economics to include the institutions—understood as formal and informal rules—that structurate economic activity in society. The term New Institutional Economics is usually ascribed to Oliver E. Williamson (1975) and builds on the concept of transaction costs in previous work by Coase (1937, 1960). Other famous scholars in this tradition are Elinor Ostrom (1990) and Douglas North (1992), but we delimit this brief review primarily to Williamson's version.

New Institutional Economics criticize neoclassical theories for neglecting the importance of institutions and for its unrealistic actor assumptions. It is broader in scope than public choice and PA models, involves higher levels of abstraction and relates to social theories of embeddedness as well as new developments in psychological theory, which breaks with the neoclassical actor assumptions. In a seminal article, Williamson relates NIE to four levels of social analysis (Williamson 2000: 597):

- L1. Social theory—Embeddedness: Informal institutions, customs, traditions, norms, religion
- L2. Economics of property rights/positive political theory—Institutional environment: Formal rules of the game—esp. property (polity, judiciary, bureaucracy)
- L3. Transaction cost economics—Governance: Play of the game, esp. contract (aligning governance structures with transactions)
- L4. Neoclassical economics/agency theory—Resource allocation and employment (prices and quantities; incentive alignment)

New Institutional Economics has mostly focused on the institutional environment ("the formal rules of the game") and governance ("the play of the game") (levels 2 and 3) and has elaborated a number of interesting theoretical ideas at these levels. In most NIE approaches, assumptions of the actor build on Simon's "bounded rationality" model rather than the utility-maximizing actor of neoclassical economics (Simon 1976). Essential concepts in the NIE tradition are transaction costs, contracts and property and decision rights. Transaction costs are the costs in making any economic trade when participating in a market (North 1992). Types of transaction costs include (a) search and information costs, (b) bargaining costs and (c) policing and enforcement costs. In the marketization perspective of this book, the transaction costs of transforming the traditional hierarchical bureaucratic structures of Public Administration into relations with purchasers, providers and contracts resembling quasi-markets are likely to be substantial. An important insight from this tradition is that contracts are usually incomplete (more or less based on tacit understandings) and thus "opening room for potential maladjustments" (Ménard 2018: 4) when paired with opportunism which may manifest itself as the "adverse selection, moral hazard, shirking, subgoal pursuit, and other forms of strategic behaviour" (Williamson 2000: 601) like in the assumptions of the Principal–Agent model above. Thus, sometimes the transaction costs of a market are too high and a hierarchical solution is more efficient—it depends on the specific situation.

It is primarily in relation to transaction costs that institutions enter the NIE analysis. A crucial notion is that institutions that facilitate low transaction costs boost economic growth and that societies with such institutions are more efficient than societies with institutions imposing high transaction costs. Thus, for instance high trust societies are expected to be more efficient than low trust societies because of lower transaction costs. Another basic notion is that "all feasible forms of organization – government included – are flawed" (Williamson 2000: 601). Thus, the remediableness criterion states that "… an organization for which no superior feasible alternative can be described and implemented with expected net gains is presumed to be efficient" (Williamson 2000: 601). Thus, the efficiency criteria of better feasible alternatives replace the optimization criteria of neoclassical economics.

### *Exit, Voice and Loyalty and Marketization*

In liberal democracies, public services are delivered within the institutional setting of representative democracy. In the empirical studies of this book, the services of road maintenance and park services are the responsibility of local governments headed by municipal boards of elected politicians. This poses questions concerning the dynamic relations between the market-type mechanisms of marketization and representative democracy. In an influential seminal book (Hirschman 1970; John 2017), Hirschman provides a generic framework, based on the concepts of exit, voice and loyalty, for analysing and understanding how markets and competition are dynamically related to political representation and public debate.

The point of departure of his analysis is the declining performance of some social system (e.g. a group, an organization or a country). Members of a group, consumers of a product or inhabitants of a country may react to deteriorating quality, quantity or both of a social unit in one or a combination of three ways by either:

- leaving—(exit)
- criticizing the declining performance—(voice)
- staying and awaiting/hoping for future improvements—(loyalty)

In a classical sector understanding of society, exit may be seen as the competitive mechanism of the market, voice as the deliberative mechanism of representative democracy and the state and loyalty as the social bond of the family/clan. The strength of Hirschman's approach is that he convincingly demonstrates that most social systems tend to be influenced more or less by all three mechanisms and that the dynamics between them will influence the likelihood of the system to remedy its deteriorating performance. The strength of the Exit, Voice, Loyalty (EVL) framework is "the integration of what is of interest to economists—choice and competition—with those features of the world that are of more concern to political scientists—individual and collective voice" (John 2017: 525). Since marketization in public management reforms very much has been about enhancing the exit mechanism in a public sector characterized by strong voice and loyalty mechanisms Hirschman's approach is of particular relevance for public services.

### *Contestable Markets and Marketization*

The theory of contestable markets (Baumol 1982) suggests that the threat of entry of other service providers into a market rather than the actual presence of them may be sufficient to enhance efficiency by competition (Albalate et al. 2012; Baumol 1982; Bel and Fageda 2011; Knott and Posen 2005; Schlesinger et al. 1986). A perfectly contestable market is one in which "entry is absolutely free, and exit is absolutely costless" (Baumol 1982: 3). Such a model world is vulnerable to a hit and run entry of firms if there is even the most transient profit opportunity. It does not exist in real world market structures, but technological changes and/or deliberate public policies may lower the barriers of entering a market and thus make the markets of for instance public services more contestable to outside intruders.

Thus, once an alternative provider starts to be a realistic alternative due to deteriorating barriers of entrance, the threat of entry may work to enhance efficiency. For instance, once technological changes removed the barriers of the natural monopolies of telephone companies and made competition possible, they started to improve efficiency due to the threat of entry even before alternative providers had entered the market. Contestable market notions have been incorporated in theories of strategy (Porter 2008) and has been suggested as an alternative strategy for public sector purchaser agencies in some circumstances. Based on the theory it can be argued that for instance public monopolies in some cases are subject to indirect competition due to realistic threats of alternative providers. Furthermore, if a private provider of public services is not confronted with sufficient competition from other private providers the realistic threat of insourcing (Hefetz and Warner 2004, 2012)—that a public provider may produce the service—may provide sufficient incentives for efficient service production.

### *Typology of Goods and Marketization*

Some of the arguments of the division of labour between the public and private sector are related to the characteristics of the goods (Samuelson 1954). One important typology is elaborated based on two dimensions. Whether goods are rivalrous or non-rivalrous and whether they are excludable or not excludable, producing a two-by-two matrix with four types of goods. Pure private goods, presumed to be best suited for market provision, are both rivalrous (if one person uses it another person can't) and excludable in the sense that other users can be excluded. Classical examples often given are food and clothes. Pure public goods, presumed to be best suited for public provision, are characterized by being non-rivalrous (all people can use it without diminishing its value to the user) and not excludable in the sense that it is impossible to exclude people from using it. Classical examples often given are a lighthouse and national defence. Club-goods are characterized by being non-rivalrous but excludable and examples are cinemas, private parks and pay-per-view television. Common-pool resources are characterized by being rivalrous and non-excludable and examples given are usually resources such as fish stocks, timber and coal.

To what extent specific goods qualify to be rivalrous, excludable or both can be difficult to decide in practice and may change over time due to technological innovations. Road maintenance, one of our two policy cases, may be considered somewhere between public good and a club good since it until recently has been difficult and expensive to make users pay for how much they use the good. Recent digital innovations however, may change this in the near future. On the other hand, roads are only non-rivalrous goods up to a point since rush hour traffic clearly diminishes the usefulness of the roads.

Two other important concepts from economic theory, are merit goods and externalities (Hughes 2018: 22–24). Merit goods are goods with important positive or negative societal externalities related to them. Societal externalities are the outcomes not directly accounted for by direct user utility and may also be referred to as general outcomes (Jorgensen et al. 1998). In our cases, it can be argued that it has merits to society, not just to each individual user, that the roads are maintained and the parks are ensured to be good recreational areas. In general, it can be argued that the stronger specific goods are characterized by societal externalities the stronger arguments for some kind of public regulation or provision.

### *Summing up Economic Theory and Marketization*

The theories and concepts presented above have been extremely influential in public management reforms and public sector governance in recent decades. They have both provided normative arguments in favour of marketization and privatization and they have provided theories to explain patterns of marketization. We have presented them in some detail here because they represent important global theorizing that paved the way for international trends towards marketization and privatization (Lee and Strang 2006; Meyer et al. 1997; Strang and Meyer 1993, see next section on sociological institutionalism). In many ways, they represent the intervention theories of marketization (Hansen and Vedung 2010). They provide more or less plausible answers to questions such as: Why should marketization work? Why should we prefer a situation with marketization to a situation without? In a public administration perspective they represent a strong normative focus on efficiency, while considerations concerning other important criteria for good governance such as equity, equality and politics (Rosenbloom 1983; Rosenbloom et al. 2015) are by and large neglected or subordinated the purpose of efficiency.

## Sociological and Historical Institutionalism: Diffusion and Path Dependencies

Above we have reviewed important economic theorizing related to marketization. These theories have both delivered important positive theories concerning how to describe and explain marketization and they have provided normative arguments concerning why marketization may be a good idea (and less so why it's sometimes not) when trying to enhance the efficiency of public service delivery. The primary driver in these theories is envisioned to be efficiency and they all build on optimizing or satisficing actor notions of rational choice. The New Institutional Economics emphasize the importance of institutionalized "rules of the game" to societal efficiency and has in that respect been part of a broader movement towards institutional perspectives within social science (Hall and Taylor 1996; March and Olsen 1989; Scott 2014). In this section, we briefly introduce two other institutional traditions—sociological and historical institutionalism—providing important theorizing to describe and explain the evolution of marketization.

### *Sociological Institutionalism: Institutionalized Cognitive Frames Enhancing and Inhibiting Diffusion*

One way to conceptually frame the adoption of marketization across national context(s) is to use a diffusion model (Lave and March 1993; Rogers 2003). In such a model, marketization reforms are seen as a global wave of novel reform ideas diffusing between countries. That is largely how the early stages of marketization are portrayed in much of the Public Administration literature (Dunleavy et al. 2006; Hood 1991; Kettl 2005). This framing, views the diffusion of marketization as initiated and spread out from so-called benchmark countries, in particular Anglo-Saxon countries, towards later adopting countries within the group of OECD countries (Bevir 2009; Salamon 1993). While this descriptive diagnosis may be questioned or added important nuances (Pollitt and Bouckaert 2011; Premfors 1998), the important contribution of sociological institutionalism is to provide a framework for understanding the drivers behind such diffusion processes. Diffusion of marketization may be enhanced by coercive, normative or cognitive mechanisms or a combination of these (DiMaggio and Powell 1991; Scott 2014). One influential version of the sociological institutionalism builds on the notion of an evolving world culture (Meyer et al. 1997) that provides the institutional conditions for the diffusion of new ways of organizing. Some management models—in our case marketization—may fit very well into this world culture and thus diffuse relatively easy into countries with very different preconditions. Other management models are less supported by global meaning systems and thus tend to diffuse in slower pace to fewer countries (Meyer 2009; Strang and Meyer 1993). In this perspective, the economic theories presented above represent globally supported ideas concerning the merits of marketization legitimized by economic theory and enhanced by international organizations like OECD and the World Bank. They become a cognitive lens that makes some observations easy to comprehend while others are harder to grasp if they don't fit into globally supported cognitive frames (Lee and Strang 2006). In early versions of sociological institutionalism (DiMaggio and Powell 1983; Meyer and Rowan 1977) this perspective led to a convergence story envisioning more similar nation states and organizations, while in later especially Scandinavian versions notions of translation and hybridization (Czarniawska and Sevón 1996; Røvik 2011, 2016; Waeraas and Nielsen 2016) suggest a more complex and nuanced outcome when globally supported ideas diffuse into local contexts.

### *Historical Institutionalism: The Importance of Path Dependencies*

While the economic and sociological institutionalism emphasize different drivers, they both tend to envision a convergence story. In the case of economic institutionalism this convergence is driven by efficiency and the notion that in the long run, the most economically efficient ways of organizing will prevail. In the case of sociological institutionalism, the convergence is enhanced by a global world culture in which science plays an important role as in the case of economic theory and marketization.

Political science and public administration traditions however tend to emphasize the importance of historically evolved national and local structures enforcing path dependencies (Lindholst et al. 2016; Mahoney and Thelen 2010; Steinmo et al. 1992) in which the nation state plays a major role. In a broad political economy perspective, the "varieties of capitalism" tradition (Hall and Soskice 2001) recognize capitalism as a global system, but emphasize the huge observable differences between ways of organizing state-market-civil society relations.

In the Public Administration literature marketization is certainly seen as a transnational phenomenon with similar governance notions diffusing across countries (Hood 1991), but much more emphasis is given to national and local contexts than in the two other institutional traditions. In general, the literature on the diffusion of public sector reforms favours the argument that local and national path dependencies tend to create divergence rather than convergence when adopting transnational organizational innovations like marketization. Different authors however emphasize different aspects of these contextual conditions. Christensen and Lægreid (2007c), for example, highlight contextual differences in formal structures (e.g. constitutions and politico-administrative systems), cultures (e.g. history and traditions) and environments (e.g. institutional and technical) as likely to produce divergence. Kuhlmann and Bouckaert (2016) highlight five contextual conditions for comparative analysis of reforms within local governments including state structure and government type (e.g. level of overall centralization and democratic system), administrative culture and tradition (e.g. legalism and rule orientation), local government responsibilities and autonomy (e.g. range of responsibilities and level of local discretion), territorial structures (e.g. size), and local democracy (e.g. distribution of power between political and administrative levels).

### *Institutional Theory and Marketization in Public Management Reforms*

From an institutional perspective, both in its economic, sociological and historical versions, marketization represents a new governance system enhancing various types of rule-systems to support the use of competition and the price mechanism in the public sector. While economic institutionalism emphasize efficiency as a driver, sociological institutionalism emphasize how marketization has been theorized as a highly legitimate governance structure in the global world culture that governments ought to implement in order to be seen as efficient. In this sociological perspective, economic theory may be seen as delivering the global cognitive driver for marketization. While sociological institutionalism emphasizes global processes enhancing the diffusion of marketization, historical institutionalism emphasizes the importance of national and local traditions and path dependencies. In this perspective, marketization will be expected to take different forms and magnitudes in different local contexts. While the general utility of marketization as a governance strategy may be accepted, it is expected to be adopted, adapted and implemented in substantially different ways in different national and local contexts.

The three institutional perspectives may be seen as competing analytical frameworks or as different perspectives that may supplement each other to enhance a more rich and nuanced understanding. In this book we primarily use the latter strategy, when we discuss our empirical findings.

## Organizing Marketization and Beyond

In this section, we introduce the basic logic of eight models for organizing marketization and we indicate how they are mutually related, as well as how they are related to the theories presented above. At its core the logic of marketization in public management reforms envisions using competition to enhance signals concerning good and bad practice in public service delivery (Hirschman 1970). In a broader sense, a number of management models and policy instruments have been introduced in recent decades which constitute the organizational basis of competition (Hansen 2011; Rainey 2009; Savas 1989) and we include these in our conceptualization of marketization. The eight models are all transnational in the sense that they have been tried out to varying extent in many countries. In a sociological institutional perspective, they can be seen as transnational organizational innovations broadly supported by a global world culture enhancing their diffusion. Below we first present the quasi-market model, since it is the model most directly resembling the market and since it encompasses most of the other models as organizing elements:

1. *The quasi-market—provider competition and user choice.* In the quasi-market model, societal engineers deliberately construct a model resembling the market. Competition between providers (public or private) and choice between several alternatives by users are enhanced by a package of organizational arrangements. Organizing public services is usually the task of the local government, which is organized in a purchaser–provider split model which separates the tasks of ordering and buying public services on the one hand and providing public services on the other (see below). The relation between the purchaser (public) and the provider (public or private) is organized as an exchange relation in a "management-by-contract" model. The basic quality of the providers may be ensured through an accreditation procedure. Users of public services are given free choice between accredited providers and often "vouchers" partly or fully financed by taxes. Thus, to the provider, the user is seen as a customer in much the same way as in a private market place. The public organizational units in this model are relatively autonomous agencies or corporations, which is supposed to compete with each other and preferably also with

private providers. The basic notion is that this organized competition enables the exit mechanism (Hirschman 1970) to work and through competition make public service delivery leaner and more efficient in both quantitative and qualitative terms. Transaction cost economics (Williamson 1998b) has delivered important theorizing concerning which conditions tend to provide the best and worst chances to make the model work.

2. *Free choice for users.* User choice is an important part of the quasi-market, but is also important in its own right. The model constructs a role for citizens as "consumers" of welfare services eluting more freedom, securing individualization of services and introducing a new value of unity through the similar rights to exercise free choices, which in turn also transforms the role of the welfare state (Rostgaard 2006). Different variants were introduced into the public context of our four countries in the 1980s and 1990s. It was later formally established as the basic rule in most public service areas. In principle and to a certain degree in practice, citizens can freely choose between day-care services, kindergartens, municipal primary and lower secondary schools, upper secondary schools, higher education, hospital treatment and elder care. The basic idea in a managerial perspective is that free choice creates a competitive situation that encourages both public and private service providers to continuously improve their services. It is an innovation that to a high degree has had formal hierarchical support in the form of legislation and normative support. In Hirschman's perspective free choice is of course essential to make the exit mechanism work, but it may weaken the voice mechanism and the dynamic relation between these two mechanisms in terms of improving organizational learning in the public sector is essentially an empirical question. Interestingly, John Clarke and Janet Newman and colleagues (2007) examined if people in Britain were becoming "citizen-consumers," and they found empirically that this was not the case. People were still able to judge when they acted as citizens and when they acted as consumers.

The two first models above have been very influential versions of marketization in the public sector in recent decades. Especially in education and health care where users are given vouchers and attempts are made to improve the transparency of the choices users face through various versions of benchmarking. The arguments supporting the models are taken from the economic theorizing presented above. They have, however, only been used partly in local park- and road services. Users usually don't pay directly for local park and road services. This may be because these public services tend to resemble public goods. Up to a point, their value to the user doesn't diminish if others use the road or the park. It is possible to make them excludable, but it's expensive. Furthermore, there are important societal externalities associated with them.

3. *Contracting (or outsourcing)—provider competition without free user choice.* In some types of public services it is difficult or impossible to organize free choice for users resembling a market. There may be only one park in the neighbourhood and everyone has to drive on the same road. In such cases users do not have a choice, but they have a voice to complain or make suggestions for change if they are dissatisfied. Still, competition between providers of public services, if more than one provider is present (concurrent contracting), can be organized to enhance efficiency and other goals (Poulsen and Hansen 2016). In the contracting model, competition between providers is organized regularly through rounds of competitive tendering, and one provider is then selected to provide the service until the next outsourcing process.
   Introduction of contracting was controversial in many countries since it was argued by both proponents and opponents of marketization of the political right and left to be an attack on the welfare state (Hansen 2011; Kristensen 1984). Today, contracting is much less controversial and politicized than previously but can nevertheless still mobilize traditional conflicts from the classic right–left scale in politics. Contracting is primarily linked to ideas of breaking down public monopolies and introducing competition mechanisms in public service provision with the aim of increasing efficiency. A recent empirical examination of contracting out in US social services found that the logic of service delivery trumped democratic concerns for citizens involved as being recipient of services (Amirkhanyan and Lambright 2017). Contracting has historically been and is presently the most important model of marketization in local park and road services in England, Denmark, Sweden and Norway.
4. *Purchaser–Provider-Split models.* These models are important preconditions of the quasi-market model and contracting, but are

also used in their own right to prepare privatization or as a way to organize the internal division of labor in public sector organizations. This model can be seen as the organizational prerequisite for outsourcing of services previously delivered by the public sector and thus constitutes a core idea of the market part of the NPM movement (Harrison 1991; Lewis et al. 1996). The basic idea is that the public sector organizations should be divided into a purchaser unit (also called an authority organization) and a provider (also called a supplier). The relation between the two organizations is formalized in written contracts and the model is thus clearly related to Management by Contract. This model makes it possible for public supplier organizations to compete with or be replaced by private supplier organizations. This organizational form is thus the organizational basis for the privatization of the supply of services where the execution of the task is still ordered and controlled by the public sector. This model is an example of organizing Principal–Agent relations in practice. The purchaser organization is the principal, the provider organization is the agent and their relations are formalized in a contract.

5. *Management by Contract.* Management by Contract can be found in respectively a "hard" and "soft" version. It is the "hard" version of Management by Contract, which is directly linked to marketization as both quasi-markets and contracting out, while "softer" versions may be considered variants of the Management by Objectives (MBO) that has been a basic model of public sector organizing since the 1980s (Greve 2000, 2005, 2008; Greve and Ejersbo 2010). In the hard version of Management by Contract, binding contracts are introduced between the public sector Purchaser/authority organizations and private or public provider/supplier organizations. When the contract has been formulated—typically for a shorter time-period of two–four years—it is the purchaser organization that must ensure that the contract requirements is met adequately. The model rests on the assumption that it is possible to specify clear expectations in the contract and that has required a great deal of adaptation in the public sector. Economic theorizing recognizes that a contract rarely if ever can specify all the aspects of the service provision. How much it is possible to specify depends largely on the complexity of the tasks, and many public services are relatively complex, leaving a great

deal to interpretation and informal negotiation and adaptation. In the "soft" version the contract is more like a communication tool, where mutual expectations are specified in writing in annual contracts, which can be characterized as internal management tools with varying degrees of openness.

6. *Yardstick competition and benchmarking.* In some contexts, user choice and/or provider competition is either impossible or difficult to organize—or simply not desirable. When economies of scale are important, and in circumstances resembling a natural monopoly due to subadditivity of costs, provider competition may be inefficient and undesirable. Even in such cases, competition may play an important role through yardstick competition (Shleifer 1985) or benchmarking (Ammons and Roenigk 2015), in which the performance of companies is compared to the performance of others, and these performance comparisons are used to improve performance through organizational learning processes. The intention is to use the comparisons for learning or control to improve practice by comparisons to "the best in the field" or some other standard (Hansen 2017). Yardstick competition supplement quasi-markets and contracting in the four countries of our study in most public service areas including park and road services. One of the arguments supporting the model is that the information generated through comparisons can enhance the transparency of the quasi-market and thus help users make informed choices. In some areas, such as district-heating (Bukh and Dietrichson 2016), it is the most important type of marketization, since it is difficult or impossible to organize other types of competition.
7. *Agencification/Corporatization—semiautonomous organizational units.* One of the basic characteristics of markets is actors with some degree of autonomy. The trend towards making organizational units in the public sector less directly hierarchically managed and more autonomous has been called agencification (Pollitt et al. 2004) or, in the case of legal autonomy, corporatization (Voorn et al. 2018). Since the 1980s, it has been an important part of NPM to enhance semi-autonomous agencies. The classical bureaucracy with clear command-and-control lines are in some, but not all, important ways substituted with semi-autonomous agencies managed through a formal contract or more informally through various versions of performance management. As long

as the agency complies with the contract or more informally delivers on the required objectives—included budget discipline—they are granted autonomy to decide how to manage and conduct their activities. This trend towards agencification of units delivering public services is an important precondition for marketization in terms of enhancing competition, but it has also been important in its own right in terms of enhancing a more decentralized management style in the public sector. A style in which local managers of service-producing units are both granted the right and the obligation to manage their organizations and adapt them to local circumstances. In recent years various types of recentralization has been seen that indicate a shift away from conventional NPM reform models towards post-NPM reform models (Christensen and Lægreid 2007c).

8. *Public–private collaboration beyond competition—Public–private partnerships.* The models above represent some of the most prominent marketization models in the public administration literature, but they sometimes run into difficulties when they are carried out in practice and varying versions of alternative models of public–private collaboration or public–private partnerships (PPPs) are tried out. PPPs came into prominence as the interest in contracting out and privatization faded in the mid-1990s. There are many different definitions of PPPs (see Hodge et al. [2010] and Stelling [2014] for overviews of the debate on how to define a PPP). It has become commonplace to note that there are many different forms of PPPs: one form is the long-term infrastructure contract (LTIC) for large infrastructure projects (or megaprojects) such as building transport infrastructure or building new hospitals. A second form is the innovation partnership where public and private actors join forces to come up with innovative ideas in public service delivery. A third form is the urban generation projects or today's "smart city" urban development projects, These forms of urban development projects have a long history in the US, the UK and other places. A fourth form is the partnership between NGOs and government organizations on constructing solutions to social problems. A good overview of the different forms of partnerships can be found in Brinkerhoff and Brinkerhoff's (2011) introductory article of Public Administration Development. What most of the partnerships focus on is tackling wicked public policy problems (see Alford and Head

2017). Some authors believe that the PPP-term is too loose to be used academically, so Donahue and Zeckhauser rejected the term and focused on "collaborative governance" instead in their 2011-book when they analysed how public actors and private actors handled pressing public policy problems.

The literature on the many forms of PPPs is quite mature now. There are several recent assessments of how many countries have used PPPs and what can be said of the policy outcomes of PPPs (Greve and Hodge 2013; Hodge and Greve 2019). One of the most continuing questions has been the discussion of the economic performance of PPPs. Here, the verdict is still out as the National Audit Office (NAO) in the UK attested to when they summed up more than three decades of the British experience with PPPs (in the so-called Private Finance Initiative). A recent overview of the performance debate for PPPs has been provided by Hodge and Greve (2018).

The notion of a PPP is acknowledging that the public sector and the private sector have to work together. Hodge and Greve (2019) call it "the enduring interdependency of politics and markets" in their most recent book. Others remain more sceptical and believe that the private sector is gaining the most from PPPs and governments are not sufficiently prepared to govern with private sector actors (Flinders 2010). In any case, PPPs became the new language that superseded the discussions on NPM or marketization, as more and more organizations started to collaborate instead of competing.

### *Synthesizing Eight Models of Organizing Marketization*

The eight models above are all transnational in the sense that public management reforms have introduced them in many countries in recent decades in different policy areas. Furthermore, some kind of decentralized decision-making in terms of agencification (model 7) seems to be a characteristic feature of all the models. The basic vision when organizing marketization is to see public sector organizations as semi-autonomous as contrasted to a traditional hierarchy.

Within park and road services, some earlier research (Lindholst 2009) indicates that the predominant model has been contracting as outlined in model 3. This has been the basic way to organize provider competition and it requires some kind of management by contract (model 5). If provider competition includes competition between public and private providers some version of a purchaser–provider-split model (model 4) is also needed to organize competition between public and private providers. Thus, combinations of model 3, 4 and 5 has been the most predominant ways to organize marketization within road and park maintenance. However, research also indicates that the introduction of the partnership agenda (model 8) has developed the contracting model from competitive towards collaborative models (Lindholst 2009).

As we shall see in Chapters 5–9, however, although NPM-versions of contracting is still a dominant model, in the most recent decades PPP models have increasingly been put to use. PPP models are more about collaboration than competition and may be conceptualized as a post-marketization or post-NPM model.

## New Public Management and Its Alternatives

The models for organizing marketization presented above all represent a group of transnational organizational innovations in public management reforms that has been introduced in many advanced economies since the 1980s and summarized under the NPM label (Hood 1991). NPM was a reaction to the growth of the public sector in the post-war decades and introduced various new ways of organizing public sector activities including marketization. The old public administration with its classical Weberian bureaucracy (Weber 2002/1921) and its focus on rule of law, hierarchy through a parliamentary chain of command and professional decision-making was supplemented, but not replaced, by marketization and modes of organizing from the private sector. In some countries like the UK this change in public management involved cutback management and rolling the state back, while in others like the Nordic countries it involved diminished public sector growth, tighter budget discipline and more focus on efficiency in the delivery of public core services. The various models for organizing marketization has been on the agenda for almost four decades and have been tried out in several countries with varying success. In a relatively recent evaluation of NPM in the UK they find little if any improvement of public performance in state administration (Hood and Dixon 2015) and various paradoxes associated with NPM (Christoffer Hood and Peters 2004) as well as post-NPM models (Christensen and Lægreid 2007a, b; Reiter and Klenk 2019) has been suggested. One of the difficulties related to NPM and marketization is its relation to the classical Weberian model of public administration. How does one combine the decentralized model of marketization with a hierarchically oriented bureaucracy?

Some North-European countries like the three Scandinavian countries analysed in this book have been characterized as representing a Neo-Weberian State (NWS) model (Pollitt and Bouckaert 2011). In a NWS perspective marketization helps, along with other reform elements, to promote a shift towards a more externally oriented public sector to meet citizens' needs and wishes, while preserving a modernized public sector rather than downsizing it.

Other alternative models of public management reform such as New Public Governance (NPG) (Rhodes 1996, 2007; Torfing and Ansell 2017) and Digital Era Governance (DEG) (Dunleavy et al. 2006) has been suggested and together the different models (or paradigms) represent an interesting but somewhat paradoxical tapestry of contemporary notions concerning how to improve public management practices (see Table 2.1) (Andersen et al. 2017).

One intriguing question is what the implications from newer reform trends have been for the models and practices of marketization across different historical contexts. From an institutional perspective, it can be

**Table 2.1** Five contemporary models for managing public sector activities

| *Model* | *OPA—Old Public Administration* | *NPM—New Public Management* | *NWS—Neo Weberian State* | *NPG—New Public Governance* | *DEG—Digital Era Governance* |
|---|---|---|---|---|---|
| Basic claim | State unique actor characterized by rule of law, neutral civil servants and a parliamentary chain of command | Marketization and modes of organizing from the private sector can make the public sector more efficient | Modernizing through marketization is OK, but the state remains a unique actor with own rules, methods and culture | Hierarchy increasingly replaced by horizontal networks of actors from many sectors | Digitalization is the meta innovation of our time and higher performance are achieved by new ways of organizing that exploits the possibilities |
| Primary coordination mechanisms | Rules, planning, bureaucracy and professions | MTMs, KPIs, goals, contracts, quasi-markets, semi-autonomous agencies | Rules, planning, bureaucracy and professions supplemented with NPM elements | Network of mutually dependent actors and coalitions | Centrally managed common standards combined with decentralization of information and decisions |

*Note* Table inspired by the following sources: (Andersen et al. 2017; Dunleavy et al. 2006; Pollitt and Bouckaert 2011; Hood 1991; Hood 2000; Rhodes 1996; Osborne 2006; Torfing and Ansell 2017; Weber 2002/1921)

expected that earlier models and practices, if not rolled back or outright displaced, are developed by integration of newer features and adaptation to contextual circumstances.

An extension of the discussions presented above Table 2.2 summarizes likely key features of marketization and privatization in three global reform phases. Compared to the core-NPM models presented above, a

**Table 2.2** Key features of marketization and privatization models in three reform phases

| *Marketization features within* | *Global reform phase* | | |
|---|---|---|---|
| | *Pre-NPM (most trendsetting 1950s–1970s)* | *Core-NPM (most trendsetting 1980s–1990s)* | *Post-NPM (most trendsetting from 2000s)* |
| Mix of providers | In-house/public as default choice, private as supplement | Private as default choice, in-house as second choice | Mix of public, private and alternative provider types (social enterprises) |
| Purposes for private involvement | Delivery of services requiring highly specialized expertise and/or equipment and/or 'buffer' role | Gaining economic benefits and increasing competition for service | Mix of purposes. Economic, benchmark, service quality, development, specialized services |
| Contracting models | Informal and relational exchange models | Formal, competitive, price/cost-oriented, conventional/simple, short term | Formal, collaborative, service oriented, user involvement, complex, long term |
| Internal organization | Informal structures, hierarchical command and control, rule-based bureaucratic and/or skill based organization | Highly formalized purchaser–provider split models, devolution of responsibilities, exposure to price competition, 'corporate-like' features | Formalized structures, performance oriented, relaxed competition |
| Interface with users | "Client" or "receiver" of services | "Costumer" endowed with choice options | Involved by voice mechanisms and "co-producers" of services |
| Overall emphasis on marketization | Low | High | Medium |

*Note* Authors' own compilation of key features and models of marketization across three reform phases. Models should be understood as Weberian ideal-types. The indicated trend-setting decades may vary between countries and regions and is probably most correct for the UK pre-NPM phase denotes an era with a limited overall role for marketization and privatization in local governments. The systematic and formal use of competitive tendering for reducing costs, for example, was introduced as part of the core-NPM models and substituted earlier and more informal practices. The post-NPM phase, on the other hand, denotes an era with a moderated role for marketization and privatization, which integrates features from newer reform trends (see Table 2.1). In particular, the post-NPM phase embraces an orientation towards reform models based on a more heterogeneous mix of provider types, contracting relations based on ideas of long-term collaboration and partnerships, a focus on solving cross-cutting policy issues, service innovations, a wider range of strategic purposes in service delivery, and more direct user involvements. However, available comparative research exploring whether newer reform trends moderate or displace marketization and privatization in local governments across several countries is scarce. Evidence from some services indicates that municipalities are reversing earlier privatizations (McDonald 2018) while evidence for other services indicates a moderation of marketization by shifts towards collaborative approaches in some countries (Greer et al. 2017).

## Conclusion

This chapter has provided key theoretical concepts and perspectives for the following chapters. The concept of marketization has been clarified and its historical context explained. Since the 1980s, marketization has been framed as key part of the broader complex of NPM models for reform. In contrast to the classical hierarchy and bureaucracy in the "pre-NPM" public sector, the construction of semi-autonomous agencies and relations based on contracts is the basic mode of organizing public sector activities under marketization. Marketization promotes certain models for organizing public sector activities and interactions with the private sector. The basic idea in conventional NPM models is to enhance efficiency in public service delivery through market-type mechanisms (MTMs)—especially competition and the use of the price mechanism. Eight related transnational models for organizing marketization have been widely used and in the empirical context of local park and road services, that we examine, the predominant model of marketization has historically been a mix of contracting and agencification. In recent years, various post-NPM models have been suggested and tried out.

Theorizing based on economic theory provides the intervention theories supporting marketization as well as notions concerning how to organize it. From the perspective of sociological institutionalism marketization is a global phenomenon, which is supported by global theorizing rooted in economic theory and diffused into multiple national and local settings. From the perspective of historical institutionalism, marketization may take many different forms due to national characteristics and local path dependencies. Thus, due to processes of national and local adaptation and translation, we expect a variety of different versions of public sector marketization in the four countries we examine in this book.

## References


Albalate, D., Bel, G., & Calzada, J. (2012). Governance and Regulation of Urban Bus Transportation: Using Partial Privatization to Achieve the Better of Two Worlds. *Regulation and Governance, 6*(1), 83–100.

Alford, J., & Head, B. W. (2017). Wicked and Less Wicked Problems: A Typology and a Contingency Framework. *Policy and Society*.

Amirkhanyan, A. A., & Lambright, K. T. (2017). *Citizen Participation in the Age of Contracting: When Service Delivery Trumps Democracy*. Routledge.

Ammons, D. N., & Roenigk, D. J. (2015). Benchmarking and Interorganizational Learning in Local Government. *Journal of Public Administration Research and Theory, 25*(1), 309–335.

Andersen, L. B., Greve, C., Klausen, K. K., & Torfing, J. (2017). *Offentlige styringsparadigmer: Konkurrence og sameksistens*. København: Jurist- og Økonomforbundets Forlag.

Ansell, C. (2011). *Pragmatist Democracy: Evolutionary Learning as Public Philosophy*. New York: Oxford University Press.

Baumol, W. J. (1982). Contestable Markets: An Uprising in the Theory of Industry Structure. *The American Economic Review, 72*(1), 1–15.

Baumol, W. J. (1993). Health Care, Education and the Cost Disease: A Looming Crisis for Public Choice. In *The Next Twenty-Five Years of Public Choice* (pp. 17–28). Amsterdam: Springer.

Bel, G., & Fageda, X. (2011). Big Guys Eat Big Cakes: Firm Size and Contracting in Urban and Rural Areas. *International Public Management Journal, 14*(1), 4–26.

Bevir, M. (2009). Marketization. In *Key Concepts in Governance* (pp. 127–131). London: Sage.

Boyne, G. A. (1998). *Public Choice Theory and Local Government: A Comparative Analysis of the UK and the USA*. Basingstoke: Macmillan.

Brinkerhoff, D. W., & Brinkerhoff, J. M. (2011). Public-Private Partnerships: Perspectives on Purposes, Publicness, and Good Governance. *Public Administration and Development, 31*(1), 2–14.

Bukh, P. N., & Dietrichson, L. G. (2016). Collaborative Benchmarking in the Danish District-Heating Sector. *International Journal of Public Sector Management, 29*(5), 502–519.

Christensen, T., & Lægreid, P. (2007a). The Whole-of-Government Approach to Public Sector Reform. *Public Administration Review, 67*(6), 1059–1066.

Christensen, T., & Lægreid, P. (Eds.). (2007b). *Transcending New Public Management: The Transformation of Public Sector Reforms.* Aldershot: Ashgate.

Christensen, T., & Lægreid, P. (2007c). Introduction - Theoretical Approach and Research Questions. In T. Christensen & P. Lægreid (Eds.), *Transcending New Public Management: The Transformation of Public Sector Reforms* (pp. 1–16). Aldershot: Ashgate.

Clarke, J., Newman, J., Smith, N., Vidler, E., & Westmarland, L. (2007). *Creating Citizen-Consumers: Changing Publics and Changing Public Services.* Pine Forge Press.

Coase, R. H. (1937). The Nature of the Firm. *Economica, 4*(16), 386–405.

Coase, R. H. (1960). The Problem of Social Cost. *Journal of Law and Economics, 3,* 1–44.

Czarniawska, B., & Sevón, G. (1996). *Translating Organizational Change.* Berlin: Walter de Gruyter.

DiMaggio, P. J., & Powell, W. D. (1991). The Iron Cage Revisited: Institutional Isomorphism and Collective Rationality. In *The New Institutionalism in Organizational Analysis.* Chicago: University of Chicago Press.

DiMaggio, P. J., & Powell, W. W. (1983). The Iron Cage Revisited—Institutional Isomorphism and Collective Rationality in Organizational Fields. *American Sociological Review, 48*(2), 147–160.

Djelic, M. L. (2006). Marketization: From Intellectual Agenda to Global Policy-Making. In M.-L. Djelic & K. Sahlin-Andersson (Eds.), *Transnational Governance: Institutional Dynamics of Regulation* (pp. 53–73). Cambridge: Cambridge University Press.

Donahue, J. D., & Zeckhauser, R. J. (2006). Public-Private Collaboration. In M. Moran, M. Rein, & R. E. Goodin (Eds.), *The Oxford Handbook of Public Policy* (pp. 496–525). Oxford: Oxford University Press.

Downs, A. (1957). *An Economic Theory of Democracy.* New York: Harper & Row.

Downs, A. (1967). *Inside Bureaucracy.* Boston: Little, Brown.

Dunleavy, P. (1991). *Democracy, Bureaucracy and Public Choice: Economic Explanations in Political Science.* New York: Harvester Wheatsheaf.

Dunleavy, P., Margetts, H., Bastow, S., & Tinkler, J. (2006). New Public Management Is Dead-Long Live Digital-Era Governance. *Journal of Public Administration Research and Theory, 16*(3), 467–494.

Eisenhardt, K. M. (1989). Agency Theory—An Assessment and Review. *Academy of Management Review, 14*(1), 57–74.

Entwistle, T., & Martin, S. (2005). From Competition to Collaboration in Public Service Delivery: A New Agenda for Research. *Public Administration, 83*(1), 233–242.

Feigenbaum, H., Henig, J. R., & Hamnett, C. (1998). *Shrinking the State: The Political Underpinnings of Privatization*. Cambridge University Press.

Flinders, M. (2010). Splintered Logic and Political Debate (Chapter 6). In *International Handbook on Public–Private Partnerships*.

Gingrich, J. R. (2007). *Whose Market Is It Anyways: Making Multiple Markets in the Welfare State*. Berkeley: University of California.

Greer, I., Breidahl, N. K., Knuth, M., & Larsen, F. (2017). *The Marketization of Employment Services: The Dilemmas of Europe's Work-first Welfare State*. Oxford: Oxford University Press.

Greve, C. (2000). Exploring Contracts as Reinvented Institutions in the Danish Public Sector. *Public Administration, 78*(1), 153–164.

Greve, C. (2005). Governing by Contract: Challenges and Opportunities for Public Managers. *Public Management Review, 7*(2), 306–308.

Greve, C. (2008). *Contracting for Public Services*. London: Routledge.

Greve, C., & Ejersbo, N. (2010). Kontrakter I Kommunerne. *Politica, 42*(2), 202–217.

Greve, C., & Hodge, G. (2013). *Rethinking Public-Private Partnerships: Strategies for Turbulent Times*. London: Routledge.

Greve, C., Lægreid, P., & Rykkja, L. H. (2016). *Nordic Administrative Reforms: Lessons for Public Management*. London: Palgrave Macmillan.

Hall, P. A., & Soskice, D. (2001) An Introduction to Varieties of Capitalism. In P. A. Hall & D. Soskice (Eds.), *Varieties of Capitalism* (pp. 1–68). Oxford: Oxford University Press.

Hall, P. A., & Taylor, R. C. R. (1996). Political Science and the Three New Institutionalisms. *Political Studies, 44*(5), 936–957.

Hansen, M. B. (2011). Antecedents of Organizational Innovation: The Diffusion of New Public Management into Danish Local Government. *Public Administration, 89*(2), 285–306.

Hansen, M. B. (2017). Performance Management and Evaluation. In B. Greve (Ed.), *Handbook of Social Policy Evaluation*. London: Edward Elgar.

Hansen, M. B., & Lindholst, A. C. (2016). Marketization Revisited. *International Journal of Public Sector Management, 29*(5), 398–408.

Hansen, M. B., & Vedung, E. (2010). Theory-Based Stakeholder Evaluation. *American Journal of Evaluation, 31*(3), 295–313.

Harrison, S. (1991). Working the Markets—Purchaser Provider Separation in English Health-Care. *International Journal of Health Services, 21*(4), 625–635.

Hartley, K., & Parker, D. (1991). Privatization: A Conceptual Framework. In A. F. Ott & K. Hartley (Eds.), *Privatization and Economic Efficiency: A Comparative Analysis of Developed and Developing Countries.* Aldershot, UK: Edward Elgar.

Hayek, F. A. (1945). The use of Knowledge in Society. *The American Economic Review, 35*(4), 519–530.

Hayek, F. A. (2014). *The Road to Serfdom: Text and documents: The* (Definitive ed.). New York and London: Routledge.

Hefetz, A., & Warner, M. (2004). Privatization and Its Reverse: Explaining the Dynamics of the Government Contracting Process. *Journal of Public Administration Research and Theory, 14*(2), 171–190.

Hefetz, A., & Warner, M. E. (2012). Contracting or Public Delivery? The Importance of Service, Market, and Management Characteristics. *Journal of Public Administration Research and Theory, 22*(2), 289–317.

Hirschman, A. O. (1970). *Exit, Voice, and Loyalty: Responses to Decline in Firms, Organizations, and States.* Cambridge, MA: Harvard University Press.

Hodge, G. (2000). *Privatization. An International Review of Performance.* Boulder: Westview Press.

Hodge, G., & Greve, C. (2018). Contemporary Public–Private Partnership: Towards a Global Research Agenda. *Financial Accountability & Management, 34*(1), 3–16.

Hodge, G. A., & Greve, C. (2019). *The Logic of Public–Private Partnerships.* Edward Elgar Publishing.

Hodge, G. A., Greve, C., & Boardman, A. E. (2010). *International Handbook on Public–Private Partnerships.* Cheltenham: Edward Elgar.

Hood, C. (1991). A Public Management for All Seasons. *Public Administration, 69*(1), 3–19.

Hood, C. (1994). *Explaining Economic Policy Reversals.* Buckingham: Open University Press.

Hood, C. (1998). *The Art of State: Culture, Rhetoric and Public Management.* Oxford: Clarendon Press (2414).

Hood, C. (2000). Paradoxes of Public-Sector Managerialism, Old Public Management and Public Service Bargains. *International Public Management Journal, 3*(1), 1–22.

Hood, C., & Dixon, R. (2015). *A Government That Worked Better and Cost Less?: Evaluating Three Decades of Reform and Change in UK Central Government.* Oxford: Oxford University Press.

Hood, C., & Peters, B. G. (2004). The Middle Aging of New Public Management: Into the Age of Paradox? *Journal of Public Administration Research and Theory, 14*(3), 267–282.

Hughes, O. E. (2018). *Public Management and Administration: An Introduction* (5th ed.). London: Palgrave.

Iversen, T., & Soskice, D. (2019). *Democracy and Prosperity: Reinventing Capitalism Through a Turbulent Century*. Princeton: Princeton University Press.

Jensen, M. C., & Meckling, W. H. (1976). Theory of the Firm: Managerial Behavior, Agency Costs and Ownership Structure. *Journal of Financial Economics, 3*(4), 305–360.

John, P. (2017). Finding Exits and Voices: Albert Hirschman's Contribution to the Study of Public Services. *International Public Management Journal, 20*(3), 512–529.

Jorgensen, T. B., Hansen, H. F., Antonsen, M., & Melancer, P. (1998). Public Organizations, Multiple Constituencies, and Governance. *Public Administration, 76*(3), 499–518.

Kettl, D. F. (2005). *The Global Public Management Revolution* (2nd ed.). Washington, DC: Brookings Institutions Press.

Knott, A. M., & Posen, H. E. (2005). Is Failure Good? *Strategic Management Journal, 26*(7), 617–641. https://doi.org/10.1002/smj.470.

Knudsen, T., & Rothstein, B. (1994). State-Building in Scandinavia. *Comparative Politics, 26*(2), 203–220.

Kocka, J. (2016). *Capitalism: A Short History*. Princeton: Princeton University Press.

Kristensen, O. P. (1984). Privatisering: Modernisering at den offentlige sektor eller ideologisk korstog? *Nordisk Administrativt Tidsskrift, 65*, 95–117.

Kuhlmann, S., & Bouckaert, G. (Eds.). (2016). *Local Public Sector Reforms in Times of Crisis: National Trajectories and International Comparisons. Governance and Public Management Series*. Palgrave Macmillan. ISBN 978-1-137-52548-2.

Lave, C. A., & March, J. G. (1993). *An Introduction to Models in the Social Sciences*. Lanham: University Press of America.

Le Grand, J., Enthoven, A., & Lipsey, D. (2007). *The Other Invisible Hand: Delivering Public Services Through Choice and Competition*. Princeton, NJ: Princeton University Press.

Lee, C. K., & Strang, D. (2006) The International Diffusion of Public-Sector Downsizing: Network Emulation and Theory-Driven Learning. *International Organization, 60*(4), 883–909.

Lewis, J., Bernstock, P., Bovell, V., & Wookey, F. (1996). The Purchaser Provider Split in Social Care: Is It Working? *Social Policy and Administration, 30*(1), 1–19.

Lindholst, A. C. (2009). Contracting-Out in Urban Green-Space Management: Instruments, Approaches and Arrangements. *Urban Forestry and Urban Greening, 8*(4), 257–268.

Lindholst, A. C., Hansen, M. B., & Petersen, O. H. (2016). Marketization Trajectories in the Danish Road and Park Sectors: A Story of Incremental Institutional Change. *International Journal of Public Sector Management, 29*(5), 457–473.

Lundqvist, L. J. (1988). Privatization: Towards a Concept for Comparative Policy Analysis. *Journal of Public Policy, 8*(01), 1–19.

Mahoney, J., & Thelen, K. (2010). *Explaining Institutional Change: Ambiguity, Agency, and Power*. Cambridge: Cambridge University Press.

March, J. G., & Olsen, J. P. (1989). *Rediscovering Institutions: The Organizational Basis of Politics*. New York: Free Press.

Marshall, T. H. (1950). *Citizenship and Social Class* (Vol. 11). Cambridge: Cambridge University Press.

McDonald, D. A. (2018, May). Remunicipalization: The Future of Water Services? *Geoforum, 91*, 47–56.

McGuire, M. (2006). Collaborative Public Management: Assessing What We Know and How We Know It. *Public Administration Review, 66*(S1), 33–43.

Ménard, C. (2018). Research Frontiers of New Institutional Economics. *RAUSP Management Journal, 53*(1), 3–10.

Meyer, J. W. (2009). Reflections: Institutional Theory and World Society. In G. Krücken & G. S. Drori (Eds.), *World Society: The Writings of John W. Meyer* (pp. 36–63). Oxford: Oxford University Press.

Meyer, J. W., Boli, J., Thomas, G. M., & Ramirez, F. O. (1997). World Society and the Nation-State. *American Journal of Sociology, 103*(1), 144–181.

Meyer, J. W., & Rowan, B. (1977). Institutionalized Organizations: Formal Structure as Myth and Ceremony. *American Journal of Sociology, 83*, 340–363.

Miller, G. J. (2005). The Political Evolution of Principal-Agent Models. *Annual Review of Political Science, 8*, 203–225.

Miller, G. J., & Whitford, A. B. (2007). The Principal's Moral Hazard: Constraints on the Use of Incentives in Hierarchy. *Journal of Public Administration Research and Theory, 17*(2), 213–233.

Mitnick, B. M. (2015). Agency Theory. In *Wiley Encyclopedia of Management* (pp. 1–6). Hoboken: Wiley.

Moe, T. M. (1984). The New Economics of Organization. *American Journal of Political Science, 28*(4), 739–777.

Niskanen, W. A. (1971). *Bureaucracy and Representative Government*. Chicago: Aldine-Atherton.

North, D. C. (1992). *Transaction Costs, Institutions, and Economic Performance*. San Francisco, CA: ICS Press.

OECD. (2017). *Government at a Glance 2017*. Paris: OECD.
Olsen, J. P. (1978). *Politisk Organisering*. Oslo: Universitetsforlaget.
Ortiz-Ospina, E., & Roser, M. (2018). *Public Spending*. Retrieved from https // ourworldindata.org/public-spending from Our World in Data.
Osborne, S. P. (2006). The New Public Governance? *Public Management Review, 8*(3), 377–387.
Ostrom, E. (1990). *Governing the Commons: The Evolution of Institutions for Collective Action*. New York: Cambridge University Press.
Ostrom, E. (2009). *Understanding Institutional Diversity*. Princeton: Princeton University Press.
Oxford University Press (OUP). (2019). *Marketization*. Online dictionary. Lexico.com. https://www.lexico.com/en/definition/marketization.
Pierre, J. (1995). The Marketization of the State: Citizens, Consumers, and the Emergence of the Public Market. In B. G. Peters & D. J. Savoie (Eds.), *Governance in a Changing Environment* (pp. 55–81). Cambridge: Cambridge University Press.
Pierre, J., & Peters, B. G. (2017). The Shirking Bureaucrat: A Theory in Search of Evidence? *Policy and Politics, 45*(2), 157–172.
Pollitt, C., & Bouckaert, G. (2011). *Public Management Reform Comparative Analysis of New Public Management, Governance and the Neo-Weberian State* (3rd ed.). Oxford: Oxford University Press.
Pollitt, C., Talbot, C., Caulfield, J., & Smullen, A. (2004). *Agencies: How Governments Do Things Through Semi-Autonomous Organisations*. Basingstoke: Palgrave Macmillan.
Porter, M. E. (2008). The Five Competitive Forces That Shape Strategy. *Harvard Business Review, 86*(1), 25–40.
Poulsen, S. M., & Hansen, J. R. (2016). Contracting to Improve Public Service Provision. *Journal of Strategic Contracting and Negotiation, 2*(3), 187–205.
Premfors, R. (1998). Reshaping the Democratic State: Swedish Experiences in a Comparative Perspective. *Public Administration, 76*(1), 141–159.
Rainey, H. G. (2009). *Understanding and Managing Public Organizations*. San Francisco: Wiley.
Reiter, R., & Klenk, T. (2019). The Manifold Meanings of 'Post-New Public Management'—A Systematic Literature Review. *International Review of Administrative Sciences, 85*(1), 11–27.
Rhodes, R. A. W. (1996). The New Governance: Governing Without Government. *Political Studies, 44*(4), 652–667.
Rhodes, R. A. W. (2007). Understanding Governance: Ten Years On. *Organization Studies, 28*(8), 1243–1264.
Rogers, E. M. (2003). *Diffusion of Innovations* (5th ed.). New York: Free Press.
Rosenbloom, D. H. (1983). Public Administrative Theory and the Separation of Powers. *Public Administration Review, 43*(3), 219–227.

Rosenbloom, D. H., Kravchuk, R. S., & Clerkin, R. M. (2015). *Public Administration: Understanding Management, Politics and Law in the Public Sector* (8th ed.). New York: McGraw-Hill Education.

Ross, S. A. (1973). The Economic Theory of Agency: The Principal's Problem. *The American Economic Review, 63*(2), 134–139.

Rostgaard, T. (2006). Constructing the Care Consumer: Free Choice of Home Care for the Elderly in Denmark. *European Societies, 8*(3), 443–463.

Rothstein, B. (1998). *Just Institutions Matter: The Moral and Political Logic of the Universal Welfare State*. Cambridge: Cambridge University Press.

Røvik, K. A. (2011). From Fashion to Virus: An Alternative Theory of Organizations' Handling of Management Ideas. *Organization Studies, 32*(5), 631–653.

Røvik, K. A. (2016). Knowledge Transfer as Translation: Review and Elements of an Instrumental Theory. *International Journal of Management Reviews, 18*(3), 290–310.

Salamon, L. M. (1993). The Marketization of Welfare—Changing Nonprofit and For-Profit Roles in the American Welfare-State. *Social Service Review, 67*(1), 16–39.

Salamon, L. M. (Ed.). (2002). *The Tools of Government: A Guide to the New Governance*. Oxford: Oxford University Press.

Samuelson, P. A. (1954). The Pure Theory of Public Expenditure. *The Review of Economics and Statistics, 36*(4), 387–389.

Savas, E. S. (1989). A Taxonomy of Privatization Strategies. *Policy Studies Journal, 18*(2), 343–355.

Schlesinger, M., Dorwart, R. A., & Pulice, R. T. (1986). Competitive Bidding and States Purchase of Services—The Case of Mental-Health-Care in Massachusetts. *Journal of Policy Analysis and Management, 5*(2), 245–263.

Schumpeter, J. A. (1942). *Capitalism, Socialism and Democracy*. New York: Harper & Row.

Scott, W. R. (2014). *Institutions and Organizations: Ideas, Interests, and Identities* (4th ed.). Los Angeles: Sage.

Shleifer, A. (1985). A Theory of Yardstick Competition. *The Rand Journal of Economics, 16*(3), 319–327.

Shonfield, A. (1968). *Modern Capitalism*. Oxford: Oxford University Press.

Simmons, B. A., Dobbin, F., & Garrett, G. (2006). Introduction: The International Diffusion of Liberalism. *International Organization, 60*(4), 781–810.

Simon, H. A. (1976). *Administrative Behavior: A Study of Decision-Making Processes in Administrative Organization*. New York: Free Press.

Steinmo, S., Thelen, K., & Longstreth, F. (Eds.). (1992). *Structuring Politics: Historical Institutionalism in Comparative Analysis*. Cambridge: Cambridge University Press.

Stelling, C. (2014). An Excursion into the Public-Private Partnership Jungle: Stop Standardizing but keep on Mapping! *International Public Management Review, 15*(1), 1–28.

Strang, D., & Meyer, J. W. (1993). Institutional Conditions for Diffusion. *Theory and Society, 22*(4), 487–511.

Tanzi, V., & Schuknecht, L. (2000). *Public Spending in the 20th Century: A Global Perspective*. Cambridge: Cambridge University Press.

Tiebout, C. M. (1956). A Pure Theory of Local Expenditures. *Journal of Political Economy, 64*(5), 416–424.

Torfing, J., & Ansell, C. (2017). Strengthening Political Leadership and Policy Innovation Through the Expansion of Collaborative Forms of Governance. *Public Management Review, 19*(1), 37–54.

Tullock, G. (1965). *The Politics of Bureaucracy*. Washington, DC Public Affairs Press.

Vickers, J., & Yarrow, G. (1991). Economic Perspectives on Privatization. *Journal of Economic Perspectives, 5*(2), 111–132.

Voorn, B., van Thiel, S., & van Genugten, M. (2018). Debate: Corporatization as More Than a Recent Crisis-Driven Development. *Public Money and Management, 38*(7), 481–482.

Waeraas, A., & Nielsen, J. A. (2016). Translation Theory 'Translated': Three Perspectives on Translation in Organizational Research. *International Journal of Management Reviews, 18*(3), 236–270. https://doi.org/10.1111/ijmr.12092.

Warner, M. E., & Hefetz, A. (2008). Managing Markets for Public Service: The Role of Mixed Public-Private Delivery of City Services. *Public Administration Review, 68*(1), 155–166.

Waterman, R. W., & Meier, K. J. (1998). Principal-Agent Models: An Expansion? *Journal of Public Administration Research and Theory, 8*(2), 173–202.

Weber, M. (2002/1921). *Wirtschaft und gesellschaft: Grundriss der verstehenden Soziologie* (5th ed.). Tübingen: Mohr Siebeck.

Williamson, O. E. (1975). *Markets and Hierarchies*. New York: Free Press.

Williamson, O. E. (1985). *The Economic Institutions of Capitalism: Simon and Schuster*. New York: Free Press.

Williamson, O. E. (1998a). The Institutions of Governance. *American Economic Review, 88*(2), 75–79.

Williamson, O. E. (1998b). Transaction Cost Economics: How It Works; Where It Is Headed. *Economist, 146*(1), 23–58.

Williamson, O. E. (2000). The New Institutional Economics: Taking Stock, Looking Ahead. *Journal of Economic Literature, 38*(3), 595–613.

CHAPTER 3

# Research Design, Materials and Methods

*Andrej Christian Lindholst, Morten Balle Hansen, Ylva Norén Bretzer, Nicola Dempsey and Merethe Dotterud Leiren*

## Introduction

This book explores the phenomenon of marketization in a comparative perspective. This chapter is devoted to a presentation and discussion of the overall research design and the empirical foundations of our book. The phenomenon of marketization is no stranger to scrutiny and has been examined extensively over time through a variety of research strategies and interests (see Chapters 1 and 2). Our research strategy is comparative in its outlook and integrates longitudinal and cross-sectional

A. C. Lindholst (✉) · M. B. Hansen
Department of Politics and Society, Aalborg University, Aalborg, Denmark
e-mail: acl@dps.aau.dk

M. B. Hansen
e-mail: mbh@dps.aau.dk

Y. N. Bretzer
School of Public Administration, University of Gothenburg, Gothenburg, Sweden
e-mail: ylva.noren-bretzer@spa.gu.se



A. C. Lindholst and M. B. Hansen (eds.),
*Marketization in Local Government*,
https://doi.org/10.1007/978-3-030-32478-0_3

analyses of experiences with marketization of park and road services within and across the four-country contexts of UK (with emphasis on England), Denmark, Sweden and Norway based on combined quantitative and qualitative data. A key feature of the research strategy is that marketization is studied with a focus on the importance of contextual differences for the diffusion and evolution of local marketization practices.

The empirical foundation consists of primary data, collected through national surveys, research interviews and document analysis, and secondary data originating from earlier studies and register-based sources from the UK, Denmark, Sweden, Norway and OECD. A part of our data material has been organized in a set of case-studies. The data material was originally collected as part of a comparative research project *Innovations in Public-Private Arrangements in an International perspective with focus on technical services in Local Governments* (abbreviated to 'INOPS'). In the project we collected data from municipalities in the UK and Scandinavia. Data collection (i.e., the survey, interviews and documents) was led by the Danish research team and took place between 2014 and 2016 in collaboration between researchers in all four countries. Data materials from INOPS have been applied—and to some extent updated—for the purpose of this book.

While the INOPS survey provided data for all four countries within the UK context (England, Northern Ireland, Scotland and Wales) we mainly focus on our data for England for statistical analysis in this book (see also Chapter 4). It should be noted that findings from statistical analysis of our INOPS survey data in general do not differ whether we analyze data for England only or include data also for Northern Ireland, Scotland and Wales.

In the remainder of the chapter we first present our comparative research strategy. *Second*, we present the INOPS survey and evaluate the

N. Dempsey
Department of Landscape Architecture, University of Sheffield, Sheffield, UK
e-mail: n.dempsey@sheffield.ac.uk

M. D. Leiren
CICERO—Center for International Climate Research, Oslo, Norway
e-mail: merethe.leiren@cicero.oslo.no

data in terms of characteristics of respondents, response rates and representativeness. Methodological reservations are also discussed. *Third*, we present the research background and methods for our case-studies. We end the chapter with a short summary and a few remarks.

### *A Comparative Research Strategy*

In comparative analysis of public management reforms, general characteristics of countries and service contexts wherein reforms are implemented are recurrently revoked as important interpretive and explanatory point of references when examining and interpreting similarities and differences in the outcomes and impacts of reforms (Christensen and Lægreid 2007, 2011; Greve et al. 2016; Kuhlmann and Bouckaert 2016; Pollitt and Bouckaert 2011; Wollmann and Marcou 2010). Christensen and Lægreid (2011), for example, highlight that contextual differences across groups of countries (and services) in *structures* (e.g. constitutions and politico-administrative systems), *cultures* (e.g. history and traditions) and *environments* (e.g. institutional and technical) are likely to produce divergence in the implementation of reforms. Another example is Kuhlmann and Bouckaert (2016) which highlight *state structure and government type* (e.g. level of overall centralization and democratic system), *administrative culture and tradition* (e.g. legalism and rule orientation), *local government responsibilities and autonomy* (e.g. range of responsibilities and level of local discretion), *territorial structures* (e.g. size), and *local democracy* (e.g. distribution of power between political and administrative levels). When taking on a comparative strategy, key characteristics of the politico-administrative system, such as the local government structure, provide a filter for interpreting how the mix of policy instruments and organizational possibilities has shaped and differentiated the wider diffusion and evolution of marketization. Similarly, the characteristics of the service sectors themselves, such as their relative ease for complying with the requisites of market-based governance, can be expected to provide a second filter. In the comparative perspective of the book, the features of the country contexts are found to vary while the features of the service sector contexts are found to be relatively invariant (see Chapter 4).

The comparative research strategy in this book calls on a combination of design elements, including different comparative methods, mixed methods involving quantitative and qualitative data, and longitudinal and cross-sectional analyses: The quantitative parts, for example, allow for statistical generalizations, while the comparative and partly the case-based methods allow for, in systematic ways, to explore differences and similarities in the diffusion and evolution of marketization across country contexts with different characteristics. To our knowledge (see also Chapter 1) the book contributes method-wise to existing literature by combining a systematic focus on marketization at the municipal level based on analysis of unique and primary quantitative and qualitative data from four countries. Comparative analysis is based on a combination of statistical analyses and case-studies, guided by attention to differences and similarities in the historical-institutional contexts. The analyses are cross-sectional and longitudinal. Cross-sectional analysis compares the current characteristics of marketization across the four countries (Chapter 10) while longitudinal analysis compares the historical-institutional developments of marketization (Chapter 16).

The mixed-method approach is based on a triangulation design (Creswell and Plano Clark 2011) involving integration and interpretation of insights from several analyses ranging from analysis and discussion of findings from our single case-studies (Chapters 11–15) to statistical analysis of quantitative data collected by uniform survey items in our four countries (Chapters 5–10). A key advantage of the mixed-method research design is the opportunities to explore and illustrate in greater detail some of the defining features of marketization in each country. This is, for example, notable in the general differences in the emphasis on formal collaboration and user involvement in contractual arrangements in a comparison of England with the three Scandinavian countries. The quantitative analysis of country differences provided in Chapter 10 only shows that municipalities in England emphasize collaboration and user involvement in terms of statistically significant higher mean scores while the case-studies enable a reader more fully to comprehend the details and underlying realities of these statistical differences.

### *The INOPS Survey*

The INOPS survey data forms a key data sources for the chapters in Part II of our book (Chapters 5–10). The survey was designed to gain insights into how service provisions within the municipal park and road sectors were organized and managed and how various types of organization and management performed. The main parts of the survey were initially developed in Denmark and later adopted and translated for use in Sweden, Norway and the UK. The core of the survey included eight main questions about the general characteristics of the respondents and their organization, 19 main questions related to the use of private contractors and 19 main questions related to the use of in-house provision. Each main question was divided into a number of items and where relevant divided into items for parks and roads respectively. The survey also gave opportunity for respondents to provide comparable information for various other types of provision arrangements. The survey was furthermore structured hierarchically so that each respondent only got questions that were relevant for the respondent's organization.

Literature on marketization was reviewed in order to provide the theoretical framework for the survey and guide operationalizations of survey items. For example, the survey included items in concordance with the literature on key organizational principles of new public management, such as purchaser-provider models or competitive tendering. Another example is the use of earlier case-based research on sector-specific contract designs (Lindholst 2009) for guiding the formulation of items on contract design in the survey. Several pilot tests with respondents from the two service sectors of investigation and researchers with sector-specific knowledge were carried out in the initial design phase in Denmark. The number, wording and response scales for items in the survey were adjusted according to the provided feedback. In the final survey, most items used 11-point numeric response scales with end anchors. Both one-dimensional (e.g. from 'not at all' to 'a very high degree') and two-dimensional scales (e.g. from 'very unsatisfied' to 'very satisfied') were used pending on the individual item. The survey also included items which used categorical response scales (e.g. 'yes' or 'no') as well as some ordinal response scales (e.g. the respondent's hierarchical position in the organization). Open response options (for comments) were included for all items. Survey questions and items used for analysis in the book are documented in the individual chapters. Further documentation on the full surveys including all items and descriptive statistics is available in separate reports for each country (Lindholst et al. 2017a; Lindholst and Holt 2017; Lindholst and Nielsen 2017; Lindholst and Severin 2017).

In the subsequent adoption for the UK, Sweden and Norway, the survey was translated and tested by researchers from each country. An initial translation was first discussed and adjusted by the researchers. Second, the translated survey was tested with primary respondents in each country. Thirdly, reported issues with respondents' understanding of formulations of survey items or their purpose were discussed and addressed by the researchers. In particular, the survey was adjusted for each country to match the technical and sector-specific jargon used by respondents within the national park and road sectors. In the process a few questions and items were included or removed for each country survey, thus, the total number of questions and items was slightly different for the UK, Norway and Sweden compared to the original survey used in Denmark.

The target population—the sample frame—for the INOPS survey was municipalities in the UK, Sweden, Denmark and Norway. Respondents in the municipalities were targeted for their expected insights into strategic and operational dimensions of the provision of park and road services. The typical respondent targeted in the survey was a mid-level manager within the municipal organization endowed with formal responsibilities for roads and/or park services. Due to variations in internal organization of park and road responsibilities it was necessary in some cases to identify more than one respondent within the same municipality. Lists of contact persons and contact details were collected separately for each country. A combination of several methods was used including contact with professional associations, inspection of websites and direct contact with the municipalities (via e-mail or phone). The combination of methods was adjusted for use in each country due to slightly different possibilities and availability of contact details. Overall, accessibility to contact details was easier in Denmark and Sweden compared to Norway and the UK. In Norway, for example, a municipal structure with many very small municipalities (less than 1000 inhabitants) and the lack of available national databases with sector-specific contact details for the municipalities made it more difficult to find the relevant contact persons. In many cases, a general contact for the municipality was the only possible access point. In order for enabling ex-post evaluation of the respondents' characteristics, the survey included questions about the respondents' background and position.

After preparing master contact lists of respondents, the data collection was carried out electronically in a web-based survey program located at the same web-domain in Denmark. In all countries an initial invitation by e-mail was followed by several rounds of reminders targeted respondents that did not respond as well as respondents that had provided partial answers. Non-functioning e-mails for respondents were followed up by identification of new respondents where possible. All data collection was furthermore administered with anonymity for the participating municipalities and respondents.

The final dataset for each country consists of replies from respondents which provided complete or partially complete data entries in the online survey. In some cases, where entries from multiple respondents for a municipality were received, it was necessary to select entries from one respondent or merge partial entries (i.e. if information for only parks or roads was received). In this process one respondent was identified as primary respondent for a municipality. Key criteria for evaluation and selection of primary respondents were: position in the hierarchy, years of employment in the organization, job title and responsibilities of the respondent's department.

### *Characteristics of Primary Respondents*

Table 3.1 provides an overview of key characteristics of primary respondents in our four countries. Note that England is chosen as sample frame rather than the UK. In general, the typical primary respondent in all four countries is a middle-aged male holding a position as mid-level manager with extensive (lengthy) professional work experience at his current municipality and within the public sector more generally.

**Table 3.1** Characteristics of primary respondents

| *Country* | *Managerial level*[a] | | | | *Female (share) (%)* | *Average age years* | *Average employment history (in years)* | |
|---|---|---|---|---|---|---|---|---|
| | *Low (%)* | *Mid (%)* | *High (%)* | *Other (%)* | | | *Current municipality* | *Public sector* |
| Denmark | 3 | 87 | 9 | 1 | 23 | 52 (8) | 11 (9) | 19 (9) |
| Sweden | 7 | 65 | 19 | 9 | 25 | 50 (9) | 10 (9) | 17 (10) |
| Norway | 14 | 48 | 31 | 5 | 14 | 52 (9) | 13 (12) | 20 (12) |
| England | 44 | 46 | 4 | 4 | 21 | 50 (7) | 17 (11) | 24 (11) |

*Notes* All values are rounded. Standard deviations in brackets

[a]"Low-level" refers to a team/group leader or similar, "Mid-level" manager refers to position as head of the department or similar, "High-level" refers to a position as head of technical department or similar (or higher), and "Other" indicates a position without personnel/managerial responsibility (e.g. a specialist or internal consultant)

There are a few notable differences in respondent characteristics between the countries. For example, for England we find a large share of low-level managers while in Norway we find a relatively large share of high-level managers. The differences in the shares of managers with different ranking between England and Norway make sense as municipalities in England are substantially larger than municipalities in Norway. Overall, respondents with the longest employment history are found in England while those with the shortest employment history are found in Sweden. Although not pursued further in our book it should also be noted that the survey indicates that the service context of our study is male dominated. Despite some differences, we are content that the key characteristics of our primary respondents indicate that the INOPS survey data on the average are based on respondents with substantial insights and experiences with the subject matter of the survey. Key methodological issues related to our data will be discussed below.

### *Representativeness*

Table 3.2 provides an overview of response rates and summary of statistical tests for representativeness in our four countries (see Appendix A for further details on the statistical tests). The rate of municipalities represented in our survey ranged from approximately 22% for Norway to 77% for Denmark. The substantial differences in response rate are likely to be explained by differences between the countries in their municipal

**Table 3.2** Survey response rates and representativeness

| *Country* | *Municipalities* | | | | *Representativeness*[c] | | |
|---|---|---|---|---|---|---|---|
| | *Total number* | *With useful data*[a] | *Response rate*[b] *(%)* | *Share of population (%)* | *Municipal population* | *Municipal area* | *Regional location* |
| Denmark | 98 | 75 | 77 | 82 | Yes | Yes | Yes |
| Sweden | 290 | 115 | 40 | 53 | Yes | Yes | Yes |
| Norway | 428 | 96 | 22 | 50 | Partial[d] | No | No |
| England | 326 | 103 | 32 | 41 | No | Yes | – |

[a]The number of municipalities for which useful survey data were provided
[b]Percentage of municipalities for which useful survey data were provided
[c]See the book's appendix for statistical tests of representativeness
[d]The dataset is representative for Norwegian municipalities with more than 10,000 inhabitant

structure and/or the administration of the survey. The administration of the survey was following approximately the same procedure for all countries. However, differences in the perception of the survey may have influenced the willingness to participate and the response rates. For example, it may be more motivating to respond to questions sent out from a university in one's own country compared to responding to a questionnaire from overseas. The municipal structure also differs substantially across the four countries (see also Chapter 4). In particular, Norway and Sweden have a high number of municipalities with very few inhabitants compared to Denmark and England (and the UK more generally). Small Norwegian and Swedish municipalities are constrained and may lack the capacity to respond, as one and the same person may have several different responsibilities that are typically specialized in larger administrations. Some very small municipalities also have very limited responsibilities for park and/or road services which may have impacted the perceived relevance of participating in our survey.

In all countries, the proportions of the total national population represented by the municipalities in our survey were higher than the response rate. This indicates at first that the size of the municipalities included in the dataset is larger than the national averages. The data also show that municipalities representing substantial proportions of the national populations are included in the survey. The data for each country was further evaluated by statistical tests for representativeness with regard to municipal population (number of inhabitants), municipal area (km$^2$) and regional location (based on major national regions). Test statistics for representativeness are found in the appendix. For Denmark and Sweden, the statistical tests show that the dataset is representative according to all three categories. For Norway, the dataset mainly represents municipalities with relatively larger populations and with relatively smaller areas located in more densely populated regions. If the tests for Norway are limited to municipalities with more than 10,000 inhabitants, the dataset (for these municipalities) is representative in all categories. However, we use the full dataset for analysis. For England, the tests show that the dataset represents municipalities with slightly larger populations than the average, but no statistically significant difference is found for size in terms of area.

Of key relevance for further analysis is that the dataset reflects the country differences in the average size in the municipalities' populations. The average municipal size in the dataset is about 213,000 for

England, 45,000 for Sweden, 61,000 for Denmark and 27,000 inhabitants for Norway. Tests show that differences in population size are statistically significant ($p$-level < .05) between all countries except Sweden and Denmark and Sweden and Norway. Thus, differences in our samples roughly reflect the differences in municipal size in the sample frames (see also Chapter 4 for further details on municipal size).

### *Secondary Data Sources*

The book utilizes several secondary data sources and register-based statistics. To ensure that these data are valid for national comparisons we prioritized the use of updated standardized data, such as data made available by the OECD (2017) on local governments and data from national statistical bureaus on population and municipal size. In the book these data are particularly used for test of representativeness (this chapter) and for comparing the context for marketization in each country (Chapter 4). Data on municipal population and size are also utilized in statistical analysis of cost differences in contracting outcomes between the Scandinavian countries in Chapter 9. In addition, we use statistics from existing research to support our analysis and understanding of national context(s) (see Chapter 4). This includes, for example, the research by Ladner et al. (2016) on local autonomy in 39 countries. Some chapters in the book (Chapters 5–8) also draw extensively on available national and historical statistics in combination with findings in existing research to examine how marketization has diffused and evolved over time within a specific country.

Standardized data appeared unavailable for some key characteristics such as size of local park and road budgets or the quantity and quality of the services (e.g. road length or number of different types of parks). No statistical test is applied in these cases and only conclusions on very general patterns are drawn. In Chapter 4, for example, the lack of standardized data only allows us to conclude that local park and road budgets take up 'small fractions' of total local budgets and use highly diverging national measures to support this conclusion. The INOPS survey also contained items on local park and road budgets. However, several respondents provided no data for these items and scrutiny of comments (open survey items) indicated that the provided figures were calculated or summarized differently (e.g. with or without snow clearing). Thus, it can be said that for some local services, at least local park and road services, it is very hard to provide comparable insights on basic key characteristics—even across countries with well-developed statistical traditions. These data limitations also impose some limitations on comparative research.

### *Methodological Discussions*

#### *Measurement Equivalence*

The INOPS survey data is based on a survey instrument administered across four countries. The validity of analyses based on comparison or integration of the survey data across the four countries depends—as with other cross national or social research—on whether there is a sufficient degree of measurement equivalence. Measurement equivalence relates to the degree to which data are meaningful to compare across different contexts such as nations or ethnic groups (Davidov et al. 2014). Measurements should ideally be unaffected by respectively construct bias, method bias and item bias (Van de Vijver 1998). *Construct bias* refers to differences in the meaning of theoretical concepts across various groups were survey data is collected. *Method bias* refers to differences resulting from methodological differences in how data are collected including differences in the administration of the survey or differences in social desirability across the target populations. *Item bias* refers to issues arising from poor translations or the use of items with a highly culture-specific interpretation.

A range of preventive measures were implemented in the design and administration of the survey across our four countries which should minimize the chance for problems with measurement non-equivalence. The design and administration of the survey was deliberately replicated to ensure that respondents were fairly similar (i.e. local park and road managers with strategical and operational insights) and that item formulations were interpreted in similar ways across the countries (by pilot tests and adjustments). Most of our data are furthermore based on fairly objective 'etic' measures about administrative-technical matters likely to be understood in a consistent manner across contextual boundaries rather than context-specific 'emic' measures which are likely to possess different meanings and be interpreted differently across contextual boundaries (Johnson 1998).

*Method Biases*
Studies based on survey-based and/or perception-based data can be affected by a range of commonly known biases caused by, for example, social desirability, or the respondent's fatigue or lack of interest in a subject (Podsakoff et al. 2012). Our respondents—local managers—are similar to other key stakeholders e.g. politicians, users or contractors, as they represent a particular perspective and hold particular interests. For example, the survey included items on the (perceived) performance of in-house provision and private contractors. Given that respondents are evaluating internal stakeholders (or themselves) in the case of in-house provision and external stakeholders in the case of private contractors, such data are not easily compared and the validity of such comparison can rightly be questioned. Survey data for more objective 'facts' such as budget size or level of contracting out may also be influenced by the respondent's memory or differences in respondents' interpretations of the content of a survey item (e.g. what should be included in an estimate for a 'total park maintenance budget'?). On the other hand, register-based data may likewise be impeded by different or flawed accounting practices (Brewer 2006).

Common method bias is a special problem for analysis of associations between several constructs based on data generated from a single source or by a single method (Podsakoff et al. 2003). Common method bias can impede validity of findings by, for example, inflating or deflating, statistical associations between key variables of interest. Common method bias may arise from a respondent's inclination to provide answers congruent with prevalent social norms (social desirability) or a respondent's tendency to fill in the same response across several items. Implementation of ex ante remedies has been recommended as the best strategy for mitigating the risks of common method bias while various ex post remedies for detection (or test) and correction (or control) are found to be less certain (Jakobsen and Jensen 2015; Richardson et al. 2009). It should be noted, however, that when a survey is well-designed the risk of common method bias and method bias more generally should not be exaggerated (George and Pandey 2017).

Ex ante remedies of method biases in the INOPS survey included identification and validation of competent respondents, granting of complete anonymity for respondents and municipalities in all countries, wording of items in more specific terms rather than general terms (e.g. avoiding asking respondents to make assessment with comparisons to other local governments experiences), careful wording and pilot test of survey items, and the use different measurement scales for different variables.

Overall, despite the possible methodological issues with the use of perception-based data collected through surveys, the INOPS survey provided data of sufficient validity for further analysis. Still, presence of a degree of method bias cannot be ruled out and interpretations based on survey data should be made with some caution.

## Case-Studies

The second primary data source in our book is research interviews and documental materials used for generating a series of single case-studies. Altogether, four single case-studies, produced as a part of a larger number in the INOPS project (Lindholst 2017; Lindholst et al. 2017b), form the basis for book's Part III (Chapters 11–15). The reduction allowed for a more stringent framing and exploitation of the strengths of single case-studies for providing richness and presenting detailed insights into real-life phenomena (Yin 2003). The four selected case-studies all aim at illustrating and exploring leading national experiences—the 'forefront'—at the municipal or local level with innovative practices for marketization within park and road services. Table 3.3 provides a short overview of the case-studies.

INOPS survey data, pilot interviews and general background information were used to identify and select relevant cases within each country. For example, the case study in Holstebro Municipality (see Table 3.3) was selected due to the status of the Municipality to be the first in Denmark to contract out all park and road maintenance services and to continue with contracting out even at 'critical junctures' where circumstances allowed for taking services back in-house. The Municipality is furthermore a medium sized municipality located outside the primary conurbations in Denmark. As such the case-study represents local park and road services in a more low-key 'ordinary' setting than, for example, the case-studies in Oslo Municipality, Norway and Queen Elizabeth Olympic Park, London, England. Another example is our selection of Täby Municipality—a case-study in the context of a medium sized Swedish municipality located in the metropolitan area of Greater Stockholm. The selection was based on Täby Municipality's reputation in the sector for an early implementation (in 2004) in a Scandinavian

**Table 3.3** Overview of case studies

| *Country* | *Authority* | *Short description* | *Key data sources* |
|---|---|---|---|
| England | Queen Elizabeth Olympic Park, London Legacy Development Corporation | Contemporary experiences with outsourcing and partnership based contracting in the largest new park built in the UK for over 100 years | Phone and face-to-face interviews combined with document studies |
| Sweden | Täby Municipality | Changes and experiences with long-term partnership based contracting 2004–2016 | Group and phone interviews (from 2006 and 2016) combined with document studies |
| Denmark | Holstebro Municipality | A longitudinal case study of how the approach to contracting has evolved across four contract period 2000–2017 | Group and phone interviews with management team and contractor combined with document studies |
| Norway | Oslo Municipality | The rise and fall of a municipally owned service delivery organization 2000s–2010s | Interviews with several key persons combined with document studies |

*Notes* The table provides a short overview of the four case studies presented and discussed in Chapters 11–15

context of an innovative and radical long-term partnership approach to contracting with the private sector. The INOPS survey data collected more than a decade later confirm that such approaches to contracting, although they have become more common, are still not widespread in Scandinavia (see also Chapter 10).

By utilizing a holistic single case-study design (Yin 2003), the four cases were produced differently and are used in flexible ways to illustrate and explore our phenomena of interest within the different country contexts as well as phenomena of wider theoretical interest. A limitation from this approach is that our case-studies are less suited for making inferences through logical and direct comparative methods such as 'most similar' or 'most different' matching (Levy 2008). What the case-studies do well, however, is that they contribute and provide richness to broader discussions about the diffusion and evolution of marketization across our four countries as well as providing insights into experiences of wider theoretical and policy interest (see Chapters 15 and 16). The case-study, for example, of the contracting model used for managing and maintaining Queen Elizabeth Olympic Park for the London Legacy Development Corporation in the metropolitan area of London illuminates the latest developments in contracting practices in the second half of the 2010s which in turn provides a reference point for understanding the opportunities and the possible scope for developing these practices more generally. Compared to the characteristics of contracting practices in the three Scandinavian countries, this case study also illuminates the unique characteristics and comprehensiveness of the partnership approach to contracting found in UK/England. This can further be viewed as an expression of the general development in reforms from core-NPM toward post-NPM models of marketization as conceptually laid out in Chapter 2 and empirically evaluated by statistical analysis of INOPS survey data in Chapter 10.

The data collection for our case-studies was organized around similar main themes in terms of context (e.g. municipal characteristics), formal organizational and managerial arrangements (e.g. contract documents), perception of day-to-day collaboration and management as well as assessments of key outcomes and experiences (e.g. managerial challenges/problems or economic outcomes). Key data sources in all case-studies were research interviews and documental materials. The case-studies differ in the extent of data sources (e.g. the type of interviewees) and data materials (e.g. the number of interviewees). Content of the case-studies was developed and validated with feedback and comments from key respondents as well as comments from peers within the research group. All case-studies were carried out and reported with full identification of (and in consent with) the relevant municipalities. Original case reports, organized and presented as rich descriptive narratives, are available in two separate research reports from Aalborg University, Denmark (Lindholst 2017; Lindholst et al. 2017b).

A curious finding from the qualitative part of the INOPS project was the researchers' experience of easier access to the field and substantial greater readiness to participate among managers and municipalities in the three Scandinavian countries compared to England. Contract documents, for example, were easily accessed in Scandinavia while not made accessible for research by managers in England. This can be regarded as a methodological problem but is also an indication of differences in country-specific cultures wherein contracting practices develops and becomes shared within a larger organizational field. Based on this, admittedly very anecdotical evidence, England appears to represent a relatively closed and secretive administrative culture compared to relatively more transparent and open administrative cultures in Scandinavia.

## Final Remarks on Methods

In this chapter, we provided an overview and discussions of the overall comparative research strategy and primary data sources utilized for analysis throughout our book. *First*, the INOPS survey provides unique and comparable quantitative data on the marketization of park and road services within municipalities in England and the three Scandinavian countries. The data form basis for different types of statistical analysis in individual chapters. In the book, we use simple descriptive statistics, comparison of differences through analysis of variance (ANOVA) and regression analysis as main tools for statistical analysis. Details of these methods are provided in the chapters. The typical number of cases available for statistical analysis varies across the chapters and the topics in focus. The typical number of cases available for comparisons is between 50 and 100 cases from each country. Given the relatively low number of cases the variation (e.g. measured as standard deviations) around central values (e.g. means) is also relatively high for most data based on survey items. In consequence, rather large mean differences are required in order to reach statistical significance in the various statistical tests. Thus, throughout our book we apply relatively high $p$-levels equal to .1, .05 and .01 in our tests for statistical significance of differences.

*Second*, our case-studies provide rich accounts on how marketization practices have taken place in four selected municipalities. Insights from the case-studies are used for illustrative and explorative purposes and as a basis for discussions of wider theoretical and policy interests. The quantitative (survey) and qualitative (case-studies) parts allow for triangulation in the summarizing parts of the book (Chapters 15 and 16) through a mixed-method research design.

In addition to the primary data sources, the various parts of the book draw upon secondary data sources in different degrees. Secondary data includes, for example, statistics provided by national statistical bureaus or standardized country data from the OECD and statistics elaborated in earlier research. These data are also informing a part of the backbone for the next chapter where our four characteristics of our four countries are compared.

## References


Brewer, G. A. (2006). All Measures of Performance Are Subjective: More Evidence on US Federal Agencies in Public Service Performance. In G. Boyne, K. Meier, L. O'Toole Jr., & R. M. Walker (Eds.), *Public Service Performance: Perspectives on Measurement and Management* (pp. 35–54). New York: Cambridge University Press.

Christensen, T., & Lægreid, P. (2007). *Transcending New Public Management: The Transformation of Public Sector Reforms*. Burlington: Ashgate.

Christensen, T., & Lægreid, P. (2011). *The Ashgate Research Companion to New Public Management*. Farnham: Routledge.

Creswell, J. W., & Plano Clark, V. L. (2011). *Designing and Conducting Mixed Methods Research*. Thousand Oaks: Sage.

Davidov, E., Meuleman, B., Cieciuch, J., Schmidt, P., & Billiet, J. (2014). Measurement Equivalence in Cross-National Research. *Annual Review of Sociology, 40*(1), 55–75.

George, B., & Pandey, S. K. (2017). We Know the Yin—But Where Is the Yang? Toward a Balanced Approach on Common Source Bias in Public Administration Scholarship. *Review of Public Personnel Administration, 37*(2), 245–270.

Greve, C., Lægreid, P., & Rykkja, L. H. (2016). *Nordic Administrative Reforms: Lessons for Public Management*. London: Palgrave Macmillan.

Jakobsen, M., & Jensen, R. (2015). Common Method Bias in Public Management Studies. *International Public Management Journal, 18*(1), 3–30.

Johnson, T. P. (1998). Approaches to Equivalence in Cross-Cultural and Cross-National Survey Research. In J. Harkness (Ed.), *Cross-Cultural Survey Equivalence* (pp. 1–40). Mannheim: Leibniz-Institut für Sozialwissenschaften.

Kuhlmann, S., & Bouckaert, G. (Eds.). (2016). *Local Public Sector Reforms in Times of Crisis: National Trajectories and International Comparison*. London: Palgrave Macmillan.

Ladner, A., Keuffer, N., & Baldersheim, H. (2016). Measuring Local Autonomy in 39 Countries (1990–2014). *Regional and Federal Studies, 26*(3), 321–357.

Levy, J. S. (2008). Case Studies: Types, Designs and Logics of Inference. *Conflict Management and Peace Science, 25*(1), 1–18.

Lindholst, A. C. (2009). Contracting-out in urban green-space management: Instruments, approaches and arrangements. *Urban Forestry & Urban Greening, 8*(4), 257–268.

Lindholst, A. C. (Ed.). (2017). *INOPS Fire internationale casestudier: En undersøgelse af udlicitering af park- og vejdrift i to engelske, en svensk og en norsk kommune*. Aalborg: Department of Political Science, Aalborg University.

Lindholst, A. C., & Holt, S. (2017). *INOPS Survey Data Report for Norway: Survey Results on the Organisation, Management and Performance of Road *and Park Maintenance Service Provisions in Norwegian Municipalities.* Aalborg: Department of Political Science, Aalborg University.

Lindholst, A. C., Hansen, M. B., & Østergaard, J. (2017a). *INOPS Survey Data Report for Denmark: Survey Results on the Organisation, Management and Performance of Road and Park Maintenance Service Provisions in Danish Municipalities.* Aalborg: Department of Political Science, Aalborg University.

Lindholst, A. C., Jensen, T. H., & Kjems, T. H. (2017b). *INOPS Fem danske casestudier: En undersøgelse af udlicitering af park- og vejdrift i fem danske kommuner.* Aalborg: Department of Political Science, Aalborg University (In Danish).

Lindholst, A. C., & Nielsen, A. S. (2017). *INOPS Survey Data Report for the UK: Survey Results on Organisation, Management and Performance of Road and Park Maintenance Service Provisions in Local Authorities in the UK.* Aalborg: Department of Political Science, Aalborg University.

Lindholst, A. C., & Severin, M. C. (2017). *INOPS Survey Data Report for Sweden: Survey Results on the Organisation, Management and Performance of Road and Park Maintenance Service Provisions in Swedish Municipalities.* Aalborg: Department of Political Science, Aalborg University.

OECD. (2017). *Subnational Governments in OECD Countries: Key Data.* Paris: OECD.

Podsakoff, P. M., MacKenzie, S. B., Lee, J. Y., & Podsakoff, N. P. (2003). Common Method Biases in Behavioral Research: A Critical Review of the Literature and Recommended Remedies. *Journal of Applied Psychology, 88*(5), 879–903.

Podsakoff, P. M., MacKenzie, S. B., & Podsakoff, N. P. (2012). Sources of Method Bias in Social Science Research and Recommendations on How to Control It. *Annual Review of Psychology, 63,* 539–569.

Pollitt, C., & Bouckaert, G. (2011). *Public Management Reform: Comparative Analysis of New Public Management, Governance and the Neo-Weberian State.* Oxford: Oxford University Press.

Richardson, H. A., Simmering, M. J., & Sturman, M. C. (2009). A Tale of Three Perspectives: Examining Post Hoc Statistical Techniques for Detection and Correction of Common Method Variance. *Organizational Research Methods, 12*(4), 762–800.

Van de Vijver, F. J. R. (1998). Towards a Theory of Bias and Equivalence. In J. Harkness (Ed.), *Cross-Cultural Survey Equivalence* (pp. 41–65). Mannheim: Leibniz-Institut für Sozialwissenschaften.

Wollmann, H., & Marcou, G. (Eds.). (2010). *The Provision of Public Services in Europe Between State, Local Government and Market.* Cheltenham: Edward Elgar.

Yin, R. K. (2003). *Case Study Research: Design and Methods* (3rd ed.). London: Sage.

CHAPTER 4

# Introducing the Research Setting: Four Countries and Two Local Services

*Andrej Christian Lindholst, Morten Balle Hansen, Ylva Norén Bretzer, Nicola Dempsey and Merethe Dotterud Leiren*

## Introduction

This chapter provides an introductory overview of our research setting in terms of four countries—UK/England, and the three Scandinavian countries of Sweden, Denmark and Norway—and two local services—parks and roads. The overview focuses on relatively stable characteristics and their differences and similarities across the countries. The overview has a dual purpose. *First and foremost*, the overview provides a reader with a broad introduction to the general characteristics of the research setting which makes up the country and service context(s) in the book.

A. C. Lindholst (✉) · M. B. Hansen
Department of Politics and Society, Aalborg University, Aalborg, Denmark
e-mail: acl@dps.aau.dk

Y. N. Bretzer
School of Public Administration, University of Gothenburg, Gothenburg, Sweden
e-mail: ylva.noren-bretzer@spa.gu.se



A. C. Lindholst and M. B. Hansen (eds.),
*Marketization in Local Government*,
https://doi.org/10.1007/978-3-030-32478-0_4

It is acknowledged that the 'familiarity' with the four countries and two services will differ from reader to reader and some degree of background information is helpful for readers to make their own comparisons and judgements. *Second*, the overview provides a point of departure for discussing why the organization of marketization might or might not differ across our four countries. Thus, a guiding research question in the chapter is whether the specific characteristics of the country and service context(s) can be expected to produce differences (or similarities) in the evolution and diffusion of marketization across municipalities in our four countries. The specific characteristics we choose to highlight in this chapter correspond with many of the general characteristics highlighted in the existing comparative literature on public management reforms (see Chapters 2 and 3). Further details for each country are provided in subsequent chapters (in particular Chapters 5–8 and Chapters 11–14).

In the introductory overview and comparison we focus on, respectively, the characteristics of local park and road services, national reform trajectories, the structure and role of municipalities in the public sector, and the importance of EU regulations. *First*, we introduce and detail the service context—local park and road services—of the book. In general, the two services hold multiple key functions within the urban infrastructure and provision of proper maintenance is vital for upholding their functionality. While responsibilities for ownership, planning and finance for local parks and roads in the main case have been kept at municipal hands, responsibilities for maintenance have been framed as suitable for marketization at early reform stages in many countries. Congruently, analysis of basic service and market characteristics as well as types of economic goods (see also Chapter 2), have recurrently rendered local park and road services as suitable for marketization.

*Second*, we briefly introduce the overall reform characteristics and trajectories of our four countries. At first glance the four countries represent two main paths for public management reforms from the 1980s

---

N. Dempsey
Department of Landscape Architecture, University of Sheffield, Sheffield, UK
e-mail: n.dempsey@sheffield.ac.uk

M. D. Leiren
CICERO—Center for International Climate Research, Oslo, Norway
e-mail: merethe.leiren@cicero.oslo.no

and onward. UK/England represents an early and radical reform country with a general emphasis on 'marketization' over 'modernization' within the overall reform mix. In contrast, the three Scandinavian countries represent a group of later and less radical reform countries with a general emphasis on 'modernization' over 'marketization' within the overall reform mix. With this point of departure, it can in a comparative perspective be expected that marketization will be more pronounced within local park and road services in the context of UK/England than in Scandinavia. However, at a second glance the timing and impetus for public management reforms differ across the three Scandinavian countries. The urgency of economic crisis, for example, has been far less pronounced in Norway compared to Denmark and Sweden. Thus, it can be argued that the impact of national reform trajectories on the marketization of local park and road services are likely to differ within Scandinavia.

*Third*, we introduce and compare key characteristics of municipalities and discuss their likely importance for marketization. In particular, we take up the role of (a) local autonomy, and (b) size and territorial structure. Local autonomy of municipalities in the UK/England vis-à-vis the powers of central government are far more limited in comparison with all three Scandinavian countries. Thus, the impact of national reforms and policies on the municipal level can be expected to be more tightly coupled in the UK/England compared to the three Scandinavian countries. The size and territorial structure of municipalities also differs across the four countries. The 429 Norwegian municipalities, for example, are stretched out over a vast geography and only 13% have more than 20,000 inhabitants. All 326 (lower-tier) municipalities in England, on the other hand, have more than 20,000 inhabitants and are located within a comparatively much more densely populated country. These characteristics, which also differ substantially across the three Scandinavian countries, can also be expected to impact how marketization is organized within each country.

*Fourth* and final, we briefly touch upon the importance of the EU context for marketization within our four countries. In general, the importance of the EU context can be argued to be highly similar as EU legislation is required to be transposed into national law in all four countries. For park and road services, the EU context has provided a common procedural and legislative framework supporting a highly formal approach to public procurement and market tests.

Overall, the chapter highlights a set of relatively stable key characteristics of our research setting which differ in substantial ways across our four countries. Our main argument is that the characteristics of country and service context(s) are important for interpreting the evolution and diffusion of marketization. A complicating observation is that the combined impact of the contextual characteristics on the evolution and diffusion of marketization can be expected to be multifaceted rather than straightforward.

## Local Park and Road Services

The notion of 'parks' is not well defined in administrative practice and can include a variety of green space types referred to by terms such as 'garden parks', 'forests', 'amusement parks', 'playgrounds', 'people's parks', 'native farms' and 'castle parks'. Other types of green and open spaces commonly administered by municipal park authorities include roadsides, grass surfaces, open space between buildings, waters and cemeteries. The distinguishing characteristic of an open space as a park or green space is the dominance of 'greenery', such as plants and trees (e.g. Swanwick et al. 2003). Within urbanized environments, various types of parks and green spaces are integrated parts of a larger green infrastructure, which provides a range of urban functions of social, economic and environmental value (Reid et al. 2005). Publicly accessible urban parks, for example, have customarily been associated with the provision of recreational opportunities and an environment which can support urban residents' mental and physical health (Zieleniec 2010). Function-designed green spaces in and around urban environments also commonly integrate sports facilities, climate adaption and heat regulation functions while a range of more innovative and typically smaller urban green spaces focus on education, local identity and food production (Derkzen et al. 2017). Lack of proper planning, design or management typically result in 'degraded' non-functional green spaces representing a range of health hazards and safety issues for urban residents. In this context, proper design, planning and management becomes essential for the upkeep and development of the value and multi-functionality of urban parks and green spaces (Dempsey and Burton 2012).

Municipal roads are key parts of a larger transport infrastructure and contribute to key societal functions in terms of economic development and social welfare and play a role for environmental and climate concerns

(Hjorthol and Leiren 2016). In relation to economic development and growth, roads affect regional development as they are important for where businesses choose to locate their industry and people choose to live. Roads may reduce (e.g. commuting) costs related to distance, increase accessibility to export markets and allow the production of goods to be more concentrated where production costs are low. In terms of social welfare, roads are important in providing access to employment, as well as social, health and education services/facilities. However, the transport sector contributes significantly to environmental pollution, greenhouse gas emissions and traffic accidents.

In all of our four countries responsibilities for public park and road services are divided between local and national and/or regional authorities. In England, Sweden and Denmark, for example, central state agencies are responsible for substantial parts of the national road networks such as motorways and major highways. In Norway, however, responsibilities for the national road network are delegated to the regional (county) level. Central state authorities are also responsible for state-owned green spaces including forests, nature areas, national parks and historical gardens and parks. The central state agencies are also responsible to some degree for overall national planning and development of services and provide guidelines, assistance and know-how to the municipalities. National authorities in all of our four countries have typically contracted out part of the maintenance of parks and roads for decades. In Denmark, for example, the national road agency has contracted out all major maintenance services since the 1980s while maintenance in historical and royal parks has been contracted out since the early 2000s. Similarly, national road authorities in Sweden also contract out all maintenance services for all national roads.

Local park and road services are usually ranking low in national political agendas and attract little public attention compared to most other public services. Local park services, for example, are mostly non-statutory and often struggle with lack of political attention and poor or lacking planning and legislative frameworks (Lindholst et al. 2014). On the other hand, planning and legislative frameworks are readily available for road services given their direct importance as transport infrastructure. In comparison, activities in the local road sector are legislatively and administratively more tightly regulated than activities in the local park sector. While municipalities in all four countries are required by law to ensure a well-functioning road network as part of the overall transport infrastructure, there are no or very few legal requirements for the provision of municipal parks and green spaces. A set of specialized laws typically requires municipalities to protect existing valuable nature areas (e.g. habitats for endangered species) and some type of forests areas from alternative land uses. There are also environmental laws that are related to parks and roads. In Norway, for example, the Biodiversity Act regulates the use of plants and pesticides and the Pollution Act regulates the use of salt forde-icing roads in the wintertime.

National figures for the scale—physically and financially—of local park and road services—give an idea about the potential size of markets where competition and private contractor s can be introduced. The available statistics indicate that the two services typically take up only small fractions of the municipal budgets. However, no comparable figures are available across our four countries. The data are found to be indicative at best and only very loosely comparable as no standardized classifications and measures were found across the four countries. The amount and type of parks and green spaces, for example, are recorded differently across the four countries. The available figures, however, all indicate that park services commonly take up less than 1% of overall municipal budgets while budgets for road services take up no more than 2–4%. In Denmark, for example, the gross expenditure for all municipal services related to road maintenance was about DKK 6.5 billion in 2017—a figure more than three times higher than the gross expenditure about DKK 2.0 billion for all services related to maintenance of municipal parks and green spaces (including forest, waters and nature areas). Overall, the expenditures for park and road services (maintenance) account for approximately 3.5% of total municipal service expenditures about DKK 241.9 billion (budgeted) in 2017 (Statistics Denmark 2018b). The percentages are roughly similar to the percentages found for England. While allocations vary between municipalities in England, reported figures show that road services receive on the average about 4% and parks less than 1% of total local budgets (DCLG 2015). For England, it should further be noted that austerity policies have since 2008 substantially reduced the amount of money available for local services. Available figures for open space spending, under which green spaces belong, indicate a 33% overall reduction (NAO 2016). No reduction in this magnitude is reported for any of the other countries in our study. The Norwegian municipalities spent about NOK 6.4 billion (gross figure) on operating roads and about NOK 1.3 billion (gross figure) on operating parks and open spaces (Statistics Norway 2018). It should be noted also, that because expenditures for many municipal services are regulated by central legislation (i.e. mandatory), the budgets for road and park services often take up a larger amount of overall available 'discretionary' budgets for construction and maintenance. The expenditures vary considerably from year to year due to seasonal variations (e.g. different needs for winter services or grass cutting due to changing weather conditions) and uneven investment needs (e.g. new trees planting or new road surfaces).

Physically, available statistics for England indicate that the 326 municipalities were responsible for more than 27,000 publicly owned and accessible parks and green spaces in and around urban zones (House of Commons 2017) as well as roughly 98% of the over 395,500 km of public road network in England (DfT 2016). In, Sweden, available national statistics for the amount of parks and green spaces are based on an estimation of the total area and not the number. Estimates from 2001 showed that Swedish municipalities were responsible for about 715 km$^2$ of park and nature areas, of which about 40% (233 km$^2$) was classified as 'managed parks' including about 206 km$^2$ of grass surfaces. The remaining 60% were classified as 'nature areas' (SK 2001). While national authorities in Sweden maintain around 100,000 km of roads the municipalities maintain around 41,000 km. In addition, there are about 430,000 km of private roads of which the majority are forest roads. The 98 Danish municipalities are responsible for planning, managing and maintaining most of the country's publicly owned and accessible parks and green spaces in and around urban zones as well as roughly 95% of the 74,500 km long public road network in Denmark. Available national statistics for Denmark indicate that the total amount of area classified as parks, sports and other recreational areas at the country level was about 393 km$^2$ in 2016 (Statistics Denmark 2018a). For Norway, national estimations of the total urban land use (countrywide) show that the road infrastructure including various types such as motorways and cycle tracks takes up about 2100 km$^2$ while various park types take up about 37 km$^2$ of a total of 5440 km$^2$ of built-up area in Norway (Statistics Norway 2018). The Norwegian figure for parks appears to include only more 'traditional' park types. Substantial parts of the road infrastructure are furthermore located outside urban settlements.

Overall the figures indicate that the potential markets for local park and road services in all four countries are relatively small in absolute terms and in relative terms when compared to total municipal budgets.

The figures for physical size and type of roads and parks are inconclusive in a comparative perspective but still the figures indicate that the composition of type and the relative size of local services vis-à-vis the national level differs in some degree across the four countries.

Of key theoretical interest for the theme of our book is that the two services belong to a group of local services recurrently perceived as relatively easy to organize and provide through market-based governance (Blom-Hansen 2003; Boyne 1998; Hefetz and Warner 2012; Hodge 2000). In a comparative perspective, local park and road services are regarded as belonging to a larger group of 'hard' or 'technical' services—often contrasted to groups of 'soft' or 'human' services where marketization is more challenging. In the traditional economic typology for goods, local parks and roads can with some reservations be classified as typical *public goods* in terms of their characteristics as non-rivalrous (a person's consumption of the good does not diminish its supply) and non-excludable (a person cannot be excluded from consumption) (see Chapter 2). More specific analysis of the transactional characteristics of services related to the maintenance of parks and roads as well as many other hard services are commonly concluding these as relatively well-suited for market-based governance. A survey-based study by Hefetz and Warner (2012) of US municipal managers' perceptions, for example, found that contracting out of park and landscape maintenance was characterized by higher competition levels, and lower levels of 'contracting difficulties' and (special) investment requirements in comparison with other municipal services. In the same study services related to road maintenance (street repair) were found to require a higher degree of investments which indicates that some smaller municipalities may not have the capacity to provide these services themselves and are dependent on third party provision but also that competition can be limited and contracting difficulties may arise. In comparison with other services, in particular social services, it can still be argued that key characteristics of local park and road services indicate that marketization will work relatively well in this service context.

Park services, but in particular road services, have often been first-mover services in public reforms promoting marketization. In England (and Wales), for example, highway maintenance was one of the first public services to be put out for tender under the 1980 Local Government Planning and Land Act while grounds maintenance and other 'blue collar' services were included later under the 1988 Local Government Act (see also Chapter 5). Hence, from a research perspective the two service sectors tend to embed longer histories and a broader set of experiences with marketization compared to other public services (Blom-Hansen 2003; Lindholst et al. 2018).

Overall, we find that municipalities in our four countries share a common responsibility for a majority of public park and road services within each national context. The political attention and budgetary importance of the services at the local level is furthermore found to be relatively limited. The limited budgets for local park and road services also indicate that the potential market size of interest for private contractors is relatively small. However, in a marketization perspective, the two services appear to be relatively well-suited for marketization due to their basic characteristics. This indicates, in concordance with historical reform developments, that local park and road services have been—and in some cases still are—'spearheads' or 'first movers' in local public management reforms which rely on marketization.

### *National Reform Trajectories*

Comparative research routinely highlights that the content and trajectories of public management reforms differs substantially across countries (Christensen and Lægreid 2011; Pollitt and Bouckaert 2011). In comparisons, the UK is recurrently highlighted as a leading country in the development and implementation of public management reforms and in particular the NPM. Barzelay (2001), for example, highlighted the UK (alongside New Zealand, Australia and the USA) as one of four international 'benchmarks' in the implementation of public management reforms. Similarly, Christensen and Lægreid (2007) wrote of the UK as belonging to a group of 'trailblazers' while Hood and Dixon (2015) wrote of the UK as a 'vanguard'state. A key observation is that UK from the 1970s and onward was among the first countries where neoliberal and neoconservative politics were implemented at a fuller scale with the aim to break up mainstream political consensus on Neo-Keynesian macroeconomic policies and the role and organization of the welfare state which had emerged across Europe in the aftermath of the Second World War. The historical impetus for the rise of neoliberal and neoconservative politics was driven by the international economic crisis of the 1970s and challenges with financing the ever-expanding complex of state-led provision of welfare services. The majoritarian type of democracy in the UK, comprising a high concentration of executive and legislative powers and very few veto 'points', has made it possible for central government to pursue swift, comprehensive and radical policies and reforms (Lijphart 1999). The particular reform path and the successive policies in the UK in the late 1970s, throughout the 1980s and into the 1990s have by some scholars been described and interpreted as 'Thatcherism'—the political agenda associated with Margaret Thatcher, UK Prime Minister 1979–1990 and conservative leader 1975–1990 (Evans 2013). The consecutive reform initiatives associated with Thatcherism strongly emphasized free markets, denationalization of state-owned industries (privatization), deregulation of the economy, flexible labour markets, tax cuts, reduced government spending and centralization of powers from local to central government. These reforms gave rise to coordination of service delivery through the market-based mechanisms of choice and competition, so-called 'quasi markets', across a variety of public services at all levels of government in the UK such as health and education (Le Grand 2007).

In comparison to the UK, the Scandinavian countries have been characterized as belonging to a group of later-adopting or even 'reluctant' reform countries which have emphasized 'modernization' rather than 'marketization' or 'minimization' strategies for reform of the state apparatus (Pollitt and Bouckaert 2011). As discussed in Chapter 2, reforms in the Scandinavian and the wider Nordic context have furthermore been characterized by their embodiment of a 'Neo-Weberian State' (NWS) model as a reference point for reform—a state model which reinforce and strengthens (modernize) rather than displace (minimize) the classical hierarchical and bureaucratic state apparatus through the incorporation of elements from newer reform doctrines (Greve et al. 2016; Pollitt and Bouckaert 2011).

The impetus for managerial reform from economic crisis and financial strains on the welfare states has also differed in timing and strength across the Scandinavian countries. In Denmark, the international economic crisis of the 1970s and 1980s turned into a financial crisis of the state in the early 1980s, but already in the 1990s the country's economy was flourishing anew. Sweden was also hit by the economic crisis in the early 1980s, but this crisis was only minor compared to a substantial more severe economic and financial crisis emerging in the early 1990s. The Norwegian economy, however, has remained relatively stable and unaffected by international conjunctures by and large due to their (huge) oil resources. In the aftermath of the global financial crisis in 2008, for example, austerity policies have had severe negative consequences for the finance of services provided by municipalities in England while municipalities in Norway have been affected to a far lesser extent by the same crisis.

Finally, in the consensus democracies of Scandinavia, many central governments in modern times, especially in Denmark, have been coalitions or minority-based highly dependent on securing a wider parliamentary consensus across several and sometimes opposing political parties and interests for producing new legislation, policies and reforms (Lijphart 1999). Thus, in comparison with majoritarian democracies, such as the system found in the UK, it has been more difficult for central governments in Scandinavia to implement (if desired) more radical, swift, comprehensive and ideological oriented policies and reforms.

Given the basic differences in ideological outlook, policy orientation towards the welfare state, national political systems, and the timing of financial crisis we expect that the global marketization agenda to produce differential impacts across the four countries. Clear differences are found between UK/England and the three Scandinavian countries in the general emphasis on marketization versus modernization in public management reforms and the possibilities for central governments to pursue reforms. The overview of national reform trajectories also indicates that our three Scandinavian countries at a closer look appear with some key differences which are likely to produce differential impacts on the evolution and diffusion of marketization. Norway, in particular, stands out with a national reform trajectory with less impetus arising from economic crisis. Denmark, in contrast, was the first of the three Scandinavian countries to experience the urgency for reforms arising from economic crisis in the 1980s. The details of reform in our four countries are explored further at the country level in Chapters 5–9.

## Characteristics of Municipalities

As noted above, municipalities in all four countries share a common responsibility for a majority of public park and road services. Thus, the comparative characteristics of municipalities across our four countries provide another contextual layer which is likely to shape the evolution and diffusion of marketization. For example, the geopolitical context, the population spread and the local concentration of populations are contextual factors important to understand the preconditions for marketization (see also Chapter 2). Historically, capital cities and larger towns, where trade, markets and commercial activities have thrived, are grown out of crossroads between land, the seashore and the great rivers. Population concentrations and functioning markets tend to be scarce where the land is mountainous and where movability, transport and communication is more complicated. Thus, in studies of inter-municipal variations in the degree of marketization, population density and municipal size is sometimes used as a proxy for the strength of markets and predictor for the likelihood that municipalities rely on markets for provision of local services (Christensen et al. 2012). Municipal size can also be said to be indicative of higher specialization and managerial capacity. The literature has recurrently highlighted the built-up of specialized managerial capacity as key for successful implementation of various forms for marketization (Bhatti et al. 2009; Brown and Potoski 2003; Kettl 1993).

To guide our comparison of municipalities, Table 4.1 provides comparable data of key characteristics of municipalities in the UK context and the three Scandinavian countries. One important upshot is that while the UK and Scandinavia at a first glance may be differentiated into two country groups in terms of differences in the national context and trajectories of public management reforms the picture is immediately more blurred in terms of the characteristics of municipalities. These characteristics and discussions of their possible impact on marketization are explored further below.

In a global perspective, the level of economic development in all of our four countries should provide for relatively good and similar financial situations for provision of public services. Measured by GDP (Table 4.1, row F), the four countries are all belonging to the group of wealthy and economically highly developed European countries within the group of OECD countries. England, as part of the UK, has by far the largest economy measured by GDP of the four countries, while Norway by far is the wealthiest country measured by GDP per capita. As noted above, however, the timing and depth of economic crisis between the 1980s and 2010s has affected the countries and the impetus for reform differently in the decades. Norway, in particular, can be said to have experienced a better and more stable financial situation than the three other countries.

A comparison of the size of our four countries in terms of population and area indicate substantial differences between all four countries. Population-wise (see Table 4.1, row A), England, as part of the UK, is

**Table 4.1** Key characteristics of Local Governments in UK/England and Scandinavia

| | *UK (England)*[a] | *Sweden* | *Denmark* | *Norway* |
|---|---|---|---|---|
| A. Inhabitants, national level (billions) | 65.1 (55.0) | 9.8 | 5.7 | 5.2 |
| B. Number of municipalities (Municipal level 2016–2017)[b] | 391 (326) | 290 | 98 | 428 |
| C. Municipal size (average/median inhabitants in thousands) | 167/132 | 34/15 | 58/43 | 12/5 |
| D. Municipal size (average area in km²) | 622 (400) | 1405 | 438 | 714 |
| E. Share of Municipalities with more than 20,000 inhabitants | 100% | 42% | 93% | 13% |
| F. GDP in USD national (billons)/per capita (thousands) | 2723/42 | 469/48 | 279/49 | 322/62 |
| G. Overall public expenditures (% of GDP) | 42.9% | 50.2% | 54.8% | 48.8% |
| H. Local (subnational) expenditures (% of public expenditures) | 25.4% | 49.9% | 63.7% | 33.0% |
| I. Local (subnational) expenditures on compensation of employees (% of total compensation) | 38.1% | 76.5% | 72.5% | 55.9% |
| J. Local (subnational) taxes (% of local revenues) | 14.9% | 53.5% | 34.9% | 37.4% |
| K. Relative local autonomyAutonomy[c] | Low | High | High | High |

*Notes* Main source for data: OECD. (2017). *Subnational Governments in OECD Countries: Key Data.* Paris: OECD

[a]Figures for England in parentheses if available

[b]Figures don't include subnational governments at regional and intermediary levels or at the sub-municipal level

[c]*Source* Ladner et al. (2016)

by far the largest country of our four countries with an estimated population of about 55.0 million inhabitants in 2016 while Norway with a population of about 5.2 million is the smallest. Denmark is slightly larger than Norway with a population of 5.7 million while Sweden with a population of 9.8 million is almost twice as large as Norway. Geographically, there are also major differences between the four countries. Denmark is by far the smallest country covering an area of approximately 43,000 km$^2$ while England, Norway and Sweden covers, respectively,

130,000 (242,000 for UK), 385,000 and 447,000 km$^2$ (Table 4.1, row D). In consequence, the average population density is relatively high in England and Denmark with, respectively, 423 and 133 inhabitants per km$^2$. In comparison, Sweden and Norway's average density is very low with, respectively, 23 and 14 inhabitants per km$^2$. In perspective, area-wise Denmark is less than one-tenth of the size of Sweden.

Since the 1970s, all four countries have organized their local governments in a basic two-tier structure with multipurpose municipalities at the core and with regional authorities taking care of more specialized functions. In Denmark and Sweden, for example, regional authorities' main responsibility is health services. In Norway, regional authorities have main responsibilities for secondary education, transport and regional planning. Common responsibilities at the municipal level in all four countries include functions such as education, health, social and welfare services, city planning and environmental and urban services. However, the four countries also represent very different structural characteristics in terms of municipal size and autonomy.

At the time of our study, municipal size in terms of the average number of inhabitants was highly different among our four countries (see Table 4.1, row C). In England, the 326 lower-tier local authorities (termed 'municipalities' in this book) out of the total of 353 local governments (including 27 upper-tier authorities) have an average of 169,000 inhabitants. In Sweden, the 290 municipalities located within 21 county councils (upper-tier authorities) have an average of 34,000 inhabitants. In Denmark, the 98 municipalities located geographically within five regional counties have an average of 58,000 inhabitants. In Norway, the 428 municipalities located within 19 counties—numbers substantially higher than in any of the other three countries—have an average of 12,000 inhabitants. On the other hand, in terms of area Sweden and Norway have by far the largest municipalities with on average 1.405 km$^2$ (Sweden) and 714 km$^2$ (Norway), respectively. Given the country differences in population and area sizes, population density is markedly different across the four countries.

The population is furthermore unevenly distributed across the geographies of all four countries with population concentrated around urban centres and metropolitan areas. The uneven distribution is substantially more pronounced in Sweden and Norway compared to the situation in England and Denmark. In terms of geography, Norway and Sweden are very similar with huge stretches of mountainous and sparsely populated areas. The uneven distribution in Sweden and Norway is evident in the higher ratios between the average and median size of municipalities (see Table 4.1, rows C and E). This indicates that the Swedish and in particular the Norwegian population is clustered highly unevenly in few relatively large municipalities and many small municipalities.

Given the comparative territorial characteristics, we expect that preconditions for marketization and formation of strong and competitive markets differ substantially across and within our four countries. Among our countries, for example, we would expect that Norway and partly Sweden constitutes a more challenging context for marketization while Denmark and in particular England constitute more supportive contexts.

In an international comparison, the municipal importance in the public economy (Table 4.1, rows H, I and J) and degree of local autonomy (Table 4.1, row K) vis-à-vis central government is high and relatively similar among the Scandinavian countries. In contrast, the municipal importance in the public economy and degree of local autonomy is substantially lower in the UK. The relatively lower local autonomy among local governments in the UK context denotes that the central government has relatively stronger leverage over local service delivery compared to the three Scandinavian countries. The higher local autonomy of local governments in Scandinavia should in principle also allow these to adapt service delivery more effectively to local circumstances and improve responsiveness to local needs and preferences. The higher degree of local autonomy in Scandinavian is also reflected in the important role the municipalities have in the public economy. Budget-wise, local governments in Denmark have the relatively largest role in terms of their share of total public budgets for services and compensation of employees. On the other hand, local governments in the UK context have the lowest share of total public budgets for services and compensation of employees. In terms of the share of total public budgets, local governments in Sweden come next to local governments in Denmark while local governments in Norway sits in between the UK and the two other Scandinavian countries.

Overall, the analysis of the comparative characteristics of municipalities across our four countries shows a highly differentiated 'municipal landscape'. Each country can be argued to represent a unique combination of characteristics. At a first glance, the high local autonomy in Scandinavia should provide municipalities with some degrees of freedom to innovate and differentiate marketization according to local circumstances, needs and preferences. However, at a second glance, the smaller municipal size in particular in Norway and Sweden also indicate a potential lack capacity for doing so. In contrast the situation appears almost opposite for municipalities in England. Denmark, however, is characterized by relatively large municipalities in terms of inhabitants, a high degree of local autonomy and a comparatively densely and evenly populated country though even in Denmark significant and increasing regional disparities has evolved in recent decades (Hansen et al. 2018). The conditions for a locally driven evolution and diffusion and higher degree of adaptation of marketization can therefore be argued to be relatively more supportive in Denmark. The combination in England of low local autonomy, a majoritarian political system, a densely populated country and very large municipalities can be argued to provide a supportive context for the implementation of marketization but in a way which is tightly coupled with the content of national reform policies.

## A Common EU Context

The supranational cooperation in Europe embodied in the contemporary European Union (EU) has since its foundation in the 1950s aimed for economic integration through establishment and support of free and open markets including markets for public services. The framework for regulation of competition and market relations was at the time of our study equally applicable in all four countries.[1] The national frameworks for regulation of public procurement and involvement of the private sector in public affairs are therefore in general aligned, although variation in the implementation exists. For example, the states are given some leeway in how to transpose EU law into national regulation. In general, EU regulations require that public procurement at all levels of the state should comply with the general principles in the EU treaty enacted in its current version (The Treaty of Lisbon from 2007) and former version

[1] At the time of the study, England, Denmark and Sweden were full members of the European Union (EU). The UK and Denmark joined the predecessor for the EU, the European Economic Community (EEC) in 1973. However, the UK decision to withdraw from the UK made after a referendum in 2016 has made the future relation and association between EU and UK unclear. Sweden joined the EU in 1995. Norway joined the European Economic Area (EEA) in 1994, which makes Norway part of the EU's internal market. This means that Norway is obliged to transpose EU laws and regulations related to the internal market, while not taking part in the decision-making processes in the EU.

(The Maastricht Treaty from 1992). The general principles include adherence to transparency, equal treatment, open competition and non-discrimination in public affairs. The principles are further enacted in the EU Procurement Directive (2004/17/EC). The procurement directive requires, for example, that all public procurements above a certain economic threshold adhere to particular rules of competition and details procedural steps in how public authorities should carry out public procurement. It follows that the EU context has been highly influential for the development of pro-market regulations and the procedures through which private sector involvement can be organized for public service delivery in all of our four countries.

## Summary

This chapter highlighted a range of relatively stable characteristics of our four countries and two services which constitute the research setting for our book. Country characteristics included structure and size of municipalities, their relative autonomy vis-à-vis the central government and the EU framework. The chapter also presented key characteristics of local park and road services. These characteristics are argued to render the two services as relatively well-suited for marketization. In addition, the EU context was found to provide a common driver for marketization across all four countries. However, the differences and the diversity in the municipal landscapes across our four countries are likely to present varying degrees of challenges for marketization. While a rough division could be made between the UK/England and the three Scandinavian countries there were also found substantial differences between the three Scandinavian countries which are likely to provide very different conditions for the evolution and diffusion of marketization.

In the following Part II of our book, four country-based chapters (Chapters 5–8) provides more detailed and longitudinal analyses of marketization and its impact on the organization of local park and road sectors. The two subsequent Chapters provide direct comparative analysis. Chapter 9 analyses and compares the economic performance from contracting out in the three Scandinavian countries. Chapter 10 compares the current use of marketization in the local park and road sectors.

In Part III of our book, Chapters 11–14 provides four single case studies of key experiences with marketization in each of the four countries. The experiences are based on analyses of longitudinal developments as well as more contemporary phenomena. Chapter 15 provides a discussion of the experiences highlighted in our four case studies. The discussion interprets and triangulates insights from the four case studies against the more general characteristics of marketization found in part two of our book. Overall, the presentation of 'between' and 'within' country analyses contributes with insights from different contexts to the overall puzzles on the evolution and diffusion of marketization within two service sectors (parks and roads) and across four countries (England and the three Scandinavian countries).

## References


Barzelay, M. (2001). *The New Public Management: Improving Research and Policy Dialogue*. Berkeley: University of California Press.

Bhatti, Y., Olsen, A. L., & Pedersen, L. H. (2009). The Effects of Administrative Professionals on Contracting Out. *Governance, 22*(1), 121–137.

Blom-Hansen, J. (2003). Is Private Delivery of Public Services Really Cheaper? Evidence from Public Road Maintenance in Denmark. *Public Choice, 115*(3), 419–438.

Boyne, G. A. (1998). Competitive Tendering in Local Government: A Review of Theory and Evidence. *Public Administration, 76*(4), 695–712.

Brown, T. L., & Potoski, M. (2003). Contract-Management Capacity in Municipal and County Governments. *Public Administration Review, 63*(2), 153–164.

Christensen, L. R., Houlberg, K., & Petersen, O. H. (2012). Udlicitering eller egenproduktion - Hvordan forklarer den politologiske litteratur de store forskelle i kommunernes brug af private leverandører i opgaveløsningen? *Politik, 15*(2), 44–55.

Christensen, T., & Lægreid, P. (2007). *Transcending New Public Management: The Transformation of Public Sector Reforms*. Burlington: Ashgate.

Christensen, T., & Lægreid, P. (2011). *The Ashgate Research Companion to New Public Management*. Farnham: Routledge.

Dempsey, N., & Burton, M. (2012). Defining Place-Keeping: The Long-Term Management of Public Spaces. *Urban Forestry and Urban Greening, 11*(1), 11–20.

Derkzen, M. L., van Teeffelen, A. J., Nagendra, H., & Verburg, P. H. (2017). Shifting Roles of Urban Green Space in the Context of Urban Development and Global Change. *Current Opinion in Environmental Sustainability, 29*, 32–39.

DCLG. (2015). *Revenue Account Budget 2015–16*. London: Department for Communities and Local Government.

DfT. (2016). *Road Use Statistics Great Britain 2016*. London: Department for Transport.
Evans, E. J. (2013). *Thatcher and Thatcherism*. London and New York: Routledge.
Greve, C., Lægreid, P., & Rykkja, L. H. (2016). *Nordic Administrative Reforms: Lessons for Public Management*. London: Palgrave Macmillian.
Hansen, M. B., Andersen, J. G., & Lassen, M. (2018). Introduktion: Regional dynamik og ulighed. *Økonomi og Politik, 91*(4): 2–6 (in Danish).
Hefetz, A., & Warner, M. E. (2012). Contracting or Public Delivery? The Importance of Service, Market, and Management Characteristics. *Journal of Public Administration Research and Theory, 22*(2), 289–317.
Hjorthol, R., & Leiren, M. D. (2016). Samferdsel – Drivkraft og Problemskaper. In I. Frønes & L Kjølsrød (Eds.), *Det Norske Samfunn* (Bind 17, pp. 108–129). Oslo: Gyldendal (in Norwegian).
Hodge, G. A. (2000). *Privatization: An International Review of Performance*. Oxford: Boulder Westview Press.
Hood, C., & Dixon, R. (2015). *A Government That Worked Better and Cost Less? Evaluating Three Decades of Reform and Change in UK Central Government*. Oxford: Oxford University Press.
House of Commons. (2017). *Public parks: Seventh Report of Session 2016–17 HC 45*. London: House of Commons.
Kettl, D. F. (1993). *Sharing Power: Public Governance and Private Markets*. Washington: The Brookings Institution.
Ladner, A., Keuffer, N., & Baldersheim, H. (2016). Measuring Local Autonomy in 39 Countries (1990–2014). *Regional & Federal Studies, 26*(3), 321–357.
Le Grand, J. (2007). The Politics of Choice and Competition in Public Services. *Political Quarterly, 78*(2), 207–213.
Lijphart, A. (1999). *Patterns of Democracy: Government Forms and Performance in Thirty-Six Countries*. New Haven and London: Yale University Press.
Lindholst, A. C., Dempsey, N., & Kreutz, S. (2014). The Politics of Place-Keeping. In N. Dempsey, H. Smith, & M. Burton (Eds.), *Place-Keeping: Open Space Management in Practice* (pp. 30–51). London: Routlegde.
Lindholst, A. C., Petersen, O. H., & Houlberg, K. (2018). Contracting Out Local Road and Park Services: Economic Effects and Their Strategic, Contractual and Competitive Conditions. *Local Government Studies, 44*(1), 64–85.
NAO. (2016). *Financial Sustainability Of Local Authorities: Capital Expenditure and Resourcing for Department for Communities and Local Government*. London: National Audit Office.

OECD. (2017). *Subnational Governments in OECD Countries: Key Data*. Paris: OECD.

Pollitt, C., & Bouckaert, G. (2011). *Public Management Reform: Comparative Analysis of New Public Management, Governance and the Neo-Weberian State*. Oxford: Oxford University Press.

Reid, W. V., Mooney, H. A., Cropper, A., Capistrano, D., Carpenter, S. R., Chopra, K., et al. (2005). *Ecosystems and Human Well-Being - Synthesis: A Report of the Millennium Ecosystem Assessment*. Washington, DC: Island Press.

SK. (2001). *Kommunernas väghållning och parkskötsel 2001*. Stockholm: Svenska Kommunförbundet (in Swedish).

Statistics Denmark. (2018a). *Arealdk1: Land by Land Cover, Region and Unit*. Available at www.statistikbanken.dk/arealdk1. Accessed May 2018 (in Danish).

Statistics Denmark. (2018b). *Regk31: Kommunale regnskaber (1000 kr.) efter område, funktion, dranst og art*. Available at www.statistikbanken.dk/reg31. Accessed May 2018 (in Danish).

Statistics Norway. (2018). *Land Use and Land Cover*. Available at www.ssb.no/en/arealstat. Accessed May 2018.

Swanwick, C., Dunnett, N., & Woolley, H. (2003). Nature, Role and Value of Green Space in Towns and Cities: An Overview. *Built Environment, 29*(2), 94–106.

Zieleniec, A. J. L. (2010). Parks. In R. Hutchison (Ed.), *Encyclopedia of Urban Studies* (pp. 583–587). Thousand Oaks: Sage.

PART II

# Country Analysis

CHAPTER 5

# In-House, Contracted Out…or Something Else? Parks and Road Management in England

*Nicola Dempsey, Mel Burton and Johanna Selin*

## Introduction

Marketization has long-driven public service management (including roads and parks) in England in attempts to enhance competition and improve quality (Boyne 1998) since the late 1970s. Within Europe, the UK has gone furthest in implementing neoliberal doctrines through privatization of previously nationalized sectors and market liberalization (Wollmann 2017). This marked a shift from the traditional bureaucratic form of public service administration based on in-house service delivery towards a range of other models (Gill-McLure 2014; Kuhlman 2010). These models include contracting-out, public procurement, public–private partnerships (PPPs) and agencification. Of all the policy instruments introduced in England to date, it is Compulsory Competitive

N. Dempsey (✉) · M. Burton
Department of Landscape Architecture, University of Sheffield, Sheffield, UK
e-mail: n.dempsey@sheffield.ac.uk

J. Selin
University of Gothenburg, Gothenburg, Sweden

 
A. C. Lindholst and M. B. Hansen (eds.),
*Marketization in Local Government*,
https://doi.org/10.1007/978-3-030-32478-0_5

Tendering (CCT), and the accompanying practice of contracting-out, which has had the most enduring legacy. This chapter reports on empirical data examining the extent to which current parks and road maintenance arrangements taken by local authorities reflect this legacy. The findings suggest a significant shift in terms of who holds the responsibility for parks maintenance where this is increasingly becoming shared between different combinations of local authorities, private, third sector and voluntary actors. This is particularly the case for parks maintenance as current austerity measures are much more acutely felt here than for roads.

## Public Service Delivery in England: 1970s–1990s

The opening up of public service delivery to the market has long shaped England's political-administrative system (Rodrigues et al. 2012), to the point where England has been viewed as a benchmark when it comes to different ways of engaging private actors to carry out public services (Barzelay 2001). A market-led approach was embraced by the Conservative Party when they came to power in the late 1970s, exemplified by the 1988 Local Government Act which stated that construction and maintenance work had to be put out for CCT. Opening up the market meant that private, public and/or third sector could deliver the service as long as the procurement process followed was competitive (Boyne 1998) and the Act covered street cleaning and grounds maintenance (Parker and Hartley 1990).

### *Compulsory Competitive Tendering*

CCT has had significant and long-lasting effects, both positive in terms of cost savings and negative in relation to quality (Barber 2005). Even if a local authority could demonstrate that delivering a service in-house was more cost-effective than contracting-out to private organizations, CCT regulations barred this from happening (Frederick 1994). Local authorities responded to this by forming "direct service organizations" (DSOs)—hybrid organizations which sat within the local authority with operational and financial quasi-autonomy as they operated as a private concern (Patterson and Pinch 1995; Wollmann 2017). DSOs tendered for contracts which actually had to demonstrate greater cost-effectiveness when compared to external competitors (Milne et al. 2012). This separation of client and contractor, often called the purchaser–provider split (see Chapter 2), was encouraged to avoid bias in the competitive process of contract tendering (Clark 1997). During the first round of CCT projects, the majority of contracts were won in-house as cost savings through redundancies and lower wages were used as a means of competing with private contractors. The terms and conditions of workers' contracts worsened under both private contracts and DSOs where rates of pay were reduced and/or hours were cut and entitlements to many statutory employment rights such as holiday pay and maternity leave were reduced (Patterson and Pinch 1995). While transparency of the process was often achieved, tendering to the lowest bidder left little scope for professional judgement and specialist knowledge in carrying out grounds maintenance. Milne et al. (2012) therefore found that parks staff on the ground felt a loss of autonomy, skill and knowledge. CCT meant tasks were increasingly controlled by the conditions of contracts, for example, grounds maintenance staff were less able to use their knowledge about timing and appropriateness of maintenance work (e.g. pruning) (Patterson and Pinch 1995).

The local authority-DSO arrangements sometimes resulted in antagonistic relations as well as mistrust between service deliverers and commissioners (Milne et al. 2012). Long-term relationships were not always feasible as local authorities were forced to accept bids from "better" contractors once contracts were up for renewal (Osborne 2010). Market liberalization driven by the 1980s legislation led to the demise of the quasi-monopoly held by local authorities and the expansion of private sector providers (Wollmann 2017). According to Clark (1997), parks officers surveyed in the early 1990s claimed that the money saved after competition was introduced was not being reinvested, indicating that parks had lost approximately £80 million per year since the introduction of CCT.

### *Public–Private Partnership*

PPP has a very long history in England with privateer shipping on behalf of the British Empire going back to the sixteenth century. But the term began to be widely recognized in the 1990s in England (Bovaird 2010) as a form of public investment (Grimsey and Lewis 2005) forming a partnership between public, private and sometimes third sector organizations, based on flexible methods of finance and operation of facilities and/or services (Whitfield 2001). Driven by the problems of publicly procured projects in England running overtime and over-budget, the Private-Finance Initiative

(PFI—a form of PPP) was introduced in 1992 as a financial mechanism of securing private finance to "increase investment in [...] infrastructure without affecting public borrowing" (Whitfield 2001: 5), which is of particular relevance to roads in England. Proponents of PPP claim it can enable long-term projects without increasing public spending, bringing in expertise from the private sector through a competitive process (Sunderland and O'Day 2012). However, it became clear after projects were implemented that PFI was not cost-effective for the public sector (Whitfield 2001). The 2008 financial crises meant there was so little lending by banks that PFI contracts were untenable, and the costs were passed on to the taxpayer (NAO 2014). The PPP model has therefore been severely criticized for falling far short of the claimed efficiencies it brings (e.g. Nisar 2007; Carpintero and Petersen 2014). There is also criticism for the lack of transparency in contracts signed between client and contractor, such as those made between the Amey (private infrastructure service provider[1]) and Birmingham and Sheffield City Councils which led to court proceedings in both cases.[2] The PPP model, however, continues to be a primary vehicle for the delivery of public sector services in England, and some other countries have dedicated PPP units, potentially "undermining the case for other viable procurement methods" (Hawkesworth 2010). Academic studies have found that PFI with a not-for-profit (rather than a for-profit) firm would always yield greater social benefits (Bennett and Iossa 2005).

### *Public Service Delivery in England: Late 1990s–2010s*

The New Labour Government (elected 1997) criticized CCT for its inflexibility, compromise on quality and overemphasis on competition and efficiency (Hefetz and Warner 2007). New Labour marked the end of CCT by introducing the 1999 Local Government Act making it was no longer mandatory to contract out local services to the lowest bidder and highlighted quality as the overriding goal regardless of who

[1] Amey is a subsidiary of Spanish company Grupo Ferrovial, S.A.

[2] In Birmingham, the council attempted to invoke penalty clauses in contract as it was not satisfied with the quality of repairs and road resurfacing work (Elkes 2016). In Sheffield, some residents have been protesting the felling of street trees as part of the Amey contract and in summer 2017, the council 'obtained a high court injunction in an attempt to prevent protesters from standing in the way of tree-felling contractors' (Halliday 2017).

delivered public services (Bevir 2012). Best Value was introduced as a policy reform to ensure that local people were provided with efficient and effective services through the principles of quality and value-for-money. In reality, the shift towards "best value" led to performance targets and monitoring by central government auditors (the now defunct Audit Commission). Often these centrally-controlled performance indicators meant expensive evaluation processes and heavier workloads for local government (Kuhlman 2010).

Strategic commissioning also developed at this time constituting "a central concept in UK public management for almost a decade" (Bovaird et al. 2014: 541). The advantage of strategic commissioning is that it is not simply outsourcing or contracting-out, but it directly involves third sector organizations, marking a focus on end-users (Localis 2011). Strategic commissioning has been advocated by the English government and so is used by local authorities as a model for public sector service delivery, providing opportunities for organizations such as social enterprises to provide public services (Localis 2011). Taking a holistic approach is distinct from the traditional form of public procurement, e.g. contracting-out, and has led to greater externalization of public service delivery to create partnerships and mutual agreements with non-governmental actors (Bovaird et al. 2014).

The Conservative-Liberal Democrat Coalition Government, which came to power between 2010 and 2015, led the way for the most significant budget cuts to the public sector since 1945 (Cowley et al. 2011) which the current Conservative Government (elected 2015) continue. After the financial crises of 2008, minimizing public expenditure and state power have been proposed as solutions to the national economic problem. The Conservatives conceptualized this as the "Big Society" which, among other things, relies on greater involvement of third and private sector to reduce government spending and the size of the public sector (after Richards 2011). The ensuing public sector budget cuts have led to an effective replacement of skilled workers with volunteers (e.g. in the library sector; Platts-Fowler and Robinson 2016) raising concerns about both the quality of service provision and the capacity of communities to deliver (Casselden et al. 2015). It has been highlighted elsewhere that the biggest obstacle for greater community involvement is the dominance of the market-based model for public service delivery, because power is not effectively being transferred: it "does not correct the inevitable imbalance of power between...those who have most power in society and those who have least" (Slocock et al. 2015: 62).

## The State of Contemporary Parks and Roads and the Legacy of Past Policies

Both the road and park sectors have challenges ahead. A recent report from the Local Government Association (LGA) (2017) forecasts a 42% rise in traffic level and a rise of 61% of the congestion levels on the UK roads by 2040. The state of the roads in the country today is claimed to be in bad condition, with issues including potholes and poor management of ageing roadside trees. This constitutes a huge task for local authorities: the backlog of maintenance is calculated (as of 2012) at around £12 billion (LGA 2017). While funding is readily available for roads and highways, there are ongoing budget cuts for park services. According to national surveys from 2014 to 2016, a total, 92% of park managers have seen cuts in their budgets since 2010 and 81% of local authority Parks Departments have lost skilled management staff (HLF 2014, 2016). Half the local authorities surveyed in 2016 were considering selling parks and green spaces, and the same proportion had transferred their management of outdoor sports facilities to other organizations (including community groups).

It is worth reflecting on the legacy of policies which led us to a situation where local authorities consider selling off their public parks as a viable and acceptable course of action. It is largely because parks have been mostly ignored by central government with the exception of New Labour's raft of urban regeneration programs of the 2000s (HLF 2014). The most prominent and renowned national support for park services in England is the now defunct national advisory body CABE Space. The (New Labour) government-funded organization was in operation in the 2000s (until it was axed by the coalition government in 2010) and produced a series of valuable status reports and guidelines on park services, some of which are still used by local authorities today. That CABE Space as a national voice no longer operates is a sign of the low status of parks and green space in the English national policy context, when statutory services such as health and education take precedence, particularly in times of financial austerity.

Between the late 1970s–1990s, the Conservatives lowered local government expenditure meaning that parks were an easy—non-statutory—target. CCT played an important role in this development. While CCT was underpinned by a market-oriented approach to provision, parks provide a public service with a non-market value (i.e. the environmental, social and cultural values of green space were never quantified). While this has been addressed more recently through a move towards monetary valuation of green space (e.g. Mell et al. 2016), the value of long-term management of parks and green space is consistently underestimated (Dempsey et al. 2014). Implications of CCT, alongside cost reductions, include a loss of (horticultural) skills as tasks became over-simplified and effectively reduced to grounds maintenance such as grass mowing. A loss of community contact has also been found where the dedicated park-keeper is a relic of the past now staff must work over multiple sites (English Heritage 2005), along with a lack of a long-term perspective taken by contractors and cash-strapped local authorities (Jones 2000).

When Best Value was introduced under New Labour to gain better quality in contracts, parks fared better and citizens were included in the decision-making process. But while there were improvements to many parks through capital investment, it was difficult for local authorities to achieve benchmarking targets when they did not also receive accompanying revenue funding, continuing and having to demonstrate financial viability and accountability. The lack of national government focus on ongoing maintenance of parks, coupled with the non-statutory nature of parks management and accompanying budget cuts made to parks management post-2010, means that managers expect park standards to fall over next three years (HLF 2016). This has led local authorities to seek new sources and ways of funding parks beyond the public sector. The national government became involved in this debate through a House of Commons Select Committee Inquiry into the future of public parks (2016). Its response to the Inquiry report underlines the current government's position to not make green space management and maintenance a statutory duty for local authorities. Rather it anticipates a proliferation of "alternative management models or funding arrangements" with the Inquiry asking government to help remove (e.g. institutional/legal) barriers and manage risks involved in, for example, transferring the management of land to non-public sector stakeholders (HM Government 2017).

The rest of this chapter calls on INOPS survey data from 2015. The survey was distributed among 326 local authorities in England. In total, 103 valid responses were received constituting a response rate of 32% (see also Chapter 4).

### *The Extent of Contracting-Out Parks and Roads Maintenance in England*

Table 5.1 shows who carries out maintenance for parks and roads and how the budgets are allocated, according to the public sector respondents to our questionnaire survey. For parks, 60% of local authority respondents use private contractors for parks maintenance and 64% make use of in-house green space maintenance services, indicating that there is not necessarily one single management provider in a given local authority. The HLF 2014 study found that 23% of local authority respondents reported contracting-out parks maintenance. HLF also found that over half of UK local authorities surveyed (56%) maintained their parks through in-house services, and the APSE 2013 study found that this number was higher at that time (83%). Examined together, these findings suggest that contracting-out of parks maintenance is on the increase across local authorities, which echoes the prediction by HLF findings of "a greater mix of service delivery models including external trusts and partnerships with other organizations". We found that respondents reported widespread use of other green space maintenance providers, including community groups (44% of respondents), third sector organizations (20%), public–private ventures (7%) and social enterprises (5%). For roads maintenance, over a quarter of local authority respondents reported using private contractors., while only 36% of respondents reported using in-house providers and 9% using other types of providers. Of the other providers, these included public–private ventures (4%) and community group involvement (2%). It is difficult to find comparable historical data but Clark's study on parks management (1997) reported that 21% of survey respondents in 1996 indicated that grounds maintenance tasks constituted over half of all contracted out activity that their local authority offered. This points to an upward trend of contracting-out over time, although the involvement of not-for-profit organizations in parks management is an interesting and relatively new variation in this trajectory that was not seen in the late 1990s.

A similar distribution was not found when we examined how budgets are distributed across these different providers. Over 40 and 50% of parks maintenance budgets are distributed respectively to private and in-house contractors, which is not particularly surprising given the high proportions of local authorities who use these providers for parks maintenance. However, the large proportion of respondents (56%) who report

**Table 5.1** Maintenance and budgets in parks and roads: survey findings

| *Type of provider* | *Who carries out maintenance in parks and roads for your department?* | | *How are your budgets for maintenance distributed among different organizations?* | |
|---|---|---|---|---|
| | *Park maintenance* (N = *103) (%)* | *Road maintenance* (N = *73) (%)* | *Average of Park maintenance budget* (N = *103) (%)* | *Average of Road maintenance budget* (N = *59) (%)* |
| Private contractors | 60 | 26 | 41 | 37 |
| In-house providers | 64 | 36 | 52 | 52 |
| Other type of provision | 53 | 9 | 8 | 9 |
| *Public–private venture* | 7 | 4 | 5 | 4 |
| *Local social enterprise* | 5 | – | <1 | – |
| *Other public authority* | 3 | 1 | <1 | 1 |
| *National/local third sector organization (e.g. trust)* | 20 | – | <1 | – |
| *Community groups* | 44 | 2 | 1 | 2 |
| *Other (not specified in the survey)* | 7 | 2 | 1 | 2 |

*Note* Figures (rounded) add up to more than 100%

using other organizations for parks maintenance allocate only 8% of their budgets to them. The findings suggest that the kinds of activities engaged in are smaller-scale and less costly than those done by in-house and private contractors, and/or may be based on work by unpaid ("free") volunteers. It is a simpler state of affairs when we look at the budget breakdown for road maintenance, Table 5.1 also shows that the budgets are similarly distributed according to who carries out the work. 37% of local authority budgets are distributed to private contractors, 52% to in-house providers and 9% to other types of provision.

We asked respondents about the extent to which the contribution of different organizations had changed over the last five years, to test our hypothesis that private contractors are increasingly used to deliver parks and road maintenance. While not all respondents answered these questions, there were some interesting findings (see Dempsey et al. [2016] for a fuller examination). We found that similar proportions of respondents reported increases and decreases in using private contractors over the last five years and the longstanding influence of CCT may explain the high proportion of respondents (29%) reporting that this has stayed the same. There were broadly similar figures for in-house provision with an increase (12%) and decrease (18%) in contribution to maintenance over the last five years and a higher proportion (34%) of respondents reporting that this has stayed the same. In particular we want to highlight that a quarter of respondents reported increases of involvement of community groups in parks maintenance over the last five years, which is unsurprising in light of findings reported in Table 5.1 even though the table also shows how involvement is not replicated in financial terms. The contribution of private and in-house contractors for *roads maintenance* has not really changed significantly across the different providers, with larger proportions of the sample reporting that providers have stayed the same (Dempsey et al. 2016).

Table 5.2 compares the responses from respondents about why in-house providers and/or private contractors are used by local authorities for parks and roads maintenance. The reasons for using private contractors were mostly around five main reasons: cost-effectiveness, testing and benchmarking prices, responding to changing budget pressures, achieving high maintenance quality and flexibility of delivery. This focus on budget-related issues is consistent with the pressures experienced by English local authorities reported elsewhere (HLF 2014). We did not find any significant differences in responses between urban or rural local authorities, geographical region or local authority type, or change in

**Table 5.2** Reasons for using in-house providers and private contractors (parks and roads combined)

| | *In-house providers* | | *Private contractors* | |
|---|---|---|---|---|
| *To...* | *Mean* | *SD* | *Mean* | *SD* |
| Achieve cost-effective maintenance | 8.1 | 1.8 | 7.8 | 2.2 |
| Test and benchmark prices[a] | – | – | 6.3 | 2.6 |
| Address changing budget pressures | 8.2 | 2.4 | 6.3 | 3.1 |
| Achieve high-quality maintenance | 8.2 | 1.7 | 6.3 | 2.7 |
| Ensure flexibility of delivery | 9.0 | 1.4 | 6.1 | 2.6 |
| Carry out work that others cannot do[b] | 5.5 | 3.2 | 5.5 | 3.8 |
| Allow the department to focus on strategic management (instead of day-to-day maintenance) | 4.8 | 3.3 | 5.2 | 3.3 |
| Develop and renew sites and services | 6.8 | 2.6 | 4.4 | 3.2 |
| Develop/improve internal working methods | 7.5 | 2.3 | 4.2 | 3.1 |

*Notes* Based on INOPS survey data. $N$=51–54 (in-house) $N$=44–47 (private contractors). The figure shows the mean for responses to the question: 'Specify on a scale of 0 [not at all] to 10 [to a very high degree] the degree to which you think that the following purposes are a central part of your municipality's considerations for using in-house provision/private contractors for maintenance ..'

[a]Respondents were not asked the 'test and benchmark prices' about in-house providers

[b]When asked about private contractors, this question was phrased: Carry out work that the municipality cannot do

different organizations' contribution to service provision over the last five years. We did however find a medium and significant correlation (coefficient 0.530) indicating that respondents who reported an increase in private sector involvement were more likely to report testing and benchmarking prices as a reason for using private contractors. The main reasons overlap with those cited for the use of private contractors except for "testing and benchmarking prices" which was not a relevant question to ask regarding in-house providers. Interestingly, these main reasons were more readily cited in relation to in-house providers than in relation to private contractors, indicating the importance of cost-effectiveness, high-quality service provision and flexibility of delivery when the public sector is delivering parks and roads management. This might perhaps be because the council-employed respondents perceive more in-house scrutiny than when contractors are used. The development of internal working methods and renewal of sites and services were also cited as reasons for using in-house providers to a greater extent than using private contractors, tentatively suggesting that respondents considered that in-house providers—at the time of this survey—have the capacity to provide cost-efficient, flexible and high-quality service provision. As one respondent commented: "It makes us more flexible and we can move resources around". However, in light of the ongoing budget cuts to parks (highlighted in the HLF 2016 survey findings), if we were to conduct this survey again, we suspect that these scores would be quite different (and the sample size would probably be much reduced given the detrimental impact the cuts are having on staff numbers).

## Conclusions

Our findings suggest that past policies (e.g. CCT), and the practices they introduced, have had a lasting effect on public service delivery and the propensity of local authorities to contract this out. Some policy instruments (e.g. Strategic Commissioning) have influenced practice insofar as not-for-profit NGOs are increasingly being used as service providers. The analyses we conducted indicate that, overall, parks and roads maintenance are shifting towards shared responsibilities between different combinations of local authorities, private, third sector and voluntary actors. This broadly supports findings in the literature review which showed increased policy focus towards collaborative approaches in public service delivery (Rodrigues et al. 2012), i.e. not only local authority or private contractor. It should be noted that this relates more to parks and, to a much lesser extent, roads maintenance.

The reasons why local authorities use private contractors are closely correlated with the underlying aims contracting-out, namely to reduce budgets and increase cost-effectiveness. Survey respondents also highlighted how flexibility was an important reason for using private contractors, suggesting a need to respond to the ongoing context of austerity in the English public sector (after Mathers et al. 2015). It is not clear at this stage how much importance that respondents attached to these inter-related aspects in light of the new EU Directive and how it might affect public service delivery in the future (which is of course muddied by the UK's Brexit decision). It is not at all clear if this flexibility will be enhanced or hindered by the EU Directive (or negated completely in light of Brexit).

But regardless of European level political decision-making, it appears clear that the contracting-out of public service delivery is likely to continue. In England, this extends well beyond parks and roads maintenance to the marketization of the health sector, policing and education to name a few. When this drive to reduce budgets and increase efficiency is applied to statutory services, the non-statutory services fall further down the priority list. We can see how this happens very clearly for parks maintenance, where budgets continue to decrease. The implications of depleted funding streams for the long-term provision and management of parks are still not fully understood and flexibility will be important in the future as different models are explored and developed by local authorities and a growing range of service delivery organizations. For example, if the engagement of third sector organizations and community groups in parks maintenance continues, will this bring with its budget increases in their contracts? At the moment, this is not the case, perhaps because of the value that unpaid volunteers bring. The increasing reliance on community groups and the third sector by local and national government in England comes with a presumption that they have the capacity to deliver public services such as parks maintenance. How realistic is this reliance on community resilience as austerity measures continue? Third sector organizations are reliant on public funding and grants, and their position becomes increasingly precarious when these budgets are under threat. While the UK has a long tradition of volunteering where people give up their time willingly and for free, the pool of public services that volunteers are delivering is widening. Beyond parks, volunteers are now being asked (and, to some extent, expected) to deliver a wider set of publicly provided cultural services including running local libraries. It is not clear how realistic such reliance on volunteers is as their demographic make-up changes, with, for example, the increasing retirement age. As the impact of the 2008 economic recession continues its hold, it is perhaps likely that we will see an increasingly fragmented approach to public service delivery, which will see local authorities overseeing, rather than leading, partnerships of different stakeholders.

## References

Barber, A. (2005). *Green Future. A Study of the Management of Multifunctional Urban Green Spaces in England*. Reading, MA: GreenSpace Forum.

Barzelay, M. (2001). *The New Public Management: Improving Research and Policy Dialogue*. Jackson, MI: University of California Press.

Bennett, J., & Iossa, E. (2005). *Contracting Out Public Service Provision to Not-For-Profit Firms* (Working Paper No. 05/124). Bristol: Centre for Market and Public Organisation. Available at http://www.bristol.ac.uk/media-library/sites/cmpo/migrated/documents/wp124.pdf. Accessed April 2018.

Bevir, M. (2012). *New Labour: A Critique*. London: Routledge.

Bovaird, T. (2010). A Brief Intellectual History of the Public-Private Partnership Movement. In G. A. Hodge, C. Greve, & A. Boardman (Eds.), *International Handbook on Public-Private Partnerships* (pp. 43–67). Cheltenham: Edward Elgar.

Bovaird, T., Briggs, I., & Willis, M. (2014). Strategic Commissioning in the UK: Service Improvement Cycle or Just Going Round in Circles? *Local Government Studies, 40*(4), 533–559.

Boyne, G. A. (1998). Competitive Tendering in Local Government: A Review of Theory and Evidence. *Public Administration, 76*(4), 695–712.

Carpintero, S., & Petersen, O. H. (2014). PPP projects in Transport: Evidence from Light Rail Projects in Spain. *Public Money & Management, 34*(1), 43–50.

Casselden, B., Pickard, A. J., & McLeod, J. (2015). The Challenges Facing Public Libraries in the Big Society: The Role of Volunteers, and the Issues That Surround Their Use in England. *Journal of Librarianship and Information Science, 47*(3), 187–203.

Clark, L. (1997). *The Effects of Compulsory Competitive Tendering on Grounds Maintenance*. Glasgow: Institute of Leisure and Amenity Management (ILAM).

Cowley, P., Hay, C., & Heffernan, R. (2011). Introduction: A Landscape Without a Map? British Politics After 2010. In R. Heffernan, P. Cowley, & C. Hay (Eds.), *Development in British Politics* (pp. 1–7). Hampshire: Palgrave Macmillan.

Dempsey, N., Burton, M., & Selin, J. (2016). Contracting Out Parks and Roads Maintenance in England. *International Journal of Public Sector Management, 29*(5), 441–456.

Dempsey, N., Smith, H., & Burton, M. (Eds.). (2014). *Place-Keeping: Open Space Management in Practice*. London: Routledge.

Elkes, N. (2016, July 13). Legal Dispute Could Cost Birmingham Roads Contractor £55 Million. *Birmingham Mail*. Available at https://www.birminghammail.co.uk/news/midlands-news/legal-dispute-could-cost-birmingham-11609054. Accessed 21 January 2018.

English Heritage. (2005). *The Park Keeper*. London: English Heritage. Available at: https://historicengland.org.uk/images-books/publications/the-park-keeper/the-park-keeper/. Accessed 20 October 2019.

Frederick, D. (1994). *Why Compulsory Competitive Tendering for Local Government Services Is Not as Good as Privatisation*. London: Libertarian Alliance.

Gill-McLure, W. (2014). The Politics of Managerial Reform in UK Local Government: A Study of Control, Conflict and Resistance 1830s to Present. *Labor History, 55*(3), 365–388.

Grimsey, D., & Lewis, M. K. (2005). Are Public Private Partnerships Value for Money? Evaluating Alternative Approaches and Comparing Academic and Practitioner Views. *Accounting Forum, 29*(4), 345–378.

Halliday, J. (2017, September 28). Michael Gove Seeking Way to End 'Bonkers' Felling of Sheffield Trees. *The Guardian*. Available at https://www.theguardian.com/uk-news/2017/sep/28/michael-gove-seeking-way-to-end-bonkers-felling-of-sheffield-trees. Accessed 21 January 2018.

Hawkesworth, I. (2010). *Public-Private Partnerships*, OECD Observer, No. 278 March 2010, OECD.

Hefetz, A., & Warner, M. (2007). Beyond the Market Versus Planning Dichotomy: Understanding Privatisation and Its Reverse in US Cities. *Local Government Studies, 33*(4), 555–572.

Heritage Lottery Fund (HLF). (2014). *State of UK Public Parks 2014—Renaissance to Risk?* London: Heritage Lottery Fund.

Heritage Lottery Fund (HLF). (2016). *State of UK Public Parks 2016*. London: Heritage Lottery Fund.

House of Commons, Communities and Local Government Committee. (2016). *Inquiry into Public Parks: Seventh Report of Session 2016–17, HC45*. London: House of Commons.

HM Government. (2017). *Government Response to the Communities and Local Government Select Committee Report: The Future of Public Parks, Cm 9503*. London: DCLG.

Jones, R. (2000). Managing the Green Spaces: Problems of Maintaining Quality in a Local Government Service Department. *Managing Service Quality, 10*(1), 19–31.

Kuhlman, S. (2010). Between the State and the Market: Assessing Impacts of Local Government Reforms in Western Europe, *Lex Localis—Journal of Local Self-Government, 8*(1), 1–21.

Localis. (2011). *Strategic Commissioning Is the Future*. Available at www.localis.org.uk/news/strategic-commissioning-is-the-future/. Accessed 27 October 2017.

Local Government Association (LGA). (2017). *A Country in a Jam: Tackling Congestion in Our Towns and Cities*. London: LGA. Available at https://www.local.gov.uk/tackling-congestion, https://www.local.gov.uk/sites/default/files/documents/5.16%20Congestion_report_v03.pdf. Accessed 20 October 2019.

Mathers, A., Dempsey, N., & Molin, J. F. (2015). Place-Keeping in Action: Evaluating the Capacity of Green Space Partnerships in England. *Landscape and Urban Planning, 139*, 126–136.

Mell, I., Henneberry, J., Hehl-Lange, S., & Keskin, B. (2016). To Green or Not to Green: Establishing the Economic Value of Green Infrastructure

Investments in the Wicker, Sheffield. *Urban Forestry Urban Greening, 18*, 257–267.

Milne, R. G., Roy, G., & Angeles, L. (2012). Competition, Quality and Contract Compliance: Evidence from Compulsory Competitive Tendering in Local Government in Great Britain, 1987–2000. *Fiscal Studies, 33*(4), 513–546.

National Audit Office (NAO). (2014). *The Impact of Funding Reductions on Local Authorities*. London: National Audit Office. Available at www.nao.org.uk/report/the-impact-funding-reductions-local-authorities/. Accessed 27 October 2017.

Nisar, T. M. (2007). Value for Money Drivers in Public Private Partnership Schemes. *International Journal of Public Sector Management, 20*(2), 147–156.

Osborne, S. P. (2010). The (New) Public Governance: A Suitable Case for Treatment? In S. P. Osborne (Ed.), *The New Public Governance? Emerging Perspectives on the Theory and Practice of Public Governance* (pp. 1–16). Abingdon: Routledge.

Parker, D., & Hartley, K. (1990). Competitive Tendering: Issues and Evidence. *Public Money & Management, 10*(3), 9–16.

Patterson, A., & Pinch, P. L. (1995). Tendering and the Restructuring of British Public Sector Services. *Environment and Planning A, 27*(9), 1437–1461.

Platts-Fowler, D., & Robinson, D. (2016). Community Resilience: A Policy Tool for Local Government? *Local Government Studies, 42*(5), 762–784.

Richards, D. (2011). Changing Patterns of Executive Governance. In R. Heffernan, P. Cowley, & C. Hay (Eds.), *Development in British Politics* (pp. 29–48). Hampshire: Palgrave Macmillan.

Rodrigues, M., Tavares, A. F., & Araujo, J. F. (2012). Municipal Service Delivery: The Role of Transaction Costs in the Choice Between Alternative Governance Mechanisms. *Local Government Studies, 38*(5), 615–638.

Slocock, C., Hayes, R., & Harker, D. (2015). *Whose Society? The Final Big Society Audit*. London: Civil Exchange. Available at http://www.civilexchange.org.uk/wp-content/uploads/2015/01/Whose-Society_The-Final-Big-Society-Audit_final.pdf. Accessed 21 January 2018.

Sunderland, J., & O'Day, P. (2012). More for Less Through Private Finance Highway Maintenance. *Proceedings of the Institution of Civil Engineers: Civil Engineering, 165*(CE3), 138–143.

Whitfield, D. (2001). *Private Finance Initiative and Public Private Partnerships: What Future for Public Services?* County Kerry: European Services Strategy Unit.

Wollmann, H. (2017). Provision of Public and Social Services in European Countries. Any Lessons to Learn for the Asia-Pacific Region? *Journal of Asian Public Policy, 11*(3), 299–315.

CHAPTER 6

# Sweden: Local Marketization 1980–2018, Incremental Tendencies and Deviances

*Ylva Norén Bretzer, Bengt Persson and Thomas Barfoed Randrup*

## Introduction

It is generally understood that Anglo-American countries were early NPM reformers, while Continental Europe and Scandinavia were reluctant adopters (Christensen and Lægreid 2011: 2). In a general sense, this statement also applies to Sweden, but the opposite can also be argued. Seen from the outside, the Scandinavian countries have a similar governmental structure, and are all strong unitary states with local governments

Y. N. Bretzer (✉)
School of Public Administration, University of Gothenburg, Gothenburg, Sweden
e-mail: ylva.noren-bretzer@spa.gu.se

B. Persson · T. B. Randrup
Department of Landscape Architecture, Planning and Management, Swedish University of Agricultural Sciences, Alnarp, Sweden
e-mail: bengt.persson@slu.se

T. B. Randrup
e-mail: thomas.randrup@slu.se



A. C. Lindholst and M. B. Hansen (eds.),
*Marketization in Local Government*,
https://doi.org/10.1007/978-3-030-32478-0_6

having their own tax-collecting competences. Nonetheless, at a closer glance they are each unique in their own terms and clearly diverge from one another (Foss Hansen 2011).

Sweden consists of a two-tier local government structure with directly elected governments in both regions (*landsting*) and municipalities (*kommuner*). Both levels collect their own taxes, but the regional governments are responsible for hospital services while the local governments oversee schools, elderly- and child-care, as well as overall planning, local planning, culture and management of grey and green infrastructure. There is a total of 290 municipalities, including three large cities, and 116 suburban, 116 mid-sized and 55 rural municipalities (SKL 2017).

Marketization was not a new phenomenon in Sweden when the marketization debate took off in the early 1980s. The Social Democrats at the time actually prepared reforms which were in line with the Hood doctrines, later described as the NPM reform movement in the UK (Knutsson et al. 2017; Hood 1991). However, the marketization reforms impacted quite differently at the national and the local levels. At the national level there had been budget crises and several devaluations of the currency throughout the 1970s, and again in 1982. The public sector continued to grow, as care of the elderly, children and public health expanded between 1965 and 1985. In the early 1980s, there was an urge to take control over the budgetary growth and rationalize the public sector.

Against this backdrop the chapter aims primarily to highlight two aspects that have not been critically discussed in the previous literature. First, it seems that in the literature marketization and NPM are often discussed as cross-section snapshot from its own time-perspective. Yet the marketization debate has now been going on in Sweden for almost 40 years; therefore we aim to revisit various reports[1] from different points in time with the following questions in mind: *How has the marketization 'talk' developed over time—and can we find evidence of any significant change in private sector involvement in this regard?* These two questions will direct the first section, which reviews the Swedish national perspective.

A second aspect which has not been explored satisfactorily in the literature is *the local practice* of this 'new' set of business-inspired public–private relations. It is somewhat surprising to find that most of the analyses of contracting-out conducted in the Swedish context are based

[1]This exercise has been conducted by following up on references in known reports, to find out what has been written since the 1980s about marketization in general, but also about the park and road sectors specifically. In particular, we have been looking for 'trends', 'the talk', numbers and quantitative indicators.

on national agencies because, given that 4 out of 5 publicly employed persons in Sweden are employed by either a municipality or a region, the bulk of the 'public' sector is inherently local (Statskontoret 2015; Norén Bretzer 2017: 132). Therefore, for those interested in how marketization works in the Swedish case, it is a necessity to study these practices in the local context. In order to reduce complexity, we will further focus in on *parks* and *roads*, which are well researched in the international literature (e.g. Lindholst et al. 2017; Norén Bretzer et al. 2016; Lindholst 2009; Randrup and Persson 2009; Randrup et al. 2006; Blom-Hansen 2003). Following up on the INOPS study (2015) and the findings of previous reports, the leading question for this section are: *What have been the dominant management forms in Swedish municipalities—and to what extent have private providers been engaged in the road and park sectors?*[2] The overall findings from Sweden will be discussed in the closing section.

## Marketization Waves in Sweden, 1980s to 2018

Already in the 1600s Sweden developed a relatively modern and functionally divided state apparatus in order to raise taxes for wars (Jacobsson et al. 2015).[3] After the WWII era, during which Sweden's infrastructure was left largely unaffected, an unparalleled industrial expansion and societal growth took place.[4] By the early 1980s it was time for stabilization and tighter economic controls. The contraction that set in was commonly perceived as a crisis.

[2]Results from the *Innovation in public and private collaboration project* (INOPS) can be found at https://vbn.aau.dk/da/projects/innovationer-i-det-offentlige-private-samspil-inops. INOPS was co-financed by Aalborg University, Denmark, and Hedeselskabet—a large Danish non-profit foundation. Also relates to Chapters 3 and 4 of this book.

[3]The independence of the administrative agencies in Sweden is still today protected by the constitution. Their primary tasks are to implement the decisions and laws that have passed the parliament (*the Riksdag*). However, the Government also gives the agencies yearly instructions through annual "budgetary letters" (*regleringsbrev*), finally decided upon by the parliament in December every year. No minister is allowed to point out directly what the agencies should do or decide, which stands out in contrast to the Danish and Norwegian traditions (Foss Hansen 2011: 123).

[4]The municipal sector had expanded from 11% of GDP in 1960 to 24% of GDP in 1978, often financed by increasing municipal taxes (Agurén and Broms 1982). This was a result of the expansion of child-care and elderly care, which had often been delivered by housewives and servants in the past. When more female labour was demanded in the industrial sector during the 1970s and 1980s, the care sector developed at the municipal level.

The decade opened with a devaluation of the currency in 1982 (see Table 8.1). The 'industrial policy era' (1970–1982) came to a close, and a crisis group was installed under the Prime Minister Olof Palme (Andersson 2006: 113). The administrative political strategy adopted by the Social Democrats followed two partly-conflicting paths (Pollitt and Bouckaert 2011; Premfors et al. 2009). One aimed to improve administrative efficiency, under the direction of the Ministry of Finance. The other, headed by the Ministry of Regional and Local Development (*Civildepartementet*), proclaimed improved services, transparency, decentralization and increased user participation (Andersson et al. 2017: 40; Montin 1992; Elander and Montin 1990). The timing matched the international influences well (Rhodes 1996; Pollitt 1993; Osborne and Gaebler 1992; Hood 1991). These trends also coincided with the neoliberal influences that proliferated in those days, which prescribed a minimal state and stricter economic frames (Boréus 1994). The large number of state-owned companies came under criticism. 'The Swedish model', which for decades had been built upon close collaboration between industrial representatives and their union counterparts on the boards of the state or in private rooms, came to an end in 1987 when the Swedish Employers' Association (SAF) broke this collaborative understanding (Rothstein and Wahlne Westerhäll 2005; Johansson 2000). Table 6.1 provides an overview of the marketization waves.

One of the major reforms with the largest consequences was the de-regulation of the capital markets decided in 1985–1989 (Andersson et al. 2017: 45; Lindvall 2004). From being a closed northern Scandinavian economy, Sweden suddenly became exposed to the global financial market. Turning to the municipal level, the 1980s was a time of administrative innovations in which sub-municipal neighbourhood councils were introduced, especially in larger cities (*kommundelsnämnder*), so that citizens would come closer to the administrations and local politicians. Additionally, purchaser–provider models were introduced. Supplementary reforms were introduced focusing on budgetary objectives rather than detailed regulations, and tasks were decentralized from the state to the municipalities. In 1986 the Ordinance on Public Procurement was introduced, to apply at state level only, which would formalize the relations between purchasers and producers/contractors.

After some financially booming years at the end of the 1980s, the 1990s opened with a severe economic crisis. The currency had to be defended severely in September 1992, and at one point Sweden's Central bank (the *Riksbank*) raised the internal rent for the banks to 500%. Nevertheless, the Swedish currency would fall about 25%, and the financial crisis was a state

**Table 6.1** Marketization waves in Sweden, 1980s–2018

| *Decade* | *Administrative level* | |
|---|---|---|
| | *National* | *Municipal* |
| 1980s | • Growing public expenditure<br>• NPM reforms initiated by Social Democrats, but prepared by the right-wing parties<br>• Detail budgeting abandoned, block budgeting<br>• Ordinance on public procurement (1986: 366), state level<br>• 1987: Corporatist model broken apart<br>• Decentralization reforms strengthened municipal autonomy<br>• Detailed regulation replaced with management by objectives<br>• Financial deregulation | • Sub-municipal geographical neighbourhood councils introduced (***kommundelsnämnder***)<br>• In late 1980s, the purchaser–provider model became popular in regions and municipalities (see case study of Täby in Chapter 12) |
| 1990s | • 1991 state financial crisis<br>• Law on Public Procurement (LOU) (1992: 1528), applied to all public organizations<br>• Framework budgeting introduced by prime minister Göran Persson (Parliamentary Bill 1995/1996: 220)<br>• 1994: The beginning of the privatization of national agencies (railways, post, telecom, electricity market and national airlines)<br>• 1995: Sweden became a full EU member<br>• 1999: The first PPP project Arlandabanan started to operate, in 2000 the Øresund bridge opened (also PPP) | • Decentralization and management by objectives were major trends<br>• Municipal administration of the primary and secondary schools effectuated in 1991, after twenty years of debate. Also, elderly care and care of handicapped people decentralized.<br>• 25% of the municipalities practiced the purchaser—provider model (1991).<br>• 1993: new system of grants to the municipalities, fixed central budgets |

(continued)

**Table 6.1** (continued)

| *Decade* | *Administrative level* | |
|---|---|---|
| | *National* | *Municipal* |
| 2000s | • Functional fragmentation and coordination of needs<br>• 2005: The European Court judged that the state drugstore monopoly Apoteket was against the EU legal rules<br>• 2006: Continued privatization of national monopolies such as *V&S Group* and *Apoteket*<br>• Update of LOU (2007: 1091)<br>• The Responsibility Committee (SOU 2007: 10)<br>• 2008: Law on Free Choice Care (LOV 2008: 962) | • 'NPM-light', no clear transfer from public to private production, but market-inspired production 'lines' with increased output focus<br>• Alternative forms of service production increased, such as elderly- and child-care<br>• Regional development policies emerged |
| 2010s | • Increased competition widen the service qualities in various parts of the country<br>• The total number of state employees did not decrease 1999–2013 (Andersson et al. 2017: 15)<br>• 2010–2014, an increase of private service delivery of 32% (SCB 2016a; LOU 2016: 1145)<br>• Coordinators were introduced in national policy-administrative streams, such as gender, crime prevention, environmental and energy (Svensson 2017) | • 2016: Purchasing/provider model taken away in Uppsala municipality<br>• Municipal coordinators needed in health, gender, diversity, ICT, quality, GIS, transport, etc. (*samordnare*) |

*Sources* Compiled by the authors. Important sources of inspirations have been Andersson et al. (2017), Elander and Montin (1990), Lapsley and Knutsson (2017), Montin (2000, 2017), Santesson-Wilson and Erlingsson (2009) and Svensson (2017)

of fact. Since 1982 the Social Democrats had run the government, with the exception of the right-wing Bildt government of 1991–1994; in the 1994 elections the Social Democrats re-entered the governmental office. The unemployment numbers had skyrocketed from 1.5–2.0% in 1990 to over 8.0% in 1994. In terms of economic reform agendas, there were hardly any differences between the two political camps, and in 1994 the new government started to sell-off 35 national companies, such as the steel producers SSAB and LKAB, the defence material producers Celsius Industries, the mixed production at Procordia AB[5] and various forestry-related companies (Andersson et al. 2017: 54). Additionally, infrastructure was privatized, including the railways, post, electricity, etc. The municipalities took over responsibility for primary and secondary schools in 1993. Care of the elderly and of disabled persons was also decentralized to the municipalities (the ÄDEL-reform). 'Steering by objectives' and 'decentralization' were the code words of the 1990s. Even so, in the midst of the financial crisis, two demanding Private Public Partnership projects (PPP) were brought forward: the *Øresund Bridge* (between Sweden and Denmark) had been discussed for over 100 years and could potentially provide many job-opportunities, much needed at the time; the *Arlanda Railway* had a shorter planning history but was a key issue for the Bildt government, linking the capital of Stockholm to the country's primary airport.

The reform pathway set during the 1990s continued into the 2000s. Other trends of the time were a reduction in the number of politicians and functional devolution to professional managers (SCB 2016a; Montin 2000: 10–12). Delegation, autonomy and entrepreneurship continued to be emphasized. Administrative units were supposed to 'sell' their services, and 'citizens' were transformed into 'customers'. Purchasing-provider models were further implemented, as were 'freedom of choice' models. However, in the popular debate numerous examples emerged of quality standards that were not met and public opinion clearly wished to keep the size of the public sector intact (38% in favour of maintaining the present size, against 27% in support of reducing it) (Nilsson 2011). Further measurements of public attitudes towards privatization between 1987 and 2010 indicated a majority against most of the privatization initiatives of the period, with the early exception of increased private alternatives in healthcare (ibid.: 287). In parallel, satisfied-customer data (NKI) indicates that the service satisfaction improved for elderly care, housing, rescue

[5] The business spanned industries from mining to forestry and wharfs.

services, water supply, road maintenance and garbage collection, whereas it decreased for environmental care (Arnek 2014: 88). Overall, citizens seem to be more satisfied with the services in 2012 compared with their attitudes in 2002, despite their dislike of privatization measures.

The introduction of competition mechanisms continued to be emphasized by the right-wing government in office from 2006 to 2014. The drugstore monopoly *Apoteket* was privatized due to an EU court case in 2010, as was the liquor Monopoly (*Vin & Sprit, V&S Group*) in 2008. The law on public procurement now also applied to the local level (LOU 2007), as did the Law on Freedom of Choice in welfare (LOV 2008: 962). The LOV-regulations provide a framework for the private provision of public services within elderly care and parts of the healthcare sector. Market relations were strengthened, for example in terms of the public surveillance and inspections of the producers, but also boosting the production and distribution conditions.

The actual costs are complicated to evaluate, but a report from the Swedish Local Authorities and Regions (SALAR) covering the period 1980–2012 indicates that the municipal costs underwent a yearly increase of around 1% in fixed prices, elderly care excluded—especially in areas where profound reforms had been made (SKL 2014: 24). This result was not related to demographic changes, but to an increasing number of service activities. Cost per pupil in schools increased from 62 to 80 (KPI measured 2002 and 2012, Arnek 2014: 74). Only for the elderly, aged 65+, were fewer resources used per client in 2012 than in 2002. Andersson et al. (2017) also point out that at the national level there were more government employees in 2013 than in 1999 (p. 15).

Increased focus on consumer perspectives marked this period (Andersson et al. 2017: 66), as did some additional keywords such as 'innovation', 'entrepreneurship', 'triple-Helix' and 'collaboration', both nationally and locally. Since the 2010s the marketization reform picture has become rather ambiguous. To sum up some important evidence relating to the promises set out initially, we have made the following major findings at the national level.

## Four Decades of Swedish Marketization—What Did We Get?

*First*, in order to follow up on 'the talk' about marketization in the sense of transferring activities from the public sphere to the private sector, we can conclude that reforms over the period 1980 to 2018 have reduced the number of nationally-owned companies quite extensively. Today there are 48 fully or partly state-owned companies, compared to over 800 in 1980 (Parliamentary Bill 1980). The public sector does not seem to have been eroded, however, rather it has transformed into silos, with increased controls of the content and costs of the processes therein, and a meta-governance function (Hall 2012; Sørensen 2006).

*Second*, it comes quite as a surprise that public sector services actually cost more in 2012 than they did in 2002—*especially in reformed areas*—which indicates that the cost efficiency theory did not deliver. Further in-depth analyses need to be done in this regard. However, we should keep in mind that the public share of GDP has hardly increased, the overall public share of GDP (including state expenses and social insurances) decreased from 44% in 1980 to 43% in 2015 (Norén Bretzer 2017: 69). The municipal share of GDP was 18% in 1980 and 19% in 2015. The total number of state employees was greater in 2013 than in 1999 (Andersson et al. 2017: 15). This may be interpreted as indicating that the NPM reforms did not diminish the state or reduce the costs of public services, but simply organized both in alternative ways.

*Third*, citizens at least seem to be more satisfied today than in 2002, possibly as a result of higher service-levels and more 'service activities', in spite of scepticism towards the increasingly privatized production of welfare services. Today, we have a population with a much higher educational level than in 2002, which might be more demanding than previously; it is possible that this development relates to the failure to decrease costs.

On the issue of increased contract steering, or tendering with the LOU tools, it is often observed that over 60 billion € in private contracts are subject to public procurement (Konkurrensverket 2016). Unfortunately, it has proven hard to evaluate such a number over time. One major reason is that the procurement databases are themselves privatized and, consequently, comparable data is difficult to extract systematically. The Swedish Competition Agency (Konkurrensverket 2016: 7) writes:

> At present, no Swedish authority collects data on the public procurements taking place in Sweden. There is no central announcement place for public procurements; instead they are privately announced, which differs from most other EU member states.

This fact is further underlined by a 2012 study by Houlberg and Petersen, which concluded that: 'unlike in the Danish situation, it is not possible to analyse the Swedish data and make one's own calculations' (2012: 25). Overall, in 2015 only 1% of the contracts were won by foreign (EU) firms (Konkurrensverket 2015: 33; EU 2014), and by the 1980s, 19% of all tendered services were sub-contracted (SCB 1980; Ds Fi 1985: 5). The municipalities have become a very important area for public procurement, initiating approximately 2/3 of actual procurements. As municipal companies are also buyers of services and materials, sub-contracting is also a vital part of the delivery chain.

The first question—*How has the marketization 'talk' developed over time?*—can best be answered with reference to three categories: 'transferring public activities to the market', 'contract steering' and 'control' (Almqvist 2006). The data presented in Table 6.1 conform to the three categories described by Almqvist, and we have given examples of how these have evolved. At the beginning of the period, marketization was the primary aim, while the focus on control has increased towards the end. Citizens also seem to be happy with most of the services, but costs have not clearly decreased (Arnek 2014; SKL 2014).

On the second question—*Is there are any evidence of significant change in private sector involvement in this regard?* The immediate response is both 'yes' and 'no'. Yes, because the number of national enterprises has been reduced significantly. Yes, also, as the private share of welfare production has increased (SCB 2016b). The 'no' relates to the fact that it is not possible to evaluate the public procurement statistics and follow the share of the overall private sector involvement over time in order to estimate whether this share has actually increased. Perhaps, though, the response to this question might be clearer when we turn to the local level?

## Public Sector Reforms in the Swedish Local Park and Road Sectors

Let us now turn to the municipal level, in order to further investigate what happened when the marketization reforms were introduced in two 'hard' sectors.[6]

[6]By doing this, we have in part been searching in the archives, specifically for reports and surveys dealing with the park and road sectors from the 1980s onwards. Reports were found at the National Archive, Kungliga Biblioteket, Stockholm. Searches were made in

The municipalities went through a large process of merger and reform in 1952–1974, when 2498 municipalities were reduced to barely 300. It was the largest reform since the municipalities replaced church parishes in 1862. Slowly, throughout the twentieth century, the municipalities who could afford it developed and invested in critical infrastructures such as water, sanitation, roads, parks, energy supplies and urban developments.[7] Smaller and mid-sized municipalities often had occasional needs but could not afford a full in-house technical department for its road maintenances throughout most of the 1900s. Such services were often bought from local private contractors, larger professional companies, or from a public national supplier.[8] When the contraction phase set in in the late 1980s, the arguments pursued were that the municipal administrations had to be more competitive and exposed to competition. Paradoxically for the municipal local organizations this became the moment for expansion, as education tasks and various forms of caretaking were decentralized from the state to the municipalities. Nonetheless, for technical matters the situation was quite the reverse.

Various technical activities were merged together into one overarching authority—water and road management were increasingly grouped together with urban planning, architecture, building maintenance and sport facilities, as well as with roads and parks. Often the new authority was labelled as *the city building office*, sometimes even including environmental inspection and management. These concentration tendencies had already started in 1975, especially in the mid-sized municipalities (Hansson and Knutsson 1991: 18), but the merging processes continued throughout the next three or four decades (*nämndsammanslagningar*).

LIBRIS. Search codes were 'municipal parks' and 'municipal roads'. Reports found often included references that were followed-up. Together with the INOPS data, these various sources of data will be contrasted over time and across the two sectors.

[7] In earlier, peasant societies, private provision was the norm. Still today, water provision in the countryside is a responsibility of the home-owner. Moreover, roads in the countryside have for a long time been the responsibility of local road associations, even if the municipality plays the dominant role in local road management (cf. Hansson and Knutsson 1991: 7). See also *The National Association for Private Roads*, www.revriks.se.

[8] One such example was *Vägverket* (the former Road Agency, today the Transport Agency) from whom the local municipality would frequently buy road maintenance services in the 1970s.

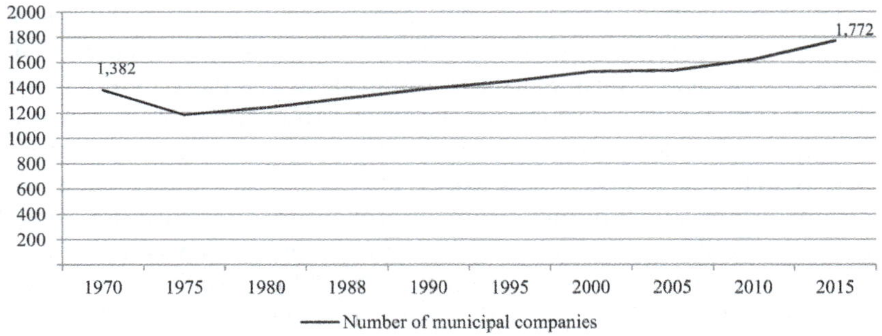


**Fig. 6.1** The corporatization trend in Swedish municipalities (total number per year) (*Sources* SCB 2001, 2014; Hallgren 1997; Jansson and Forssell 1995; SCB data on existing publicly owned enterprises)

One important trend which has to be taken into account was 'corporatization' (*företagiseringen*), also called 'agencification' (see Chapter 2), which meant that classical (local) administrative infrastructure services were reorganized into companies owned, in general, by the municipalities.[9] Today, 53% of the municipal companies in Sweden provide public housing,[10] 25% provide energy and water, 9% provide transport and communication and the remainder are engaged with education, hotels in remote areas, etc. (SCB 2014). In 2016 the municipal companies had a turnaround of 195 billion SEK, employing some 52,000 persons. The term 'municipal corporatization' can include voluntary associations and foundations, but 98% are ordinary Ltd companies, run under the limited shareholders act, but publicly owned. In addition, the municipal enterprises must be owned 50% or more by one or several municipalities; in fact, the vast majority is fully owned by a single municipality (Fig. 6.1).

[9] Municipalities already provided services to their citizens through local enterprises in the mid-1850s (Hallgren 1997: 9). Services traditionally supplied such companies included railways, trams, harbours, water and sewage systems, garbage, slaughterhouses, market-halls (*saluhallar*), electricity, swimming halls, sport arenas and housing.

[10] For decades the municipalities have had a responsibility to ensure that all citizens are provided with housing. Hence, the public housing-stock in Sweden is constituted by larger volumes than just *social housing*, which relates to the European norm. 43% of Swedes live in detached houses, while 51% live in an apartment. Within the category of apartments, 29% are publicly owned and rented (SCB 2015).

It is not unusual that several municipalities co-own, for example, a garbage treatment plant, or an electricity production site. One example is *Renova*, a waste management company co-owned by ten municipalities in the greater region of Gothenburg. Occasionally, municipalities may also sell companies, which happened to the Gothenburg Harbour and several housing companies in Stockholm and in the northern municipalities. Overall, though, the trend suggests a stable long-term increase in this activity form, rather than a turnover to the private market. Another trend in recent years is that municipalities amalgamate their companies into one major group, or business group, which controls the various companies.

## Municipal Park and Road Developments, 1980–2015

By tradition, the municipalities have had the primary responsibility for most of the technology and infrastructure in the local communities. Furthermore, the responsibility for maintenance of parks and roads traditionally lies within the public sector in most countries around the world (Dempsey et al. 2014). *Park maintenance* is part of the traditional maintenance responsibilities of 'common space',[11] or urban open spaces (UOS). Today, *parks* are often more broadly defined, which is reflected in the organization of municipal park maintenance. 'Parks' are now often defined as being 'green spaces' (WHO 2017) or 'open spaces', which includes spaces dominated by grey areas such as squares and pedestrian streets (Thompson 2002; Thwaites et al. 2005), or even blue areas such as lakes, waterfronts and beaches (Vierikko and Niemelä 2016; Roebeling et al. 2017). In the following we denote all UOS as part of the park sector.

Traditionally the organization of UOS maintenance has been related to the size of the municipality. UOS responsibilities may be integrated into or closely connected to public housing, hospitals, schools, sport facilities and other institutions (Hansson 1990: 2).[12] Hansson described

[11] Examples of 'common space' include roads, parks, squares, public parking and biking-lanes. All public areas should be defined in detailed local planning documents (PBL 2010: 900).

[12] Green spaces were governed by the following actors, according to Hansson (1990): Municipalities (49%), single-homes (31), cooperative housing (12), the church (3), the regions, *landsting* (2), national defence (2), and the folkparks, NGO and semi-municipal management (1).

the park management in the early 1990s as characterized by dispersal among a large number of departments that each had a focus other than maintenance of the UOS. This resulted a lack of 'the big picture' and professional skills in UOS maintenance operations in many municipalities. This trend is seen even today, where the Swedish green sector is estimated to hold approximately 40,000 individual actors, of which the 290 municipalities may hold several individual organizations related to, for example, the social sector (green spaces around elderly care homes, child-care centres, etc.), the cultural sector (sports grounds), or the technical sector (road side trees, parks, etc.).

*Road maintenance* most often concerns and includes the maintenance of the road surfaces, including the areas adjacent to the roads (e.g. road median strips, road side grass areas, parking lots and related vegetation). Thus, a road maintenance contract may often include significant elements of green space maintenance. The actual maintenance of the road (including rebuilding and paving of surfaced areas) will usually be provided for in separate contracts; therefore, in a municipal context, road maintenance and green space maintenance are often tendered in a combined contract.

In the early 1990s contracting-out continued to be emphasized as the public procurement regulations tightened and became mandatory for municipalities as well (LOU 1992).[13]

Furthermore, several organizational *forms* presented themselves to decision-takers at the time, who were choosing between the following (Hansson and Lind 1998; Hansson and Knutsson 1991):

- Increased contracting-out to sub-contractors.
- Reorganization, from municipal responsibility to user-production (e.g. a football club that maintains a playing arena). This alternative is not a viable option in most modern cases because there are increasing legal restrictions around, for example, the standards of football arenas.[14]

[13]There have been regulations on public procurement in Sweden since at least the 1800s, which were updated in 1952, 1973, 1980 and 1986. In 1973 the Swedish Association for Local Authorities (SKL) recommended general public procurement procedures, but these recommendations were not mandatory (Sundstrand 2013: 39).

[14]Under situations of austerity and cutbacks, these responsibilities are very likely to be re-negotiated with the local civil society. Other examples are snow-cleaning, playground maintenance, electric jogging paths, swimming sites and housing maintenance, sport arenas

- Running the technical or park affairs in the form of a foundation, a limited but existing phenomenon.
- Run the technical affairs in municipal Ltd company forms, owned by a single municipality.
- Run the technical affairs in municipal Ltd company forms, co-owned by several municipalities.
- Run the technical affairs as an inter-municipal collaboration, similar to the point above.

We have not been able to detect the composition of management forms from the early years of the period, even though Hansson and Knutsson (1991) noted that 'almost 10% of the municipal employees work in municipal enterprises, turning around some 50 billion SEK which relates to 25% of the total municipal turnaround'. Hansson (1991) discussed various forms but did not calculate the frequency of the different forms among the municipalities. The same goes for Hansson and Mattisson (1993) and for Hansson and Lind (1998). From the INOPS study (2015) we can conclude that the municipalities most often exercise mixed forms in relation to maintenance organizations (Fig. 6.2).

From Fig. 6.2 we learn that mixed forms of management provision are the most common practice. The binary kind of language that from time to time has been exercised implies that activities either are 'municipal' or 'private'. This probably applies better to the national level—a much more complex and nuanced reality has been found to exist at the local level. This diversity of mixed organizing forms is confirmed in both the park and road sectors. We also find that co-owned public companies and 'public–private partnerships' are rare, if they exist at all for parks or roads. 'In-house-only' is more common than 'private provision only' for parks in 2015. For roads, these two categories are both limited but equally frequent, as entirely 'in-house'-management is found in 18% of the municipalities and 'private provision only' in 19% of the municipalities (Norén Bretzer et al. 2016).

and parks (Hansson and Knutsson 1991: 37). A drawback of this management form is that the users normally lack the competence needed or the long-term responsibility. Hansson and Knutsson reported that in two-thirds of the municipalities a share of their technical maintenance was dependent on user production.

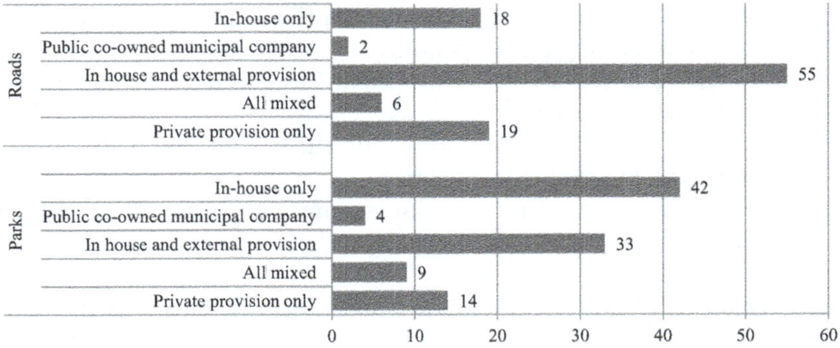


**Fig. 6.2** Maintenance forms in Swedish municipalities 2015 (per cent) (*Notes* Total number of responses for parks was $n = 100$, total number of responses for roads was $n = 106$. The initial question was: Who provides management tasks for your organization? *Source* INOPS survey 2015; Norén Bretzer et al. 2016)

**Table 6.2** Marketization in local park and road sectors in Sweden, 1980s–2018

| *Decade* | *Sector* | |
|---|---|---|
| | *Local parks* | *Local roads* |
| 1980s–1990s | '56 per cent of 253 municipalities responded that they had bought [*park*] maintenance services… Mean share of the maintenance budget was 3 per cent' (Hansson 1987: 66) | 'Building of municipal roads is done in-house to the extent of 50%' (1978–1982) (Ds Fi 1985: 12, 9–10) |
| 2000s–2018 | 28% of municipal park maintenance budgets contracted out (INOPS 2015) | 49% of municipal road maintenance budgets contracted out (INOPS 2015) |

*Notes* Estimations based on INOPS survey data for shares of maintenance budgets contracted out for parks and roads builds on unweighted averages

A different but related question is whether the public procurement directive and other competition-oriented reforms have resulted in any significant changes in practice since the early 1980s and 1990s? Information gathered from archives of earlier reports are included in Table 6.2.

The results indicate that an increase in contracting-out has taken place in the park sector since the early period, from around 3% in 1987 to around 28% in 2015. The results for the road sector point to a more stable situation, as around 50% was contracted out in 1978 and 49% in 2015, according to the INOPS study. This is quite a surprising result for the road sector, but it may be that the marketization gains had already been accounted for in the road sector in the mid to early 1980s, as in this sector it had been common practice to buy services on the open market even decades before. Arguably, the park management sector is to be seen as having learned from the road sector's prior adoption of such practices.

## Summing Up 40 Years of Local Marketization in Sweden: A Few Initial Lessons

The overall lesson from almost 40 years of national and local marketizations in Sweden is that the Swedish public sector has been modernized and reformed along lines inspired by a multitude of techniques imported from the private sector. In times of economic crises the reform process seems to have gained momentum, driven by left-wing and right-wing governments alike. The transformation has in fact been an issue of technical necessity, rather than a political debate. Andersson et al. (2017: 207) showed that a primary task for nearly a fourth of the government agencies is to affect markets through regulation, surveillance, sanctions, memberships and creation of hierarchies between various purchasers and providers. A large percentage of the state agencies have emphasized increased competition; discussions of management forms were dominant during the early period, while questions about quality control and thorough revision and surveillance came into focus at the end of the period. The most evident marketization effect—the transfer of public activities to the market—occurred on the national level when most of the state-run companies were sold off between 1992 and 2009. The second most evident marketization reform in Sweden was the decentralization of the education and welfare systems to the local level, and the opening for private welfare producers that emerged from 1993 and on. Generally, it seems that in most areas the customers, or the citizens, are happier with the various services they are paying for today than they were in 2002 (SKL 2014; Arnek 2014).

At the local level, where the bulk of the public sector is located, 'marketization' may more correctly be described as *market imitation*. The binary transfer of activities from the public to the private sphere which took off at the national level was rarely copied at the local level, though it happened in certain municipalities such as Täby (see Chapter 12). Due to the decentralization trends, the municipal sector has expanded significantly from the 1980s to the present. In addition, the municipal bureaucracy is more standardized today than 40 years ago, with clear regulations and budgetary controls for each and every unit. There is undoubtedly a more professionalism today, even though in 2016 only 25% of all Swedish municipal park administrations had a strategic plan for their green spaces (Randrup et al. 2017). However, the NPM movement has led to an increased focus on production processes and outputs, thus also an increase in tendering practices, quality controls, and evaluation and revision processes. Many of these managerial innovations derived from production-lines in the private sector, and were introduced into local state activities during recent decades, a trend which we have interpreted as a *market imitative process*.

One of the *imitation tendencies* is that municipalities throughout these four decades have continued to develop in-house enterprises (Fig. 6.1), from whom they can buy their services without a formal tendering process and thus without really involving private market actors. Other alternatives are to contract out some or all of the maintenance functions. Increased use of standardization, quality manuals and post-controls are examples of imitations of industrial processes. The increase in contracting-out in the park sector, from 3 to 28% (Table 6.2), may be understood as an imitation of what had already been going on for decades in the roads sector. The INOPS 2015 results show that mixing and combination of purchasing relations characterize these sectors, rather than one single form dominating. The organization of municipal production is indeed a complex matter in Sweden, as we have learned.

## References

Agurén, M., & Broms, I. (1982). *Kommunen och serviceföretagen – Hur kommunen väljer att organisera samhällsservice*. Stockholm: Management Media (in Swedish).

Almqvist, R. (2006). *New Public Management – om konkurrensutsättning, kontrakt och kontroll*. Stockholm: Liber (in Swedish).

Andersson, J. (2006). *Between Growth and Security: Swedish Social Democracy from a Strong Society to a Third Way*. Manchester and New York: Manchester University Press.

Andersson, C., Erlandsson, M., & Sundström, G. (2017). *Marknadsstaten. Om vad den svenska staten gör med marknaderna – och marknaderna med staten*. Stockholm: Liber (in Swedish).

Arnek, M. (2014). *Med nya mått mätt – en ESO-rapport om indikationer på produktivitetsutveckling i offentlig sektor* (Report Number 2014:7). Rapport till expertgruppen för studier i offentlig ekonomi (in Swedish).

Blom-Hansen, J. (2003). Is Private Delivery of Public Services Really Cheaper? Evidence from Public Road Maintenance in Denmark. *Public Choice, 115*, 419–438.

Boréus, K. (1994). *Högervåg. Nyliberalism och kampen om språket i svensk offentlig debatt 1969–1989*. Stockholm: Tiden (in Swedish).

Christensen, T., & Lægreid, P. (Eds.). (2011). *New Public Management*. Burlington: Ashgate.

Dempsey, N., Smith, H., & Burton, M. (2014). *Place-Keeping: Open Space Management in Practice*. New York: Routledge.

Ds Fi. (1985). *Egen regi eller entreprenad i kommunal verksamhet – möjligheter, problem och erfarenheter* (Report Number 1985:12). Stockholm: Rapport till expertgruppen i ekonomi (in Swedish).

Elander, S., & Montin, S. (1990). Decentralisation and Control: Central-Local Government Relations in Sweden. *Policy and Politics, 18*(3), 165–180.

EU. (2014). *Public Procurement—Study on Administrative Capacity in the EU: Sweden Country Profile*. http://ec.europa.eu/regional_policy/sources/policy/how/improving-investment/public-procurement/study/country_profile/se.pdf/. Accessed April 2018.

Foss Hansen, H. (2011). NPM in Scandinavia. In T. Christensen & P. Lægreid (Eds.), *New Public Management* (pp. 113–129). Burlington: Ashgate.

Hall, P. (2012). *Managementbyråkrati*. Malmö: Liber (in Swedish).

Hallgren, T. (1997). *Fakta och Argument om Kommunala företag*. Stockholm: Svenska kommunförbundet (in Swedish).

Hansson, L. (1987). *Den kommunala parkenhetens organisation och verksamhet – en enkätstudie*. Alnarp: Stad & Land nr. 52 (in Swedish).

Hansson, L. (1990). *Grönsektorns organisation – en spekulativ analys av olika utvecklingsinriktningar*. Alnarp: Stad & Land nr. 82 (in Swedish).

Hansson, L. (1991). *FoU om de kommunala tekniska kontorens ekonomi, organisation och administration – projektbeskrivning* (Rapport nr. 1). Lund: Institutet för ekonomisk forskning vid Lunds universitet (in Swedish).

Hansson, L., & Knutsson, B. O. (1991). *Organisation av kommunal teknisk verksamhet – en enkätstudie i början av 1990-talet* (Rapport nr. 2). Lund: Institutet för ekonomisk forskning vid Lunds universitet (in Swedish).

Hansson, L., & Lind, J. I. (1998). *Marknadsorientering i kommuner och landsting – erfarenheter från pionjärernas kamp*. Stockholm: Nerenius & Santérus (in Swedish).

Hansson, L., & Mattisson, O. (1993). *Kommunal teknik en marknad för entreprenörer? – förutsättningar och alternativa strategier* (Rapport nr. 25). Lund: Institutet för ekonomisk forskning vid Lunds universitet (in Swedish).

Hood, C. (1991). A Public Management for All Seasons? *Public Administration, 69*(1), 3–19.

Houlberg, K., & Petersen, O. H. (2012). *Indikatorer for kommunernes køb af externe ydelser i Danmark og Sverige*. København: AKF Notat (in Danish).

Jacobsson, B., Pierre, J., & Sundström, G. (2015). *Governing the Embedded State*. Oxford: Oxford University Press.

Jansson, D., & Forssell, A. (1995). Ord som fångslar: Om kommunernas företagisering. *Statsvetenskaplig tidskrift, 98*(3), 346–361. (in Swedish).

Johansson, J. (2000). *SAF och den svenska modellen – En studie av uppbrottet från förvaltningskorporatismen 1982–91*. Uppsala: Avhandling i statsvetenskap (in Swedish).

Knutsson, H., Mattisson, O., Näsi, S., Nyland, K., & Skærbæk, P. (2017). New Public Management in a Scandinavian Context. In I. Lapsley & H. Knutsson (Eds.), *Modernizing the Public Sector: Scandinavian Perspectives* (pp. 18–34). London: Routledge.

Konkurrensverket. (2015). *Facts and Figures on Public Procurement in Sweden*. Stockholm: The Swedish Competition Authority's Report Series.

Konkurrensverket. (2016). *Statistik om offentlig upphandling 2016* (p. 7). Konkurrensverket, Upphandlingsmyndigheten.

Lapsley, I., & Knutsson, H. (Eds.). (2017). *Modernizing the Public Sector: Scandinavian Perspectives*. London: Routledge.

Lindholst, A. C. (2009). Contracting-Out in Urban Green-Space Management: Instruments, Approaches and Arrangements. *Urban Forestry & Urban Greening, 8*(4), 257–268.

Lindholst, A. C., Randrup, T. B., Kristoffersson, A., Hansen, M. B., & Persson, B. (2017). Evaluating the Complexities of Contracting Outcomes in Urban Services: The Case of Green Space Maintenance in Denmark and Sweden. *Environment and Planning C: Politics and Space, 36*(6), 1046–1067.

Lindvall, J. (2004). *Gothenburg Studies in Politics: Vol. 84. The Politics of Purpose: Swedish Macroeconomic Policy After the Golden Age*. Gothenburg: Department of Political Science, Gothenburg University.

LOU. (1992:1528). *Law on Public Procurement* (Lag om offentlig upphandling) (in Swedish).

LOU. (2007:1091). *Law on Public Procurement* (Lag om offentlig upphandling) (in Swedish).

LOU. (2016:1145). *Law on Public Procurement* (Lag om offentlig upphandling) (in Swedish).

LOV. (2008:962). *Law on Freedom of Choice in Welfare* (Lag om valfrihet i vården) (in Swedish).

Montin, S. (1992). Privatiseringsprocesser i kommunerna: teoretiska utgångspunkter och empiriska exempel. *Statsvetenskaplig tidskrift, 95*(1), 31–57 (in Swedish).

Montin, S. (2000). Between Fragmentation and Coordination. *Public Management Review, 2*(1), 1–24.

Montin, S. (2017). *Debatt pågår! Kommunerna och förvaltningspolitiken under nästan 40 år*. Stockholm: Sveriges Kommuner och Landsting (in Swedish).

Nilsson, L. (2011). Välfärdsopinion – valåret 2010. In S. Holmberg, L. Weibull, & H. Oscarsson (Eds.), *Lycksalighetens ö* (pp. 279–296). Gothenburg: Gothenburg University, SOM Institute (in Swedish).

Norén Bretzer, Y. (2017). *Sveriges Politiska System* (3rd ed.). Lund: Studentlitteratur (in Swedish).

Norén Bretzer, Y., Persson, B., & Randrup, T. B. (2016). Is Public Procurement Efficiency Conditioned by Market Types? A Critical Test in Park and Road Sectors in Sweden. *International Journal of Public Sector Management, 29*(5), 488–501.

Ordinance on Public Procurement. (1986:366). Upphandlingsförordningen (in Swedish).

Osborne, D., & Gaebler, T. (1992). *Reinventing Government*. Reading, MA: Addison-Wesley.

Parliamentary Bill. (1980). *Om insyn i statliga företag* (1980/81:22). Stockholm: Sveriges Riksdag (in Swedish).

Parliamentary Bill. (1995). *Lag om statsbudgeten* (1995/1996:220). Stockholm: Sveriges Riksdag (in Swedish).

PBL. (2010). *Plan- och bygglag* (2010:900). Stockholm: Näringsdepartementet (in Swedish).

Pollitt, C. (1993). *Managerialism and the Public Services*. Oxford: Blackwell.

Pollitt, C., & Bouckaert, G. (2011). *Public Management Reform: A Comparative Analysis* (3rd ed.). Oxford: Oxford University Press.

Premfors, R., Ehn, P., Halden, E., & Sundström, G. (2009). *Demokrati och byråkrati*. Lund: Studentlitteratur (in Swedish).

Randrup, T. B., Nielsen, J. B., Lindholst, A. C., Nuppenau, C., & Sejr, K. (2006, March). New Trends in Outsourcing Public Green Space Maintenance—The Concept of Integrated Park Management: Ifpra World—Refereed Section. *International Federation of Parks and Recreation Administration*, 8–10.

Randrup, T. B., Östberg, J., & Wiström, B. (2017). Swedish Green Space Management—The Managers Perspective. *Urban Forestry & Urban Greening, 28*(6), 103–109.

Randrup, T. B., & Persson, B. (2009). Public Green Spaces in the Nordic Countries: Development of a New Strategic Management Regime. *Urban Forestry & Greening, 8*(1), 31–40.

Rhodes, R. A. W. (1996). The New Governance: Governing Without Government. *Political Studies, 44*(4), 652–667.
Roebeling, P., Saraiva, M., Palla, A., Gnecco, I., Teotonio, C., Fidelis, T., et al. (2017). Assessing the Socio-Economic Impacts of Green/Blue Space, Urban Residential and Road Infrastructure Projects in the Confluence (Lyon): A Hedonic Pricing Simulation Approach. *Journal of Environmental Planning and Management, 60*(3), 482–499.
Rothstein, B., & Wahlne Westerhäll, L. (Eds.). (2005). *Bortom den starka statens politik*. Stockholm: SNS Förlag (in Swedish).
Santesson-Wilson, P., & Erlingsson, G. (Eds.). (2009). *Reform: Förändring och tröghet i välfärsstaterna*. Stockholm: Norstedts (in Swedish).
SCB. (1980). *Kommunernas finanser*. Stockholm: Statistics Sweden (in Swedish).
SCB. (2001). *Kommunägda företag 2001*. OE 27 SM 0201. Stockholm: Statistics Sweden (in Swedish).
SCB. (2014). *Offentligt ägda företag 2014*. OE 27 SM 1401. Stockholm: Statistics Sweden (in Swedish).
SCB. (2015, December 31). *Bostadsbeståndet*. Stockholm: Statistics Sweden.
SCB. (2016a). *Förtroendevalda i kommuner och landsting 2015* (Demokratistatistik Rapport 22). Örebro (in Swedish).
SCB. (2016b, September 22). *Finansiärer och utförare inom vård, skola och omsorg 2014*. OE 29 SM 1601. Stockholm: Statistics Sweden (in Swedish).
SKL. (2014). *Välfärdstjänsternas utveckling 1980–2012: Ökande resurser och växande behov*. Stockholm (in Swedish).
SKL. (2017). *Kommungruppsindelning 2017*. https://skl.se/tjanster/kommunerlandsting/faktakommunerochlandsting/kommungruppsindelning.2051.html. Accessed April 2018 (in Swedish).
Sørensen, E. (2006). The Changing Role of Politicians in Processes of Democratic Governance. *The American Review of Public Administration, 36*(1), 98–114.
SOU. (2007:10). *Hållbar samhällsorganisation med utvecklingskraft*. Final document, Ansvarskommittén. Stockholm: Fritzes (in Swedish).
Statskontoret. (2015). *Den offentliga sektorn i korthet*. Stockholm (in Swedish).
Sundstrand, A. (2013). *Offentlig upphandling – en introduction*. Lund: Studentlitteratur (in Swedish).
Svensson, P. (2017). *Cross-Sector Strategists: Dedicated Bureaucrats in Local Government Administration*. Gothenburg: Gothenburg University, School of Public Administration.
Thompson, C. W. (2002). Urban Open Space in the 21st Century. *Landscape and Urban Planning, 60*(2), 59–72.
Thwaites, K., Helleur, E., & Simkins, I. M. (2005). Restorative Urban Open Space: Exploring the Spatial Configuration of Human Emotional Fulfilment in Urban Open Space. *Landscape Research, 30*(4), 525–547.

Vierikko, K., & Niemelä, J. (2016, January). Bottom-Up Thinking—Identifying Socio-Cultural Values of Ecosystem Services in Local Blue–Green Infrastructure Planning in Helsinki, Finland. *Land Use Policy, 50*, 537–547.
WHO. (2017). *Urban Green Spaces*. World Health Organization. http://www.who.int/sustainable-development/cities/health-risks/urban-green-space/en/. Accessed April 2018.

CHAPTER 7

# Denmark: The Incremental Way Towards a Deep-Seated Marketization of Service Delivery

*Andrej Christian Lindholst*

## Introduction

The organization of service delivery in the municipal park and road sectors in Denmark has in the period from the 1980s to the 2010s been profoundly changed towards a 'marketized' model of public service delivery. While service delivery in the 1980s primarily relied on in-house provision based on professional expertise combined with some purchases of specialized services, the 2010s have witnessed widespread use of competitive tendering, private contractors and corporate principles for organizing in-house provision. The primary aim of this chapter is to address how this fundamental change in the organization of service delivery came about. For this purpose, the chapter details and interprets the changes in light of the general reform push for marketization in the Danish public sector from the early 1980s and onward. Overall, the chapter assesses the degree the marketization agenda has impacted the

A. C. Lindholst (✉)
Department of Politics and Society, Aalborg University, Aalborg, Denmark
e-mail: acl@dps.aau.dk



A. C. Lindholst and M. B. Hansen (eds.),
*Marketization in Local Government*,
https://doi.org/10.1007/978-3-030-32478-0_7

organization of municipal park and road services among Danish municipalities in a historical perspective and describes the characteristics of the particular path and forms of marketization within the two service sectors. Overall, it is found that the path towards a steadily more complex and deep-seated marketization within municipal park and road services have been characterized by incrementalism and a slow reform pace located within a 'pragmatic' rather than a 'cohesive' policy context.

The chapter relies on existing literature, earlier studies of reform and organization in the park and road sectors and INOPS survey data (see Chapter 3). The chapter is organized into three main sections. First, the chapter provides an overview of the development of the general marketization agenda in the period 1980s–2010s. Second, a chronological overview is provided for the impact of marketization on the organization of municipal park and road sectors in the period 1980s–2010s. Third, and finally, the status and characteristics of marketization in the park and road sectors are discussed and conclusions are drawn.

## The Marketization Agenda 1980s–2010s

The overall approach to public management reforms in the Danish public sector from the 1980s and onward has usually been characterized as one of 'modernizing' rather than 'marketizing' as well as one driven by incrementalism and pragmatism rather than radical change and ideology (Greve 2006; Jensen 1998; Pedersen and Löfgren 2012). In Denmark, it has even become possible to talk about a new public management 'without marketization' in reference to the implementation of a series of major administrative reforms in the 2000s characterized by a diverse set of non-market-based means such as mergers and enlargements, reliance on professions, hierarchical control and audit mechanisms, standards for compliance, statutory rights for citizens, taxation limits and hard budget restraints (Pedersen and Löfgren 2012). In consequence, the wider reform agenda has promoted and relied upon a variety of new instruments for governing more than it has replaced government itself with market-based coordination mechanisms.

A rough history of the general marketization agenda in Denmark divides the development into several major phases, starting with the 1980s (Ejersbo and Greve 2014). The first political–administrative initiatives in Denmark emphasizing marketization as a systematic strategy for reforming and running the public sector emerged under right-wing governments in the early 1980s as a core part of a wider new public management (NPM)-oriented reform agenda (Ejersbo and Greve 2014). These initiatives were introduced by an incoming right-wing-led government, which came into power on the backdrop of an emerging financial crisis of the state where a former left-wing government had failed to reach political consensus for its proposal to address increasing state deficits and restore public finances. Marketization in the first political–administrative initiatives was an integrated part of a larger political agenda for restoring public finances and was presented as a tool for achieving 'economic or administrative benefits' and ensuring services delivery in ways that were 'best and cheapest'—notably by involvement of the private sector through market tests (competitive tendering) and subsequent contracting out. The initiatives also emphasized needs for increased cost-awareness and service orientation in public service delivery. Despite policies to some extent were inspired by the Thatcher era in the UK they were formulated in a Danish political tradition for minority governments and attempts to seek consensus. Thus they were pragmatic in their formulation and overall orientation and had little immediate impact on the organization of public service delivery. The overall agenda however, spurred several ideological quarrels between political parties and protests from organized interest groups (e.g. labour unions).

A wider political and administrative consensus emerged in the 1990s when successive left-wing governments from 1993 and onward embraced marketization as a legitimate and pragmatic reform instrument. However, in contrast to the early 1980s, public finances were restored and the economy was booming. The emerging consensus was combined with experiments and learning in different service sectors but also with large-scale implementation of some types of marketization (and privatization) at the state level, such as a substantial sale of state-owned public assets within infrastructure, including telecommunications and airports (renowned as 'privatization' in a Danish context). Internal marketization (without privatization) was also introduced and promoted through government policies and administrative practice through performance-based contracting, standardization, benchmarking, agentification and corporatization (Ejersbo and Greve 2014).

Marketization found its way earlier within some municipal services—in particular within technical services—than in other services such as welfare and social services. A national survey on the use of competitive tendering within technical services in the mid-1990s (KL 2001), for example, found that competitive tendering at that time was widely used within garbage collection and road maintenance (among approximately two-thirds of the municipalities), while substantially less so for other technical services. However, some highly profiled marketization 'experiments' at the municipal level in the 1990s also went awry, such as the development of unlawful and scandalous administration practices in public–private collaborations for service delivery and local development in the right-wing-led municipality of Farum.

In the 2000s, different forms of marketization were promoted and implemented within an increasing number of services. Despite the emerging consensus in the 1990s, right-wing governments from 2001 and onward promoted the marketization agenda with greater enthusiasm and more cohesive policy instruments than left-wing governments did in the 1990s. The characterization of the Danish approach as one of pragmatism and incrementalism was also challenged by several right-wing government initiatives in the 2000s. Policies in the 2000s generally aimed at contesting in-house provision and increasing the share of private provision of public services through a mix of more or less cohesive policy instruments, ranging from stronger administrative coordination, sector-specific use of compulsory competitive tendering, private sector rights to challenge public service delivery, binding targets for the level of contracting out in local governments and recurrent political proposals concerning the implementation of compulsory competitive tendering for additional services. Cohesive policies ensuring users a choice between public and private providers were also implemented within a few key welfare sectors, notably, homecare (Rostgaard 2018; Hansen 2010), healthcare (Larsen and Stone 2015) and public employment services (Breidahl and Larsen 2015). In the latter part of the 2000s many management tools broadly associated with marketization and New Public Management (see also Chapter 2) had diffused into most Danish municipalities (Hansen 2011) with substantially stronger impact than in the Danish state administration (Hansen 2013). Right-wing governments in the 2000s also launched and promoted a systematic public–private partnership (PPP) agenda for private sector involvement and investment in infrastructure projects, while the regulative and administrative framework for contracting out was further strengthened (Christensen and Petersen

2010). However, institutional support for the PPP agenda was limited and the agenda only resulted in the initiation of a smaller number of pilot projects in the 2000s (Petersen 2015). Finally, a major structural reform reducing the number of municipalities from 271 to 98 and rearranging the organization of a number of public services aimed at improving professionalism and organizational effectiveness in the public sector but also embedded expectations for increased marketization and private sector involvement (Houlberg and Dahl 2010).

In a response to the heat of the general marketization agenda, some local initiatives were taken within the municipalities in order to reform and promote in-house provision as an alternative to contracting out. A group of technical departments in the municipalities, for example, established a supportive network in the early 2000s for development, knowledge sharing and promotion of competitive business models for in-house provision within technical services (KEF 2017).

Policies and practices matured further in the 2010s and the more complex forms of marketization such as PPPs for the provision of infrastructure found an increased use at all levels of governments. In the late 2000 and throughout the 2010s, new corporate forms were promoted within public utilities and infrastructure. New regulations, for example, opened up for a more business-oriented and corporate organization and operation of municipal harbours. The promotion of corporate forms within public utilities was at this stage often mixed with voices promoting the sale of assets to the private sector as an alternative. Despite almost four decades of normalization of marketization as policy and administrative practice, some high-profiled initiatives also spurred substantial public debate and opposition in the 2010s. Most notably, the Ministry of Finance's partial sale of ownership (shares) within the energy sector to a global investment bank in 2014 incited previously unseen public and political upheaval, ultimately resulting in a historical break-up of a left-wing government coalition (Lindholst and Hansen 2015). Congruently, a substantially more critical stance in the public support for further private involvement in public service delivery developed in the 2000s compared to the early 1990s (Stubager et al. 2013). A few sectors also experienced a 'rolling back' of highly profiled marketization policies. Public employment services, for example, were, in the 2000s, subject to a compulsory competitive tendering policy based on a rigid scheme linking price with performance targets in the delivery of various employment services. However, due to the poor performance of many private providers and recurrent 'scandals' in the media, the policy was abandoned in 2011 by an incoming left-wing-led government and replaced with a system based on collaboration and less emphasis on price competition (Breidahl and Larsen 2015). More generally, a centre-left-wing government in office in 2011–2015, rolled back the cohesive policy instruments implemented by right-wing governments in the 2000s while retaining political support and revitalizing some parts such as PPPs for welfare innovation and infrastructure projects. However, an incoming right-wing government in 2015 re-emphasized and promoted anew classical marketization doctrines such as private sector involvement, choice models and competitive tendering at the municipal level.

The general marketization agenda in the Danish public sector 1980s–2010s has mainly been driven by incrementalism and pragmatism but also with ideological differences among successive right- and left-wing governments in their emphasis on marketization in policies and the scale and scope of private sector involvement. The pragmatism reinforced by a political tradition for a high degree of autonomy for local government, has given some leeway for municipalities to differ in their implementation of marketization across various services and in their reform of in-house provision. The level of contracting out, for example, has been found to vary significantly across municipal services according to local characteristics, such as economic pressure, municipal size and ideological orientation of the city council (Foged 2015). However, an increasingly stronger undercurrent in the marketization agenda has also relied on a more cohesive policy approach, including tighter regulations and fewer degrees of freedom for municipalities.

## Marketization in the Park and Road Sectors

The road and partly the park sectors were among the first municipal service sectors where different types of internal and external marketization found their way and reshaped the organization of service delivery. Table 7.1 provides a detailed historical overview of the trajectories of marketization in the two sectors for the period 1980s–2010s. Below, the trajectories are roughly grouped and detailed according to four consecutive decades.

**Table 7.1** Trajectories of marketization in the Danish municipal road and park sectors 1980s–2010s

| *Decade* | *Sector* | |
|---|---|---|
| | *Road* | *Park* |
| 1980s | • Private provision around 40%<br>• Full-scale contracting out at the state level (state roads and highways)<br>• Low level of public procurement/competitive tendering<br>• Auxiliary use of private contractors (specialized tasks or as buffers) | • Private provision around 10–15% (for specialized tasks)<br>• Low or non-existing use of public procurement and competitive tendering |
| 1990s | • Private provision around 40%<br>• No increase in the share of private contractors<br>• Common vocabulary for service specifications is developed and integrated into a full 'paradigm' for public procurement (1999)<br>• Increased cost motives for public procurement<br>• Internal reorganizations (quality control systems, resource management, merger of in-house park and road provision) | • Slow increase of private provision from around 16 to around 20%<br>• Little use of private contractors and few cases of competitive tendering and contracting out<br>• Full-scale contracting out initiated at the state level (royal and historical parks)<br>• Common vocabulary for service specifications is developed (1998).<br>• Increased cost motives for public procurement<br>• Internal reorganizations (quality control systems, resource management, merger of in-house park and road provision) |
| 2000s | • Private provision slightly decreasing to 35% in 2007, but steadily increasing hereafter<br>• Experiments with alternative contracting concepts (long-term performance contracts and partnering)<br>• Revision of common vocabulary in 2001 and 2005<br>• Unsuccessful experiments with reforms by establishment of inter-municipal corporations<br>• Further internal reorganizations (internal contracting, provider–purchaser models, corporate-like forms) | • Private provision increases from around 20 to 30%<br>• Full 'paradigm' for public procurement of park services made available<br>• Introduction of alternative concepts for contracting out<br>• Unsuccessful experiments with reform by establishment of inter-municipal corporations<br>• Further internal reorganizations (internal contracting, provider–purchaser models, corporate-like forms) |

(continued)

**Table 7.1** (continued)

| *Decade* | *Sector* | |
|---|---|---|
| | *Road* | *Park* |
| 2010s | • Continued increase in private provision to almost 50% in 2015<br>• Long-term (+10 years) performance-based maintenance contracts become widespread<br>• First PPP project (motorway) implemented at the state level | • Private provision increases from around 30 in 2010 to almost 40% in 2014<br>• Revision of common vocabulary for service specifications<br>• Experiments with alternative contracting concepts (e.g. balanced scorecard principles, decentralized decision-making) |

*Note* Partly based on Lindholst et al. (2016)

### *The 1980s and Earlier*

Available sources on the organization of park and road services in local governments indicate that a skill-based organizational form with a low degree of formalization of management systems was pre-dominant in the 1980s and early 1990s. Gjelstrup (1991, 1992), for example, found that local governments in the early 1990s (and before) did not have formal (performance) management systems in place for road services that could document cost and service levels. Likewise, Nuppenau (2009) found that a more widespread introduction of formal management systems for park services only started in the 1990s. Furthermore, the general preference among municipalities in the 1980s was in strong favour of in-house arrangements, which were generally believed to be the best way of organizing service provisions. The private sector in the 1980s (and earlier) was mainly involved for specialized services it offers, which could not easily be delivered through in-house provision and not for cost-minimizing purposes. Case studies (Lindholst et al. 2017) show that traditional forms of organization were still in place in some smaller local governments until the mid-2000s when a structural reform created larger and more professional organizations through municipal mergers or by requirements for the few remaining small municipalities to review and reform their service delivery systems.

In a historical overview of marketization in Danish municipal road and park sectors, it is notable that developments within the road sector began early and took place in a pretext of existing large-scale private sector involvement. In the park sector, marketization took place in a pretext of very low private sector involvement (Lindholst et al. 2016). Sources indicate that around 10–15% of maintenance budgets were spent on private purchases until the early 1990s (Nuppenau et al. 2005) while maintenance of state-owned (royal) parks and gardens were provided in-house until the late 1990s. For the 1980s and earlier, historical statistics indicate that the municipalities spent around 40% of their road maintenance budgets on purchases from private contractors. Also, at the state level almost all maintenance of state-owned roads and highways were already contracted out to private contractors in the 1980s. The high spending on private purchases for road services was related to capital-intensive and costly asphalt works, the quantity of which is highly irregular from year to year for the individual municipality. However, in both sectors purchases in the 1980s were organized informally rather than through formalized and well-regulated processes for public procurement. Furthermore, until the late 1990s the road sector was suspected by national competition authorities of widespread collusion behaviour among private companies in their pricing of work for Danish municipalities (Konkurrrencestyrelsen 1999).

### *The 1990s*

In the 1990s, the park and road sectors witnessed substantial changes in the scope and scale of marketization. Internally, reorganizations related to the development and implementation of quality control systems, resource management systems and mergers of former separate park and road units (Nuppenau 2009). In both sectors, standardized professional vocabularies for specifying maintenance standards were developed in the late 1990s (published in 1998 for parks and 1999 for roads) and later revised in both sectors. State authorities with sector responsibilities spurred and supported the development in both sectors. In both sectors, the drivers were requirements to meet tighter financial conditions (e.g. limited budgets) and to support the use of competitive tendering and contracting out. The methodology for specifying maintenance standards has been based on a 'standard' approach, focusing on defining quality in measurable ways in compliance with the need for competitive pricing, control/monitoring and follow-up on service provisions—an approach also framing questions of quality as a matter of a technical-professional judgement rather than public deliberation (Lindholst et al. 2015).

While the park sector mainly witnessed a move towards internal marketization in the 1990s, the road sector also witnessed a substantial change in how private purchases were organized. In particular, the use of formal procedures for public procurement increased substantially in the road sector, while public procurement was only sporadically used in the park sector (KL 2001). As a consequence, the already substantial purchases of services from private enterprises in the road sector were permeated with intensified competition in a shift from informal and unregulated purchasing procedures towards formal and regulated ones.

### *The 2000s*

In the 2000s, marketization was intensified further in both sectors. Measured by national statistics for private purchases, the level of contracting out increased from about 20 to 30% in the park sector while the development was more uneven for the road sector. In the time around the municipal mergers in 2007, the level of private purchases dropped but has increased substantially since then. The formal regulative framework for competitive tendering was further strengthened and formalized by the implementation of the EU-procurement directive, regulating public purchases in 2004.

In both sectors, the purchaser–provider model and internal contracting were introduced in internal organizational arrangements on top of new management systems introduced in the 1990s (Nuppenau 2009). The development of internal marketization was supported by the establishment of sector-specific networks in 2004 for improving in-house provision of park and road services. The networks aimed at improving overall performance of in-house provider organizations and their competitiveness with private contractors (KEF 2017). Some high-profiled municipal attempts to reorganize service delivery into company forms working on almost equal terms as private companies also failed. For example, the two left-wing-led municipalities of Odense and Vejle established a jointly owned inter-municipal company (Infra Service I/S) in 2005, but already by 2008 they had to liquidate the company after accumulating severe and increasing deficits, which subsequently had to be covered by the two municipalities (i.e. by tax-payers' money). Among the reported reasons for the deficits were irregular and incompetent managerial and financial practices, the use of (too) low prices for winning and keeping contracts with the parent and other municipalities, and the enactments of a sudden national regulation in the mid-2000s limiting the extent that municipalities were allowed to carry out and compete for services in other municipalities. After the close-down of the failing company one municipality (Odense) decided to contract out all service provisions, while the other municipality (Vejle) reorganized most services in an in-house organization.

The development of alternative and more collaborative approaches to contracting out were also taking place in both sectors in the 2000s (Lindholst 2008). The development of collaborative approaches mirrored a growing emphasis within the national policy agenda on 'partnerships' and new ways of organizing public–private relations. In the park sector, a concept of 'integrated park management' introduced a framework for integrating strategy, user involvement, investments, service development and maintenance operations as part of a collaborative approach to contracting out (Randrup et al. 2006). In the late 2000s, the park sector also witnessed several experiments with various so-called 'holistic approaches' to contracting out, based on multiple performance measures as well as a collaborative approach between a purchaser and service providers. In the road sector, collaborative approaches for organizing maintenance contracts termed 'partnering' were developed from the early 2000s and onwards and implemented by the national road authorities as well as promoted for use in the municipalities (Lindholst 2008). Partnering denoted a formal collaborative arrangement in which partners engaged in the process under a shared vision, joint activities and mutual economic incentives. Partnering aimed at providing flexibility in medium-term maintenance contracts in primarily urban zones with relatively unpredictable service needs and coordination needs with several potential stakeholders (e.g. land owners or utilities). Partnering contracts by the municipalities have typically been used as alternatives to one-year contracts, where maintenance and production needs are unilaterally planned and decided on by municipal planning departments. The advantage of a partnering contract in this case is better forward planning and reduced costs due to a private contractor's higher future certainty about required investments in production capacity. During the early 2000s, the municipalities also started to use long-term performance-based maintenance contracts in the road sector with the purpose of ensuring a more efficient mix between investment and maintenance costs under relatively predictable service needs, particularly in rural areas. The INOPS survey data indicate that about 20% of all municipalities in the mid-2010s used long-term road maintenance contracts, typically running between 10 and 15 years, for some parts of their road networks.

A structural reform effectuated in 2007, whereby smaller municipalities were merged into larger units, further fueled the marketization agenda. INOPS case studies for Denmark (Lindholst et al. 2017) show that efforts in some of the newly established and merged municipalities firstly concentrated on the reform and integration of internal organizational systems and service provision, but were also guided by long-term strategies based on competitive tendering as a final benchmark for acceptable performance and the basis for choosing between a continuation of in-house provision or contracting out.

What is particularly notable for the park sector in the 2000s was a steep increase in the use of public procurement and contracting levels from the early 2000s and onward. In comparison, the increased use of public procurement in the park sector in the 2000s led to increased contracting levels, while the increased use of public procurement in the road sector in the 1990s 'merely' intensified competition in already existing private purchases (Lindholst et al. 2016).

### *The 2010s*

The first half of the 2010s witnessed a further development of marketization in the park and road sectors. By 2015, according to official statistics (Statistics Denmark), the degree of private purchases for maintenance services reached almost 40% for the parks and almost 50% for roads. Compared to earlier, the two sectors still exhibit some differences with regard to the levels of contracting out, although the park sector has increasingly been 'catching up' with the road sector. Official statistics also register some administrative costs on accounts for maintenance as well as some purchases that could hardly be produced by a municipality, such as materials and fuels. The actual degree of maintenance operations carried out by private contractors is therefore likely to be somewhat lower than municipal accounts indicate.

Based on INOPS survey data, Fig. 7.1 provides an overview of the reliance in service delivery in the mid-2010s on, respectively, mainly private provision (contracted out 90% or more), in-house provision (contracted out 10% or less) or mixed delivery (contracted out between 10

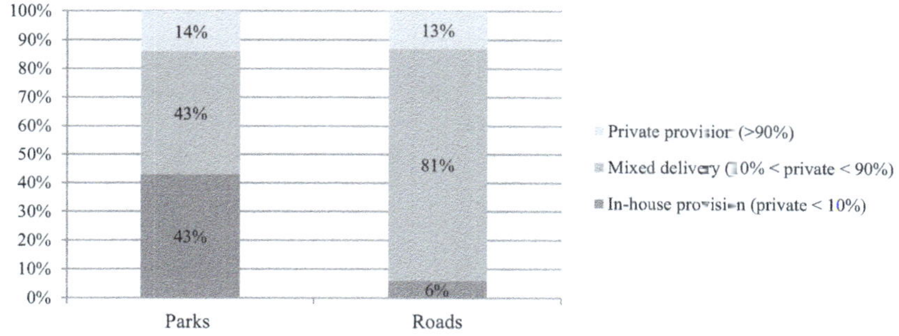


**Fig. 7.1** The mix of private and in-house provision in the Danish municipal road and park sectors (*Note* Based on INOPS survey data. $N=74$ for parks and $N=72$ for roads)

and 90%). Notably, across the two sectors the most common organization of service delivery is mixed delivery. About 14% of the municipalities rely almost completely on private delivery (90% or more) This is novel compared to the situation in the early 2000s (and before) where only one municipality was renowned for shifting completely from in-house to private provision. Still, the vast majority of the municipalities rely on in-house provision in substantial degrees for both park and road services.

In comparison with the situation in the 1980s and early 1990s the purpose for private involvement had also shifted substantially by the 2010s. Figure 7.2 reports on the importance of various purposes for using private contractors and in-house provision for road and park services for the mid-2010s. The statistics show that economic considerations in terms of *test and benchmark prices* and *cost-efficiency* (mean score=7.5) are the two most important purposes for using private contractors. *Getting (specialized) tasks done, which the municipality cannot provide* itself, is also a relatively important purpose (mean score=6.7). The mean scores for the remaining purposes with private provision are all substantially lower. The statistics also highlight that Danish municipalities evaluate the importance of purposes differently across public and private production, with significantly higher average scores for the purposes of using public service provision compared with the purposes of using private contractors. The difference in favour of in-house provision is statistically significant (tests not shown) for four items, whereas the differences between in-house and private provision for the purpose *test*

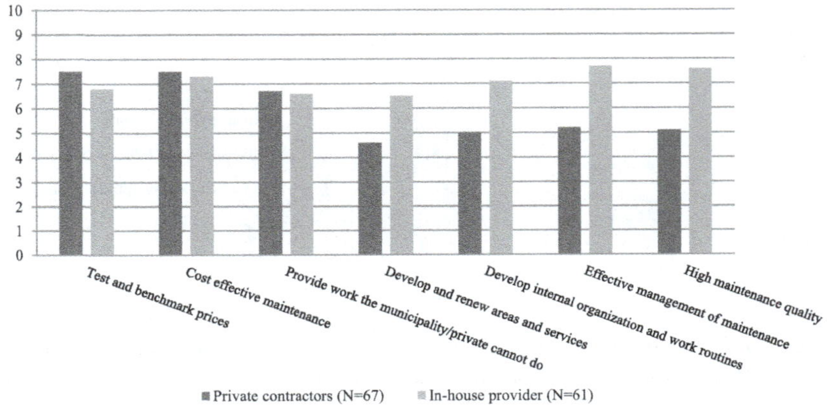


**Fig. 7.2** Importance of seven purposes for using private contractors and in-house providers (parks and roads) (*Note* Based on INOPS survey data. The figure shows the mean for responses to the question: 'Specify on a scale of 0 [not at all] to 10 [to a very high degree] the degree to which you think that the following purposes are a central part of your municipality's considerations for using in-house provision/private contractors for maintenance…')

*and benchmark prices* are significantly more important for private provision than for in-house delivery. These findings point to the overriding importance of using private contractors for primarily economic purposes in terms of *cost-effective maintenance* and *test and benchmark prices* and more secondary for provision of services that cannot be provided in-house. Furthermore, the findings indicate that private contractors in the mid-2010s are used for a narrower set of purposes compared with the broader range of purposes for using in-house provision. In comparison with the situation in the early 1990s, the main motives for using private contractors (specialized tasks and buffer) are still found to be important but are now complemented and overshadowed by economic concerns related to comparing and ensuring low costs.

The internal organization of park and road services in local governments also changed substantially in the period 1980s–2010s. Based on INOPS survey data, Table 7.2 provides an overview of the use of eight formal instruments related to the use of marketization in the organization of in-house provision of road and park maintenance services. The instruments are ordered in the table by how frequently they are used

**Table 7.2** The diffusion of formal marketization instruments for managing and organizing in-house providers in Danish municipalities in the mid-2010s

| *Formal instruments*[a] | *Frequency*[b] *(%)* |
|---|---|
| Separate top management | 90 |
| Separate budgeting/financial statement | 87 |
| Competitive tendering of services provided in-house | 75 |
| Business plans | 74 |
| Allowed to carry out tasks for other clients | 73 |
| Separate monitoring function of maintenance operations | 68 |
| Formal purchaser–provider split | 54 |
| Company ownership structure (100% owned by the municipality) | 6 |

*Note* Based on INOPS survey data. $N=64$

[a]The table shows the frequencies of positive answers ('yes') for eight key management instruments on the question: "Which of the following management instruments does the municipality use for managing and organizing the in-house service provision of parks and roads maintenance?"

[b]The frequencies count the share in the group of Danish municipalities with an in-house provider that uses a particular management instrument

among those municipalities that have a degree of in-house provision (which encompasses almost 90% of all Danish municipalities). The two most widespread instruments among the municipalities are *separate top management* (90%) and *separate budgeting/financial statements* (87%). *Competitive tendering of services provided in-house* and *allowed to carry out tasks for other clients* are also commonly used (75 and 73%, respectively). The two least frequently used instruments are *formal provider–purchaser split* (54%) and *a company ownership structure* (6%).

Overall, the data indicate that in-house providers have become organized as 'corporate-like' entities. Most in-house providers are managed as a semi-autonomous part within the overall organization. Their management is working with a degree of autonomy; they have a 'business plan' in place for their organization, and they are held accountable for their economic performance through annual budgets and financial statements. What is somehow surprising is that internal purchaser–provider models are 'only' used by around one-half of the municipalities. This model involves a formal separation of internal responsibilities for 'purchasing' services from the responsibilities for 'providing' services. In other words, decision-making for the level of operational maintenance is decentralized among one-half of the municipalities while it is centralized in the other half.

Furthermore, tasks currently carried out by in-house providers are frequently subject for market testing by competitive tendering. This indicates that direct competition between public providers and private enterprises are very common in Denmark. This interpretation is further supported by the evidence of a relatively widespread use of control bids/calculation (for in-house provision) when services are competitively tendered. INOPS survey data indicate that about one-half of all municipalities include a control bid/calculation for the cost of in-house provision when services are competitively tendered to the market. This is also reflected in the importance of price tests and benchmarking as a purpose for using in-house providers as well private contractors. Furthermore, three-quarters of all in-house providers are allowed to some degree to carry out work for clients other than the municipality (e.g. private customers or public institutions). The various findings indicate that competition between public and private service providers despite tight national regulations to some degree goes 'both ways'. However, it is rare to find examples of municipal providers in competition with private contractors bidding for and carrying out tasks in other municipalities.

## Discussions and Conclusions

This chapter has provided an overview of the general marketization agenda in Denmark and the resulting organizational changes within municipal park and road services in the 1980s–2010s period. It is found that the national agenda for marketization has contributed to and is reflected in a fundamental reorganization of service delivery in the two sectors. The changes within municipal park and road services have followed rather closely the overall developments in the central policy push for promoting marketization in the public sector more generally. Municipal park services, but in particular road services, have been part of the forefront in overall marketization efforts in Denmark and by the mid-2010s the two services are witnessing high contracting levels compared to other municipal services.

Developments have by and large reflected the dominant pragmatic approach for marketization in Denmark and taken place through slower incremental processes in both sectors, where marketization has become ever more pervasive and complex. In comparison, the road sector was marketized earlier and has in some degree matured further than the park sector. For example, in 2013, the first and so far the only PPP in the road sector delivered a new state highway, including a 20-year maintenance period. Cohesive policies supporting marketization have not been applied directly in the road and park sector as in some other municipal service sectors, such as Danish eldercare (by requirements to ensure free choice between private and public providers) or in public employment services (compulsory competitive tendering). However, cohesive instruments, such as agreements on binding targets for increased (levels of) private purchases, have indirectly affected the direction in the overall development and inherently contained a bias towards private over public provision. Still, the policies driving the marketization agenda have maintained a high degree of freedom for the municipalities in the implementation of the agenda within park and road services. To some degree, state authorities have acted as forerunners in the implementation of marketization in the park and road sectors and provided some support for the development of the marketization agenda among the municipalities.

Interestingly, the overall policy approach has prompted a 'bottom-up' response from the network of municipal in-house providers, with the aim to modernize and harness in-house providers' profiles in the competition with private contractors. A pervasive reorganization of in-house providers into competitive corporate-like internal entities has taken place and replaced former skill-based organizational forms. Interestingly, the development of internal corporate-like entities at the municipal level partly runs counter to right-wing policies at the national level seeking to promote further the involvement of private contractors in service delivery. It is notable that mixed delivery is the most prevalent form of organizing the balance between public and private provision across the two services and only a small fraction of the municipalities adheres to pure private provision. The appearance of municipalities opting for pure private provision, however, is still a novelty compared to the 1990s and earlier. Pure in-house provision is rare in road services while almost one-half of the municipalities rely on pure in-house provision for park services. It is notable that the use of private contractors providing maintenance services is mainly for cost purposes, while in-house providers are used for a broader set of purposes. In this sense, there seems to be a division of work between private and in-house providers. However, at least conceptually, there is also found a tendency to promote a more rounded approach to private sector involvement through new alternative contracting models taking off in the 2000s.

Furthermore, there is no indication in the analysis of the development undergone in the 1980s–2010s of attempts to 'roll back' marketization within park and road services as has been the case within, for example, public employment services (Breidahl and Larsen 2015), or that the development of marketization has reached a state of equilibrium, for example, between the degree of public and private service provision and in how the approach to contracting out should be organized. The analysis found an ongoing development and refinement of a set of more collaborative and diverse approaches to marketization. In the 2000s and 2010s, the two sectors seem to be in a phase of 'maturation' and 'learning', where experiences with and concepts for alternative models for the organization of contractual relations are developed and disseminated. By the 2010s, the choice for Danish municipalities is not only whether to contract or not, but also a choice among various alternative models for contracting out and organizing a division of labour between internal and external service provision. Still, the key characteristics of the development are very much in line with some of the classic NPM doctrines established in the 1980s (Hood 1991). In particular, the park and road sectors are characterized by a widespread use of intense and ongoing competition for contracts between private contractors and in-house providers combined with the reorganization of in-house providers into forms with corporate-like characteristics ('agentification'). The evidence indicates, however, that more advanced forms, such as inter-municipal companies or a true company structure, are rare. Similarly, no evidence is found for any substantial involvement of other types of organizations, e.g. community-based or non-profit organizations, in service delivery, or any broad shift towards truly collaborative approaches to contracting out.

In a short summary of the findings in this chapter it can be said that the trajectories of marketization in the municipal park and road sectors in Denmark have followed an incremental reform path with ongoing decentralized experiments resulting in profound and dynamic reorganizations of internal and external service delivery, including both standard and more advanced forms for marketization. Overall, it is found that reform and organizational change in the two sectors in the decades from the 1980s and until the mid-2010s represent a case of an increasingly wide-ranging, deep-seated and complex use of marketization. This complexity is reflected in a widespread use of long-standing models of marketization associated with the core doctrines of the NPM combined with the development of new collaborative approaches for contracting out. Still, it is important to note that in-house provision plays the major role within the organization of service delivery.

## References


Breidahl, K., & Larsen, F. (2015). The Developing Trajectory of the Marketization of Public Employment Services in Denmark: A New Way Forward or the End of Marketization? *European Policy Analysis, 1*(1), 92–107.

Christensen, L. R., & Petersen, O. H. (2010). Regulering af udlicitering og offentlige-private partnerskaber (OPP) i de danske kommuner. *Politica, 42*(2), 235–257.

Ejersbo, N., & Greve, C. (2014). *Moderniseringen af den offentlige sektor.* København: Akademisk Forlag.

Foged, S. K. (2015). Årsager til konkurrenceudsættelse i danske kommuner, 2007-2013: fra generelle til sektorafhængige forklaringer. *Politica, 47*(1), 24–45.

Gjelstrup, G. (1991). *Omstilling i den tekniske sektor - drift af veje som eksempel.* København: AKF Forlaget.

Gjelstrup, G. (1992). *Omstillingens svære kunst - den tekniske sektor som eksempel.* København: AKF Forlaget.

Greve, C. (2006). Public Management Reform in Denmark. *Public Management Review, 8*(1), 161–169.

Hansen, M. B. (2010). Marketization and Economic Performance: Competitive Tendering in the Social Sector. *Public Management Review, 12*(2), 255–274.

Hansen, M. B. (2011). Antecedents of Organizational Innovation: The Diffusion of New Public Management into Danish Local Government. *Public Administration, 89*(2), 285–306.

Hansen, M. B. (2013). Transnational organisatorisk innovation i den offentlige sektor. *Politica, 45*(3), 267–286.

Hood, C. (1991). A Public Management for All Seasons? *Public Administration, 69*(1), 3–19.

Houlberg, K., & Dahl, P. S. (2010). Konkurrenceudsættelse i danske kommuner - kommunalreformen som fødselshjælper? *Politica, 42*(2), 163–182.

Jensen, L. (1998). Interpreting New Public Management: The Case of Denmark. *Australian Journal of Public Administration, 57*(4), 54–65.

KEF. (2017). *Information brochure.* Birkerød.

KL. (2001). *Udbud og udlicitering på det tekniske område: Omfang og erfaringer.* København: kommunernes Landsforening.

Konkurrrencestyrelsen. (1999). *Konkurrence- og samarbejdsforholdene i asfalt-branchen - analyse.* København: Konkurrencestyrelsen.

Larsen, L. T., & Stone, D. (2015). Governing Health Care Through Free Choice: Neoliberal Reforms in Denmark and the United States. *Journal of Health Politics, Policy and Law, 40*(5), 941–970.

Lindholst, A. C. (2008). *Partnerskaber i parkforvaltningen: Grøn drift på kontrakt*. Frederiksberg: University of Copenhagen.

Lindholst, A. C., & Hansen, M. B. (2015). Befolkningens holdninger til markedsgørelsen af den offentlige sektor: Erkendelsesinteresser og forklaringsmodeller i politologien. *Politik, 18*(4), 47–59.

Lindholst, A. C., Hansen, M. B., & Petersen, O. H. (2016). Marketization Trajectories in the Danish Road and Park Sectors. *International Journal of Public Sector Management, 29*(5), 457–473.

Lindholst, A. C., Jensen, T. H., & Kjems, T. H. (2017). *Fem danske casestudier: En undersøgelse af udlicitering af park- og vejdrift i fem danske kommuner*. Aalborg: Aalborg Universitet.

Lindholst, A. C., Sullivan, S. G., van den Bosch, C. C. K., & Fors, H. (2015). The Inherent Politics of Managing the Quality of Urban Green Spaces. *Planning Practice and Research, 30*(4), 376–392.

Nuppenau, C. (2009). *Marketizing Municipal Park Management Organisations in Denmark: A Study of Policymaking and Organisational Change in the Period 1985–2005*. Frederiksberg: University of Copenhagen.

Nuppenau, C., Lindholst, C., & Sejr, K. (2005). *Udbud og udliciteringer af grønne driftsopgaver 1997–2003*. Hørsholm: Center for Skov, Landskab & Planlægning.

Pedersen, J. S., & Löfgren, K. (2012). Public Sector Reforms: New Public Management Without Marketization? The Danish Case. *International Journal of Public Administration, 35*(7), 435–447.

Petersen, O. H. (2015). National understøttelse af offentligtprivate partnerskaber (OPP): En komparativ analyse af 20 europæiske lande. *Politica, 47*(4), 561–579.

Randrup, T. B., Nielsen, J. B., Lindholst, C., Nuppenau, C., & Sejr, K. (2006, March). New Trends in Outsourcing Public Green Space Maintenance: The Concept of Integrated Park Management. *IFPRA World—Refereed Section*, 8–10.

Rostgaard, T. (2018). Revisiting the Public Care Model: The Danish Case of Free Choice in Home Care. In D. Pilling & K. Christensen (Eds.), *Ashgate Research Companion to Care Work Around the World* (pp. 29–44). Ashgate: Farnham.

Stubager, R., Holm, J., Smidstrup, M., & Kramb, K. (2013). *Danske vælgere 1971–2011: En oversigt over udviklingen i vælgernes holdninger mv*. Aarhus: Institut for Statskundskab.

CHAPTER 8

# Norway: The Reluctant Adopter of Marketization

*Merethe Dotterud Leiren, Julie Runde Krogstad and Ingjerd Solfjeld*

## Introduction

Norway has been characterized as a reluctant reformer when it comes to implementing marketization elements in public service delivery (Lieberherr and Leiren 2017). Yet the extent of marketization varies across sectors and political levels. In a Scandinavian context, Norway has been described as a 'follower' in technical service provision, yet when compared, for example, with the tradition of the German *Stadtwerke*,

M. D. Leiren (✉)
CICERO—Center for International Climate Research, Oslo, Norway
e-mail: merethe.leiren@cicero.oslo.no

J. R. Krogstad
TØI—Institute of Transport Economics, Oslo, Norway
e-mail: julierkrogstad@gmail.com

I. Solfjeld
Faculty of Landscape and Society,
Norwegian University of Life Sciences, Ås, Norway
e-mail: ingjerd.solfjeld@nmbu.no



A. C. Lindholst and M. B. Hansen (eds.),
*Marketization in Local Government*,
https://doi.org/10.1007/978-3-030-32478-0_8

Norway emerges as a somewhat early adopter. There is a vast literature on the development of marketization in many technical service sectors. Examples include public transport, a topic on which there is abundant international (Van de Velde 2014) and Norwegian literature (Longva and Osland 2010). Water is another area (Finger et al. 2007; Lieberherr and Fuenfschilling 2016). In contrast, with few exceptions (Durucz 2014; Randrup and Persson 2009), little has been written about local maintenance of roads and parks in Norway. Exploring the impact of marketization on the organization of these two services, we ask the following questions: How has marketization developed in Norway during the last 40 years? What organizational changes do we see at local level in the technical maintenance services for road and parks during the same decades? To what extent do the changes in municipal road and park services reflect the changes at the national level?

To answer these questions, we divide the chapter into three parts: First, we describe the general trends across sectors in Norway, including policies, administrative structure and organization of service delivery. This description is largely based on secondary literature. Second, we focus on the organization of services in park and road maintenance in Norway. The public administration and policy literature has largely neglected these sectors. There is a lack of documentation pertaining to the organization of local roads and parks in Norway in earlier periods. Historical insights draw on document studies and eight interviews: One of these represents the national interest organization for parks (*Bad, park og idrett*) and one the interest organization for municipal roads (*Norsk kommunalteknisk forening*); three employees in the municipality of Oslo are consulted (one is a former employee); one in Stavanger and one in the municipality of Trondheim, and one former employee in the municipality of Drammen. To add details and clarify uncertainties, we have also contacted two municipalities via phone or e-mail. Interviewees other than official representatives have responded to these requests. Furthermore, in an effort to quality-assess historical information, we have discussed our findings with one person who has a lengthy background in a tree care company established in 1996, and one expert who has been a municipal park manager in different municipalities since 1983. Insights into the current organization of park and road services are based on the INOPS survey conducted in Norway in 2015 (see Chapter 3).

Finally, we arrive at a conclusion about the adoption of marketization policies at the national and local level, focusing particularly on parks and roads. We find that while contracting-out to private entrepreneurs has a long tradition in Norway's technical service provision, marketization with its imperatives of competition and performance management goes only two decades back in time in the municipal road and park sectors. Central state authorities having the responsibility for roads have been key in initiating the development through early reforms of service delivery systems by splitting the responsibilities of purchaser and provider. The municipalities have followed suit within the roads and park sector to prepare the basis for competitive tendering. However, in contrast to the general development of marketization in Norway at the state level, many municipalities seem to grapple with the 'fundamentals' of marketization.

## Marketization Policies in Norway: 1980s–2010s

Historically, Norway has been a reluctant marketization adopter. To explain why this is so, Christensen and Lægreid (2001) highlight strong governmental emphasis on equality and a relatively good economic status due in large part to the lucrative national oil resources. They also argue that political turbulence and continuous negotiations, given minority governments from the 1980s until the red–green majority took office in 2005, weakened the conditions for implementing public management reforms. In addition, trade unions have been proactive in resisting marketization initiatives and successfully managed to find alternative strategies to improve welfare services (Vabø et al. 2013). The political and administrative system in Norway has traditionally included civil service unions as key participants in reform processes (Vabø et al. 2013; Christensen and Lægreid 2009).

However, reluctance towards marketization does not mean rejection. The key reform strategy in Norway has been to adapt public organizations to the market, thereby to some extent avoiding privatization of public services (Christensen and Lægreid 1998). Starting in the 1980s, marketization has been slowly implemented in the Norwegian public sector, but the forms it has taken have been reshaped to 'fit' the political administrative system. This means that public sector organizations have adapted performance management and devolution rather than privatization. For example, central agencies have been transformed into state-owned companies, thereby avoiding private ownership.

In the 1980s, the marketization agenda in Norway consisted primarily of management strategies and structural devolution (Røvik 1998). The introduction of the Norwegian system of performance management, 'management by objectives and result' was one key element of the 1984

Official Norwegian Report on how to increase efficiency in Norwegian state budgets. This principle was intended to increase the flexibility of managers in terms of how they may use resources to achieve set goals—under the slogan 'let managers manage'. The budget reform in 1986, when the right-wing government introduced a 'modernization programme', gave local authorities more freedom in terms of how to prioritize services and implement cost-effective solutions across sectors. The national government altered the complicated funding scheme to local governments and turned earmarked grants into block grants. The reform increased the focus on result reporting and evaluation (Christensen and Lægreid 1998). One additional consequence of this was that many municipalities had to curb expenditures due to cuts in subsidies (Vabø et al. 2013).

With regard to structural devolution in the 1980s, many organizations inside the central administrative apparatus as well as public enterprises increased managerial and organizational discretion by moving responsibilities to the lower levels of the organization, or they separated administrative functions and policies by transferring responsibilities to more or less autonomous units. One purpose was to transfer responsibility for service quality and budgets to separated or decentralized service providers. The government introduced geographical, semi-autonomous units responsible for their own results and budgets within large public enterprises that had formerly been monopolies in sectors such as telecommunications and the post office (Røvik 1998). The government also introduced more flexible administrative rules at the central government level and gave agencies at the central level more autonomy in personnel and financial matters (Christensen and Lægreid 2009). An important doctrine was to relieve the ministries of administrative and technical tasks so that they could fully act as secretariats for political leadership. This increased the number of central agencies (directorates) from 74 to 81 during the 1980s (Lægreid et al. 2013).

Massive reorganizations were carried out at the local level. In 1992, the parliament adopted a new Local Government Act, enabling the municipalities to structure their administrations to meet local needs (Fimreite and Lægreid 2005), i.e. to ensure effective services. In the mid-1990s, more than 80% of the municipalities had reorganized their political and/or administrative organization (Christensen et al. 2014: 163). Many municipalities adopted flat organizational structures and reduced middle management levels. Municipalities increasingly established more or less autonomous local service provider units that were responsible for their own cost-efficiency (Vabø et al. 2013). In the 1990s, the government added new elements such as the introduction of statutory rights for the access to welfare services (e.g. patient rights and the right to secondary education) and the establishment of independent control authorities.

Mixed policies towards marketization characterize the period from 2000 to 2010. On the one hand, the centre-conservative government, which was in power from 2001 to 2005, privatized many central public enterprises: the number of state-owned companies (i.e. corporations) almost doubled (Lægreid et al. 2013). On the other hand, the red–green majority coalition, which won the election in 2005, promoted an anti-marketization agenda (Christensen and Lægreid 2009). It should be mentioned, however, that the Labour Party in the 1990s also promoted marketization policies. Labour formed the government in 2000 and had to step down one year later. During this one year, the Labour government partly privatized the public telecommunications company and the state oil company (Christensen and Lægreid 2009).

The Centre-Conservative government, during the years 2001–2005, promoted economic liberalization, but also included reforms of a 'hybrid' nature (e.g.: the hospital reform which re-centralized hospitals to the national level, reorganized them into health enterprises and adopted the money-follows-the-patient principle; and the reform of the employment and welfare administration, which merged the central administrative sectors of employment and national insurance administration into a new agency for work and social welfare) (Christensen and Lægreid 2009). In the 2005 elections, the red–green coalition argued that marketization reforms should be stopped or modified because of the negative consequences of increasing fragmentation and decreasing political control. During the eight-year term of office, the red–green coalition slowed marketization reforms, but did not reverse them (Bezes et al. 2012).

The 2010s have been characterized by marketization and centralization. The Conservative minority government, which took office in 2013, aimed to increase efficiency in the public sector. Marketization elements were again put on the political agenda, but directed towards specific sectors like transport where the Government, among other initiatives, unbundled the Norwegian railway. In 2016, the government also established a new state-owned corporation ('New Roads') for the purpose of

**Table 8.1** Trajectories of marketization in municipal road and park sectors in Norway, 1980s–2010s

| *Decade* | *In general* | *Sector* | |
|---|---|---|---|
| | | *Local roads* | *Local parks* |
| 1980s | Decentralization strengthened municipal autonomy<br>1987: Performance management system<br>Modernization programme | Low or non-existing use of public procurement and competitive tendering<br>Private and in-house provision | Low or non-existing use of public procurement and competitive tendering<br>Private and in-house provision |
| 1990s | Increasing marketization<br>The New Local Government Act gave the municipalities opportunities to re-structure their administrations<br>Costs were important for introducing public procurement | Private and in-house provision<br>Stable share of private contractors<br>1996: Drammen (first known example) established a public maintenance operator and introduced competitive tendering | Private and in-house provision<br>Internal contracting, provider–purchaser models<br>1996: Drammen (first known example) established a public maintenance operator (Drammen drift KB) and prepared for introducing competitive tendering<br>Development of a Norwegian standard NS 3420 ZK for service specifications |
| 2000s | Full-scale contracting-out of national roads<br>2003: Reorganization of the Norwegian Public Roads Administration into a purchaser and transfer of operations and maintenance to a publicly owned limited company, *Mesta AS*. | Internal reorganizations (e.g. Oslo's public road maintenance company 2001–2012)<br>Developments in the EU and at the national level inspired the introduction of a purchaser–provider model in municipalities<br>Increasing contracting-out | Internal reorganizations<br>Contracting-out occurred at slow pace<br>2001: Drammen (a pioneer) launched its first competitive tender<br>Mid-2000s: Preparation for contracting-out with procurement bodies and independent enterprise divisions (e.g. the municipal operational enterprise for park maintenance in Oslo 2004–2009) |
| 2010s | 4/5 municipalities adopt competitive tendering | Internal reorganizations (e.g. merging of parks and roads in Oslo)<br>40% of municipalities use competitive tendering for road maintenance (Monkerud et al. 2016)<br>88% use private companies to some extent (INOPS)<br>5% use only in-house providers for maintenance (INOPS) | Internal reorganizations (e.g. Oslo contracts out all its park maintenance)<br>4% of municipalities never use contracting-out, 47% seldom, 16% sometimes and 6% often (Durucz 2014)<br>41% use private companies to some extent (INOPS)<br>38% use only in-house providers for maintenance (INOPS) |

speeding up the planning of national roads. However, the Conservative minority government since 2013 has primarily been the promoter of centralization. One example is the 2017 municipal reform, which seeks to strengthen municipal service delivery by reducing the number of municipalities from 428 to 354, counties from 19 to 11, and police districts from 27 to 12 (Government 2017). The municipal reform will be implemented in 2020.

To sum up, Norwegian marketization policies over the past decades have strengthened the autonomous role of municipalities, semi-autonomous agencies and state-owned companies. This has challenged the traditional Norwegian centralized state (Christensen and Lægreid 2009). However, new regulatory tools have been introduced, such as performance indicator systems, regulations and standards for welfare services (Pollitt and Bouckaert 2011; Vabo 2014). Since 2013, there is a tendency towards more centralization. Table 8.1 gives an overview of the general tendencies in phases, including the development in the municipal park and road sector.

## Park and Road Sector

This section provides a historical overview of how municipalities have organized local road and park services. In general, Norwegian municipalities are free to plan and organize their services in ways that accommodate local conditions. However, if they choose to contract out services, they have to make use of competitive tendering, in line with the Norwegian Public Procurement Act. In 2016, four out of five municipalities used competitive tendering when purchasing services (Monkerud et al. 2016). In road and park maintenance, almost 2/3 of the municipalities ($N = 73$) make use of competitive tendering, although they provide the services in-house (INOPS survey).

There are three common ways of organizing operational tasks in Norwegian park and road maintenance: contracting-out, in-house provision and a combination of contracting-out and in-house provision. *First*, in cases of contracting-out, the local authority arranges competitive tendering, manages contracts and controls the service provision. One example is Oslo, which contracts out its entire road and park services (Chapter 14).

*Second*, in cases of full in-house provision, the municipality has its own service unit to carry out the operational tasks. One example is Stavanger

(132,102 inhabitants), which has its own municipal service enterprise. In the INOPS survey, 32% of all the municipalities that make use of in-house provision responded that they have a formal split between provider and purchaser (see Table 8.2). In some municipalities, such a split has been a first step in the direction of introducing competitive tendering, where the municipal service unit has to compete with private actors. The municipal enterprise participates in competitive tendering procedures and has won maintenance contracts in neighbouring municipalities, with private companies and from private persons. The enterprise is organized in different units that handle municipal tasks and external contracts, as it has been challenging to maintain sufficient resources for municipal tasks when the enterprise won external contracts.

*Third*, in cases of combined contracting and in-house performance, the municipalities often buy services on the market, independently of their own service organizations (Leiren et al. 2016). This is often practised in mid-sized and small municipalities, where contracting-out is typically related to machine-intensive tasks like snow mounding, or relates to services that require special competence, for example, tree care operations. Larger municipalities also do this, for example Trondheim (184,960 inhabitants), in which an internal unit ensures the majority of its park and road operations.

**Table 8.2** The diffusion of formal marketization instruments for managing and organizing in-house providers in Norwegian municipalities in the mid-2010s

| *Formal instruments*[a] | *Frequency*[b] *(%)* |
|---|---|
| Autonomous top management | 64 |
| Autonomous budgeting/financial statement | 80 |
| Competitive tendering of services provided in-house | 61 |
| Business plans | 73 |
| Allowed to carry out tasks for other clients | 38 |
| Separate monitoring function of maintenance operations | 36 |
| Formal purchaser–provider split | 32 |
| Company ownership structure (100% owned by municipality) | 6 |

*Notes* Based on INOPS survey data. $N=73$

[a]The table shows the distribution of positive answers ('yes') for eight key management instruments on the question: 'Which of the following management instruments does the municipality uses for managing and organizing the in-house service provision of parks and roads maintenance?'

[b]The frequencies count the share in the group of Norwegian municipalities with an in-house provider that uses a particular management instrument

### *The 1980s and 1990s*

Norwegian municipalities have traditionally kept maintenance of roads and parks in-house. Seasonal tasks that demand a large workforce, machines and equipment during a limited period, such as snow removal and gritting, have normally been awarded to farmers and private entrepreneurs, e.g. 'those who have been around'. For example, farmers have cleaned roads and removed snow during winter and carried out special tasks such as tree-safety assessments and tree care operations. Contracts have been small and negotiated, i.e. private operators have not been awarded contracts via competition, but through negotiations with the public authority on price and quality of the delivery. Contracts have been awarded to those who have previously carried out the tasks. Presumably, there has also been a spark of local patriotism in the sense that having local private operators maintain municipal parks and roads is deemed a good thing. The use of various private service providers has resulted in differences in service quality depending on equipment and professionality.

In the 1990s, many municipalities reorganized their administrations, adopted flat organizational structures and service provider units according to the purchaser–provider model, primarily so as to increase efficiency. Some municipalities established their own technical service enterprises, aiming to compete for contracts in the market. The first known example is from 1996, when Drammen, a mid-sized municipality, separated its technical services into a municipal operational enterprise, *Drammen drift KB* (Drammen 1997). The enterprise was expected to carry out services for Drammen municipality but also for other public and private actors. When Drammen introduced competitive tendering, the enterprise lost contracts to other entrepreneurs, and eventually operated on a deficit budget (see Chapter 14 for a similar development in Oslo).

Some municipalities made their first small-scale attempts at competitive tendering in the late 1990s. One example is Trondheim, which introduced competitive tendering for all winter maintenance in one neighbourhood as a pilot project but decided to continue to use internal employees in combination with private entrepreneurs. One reason for this was the high costs related to preparedness, which the municipality covered in the early generation of contracts (since the 2010s, the operators typically have to cover such costs themselves, i.e. calculate the risk in the bids).

### *The 2000s*

In the 2000s, local authorities increasingly managed service provision units at arm's length and defined goals for the units to implement. This was inspired by developments at the EU level and at the national level, but there were also some 'early movers' at local level, who introduced a purchaser–provider split before the national road authorities underwent a similar development and before EU competition rules were transposed into the Norwegian Public Procurement Act.

Several mid-sized municipalities that had previously awarded contracts through negotiations to local farmers and small entrepreneurs began to award contracts through competitive tendering because of changes in the public procurement statute. With increasing demands (e.g. the move from negotiations to competitive procedures increases the administrative burden on the operators; the calls for tenders sometimes require a greater number or different types of tasks in the same 'package'), many of the small companies disappeared from the market.

Contracting-out occurred at a slower rate for parks than for roads. For roads, one informant suggests that the development towards increased contracting-out of local responsibilities was inspired by developments at the national level. In 2003, the government decided to split the Norwegian Public Roads Administration into one purchaser unit and one service provider. The latter became a limited company, *Mesta AS*, owned by the Ministry of Transport and Communications. At national and regional level, this purchaser–provider split was the first step towards introducing competitive tendering of road services. The first competitive tender at national level was carried out in 2003, with one aim, among others, being to achieve cost-efficiency. Indeed, in the initial rounds, the price dropped. A consultancy concluded that the early low prices, followed by a sharp cost increase in 2008/2009, was a consequence of an immature market, i.e. large companies set the price too low in order to win and establish themselves in a new market (Dovre Group 2010).

However, some municipalities introduced a purchaser–provider model prior to the mentioned separation at the national level. Two early movers in introducing competitive tendering of technical services were Drammen and Oslo (see Chapter 15 about Oslo). Both put park and road maintenance out to tender as part of a reorganization of such services into municipal enterprises, and eventually both dissolved these enterprises. In 2003/2004, Drammen contracted out all park and road maintenance services to private entrepreneurs. In the road sector, Drammen had dozens of small contracts, but decided to merge them into a single large one. The daily road maintenance services were put to tender in two contracts. Three entrepreneurs competed; one won both contracts. In other words, the result was a weakening of the competitive element and a situation with a limited number of suppliers. In later rounds, Drammen improved its contracts and looked to the national level for lesson-drawing.

In contrast to Drammen and Oslo, Trondheim and Stavanger continued to provide services in-house. In the 2000s, these two municipalities began to prepare for contracting-out by dividing the units into a procurement body and an independent enterprise. However, while they introduced pilots, they never introduced full-scale competitive tendering. Trondheim came close to organizing city operations in a municipal enterprise in 2003 (but up until the present time has kept almost all operations within the municipal administration). In 2002, the conservative local government in Trondheim proposed reorganizing city operations, including park and road maintenance, into a municipal enterprise, but the red–green coalition elected in 2004 abandoned this plan.

Stavanger established a municipally owned service enterprise for parks, sports and roads in 2006, but never took the leap to competitive tendering. The aim was to make a clear division between the roles of purchaser and provider and associated costs. The purchaser unit in the municipality awards contracts directly to this enterprise, which is considered as being part of the municipal organization. This arrangement receives political support because it is seen as important for maintaining local jobs and political control.

After an increase in public procurement since the early 2000s, the proportion of municipalities with tendered services for operation and maintenance of road services was stable at around 40% of the municipalities until the beginning of the 2010s (Monkerud et al. 2016). We do not have numbers for parks in the same period.

### *The 2010s*

In the 2010s, competitive tendering for operation and maintenance of road services increased from 40% of Norwegian municipalities in 2008 to 66% in 2012. This share was still 66% in 2016 (Monkerud et al. 2016). In a survey among Norwegian municipalities from 2013, 16% responded

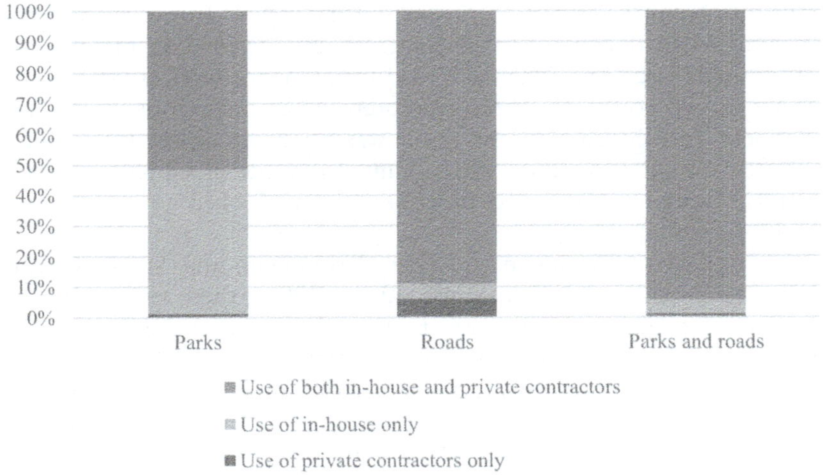


**Fig. 8.1** The use of private contractors and/or in-house providers for park and road maintenance ($N = 95$) (*Notes* Based on INOPS survey data)

that they sometimes contract out park maintenance and 6% that they often do (Durucz 2014).

Many municipalities, which in the 2000s provided road and park maintenance services primarily in-house or in a combination of in-house and contracting-out, initiated competitive tendering pilots in the 2010s. For example, in 2013 Trondheim decided to test competitive tendering of all winter maintenance in one large neighbourhood (this will be evaluated in 2018). In 2014, Stavanger initiated a competitive tendering pilot for park maintenance in one neighbourhood (the results will be benchmarked and compared with the results in other neighbourhoods).

Our INOPS survey from 2015 provides data of Norwegian municipalities' use of different provider types for provision of park and road maintenance services (see Fig. 8.1). The percentage of municipalities that only partially use private contractors is higher for road (88%) than park maintenance services (41%). The percentage of municipalities that only use in-house providers is higher for park (38%) than road maintenance services (5%). Use of other types of provision for park and/or road maintenance is less widespread. Although inter-municipal companies are common in remotely located municipalities with small populations (Bjørnsen et al. 2015), our INOPS survey data shows that this organizational form

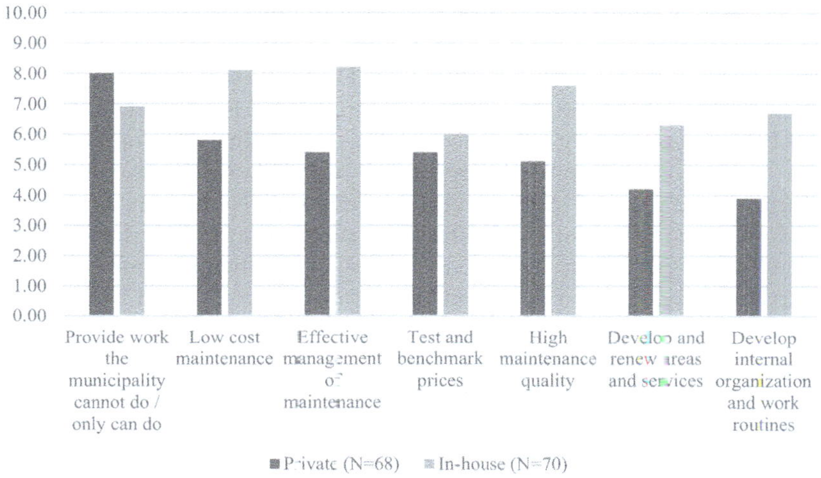


**Fig. 8.2** Importance of seven purposes for using private contractors and in-house providers (parks and roads) (*Notes* Based on INOPS survey data. The figure shows the mean for responses to the question: 'Specify on a scale of 0 [not at all] to 10 [to a very high degree] the degree to which you think that the following purposes are a central part of your municipality's considerations for using in-house provision/private contractors for maintenance…')

has not been common for local park and road maintenance services. Only 13% of the respondents answered that they had established other types of provision than in-house or contracting-out (i.e. 'public–private company', 'other municipal provider', 'inter-municipal company' and 'other arrangements'). The evidence suggests that a mix of different providers is common for the provision of both park and road maintenance. However, mixed provision is more dominant for road than for park maintenance.

Figure 8.2 provides an overview of how the respondents evaluate the importance of different purposes for using private contractors as well as for using in-house provision. The most important purpose for *using private contractors* is to 'provide work the municipality cannot do' (mean score = 8.0). 'Low-cost maintenance' (mean score = 5.8) is the second most important purpose for using private contractors. The score difference between the two purposes is statistically significant.

The two most important purposes for *using in-house provision contractors* are 'effective management of maintenance' (mean score = 8.2) and 'low-cost maintenance' (mean score = 8.1). The results indicate that the choice of private contractors or in-house provision is relatively independent of the development of services and organizational development. The low ranking of development purposes for using private contractors (mean scores of 6.3 and 4.2 respectively) suggests that Norwegian municipalities focus on low costs and effective maintenance rather than gaining inputs from the private market. Furthermore, contracting-out is used to a greater extent than in-house provision for services that can be provided only through one type of arrangement, referring to the response to 'provide work that the municipality cannot do or only can do' (score difference = 1.1). The difference is statistically significant ($p < .01$). In-house provision is used to a greater extent for the purpose of 'low-cost maintenance' compared to contracting-out (score difference = 2.3). The difference is statistically significant ($p < .01$).

When it comes to *formal management of in-house providers*, Table 8.2 shows that the two most widespread instruments that Norwegian municipalities use are 'separate budgeting/financial statements' (80% of all municipalities) and 'business plans' (64% of all municipalities). The least frequently used instruments are 'separate monitoring function of maintenance operations' (36% of all municipalities), 'formal provider–purchaser split' (32% of all municipalities) and 'company ownership structure' (6% of all municipalities). While the use of separate budgeting and business plans are in line with the general development of marketization, the fact that only one-third of the municipalities make use of separate monitoring functions and less than one-quarter have a formal purchaser–provider split contradicts the general development. These low shares suggest that many Norwegian municipalities have not made use of many of the typical marketization measures in the local roads and parks sectors.

## Conclusions

Since the end of the 1980s, there has been an increased focus on marketization reforms in Norway, starting with management strategies and devolution. Both left-wing and right-wing-oriented governments supported the introduction of marketization elements. Initially such changes did not embody a large degree of privatization as such but were rather geared towards making public companies more efficient. In more recent decades, there is a tendency to counteract fragmentation issues by centralizing responsibilities that had been split up under the banner of marketization.

In the local roads and park sector, the marketization development has been much slower than at the national level. The evidence shows that the extent and the manner in which local road and park authorities cooperate with private service providers vary. Historically, there has always been a segment of private operators involved in carrying out local road services, including for example farmers who have removed snow from the streets. In larger municipalities, this has also been the case for parks. Yet, marketization with its imperatives of competition and performance management is only two decades old in these two sectors.

At local level there have been some early movers among mid-sized (e.g. Drammen) and large cities (e.g. Oslo). In addition, the national level having responsibility for roads has been key in inspiring marketization in the municipal park and roads sector. This has been particularly clear since the unbundling of the national road administration into a purchaser and provider in 2003 and later by imposing competition rules via procurement regulations. Given pressures on performance and cost-efficiency, local public authorities have followed suit to prepare the grounds for competitive tendering. The development has resulted in a professionalization of the procurement role.

However, in the park and road sectors, many Norwegian municipalities continue to grapple with the 'fundamentals' of marketization, e.g. fostering competition and using competition to benchmark or motivate performance. This might be related to the fact that municipalities in Norway are small road and park owners—the vast majority of roads are a regional responsibility. Norway is also unique in the sense that the country—with its 428 municipalities (354 as of the year 2020)—has more municipalities than any other Scandinavian country, and many of these are sparsely populated.

Under such conditions, it is more difficult to ensure a well-functioning market, which is one key principle on which marketization is based (see also Chapters 2 and 4). Small municipalities do not have many parks, and this makes it less interesting for entrepreneurs to participate in procurements. Similarly, large municipalities have more kilometres of roads to maintain and therefore may be more interesting to entrepreneurs. Norwegian municipalities also perceive contracting-out of road and park services as not necessarily beneficial in terms of costs or performance, but rather as something they have to do due to a need for complementary capabilities: Cost-efficiency, as a reason for contracting-out, is mentioned less prominently among the respondents than is the lack of a possibility to provide services in-house.

Such market and capability conditions contribute to explain why Norway is a reluctant adopter of marketization of municipal park and road services. The evidence shows that, in 2015, a combination of in-house provision and use of private operators is the most common organizational form in the municipal parks and roads services in Norway and that the use of private contractors takes place to a larger extent in the road sector than the park sector.

## References


Bezes, P., Fimreite, A. L., Lidec, P., & Lægreid, P. (2012). Understanding Organizational Reforms in the Modern State: Specialization and Integration in Norway and France. *Governance, 26*(1), 147–175.

Bjørnsen, H. M., Klausen, J. E., & Winsvold, M. (2015). *Kommunale selskap og folkevalgt styring gjennom kommunalt eierskap* (NIBR-rapport 2015:1). Oslo: NIBR (In Norwegian).

Christensen, T., Egeberg, M., Lægreid, P., & Aars, J. (2014). Forvaltning og politikk. Universitetsforlaget.

Christensen, T., Fimreite, A. L., & Lægreid, P. (2007). Reform of the Employment and Welfare Administrations—The Challenges of Co-Coordinating Diverse Public Administrations. *International Review of Administrative Sciences, 73*(3), 389–408.

Christensen, T., & Lægreid, P. (1998). Administrative Reform Policy: The Case of Norway. *International Review of Administrative Science, 64*(3), 457–475.

Christensen, T., & Lægreid, P. (2001). New Public Management: The Effects of Contractualism and Devolution on Political Control. *Public Management Review, 3*(1), 73–94.

Christensen, T., & Lægreid, P. (2009). Public Management Reform in Norway: Reluctance and Tensions. In S. F. Goldfinch & J. L. Wallis (Eds.), *International Handbook of Public Management Reform* (pp. 300–316). Cheltenham: Edward Elgar Publishing.

Dovre Group. (2010). *Evaluering av konkurranseutsetting av drift- og vedlikehold i Statens vegvesen*. Oslo: Dovre Group AS. (In Norwegian).

Drammen. (1997). Drammen municipality, The alderman 1997. (In Norwegian).

Durucz, M. (2014). *Grøntanleggsforvaltning i norske kommuner: Status og utvikling (1989–2014)* (Master thesis). Norwegian University of Life Sciences, Ås. (In Norwegian).

Fimreite, A. L., & Lægreid, P. (2005). *Specialization and Coordination: Implications for Integration and Autonomy in a Multi-Level System* (Working Paper No. 7). Bergen: Rokkansenteret.

Finger, M., Allouche, J., & Luis-Manso, P. (2007). *Water and Liberalisation: European Water Scenarios*. London: IWA.

Government. (2017). *Kommunereform*. Available at: https://www.regjeringen.no/no/tema/kommuner-og-regioner/kommunereform/kommunereform/id2548377/. (In Norwegian).

Lægreid, P., Roness, R. G., & Rolland, V. (2013). Agencification and Corporatization in Norway 1947–2011. *International Journal of Public Administration, 36*(9), 659–672.

Leiren, M. D., Lindholst, A. C., Solfjeld, I., & Randrup, T. (2016). Capability Versus Efficiency: Contracting Out Park and Road Services in Norway. *International Journal of Public Sector Management, 29*(5), 474–487.

Lieberherr, E., & Fuenfschilling, L. (2016). Neoliberalism and Sustainable Urban Water Sectors: A Critical Reflection of Sector Characteristics and Empirical Evidence. *Environment and Planning C: Government and Policy, 34*(8), 1540–1555.

Lieberherr, E., & Leiren, M. D. (2017). Privatization, Outsourcing and Public Service Objectives: An Explorative Analysis of Two Network Industries. *Case Studies on Transport Policy, 5*(4), 681–689.

Longva, F., & Osland, O. (2010). «Anbud på norsk». Effekter av konkurranse i lokal kollektivtransport. *Tidsskrift for samfunnsforskning, 51*(3), 387–415. (In Norwegian).

Monkerud, L. C., Indset, M., Stokstad, S., & Klausen, J. E. (2016). *Kommunal organisering 2016* (NIBR-rapport 2016:20). Oslo: NIBR. (In Norwegian).

NOU 1984:23. (1984). *Produktivitetsfremmende reformer i statens budsjettsystem*. Available at: http://www.nb.no/statsmaktene/nb/761f37b928d9266e5b536dce73dd79b5?index=1#5. (In Norwegian).

Pollitt, C., & Bouckaert, G. (2011). *Public Management Reform: A Comparative Analysis – New Public Management, Governance, and the Neo-Weberian State* (3rd ed.). Oxford: Oxford University Press.

Randrup, T. B., & Persson, B. (2009). Public Green Spaces in the Nordic Countries: Development of New Strategic Management Regime. *Urban Forestry & Urban Greening, 8*(1), 31–40.

Røvik, K. A. (1998). *Moderne organisasjoner. Trender i organisasjonstenkningen ved tusenårsskiftet*. Bergen: Fagbokforlaget. (In Norwegian).

Vabø, M., Christensen, K., Jacobsen, F. F., & Trætteberg, H. D. (2013). Marketisation in Norwegian Eldercare: Preconditions, Trends and Resistance. In G. Meagher & M. Szebehely (Eds.), *Marketisation in Nordic Eldercare: A Research Report on Legislation, Oversight, Extent and Consequences*. Stockholm: Stockholm University.

Vabo, S. I. (2014). Flernivåorganisering – lokal skreddersøm og nasjonale standarder. In M. Vabø & S. I. Vabo (Eds.), *Velferdens organisering*. Oslo: Universitetsforlaget. (In Norwegian).

Van de Velde, D. (2014). Market Initiative Regimes in Public Transport in Europe: Recent Developments. *Research in Transportation Economics, 48*, 33–40.

CHAPTER 9

# Economic Effects of Contracting Out in Scandinavia, and the Importance of Country Context

*Andrej Christian Lindholst, Ole Helby Petersen and Kurt Houlberg*

## Introduction

The organization of public service delivery in the Scandinavian countries has undergone major changes since the 1980s, as a result of the continuous flow of reforms that have emphasized different forms of privatization and marketization. A major trend in this development has been the expanded use of competitive tendering and contracting out across

A. C. Lindholst (✉)
Department of Politics and Society, Aalborg University, Aalborg, Denmark
e-mail: acl@dps.aau.dk

O. H. Petersen
Department of Social Science and Business,
Roskilde University, Roskilde, Denmark

K. Houlberg
VIVE—The Danish Center for Social Science Research,
Copenhagen, Denmark



A. C. Lindholst and M. B. Hansen (eds.),
*Marketization in Local Government*,
https://doi.org/10.1007/978-3-030-32478-0_9

many areas of public service delivery and in technical services, particularly municipal park and road services (see also Chapter 2). As in many other western countries, the driving forces behind these reforms have been a combination of political, administrative and economic objectives. Politically, approval of the private provision of publicly funded services has gradually increased, and the contracting out of technical services such as park and road maintenance is nowadays widespread across Scandinavian municipalities. From an administrative perspective, there is a perception that using competition and private management principles has the potential to improve organizational performance and management in the public sector. Finally, from an economic perspective, contracting out has been promoted as a tool for reducing costs and improving efficiency in public service delivery (Lindholst et al. 2018).

Contracting out in the context of the welfare state in Scandinavia differs in many ways from the situation in other countries. The important role of the public sector in the economy, combined with a historical tradition of tax-funded public service delivery, strong public service unions and a general reform orientation towards a Neo-Weberian State (NWS) model, has in many ways made the public sector resilient to the pressure for more radical shifts towards a greater reliance on market-based solutions. From this perspective, one can expect limited effects of contracting out, because the Scandinavian model shields the public sector and its employees from the competitive forces of the market. However, from another perspective, the fact that the public sector has been more protected from the market than in most other countries may result in significant effects when public services are eventually exposed to competition from the private market. Reviews of the scholarly literature indicate that marketization is, on average, associated with lower costs for technical services but not for welfare services (Petersen et al. 2018). In the context of park and road services, cost reductions from contracting out are relatively well-documented in Denmark (Blom-Hansen 2003; Lindholst et al. 2018) and to some extent in Sweden (Bretzer et al. 2016), whereas empirical evidence from Norway indicates higher costs as a result of contracting out (Leiren et al. 2016). While studies have indicated significant country differences, however, there has been very limited systematic comparison of contracting outcomes and the factors explaining those outcomes across national institutional contexts.

This chapter aims to contribute to the contracting literature by conducting a comparative statistical analysis of the economic outcomes of contracting for municipal park and road services in Denmark, Sweden and Norway. Our analysis draws on a uniform cross-national dataset based on the INOPS survey (see also Chapter 3) and is, to the best of the authors' knowledge, the first statistical comparison of the economic outcomes of contracting across the Scandinavian countries. More specifically, the purpose of this chapter is to shed light on differences and similarities between countries in the economic outcomes of contracting out, and the factors that influence these outcomes. With this purpose in mind, we first discuss a set of theoretical arguments about the effects of contracting out across and within the Scandinavian countries, and test the theoretical propositions in a comparative statistical analysis.

The chapter addresses the following two research questions:

- Does contracting out in municipal park and road services lead to different cost changes across national contexts?
- Do the factors explaining cost changes from contracting out differ across national contexts?

The chapter addresses discussions in the contracting literature about the importance of the institutional, regulatory and market context for the outcomes of contracting out. Although the Scandinavian countries are often regarded as a relatively homogeneous group of countries characterized by large tax-financed public sectors and high levels of autonomy delegated to the municipalities (e.g. Sellers and Lidström 2007), there are important national differences as well (see Chapters 4 and 6–8). Since the 1980s, Danish municipalities have expanded the use of competitive tendering and contracting for the delivery of park and road services. The Swedish municipalities embarked on contracting somewhat later, and to a slightly lesser degree, but the focus and content of the marketization reforms have been largely similar in the two countries. In contrast, Norway embarked on marketization reforms relatively late and to a more modest degree. Another difference is that municipalities in Sweden and Norway are geographically dispersed and of highly differing size, whereas Danish municipalities are relatively homogeneous in terms of both size and geography. The Scandinavian countries thus provide an empirical setting for examining the outcomes of contracting out with several key differences of interest for a comparative perspective.

In the remainder of the chapter, we first discuss the importance of country differences for contracting outcomes. Second, we describe the variables and methods used in our statistical analysis. Third, we present the results of the comparative statistical analysis. Finally, we discuss the implications of our findings.

## The Importance of Country Differences

A theory of contracting out as a cost-focused strategy can be extracted from the public management literature. In the literature, contracting out as a cost-focused strategy is usually characterized by the establishment of ex ante price competition by putting services out for tender in an auction-like process in which competing providers are invited to submit bids for contracts with public clients (e.g. Domberger and Jensen 1997). Various scholars have studied the conditions under which contracting out should (or should not) work relatively well. According to Dehoog (1990), contracting with the private market is likely to yield positive outcomes when: (a) competition can be fostered, (b) organizational resources are adequate and (c) certainty about future needs and circumstances is high. Similarly, Donahue (1989) highlights the prospects for the success of contracting out when competition is available, services can be unambiguously specified in a contract and the contracting processes can be managed. Domberger and Jensen (1997) add to the insights by framing the importance of competitive markets, the significance of the quality characteristics of a service that it is impossible to cover in the contract, and the magnitude and specificity of the physical assets required to provide a service. Later works by Brown and Potoski (2005) and Hefetz and Warner (2011) have further reaffirmed and elaborated on the conditions under which contracting out can be expected to work well. Hefetz and Warner (2011), for example, add the level of citizen interest as an important factor complicating the use of contracting out. Findings in the studies by Brown and Potoski (2005) and Hefetz and Warner (2011) also indicate that park and road services are relatively well-suited for contracting because of their characteristics with regard to transaction costs and service measurability. Further features have been added to the list of factors that influence contracting outcomes, such as local place characteristics like organizational size, degree of urbanization and market maturity (Bel and Fageda 2009).

In the account above, the theory of contracting out is elaborated as a universal model that is expected to work well when particular conditions are fulfilled. However, the model can be further developed and refined, in comparisons across different country contexts, by incorporating insights from new institutional economics (NIE) on the importance of the broader institutional environment (Williamson 2000). Overall, with a point of departure in insights from NIE, the stage of general development consisting of contracting out as an institutionalized arrangement within a particular context can be expected to play a role in overall performance. In NIE, economic exchanges are seen as taking place within a broader and multilayered environment of institutions of higher and lower orders. The efficiency of a particular mode of organizing economic exchanges, such as contracting out, is argued to be contingent upon the characteristics and supportiveness of the overall institutional environment. Differences in national regulation and trajectories of marketization, for example, may thus provide explanations for differences between countries in the economic performance of contracting. More specifically, Williamson (2000) proposes four institutional layers: (1) a layer of embeddedness in informal institutions, norms, customs and traditions; (2) a layer of formal 'rules of the game', such as constitutional rights, contract law and legal regulations; (3) the available modes of organizing economic exchange (governance structures), and their possible alignment with the transactional characteristics of the exchange; and (4) the instruments for the ongoing adaptation of exchange within a particular mode of economic exchange.

The consequence for our analysis is that differences in country context are likely to matter for contracting outcomes. The outcomes of contracting out are contingent not only on local structural conditions and contracting strategies, but also on national regulations, institutional arrangements and the marketization history of the country in question. As part of this, the impact of some lower order institutions, like formal contracts, depends on the characteristics of higher-order institutions. The relative efficiency of particular modes of organizing economic exchange is thus likely to differ according to differences in the broader institutional environment. In a longitudinal or historical perspective the argument in NIE also applies to shifts or developments in institutional environments (parametric shifts), as these affect the impact of specific arrangements for organizing economic exchanges (e.g. market-based exchanges). Taking the insights of new institutional economics as our point of departure, we hypothesize that contracting out will produce different outcomes across national contexts that have different institutional and regulatory environments.

One would initially expect that contracting out is most likely to produce cost savings in contexts with well-developed institutional environments and longstanding contracting experience. In such contexts, the different institutional layers supporting the use of contracting out are well developed, stable and familiar to all parties, and they may therefore provide a more efficient way of organizing economic exchange. However, a 'muddy' picture may also arise. In highly developed institutional contexts, the recurrent use of contracting may produce no further marginal improvements, as potential economic gains may already have been harvested at an earlier stage (Bel and Costas 2006).

### *Importance of Country Differences in Scandinavia*

In international comparisons, the three Scandinavian countries are often characterized as universal welfare states whose welfare state systems and politico-administrative structures are organized in a rather similar way (Sellers and Lidström 2007). Legislation and market regulations in the three countries are also heavily influenced by European Union (EU) regulations.[1] Common EU public procurement directives are implemented through national legislation in all three countries. The Scandinavian countries, as well as those in the wider Nordic context, are also renowned for embedding an orientation towards a Neo-Weberian State (NWS) in their reform trajectories (Greve et al. 2016). However, the three countries also demonstrate different national policies and trajectories in the involvement of private providers in public service delivery. In line with the NIE arguments above, these differences can be expected to be mirrored in different contracting outcomes as well as in the factors influencing these outcomes.

Moreover, the structural characteristics of the municipalities also differ between national contexts. Such differences in municipal characteristics produce different contracting levels, provider markets and contracting outcomes (Foged 2016; Lindholst et al. 2018). Large municipalities and more densely populated municipalities may, for example, be able to

[1] Denmark and Sweden are both members of the EU, whereas Norway is not an EU member but is closely affiliated with the EU through its membership of the European Economic Area (EEA).

manage markets more efficiently and obtain larger cost savings (Brown and Potoski 2005). In addition, systematic differences in the level of competition, use of contracts, skill of the municipality in managing the contracting processes and emphasis on contracting out as a cost-focused strategy will also affect the outcomes of contracting out. Below, the most important differences between the three Scandinavian countries are discussed (further details are found in Chapters 6–8 and 10).

In comparison with Denmark and Sweden, the Norwegian context stands out as being characterized by a briefer history of marketization and organizational restructuring in the municipal sector. Thus, the Norwegian municipalities have, in comparison with their Scandinavian siblings, had less time to become familiarized with contracting or to adopt tools such as contract and service standards. The use of contracting out in Norway in the mid-2010s to some degree resembled earlier uses of contracting out in Denmark in the 1980s and 1990s, with contracting out mainly being used for purchasing services that could not be produced in-house, rather than the markets being used to compare costs and/or drive down the cost of service provision (see also Leiren et al. 2016). Furthermore, the administrative structure in Norway is characterized by the existence of many municipalities with a small number of inhabitants spread out over a vast geographical area.

In contrast, Denmark and Sweden have substantially longer histories of marketization in the municipal sector in general, and in the park and road sectors in particular. Consequently, marketization has gradually become more institutionalized, and competitive markets have matured over a longer time span. One argument could be that the shorter history of marketization in Norway would be reflected in relatively higher cost savings from contracting out than in Denmark and Sweden. On the other hand, the shorter history of marketization in Norway may also imply that the institutional framework and municipal contracting expertise is less developed, thus posing a barrier to cost savings. Lastly, Sweden represents a 'middle' position between Denmark and Norway. Many municipalities in Sweden are relatively small and remotely located in comparison with the municipalities in the three densely populated regional centres (Malmo, Gothenburg and Stockholm). Within the context of these Scandinavian countries that are relatively homogeneous from a welfare perspective, they thus display a number of differences in their marketization history, contracting experience and municipal structure that could lead to divergent outcomes of the contracting out of municipal park and road services.

## Methods and Data

### *Data Sources and Dataset*

Our comparative analysis of contracting outcomes builds on INOPS survey data combined with register-based data for the three Scandinavian countries. The dependent variable is the cost change from the last tender in either road or park services, as reported by municipal managers in the INOPS survey. Deviating from the country context of this book, England is omitted from the analysis because of its adoption of a different response scale (categorical) for the dependent variable in the INOPS survey. In total, 152 Scandinavian municipalities provided information for our dependent variable in park and/or road services. As some municipalities provided information for both park and road services, the initial number of cases with valid data for the dependent variable (cost change) was 213. However, the initial number of cases was reduced because of missing data for one or more independent variables or because of diagnostics for influential outliers. The final dataset thus contains 179 cases, consisting of 38 cases from 35 Norwegian municipalities, 65 cases from 46 Swedish municipalities and 76 cases from 44 Danish municipalities. In addition to the INOPS survey data, we obtained register data on municipal population and geographical area from the national statistical bureaus in Denmark, Sweden and Norway.

### *Variables*

The dependent variable *cost change from the last tender* measures the change in maintenance costs from the last time the municipality put park or road services out to tender. In the INOPS survey the respondents were asked the following question separately for park and road services: *To what degree do you estimate that the tendered services have become cheaper or more costly since the last time they were tendered? (Consider changes in the total estimated operational costs before and after the tender).* Respondents were asked to choose the percentage by which the services had become (a) cheaper or (b) more costly, or to state that they had become (c) neither cheaper nor more costly (i.e. no cost change).

Six independent variables are included in the analysis (see Lindholst et al. [2018] for further theoretical discussion). *Cost-focused contracting* is a single survey-based item measuring the municipality's emphasis on 'low maintenance costs' as the objective of contracting out. *Competition level* is a single survey-based item measuring the manager's assessment of whether the municipality usually receives a sufficient number of qualified bids in tenders for road and/or park services. *Transactional and collaborative contract features* are two additive indices measuring the municipality's emphasis on transactional and collaborative dimensions in contracts with private providers. Questions linked with transactional contract features measure the importance of legal clauses, formal specifications and sanctions. Questions linked with collaborative contract features include items related to the importance of formal collaboration, requirements for user involvement, economic incentives and competence requirements. *Tender history* is a single survey-based item measuring the number of municipal tenders in road or park services over the last ten years, ranging from 'once' to 'four times or more'. For the multivariate analysis, this ordinal-scaled item is transformed to a set of dummy variables. Finally, a dummy variable for *Sector* (parks = 0; roads = 1) controls for possible differences in outcomes across park and road services.

Furthermore, two controls, *municipal population* and *municipal area*, are included to control for structural differences in municipal characteristics between the three Scandinavian countries. To account for skewness, both of these variables are transformed to natural logarithmic scales (LN). Finally, in the pooled analysis of all three countries, we include country dummies to test for country differences not measured by our independent and control variables.

A number of validity issues should be noted (see also the discussion in Chapter 4). First, the dependent variable is based on the self-reported and retrospective assessment of cost changes by the respondent. While the exact size of cost savings may not always be remembered, contracting is used on a regular basis, and, as cost savings from tenders are normally reported to administrative and political leaders in the municipalities, we expect respondents to have a sufficiently precise knowledge of the cost changes from the previous tender. Second, our reliance on data from a single survey for both the dependent and the independent variables may raise issues related to common source bias. However, common source bias should be of less concern in our analysis as the included variables are based on different types of response scales, mostly focusing on factual

**Table 9.1** Descriptive statistics and difference tests

| | | *Country* | | | |
|---|---|---|---|---|---|
| *Variable* | *Scale* | *Norway* | *Denmark* | *Sweden* | *Scandinavia*[a] |
| Cost change from last tender | Pct. change | 8.9 | −4.6 | −2.2 | −.9*** |
| CI95% (upper/lower) | | 3.3/14.3 | −6.7/−2.5 | −4.8/0.5 | −2.7/1.0 |
| Min/Max values | | −33.0/50.0 | −30.0/16.0 | −30.0/30.0 | −33.0/50.0 |
| Test of pairwise differences[a] | | Sweden*** | Norway*** | Denmark | – |
| Cost-focused contracting | 0–10[b] | 7.1 | 7.5 | 7.5 | 7.4 |
| Competition | 0–10[b] | 5.8 | 7.4 | 6.8 | 6.8** |
| Transactional contract features | 0–10[b] | 7.2 | 7.7 | 6.9 | 7.3 |
| Collaborative contract features | 0–10[b] | 4.5 | 5.2 | 4.6 | 4.8 |
| Tender history | 1–4 | 3.2 | 3.0 | 3.1 | 3.1 |
| Sector | 0 = parks, 1 = roads | .8 | .6 | .6 | .6** |
| Municipal population | LN | 9.4 | 10.8 | 10.3 | 10.3*** |
| Municipal area | LN | 5.8 | 5.7 | 6.8 | 6.2*** |
| *N* | | 38 | 76 | 65 | 179 |

*Notes* Significance levels: $^{*}p<.1$, $^{**}p<.05$, $^{***}p<.01$. The variables for contracting purpose, transactional and collaborative features, municipal population and area are common for the road and park sectors, while the variables for cost change, and tender history are measured for each service

[a]Includes tests of country differences based on Welch's t-test and the Games–Howell post hoc test

[b]11-point scale (0 = not at all, 10 = to a very high degree)

information, and are not assessing the respondents' personal performance or the performance of their organization. Thirdly, the lower *N* for Norway (*N*= 38) should be noted. This implies that the results for Norway have low statistical power and are more sensitive to responses from single municipalities (i.e. there is a small-*N* bias).

Table 9.1 provides descriptive statistics for all the variables and reports the results of our test of country differences. Significant country differences are seen for five variables, including our dependent variable. The statistics for contextual characteristics reflect the general differences in municipal population and area across Scandinavia (see also Chapter 4). The smallest populations are found among the Norwegian municipalities, while the largest are found among the Danish municipalities. The largest areas are found in the Swedish municipalities, while the Danish and Norwegian municipalities are, on average, of similar geographical size.

## Results

In this section, we first report the results regarding differences in cost changes across countries, and then report the results regarding differences in the factors explaining the cost changes.

Figure 9.1 shows boxplots of the variation in cost changes from the last tender in each of the three Scandinavian countries. The boxplots illustrate the same pattern in country differences as the statistics reported in Table 9.1. In Norway, there is substantially higher variation in the cost changes compared to Sweden and, in particular, compared to Denmark. Additionally, in about two-thirds of the Norwegian cases the last tender resulted in a cost increase. A test of country differences in cost changes shows that the average cost changes are significantly lower than zero (indicating an average cost reduction) in Denmark, while we cannot say whether the average cost change is different from zero in Sweden. In Norway, the average cost change is significantly higher than zero, indicating that the average outcome of contracting out in park and road services is a cost *increase*. The most important finding relating to our first research question, however, is that the cost changes from contracting out vary substantially across national contexts. The average cost savings in Denmark and Sweden are significantly different from the average cost increases in Norway, as reported in Table 9.1.

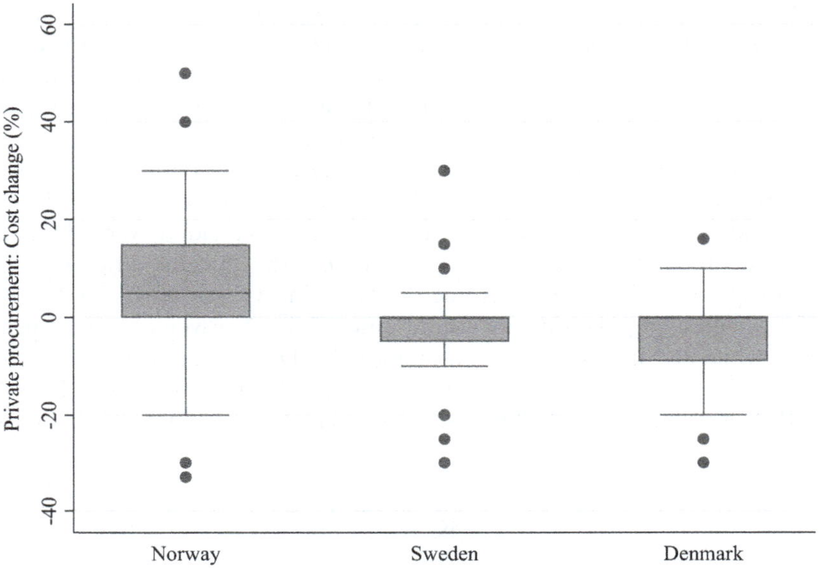


**Fig. 9.1** Boxplot for cost changes from last tender in three Scandinavian countries (*Note* $N = 179$ [Norway = 38, Denmark = 76, Sweden = 65])

Descriptive statistics and our test of differences for the independent variables (Table 9.1) show significant differences that may account for some of these country differences in contracting outcomes. Most notably, Norway represents a context with a relatively low level of competition. In addition, as noted in the methods section, Norwegian municipalities on average have the smallest populations, while the largest average area is found in the Swedish municipalities. The differences in contract features, cost-focused contracting and tender history are statistically insignificant ($p > .1$) across the three countries.

We now turn to the results regarding factors that explain differences in the outcome of contracting out across national contexts. Table 9.2 shows the results of our analysis based on four OLS-regressions: three regressions for Norway, Denmark and Sweden, respectively, and one pooled analysis for the three countries. As our prime interest concerns the variations in the impact of explanatory factors across national contexts, we focus on the regressions for the individual countries. However, at the end of the results section, we comment briefly on the pooled

**Table 9.2** OLS-regressions: Cost change from last tender (percentage change in maintenance costs)

| Explanatory variables | *Unstandardized beta-coefficients* | | | |
|---|---|---|---|---|
| | *Norway* | *Denmark* | *Sweden* | *Scandinavia* |
| Cost-focused contracting | −1.84 | −1.37*** | −.76 | −.1.01** |
| Competition level | .89 | −.14 | −1.26** | −.79** |
| Transactional contract features | −2.87* | −.64 | −1.24* | −1.41*** |
| Collaborative contract features | −1.71 | .28 | .86 | .21 |
| Tender history ('four tenders or more' as reference) | | | | |
| One | 26.79 | −7.80*** | −3.54 | −4.18 |
| Two | −10.09 | 5.91** | 3.83 | −2.27 |
| Three | −.61 | −.01 | 1.84 | 1.66 |
| Sector (road=0, park=1) | −1.42 | −.46 | −1.42 | −1.37 |
| Municipal population | −1.54 | −5.78*** | 1.61 | −.22 |
| Municipal area | 2.87 | 1.44** | 1.27 | 1.23* |
| Country (Norway as reference) | | | | |
| Sweden | | | | −11.47*** |
| Denmark | | | | −10.33*** |
| *Model summaries* | | | | |
| Constant | 45.41 | 67.07*** | −8.81 | 25.70** |
| *N* | 38 | 76 | 65 | 179 |
| Max VIF | 2.113 | 1.883 | 2.047 | 2.471[a] |
| Adj. $R^2$/F-test | .24/2.18* | .34/4.89*** | .12/1.88* | .30/7.41*** |

*Notes* A negative sign indicates a higher level of cost reductions (or lower level of cost increases)
Significance levels: $*p<.1$, $**p<.05$, $***p<.01$
Influential outlier diagnostics carried out for each model resulting in removal of two cases for Denmark, two for Sweden, and five for Norway
[a]Max VIF value is related to country dummies

analysis for Scandinavia. Overall, Table 9.2 shows that the explanatory factors vary markedly across the three countries.

Starting with *cost-focused contracting*, the signs of the coefficients are negative (indicating a cost reduction), and are thus aligned with our theoretical expectations. However, the parameter estimate is only statistically significant in Denmark, meaning that we cannot conclude that cost-focused contracting is associated with cost reductions in Sweden and Norway.

For *competition level*, the parameter estimates are negative and aligned with theoretical expectations for Denmark and Sweden. The estimate is only significant, however, for Sweden. For Norway, the sign is opposite to our theoretical expectations and the estimate is statistically insignificant.

For *transactional contract features*, the parameter estimates are negative and consistent with the theory, but are only statistically significant in the models for Norway and Sweden. For *collaborative contract features*, the sign of the parameter estimates differs across the countries and is not statistically significant in any of the models.

For *tender history*, the parameter estimates for Denmark are aligned with our theoretical expectations and are statistically significant for the categories with one and two tenders compared to the reference category with four or more tenders in the past ten years. In Denmark, higher cost savings are achieved the first and second time road or park services are put out for tender. In Sweden and Norway, the parameter estimates are insignificant. The positive but insignificant coefficient for one tender in the past ten years in Norwegian municipalities deviates from our theoretical expectations but is highly sensitive to the low number of observations (only two municipalities in this category).

The parameter estimates for *municipal area* indicate that geographical dispersion is associated with higher costs across the models. However, the estimates are only statistically significant for Denmark. For *municipal population*, the parameter estimates indicate a negative association between population size and costs in Denmark and Norway, whereas in Sweden the estimate indicates the opposite association. However, the estimate for municipal population is only statistically significant in the model for Denmark.

The parameter estimates for *sector* indicate larger cost savings in the road sector compared with the park sector, but the estimate is insignificant in all three countries.

Overall, we find that the importance of the explanatory factors varies strongly across the three Scandinavian countries. In Norway—where the latest park and road tenders on average resulted in cost increases—only one factor contributes significantly to explaining differences in cost changes: the emphasis on transactional contract features. The same association is found for Swedish municipalities, but, in addition, intermunicipal differences in competition level contribute to explaining the variations in cost changes. In Denmark, other factors apply, namely cost-focused contracting, tender history, municipal population and geographical size. In Denmark, cost savings are reported to be higher in municipalities with a stronger focus on cost containment, in municipalities that have tendered the service once or twice during the past ten years, and in municipalities with larger populations and smaller geographical size.

Turning finally to the pooled model for Scandinavia in Table 9.2, the key result contributing to our two research questions is that cost savings are higher in Denmark and Sweden than in Norway *after* controlling for country differences in local place characteristics, contract features, competition level and emphasis on low cost as the purpose of contracting. The findings indicate that other potential explanatory factors for the inter-Scandinavian differences in cost changes need further scrutiny. We briefly turn to this discussion in the concluding section below.

## Concluding Remarks

In this chapter, we asked whether contracting out in municipal park and road services leads to different cost changes across national contexts. Second, we asked whether the factors explaining cost changes from contracting out differ across national contexts. The INOPS survey data collected from municipal park and road managers in Norway, Denmark and Sweden indicate that the average change in operational costs since the last tender for municipal park and road services differs substantially across the three countries. The average change in operational costs in our sample of Norwegian municipalities is a cost increase, there is no cost change among the Swedish municipalities, and there are reduced costs among Danish municipalities. Even after controlling for key factors such as competition level, contracting purpose and municipal characteristics, we find statistically (and substantially) significant differences in the economic outcomes of contracting for park and road maintenance services across the three countries. According to the parameter estimates in our pooled Scandinavian model, the difference in cost savings between the Norwegian cases and the cases in Denmark and Sweden is of a magnitude of 10–11 percentage points.

Furthermore, the explanatory factors that are associated with cost changes differ across the three national contexts. The most consistent result is found for our variable for transactional contract features, which has the same sign in all countries and is significantly correlated with cost change in Sweden and Norway, but not in Denmark. No other explanatory variables are significantly correlated with cost changes in more than one country. The variation in explanatory factors associated with cost changes across the three countries is noteworthy and raises several questions for further theoretical and empirical research into the importance of national contextual factors in explaining contracting outcomes.

The comparative analysis based on statistical analysis provides modest support to the theoretical explanations of contracting outcomes discussed in the previous contracting literature. The empirical evidence is most consistent with theoretical explanations of contracting outcomes in the context of Denmark, while the findings for Norway deviate most from the established theoretical expectations and the empirical findings in other contexts. It is also of key interest that Scandinavia, where there are relatively similar welfare state and politico-administrative systems and where common EU regulations have been implemented, has not experienced similar results in terms of economic outcomes from contracting out. Further explanation for the differences in contracting outcomes may be found by following arguments in NIE on the importance of the characteristics and supportiveness of several institutional layers (Williamson 2000), along with service and structural place characteristics (Bel and Fageda 2009; Hefetz and Warner 2011). For example, in countries with well-developed institutions, competition, contracts and expertise, such as Denmark, the existence of cost savings is more likely to depend on whether they are actively pursued as part of the contracting strategy. In contexts with well-developed markets, these markets are able to 'deliver instantly' when a municipality chooses to expose its in-house provision to competition (as discussed in the theory section). In countries with less developed institutions, such as Norway, the outcomes from the pursuit of cost-focused strategies may be more arbitrary. An alternative explanation for the deviant outcomes in the Norwegian case may be structural place characteristics related to smaller municipalities, which affect not only a municipality's capacity for its own production but also the attractiveness of the market for private providers. Further insights into the interplay between the institutional and the structural environment may thus improve our understanding of differences in cost changes across national contexts.

Our findings on the importance of country context complement the longstanding interest in studying differences in contracting outcomes across service contexts (e.g. Bel et al. 2010). The importance of service context has often been addressed and invoked as a key theoretical explanation for differences in economic outcomes across different public services (Hodge 2000; Petersen et al. 2018). In contrast, there has only been scant attention paid by researchers to the importance of country context, and few theories have been proposed. A key finding from our analysis is that differences in country context between the three Scandinavian countries are important for understanding the economic effects of contracting out the same service (a municipal park or road service) and the factors that influence these outcomes in different national contexts. These findings could spur a more general interest in scrutinizing the history and characteristics of the national context(s) in which contracting out takes place, and motivate searches for explanations beyond the standard ones found in the contracting literature.

## References


Bel, G., & Costas, A. (2006). Do public sector reforms get rusty? Local privatization in Spain. *The Journal of Policy Reform, 9*(1), 1–24.

Bel, G., & Fageda, X. (2009). Factors explaining local privatization: A meta-regression analysis. *Public Choice, 139*(1–2), 105–119.

Bel, G., Fageda, X., & Warner, M. E. (2010). Is private production of public services cheaper than public production? A meta-regression analysis of solid waste and water services. *Journal of Policy Analysis and Management, 29*(3), 553–577.

Blom-Hansen, J. (2003). Is private delivery of public services really cheaper? Evidence from public road maintenance in Denmark. *Public Choice, 115*(3), 419–438.

Bretzer, Y. N., Persson, B., & Randrup, T. B. (2016). Is public procurement efficiency conditioned by market types? A critical test in park and road sectors in Sweden. *International Journal of Public Sector Management, 29*(5), 488–501.

Brown, T. L., & Potoski, M. (2005). Transaction costs and contracting: The practitioner perspective. *Public Performance & Management Review, 38*(3), 326–351.

Dehoog, R. (1990). Competition, negotiation, or cooperation: Three models for service contracting. *Administration and Society, 22*(3), 317–340.

Domberger, S., & Jensen, P. (1997). Contracting out by the public sector: Theory, evidence, prospects. *Oxford Review of Economic Policy, 13*(4), 67–78.

Donahue, J. D. (1989). *The privatization decision: Public ends, private means.* New York: Basic Books.

Foged, S. K. (2016). The relationship between population size and contracting out public services: Evidence from a quasi-experiment in Danish municipalities. *Urban Affairs Review, 52*(3), 348–390.

Greve, C., Lægreid, P., & Rykkja, L. H. (2016). *Nordic administrative reforms: Lessons for public management.* London: Palgrave Macmillan.

Hefetz, A., & Warner, M. E. (2011). Contracting or public delivery? The importance of service, market, and management characteristics. *Journal of Public Administration Research and Theory, 22*(2), 289–317.

Hodge, G. A. (2000). *Privatization—An international review of performance.* Oxford and Boulder: Westview Press.

Leiren, M. D., Lindholst, A. C., Ingjerd, S., & Randrup, T. B. (2016). Capability versus efficiency: Contracting out park and road services in Norway. *International Journal of Public Sector Management, 29*(5), 474–487.

Lindholst, A. C., Petersen, O. H., & Houlberg, K. (2018). Contracting out local park and road services: Economic effects and their strategic, contractual and competitive conditions. *Local Government Studies, 44*(1), 64–85.

Petersen, O. H., Hjelmar, U., & Vrangbæk, K. (2018). Is contracting out of public services still the great panacea? A systematic review of studies on economic and quality effects from 2000 to 2014. *Social Policy & Administration, 52*(1), 130–157.

Sellers, J. M., & Lidström, A. (2007). Decentralization, local government, and the welfare state. *Governance, 20*(4), 609–632.

Williamson, O. E. (2000). The new institutional economics: Taking stock, looking ahead. *Journal of Economic Literature, XXXVIII*(September), 595–613.

CHAPTER 10

# Patterns and Variations of Marketization Compared

*Andrej Christian Lindholst, Morten Balle Hansen, Ylva Norén Bretzer, Nicola Dempsey and Merethe Dotterud Leiren*

## Introduction

In Chapters 5–8, we provided overviews of the trajectories of marketization and the impact on the organization and provision of municipal park and road services in a single-country perspective for respectively England, Sweden, Denmark and Norway. One key finding appearing from a cross-reading of the four chapters is that contemporary marketization is characterized by substantial variations across the four countries. For example, the purposes for involving private providers and markets in public service delivery were not uniformly coupled to cost concerns

A. C. Lindholst (✉) · M. B. Hansen
Department of Politics and Society, Aalborg University, Aalborg, Denmark
e-mail: acl@dps.aau.dk

Y. N. Bretzer
School of Public Administration, University of Gothenburg, Gothenburg, Sweden
e-mail: ylva.noren-bretzer@spa.gu.se



A. C. Lindholst and M. B. Hansen (eds.),
*Marketization in Local Government*,
https://doi.org/10.1007/978-3-030-32478-0_10

across the four countries as envisioned in core new public management (NPM) reform models of marketization. Municipalities in Norway (Chapter 8) were found to involve providers due to their complementary capabilities rather than for the purpose of reducing costs, while municipalities in Denmark (Chapter 7) were found to apply intense and ongoing market-based competition between private and in-house providers with the aim to benchmark and reduce costs. Also, England, a country renowned for strong emphasis on marketization in their past reform trajectories, may not appear that marketized after all—even within 'spearhead sectors' such as municipal park and road services. For England (Chapter 5) it was found that provision of park and road services was shifting toward shared responsibilities between different combinations of local authorities, private, third sector and voluntary actors although the role of private providers remain important. Thus, private providers appear to have different, albeit still important, roles in public service delivery across countries with different reform trajectories. Lastly, the study of economic outcomes from contracting out park and road services in Chapter 9 found substantial variations, including average cost savings in Denmark, a neutral cost effect in Sweden and average cost increases in Norway, even after controlling for standard explanations in the contracting literature such as the level of competition and contracting strategy. These variations in outcome call for careful appreciation of the comparative characteristics of marketization and how it has evolved across different groups of countries. To provide a more detailed and systematic analysis of similarities and differences in the patterns and variations in contemporary marketization in a comparative perspective, we address the following research question in this chapter:

> 1) To what degree do patterns and variations in contemporary marketization within municipal park and road services differ across England and the three Scandinavian countries.

---

N. Dempsey
Department of Landscape Architecture, University of Sheffield, Sheffield, UK
e-mail: n.dempsey@sheffield.ac.uk

M. D. Leiren
CICERO—Center for International Climate Research, Oslo, Norway
e-mail: merethe.leiren@cicero.oslo.no

To answer the question, we compare patterns and variations of contemporary marketization in a series of statistical analyses of comparable INOPS survey data from each of the four countries (see Chapter 3 for details on data and methods). The data enable us to examine, on the basis of formal statistical tests, whether municipalities across the four countries differ in their implementation of features from different marketization models within the park and road services. The analysis allows us to compare the degree to which the features of marketization in each country are aligned with and differ across the 'pre-NPM' 'core-NPM' and 'post-NPM' models of marketization as presented in Chapter 2. The three models summarize key features of different marketization models including features related to the organization of internal service providers (internal marketization) and features related to involvement of external service providers (external marketization). In this chapter, the three models are employed as an interpretive frame for the comparison and discussion of country variations.

The comparison extends the analysis of the implementation of marketization within municipal park and road services from the single-country perspectives found in Chapters 5–8 toward a formalized comparative country analysis based on statistical techniques. For the comparison, we use data indicating:

a. the distribution of maintenance budgets across different types of service providers,
b. the importance of different purposes for involving private providers,
c. the characteristics of formal contract design for organizing the involvement of private service providers, and
d. the degree to which in-house providers is organized as semi-autonomous and 'corporate-like' units operating within a competitive environment.

*First*, the data on the distribution of maintenance budgets between different service provider types make it possible to test similarities and differences in the involvement of private service providers and other service provider types in public service delivery in the four countries. These data also allow for an exploration of whether municipalities across the four countries differ in the degree to which they use a strategy of mixed-service delivery as an alternative to full reliance on either in-house or private service provision. *Second*, the data on the importance of the purposes for involving private service providers gives a possibility to examine differences between the countries concerning the reasons why private providers are involved in public service delivery. The data allow us to test whether main purposes reflect cost-focused contracting strategies, lack of internal operational capacities or contracting strategies focused on quality and/or service/organizational development. *Third*, the data on contract design allow us to test whether the countries differ concerning how exchange relations with private contractors are organized. The data will show whether the municipalities across the countries differ in the degree they have implemented formal contract features associated with conventional and/or newer collaborative contracting models and how elaborated these formal contract features are across the countries. *Finally*, the data on how municipalities have organized their in-house provision makes it possible to test whether municipalities in the four countries differ when it comes to how far they have marketized and reorganized their internal operational capacities (i.e. service providers) as semiautonomous organizational units with 'corporate-like' features.

For our analysis we applied analysis of variances (ANOVA) and $\chi^2$-tests as main statistical techniques to test for similarities and differences in the implementation of the various features associated with different marketization models. ANOVA is applied for continuous scaled data and $\chi^2$-tests are applied for categorical data. ANOVA is furthermore based on Games-Howell post hoc tests due to its general robustness for differences in group sizes, deviations from normality and differences in variances (Fagerland and Sandvik 2009).

In the analysis, we selected England—a recurrent benchmark in international comparisons of public sector reforms from the 1980s and onward (e.g. Barzelay 2001)—as default reference country in statistical tests and for presentation of results in table formats. Relevant results from statistical tests of differences between the three Scandinavian countries are referred to in the text. The literature on NPM and marketization reforms in public administration clearly tend to portray England as a front-runner and the Scandinavian countries as reluctant reformers and we want to confront that myth by means of our data. This literature however, is predominantly done by scholars focusing at the state level and primarily based on empirical data from the state administration. Our study analyzes local government and public services not previously analyzed from the perspective of marketization except in previous publications from the INOPS project. Thus, our empirical analysis may uncover some surprising findings. Overall, the analysis and the chosen statistical techniques allow for focusing on differences between our four countries rather than differences within the countries.

In the closing discussion of the chapter, we return to our research question and sum up key findings from our comparisons and evaluate differences and similarities in the diffusion and evolution of marketization within the contemporary organization of the delivery of municipal park and road services across our four countries.

## Contemporary Marketization Within Municipal Park and Road Services

### *Who Provides the Services?*

Table 10.1 shows results from our comparison of similarities and differences in the mix of involved service providers within municipal park and road maintenance in England and the three Scandinavian countries. The first upper part of the table (rows A–D) shows the proportions of municipalities in each country which 'only' use *private providers* (defined by spending 90% or more of the maintenance budget on private providers), use *mixed public-private delivery* (spending between 10% and 90% on *in-house* or *private providers*), 'only' use *in-house provider* spending 90% or more), and finally the proportion which only use *other provider types* (spending 90% of their maintenance budget on other provider types). The middle part of the table (row E) shows the proportions in each country using *other provider types* to some extent (more than 0%). The bottom part (rows F–H) shows the average percentages (shares) in each country of budgets spend on respectively *private providers*, *in-house providers* and *other provider types.* Other provider types include such organizations as public-private ventures, community groups and third sector organizations.

We will discuss the findings in Table 10.1 starting at the bottom with rows F–H, which shows the average share of the maintenance budget for the three provider types, for our two services in the four countries. Several interesting patterns emerge when comparing England and the Scandinavian countries. Initially, from the general impression given in the Public Administration literature we would expect much stronger marketization patterns in England, but our findings indicate a more complex story line.

*First*, when looking at row G, we find that in-house provision after four decades of marketization is still a highly dominant form of

**Table 10.1** Privatization in delivery of municipal park and road services in England and Scandinavia

| *Involved organizations*[a] | | *Statistics and tests of difference (England as reference)*[b] | | | |
|---|---|---|---|---|---|
| | | *England* (N *parks/ roads*= *103/59*) | *Sweden* (N *parks/ roads*= *100/95*) | *Denmark (N parks/ roads*= *74/72*) | *Norway* (N *parks/ roads*= *75/81*) |
| A. Proportion 'only' using private contractors (90% of services or more) | Parks | 33% | 15%*** | 14%*** | 3%*** |
| | Roads | 32% | 21%* | 13%*** | 11%*** |
| B. Proportion using mixed delivery (between 10% and 90% of services) | Parks | 18% | 32%** | 43%*** | 31%* |
| | Roads | 10% | 61%*** | 81%*** | 74%*** |
| C. Proportion 'only' using in-house provider (90% of services or more) | Parks | 44% | 48% | 43% | 65%*** |
| | Roads | 46% | 17%*** | 6%*** | 14%*** |
| D. Proportion 'only' using other provider types (90% of services or more) | Parks | 5% | 5% | 0%* | 1% |
| | Roads | 8% | 1%** | 0%** | 0%*** |
| E. Proportion using other provider types (more than 0% of services) | Parks | 47% | 13%*** | 3%*** | 8%*** |
| | Roads | 15% | 10% | 1%*** | 5%** |
| F. Percentage (unweighted) of maintenance budget spend on private contractors | Parks | 40% | 29% | 27% | 14%*** |
| | Roads | 37% | 51% | 47% | 45% |
| G. Percentage (unweighted) of maintenance budget spend on in-house provider | Parks | 52% | 63% | 73%*** | 83%*** |
| | Roads | 48% | 45% | 53% | 53% |
| H. Percentage (unweighted) of maintenance budget spend on other provider types | Parks | 8% | 8% | 0%*** | 4% |
| | Roads | 11% | 4% | 0%** | 2% |

*Notes*

[a]Proportions in respectively rows A–D and rows F–H are mutual exclusive and add up to 100%. The proportions in row E are overlapping with proportions in rows A–D. 'Other provider types' include a variety of different less frequently used provider types such as 'social enterprise' or 'inter-municipal company'

[b]England is used as a reference country for statistical test of differences between the four countries. ANOVA with Games-Howell post hoc tests are used for continuous variables (rows F–H) and $\chi^2$ tests (pairwise country comparisons) are used for nominal variables (rows A–E). Significance levels: *$p<.1$, **$p<.05$, ***$p<.01$

*Source* INOPS survey 2014–2016

organizing the delivery of municipal park and road services in all the four countries. In all the four countries, around one-half or more of the maintenance budgets for respectively parks and roads are spent on *in-house providers*. This is a somewhat surprising finding—especially in the English case. We call park and road maintenance services 'spearhead' services because they are usually considered easier to marketize than many other public services. Thus, we would expect more marketization in this area than in other public policy fields.

*Second*, differences in the averages spend on *private providers* for park and road budgets (row F) are statistically insignificant in seven out of eight cases. The exception is park services in Norway where they spend a significantly lower proportion of their budgets on *private providers* than municipalities in England (Table 10.1, row F). Keeping the traditional story of the strongly marketized English case in mind it is also interesting to note that the Scandinavian countries, in terms of road maintenance, tend to spend a larger amount of their budgets on private contractors than their English colleagues although the difference is not statistically significant (Table 10.1, row F).

*Third*, when comparing park and road services in row G, we find that the predominance of *in-house providers* is higher in park than in road services in Scandinavia. In comparison with England, the higher shares of maintenance budgets allocated to *in-house providers* for park services in Denmark (mean difference = 21 percentage points), and Norway (mean difference = 31 percentage points) are found to be statistically significant ($p < .01$). Thus, in the case of park services the usual story of England as a spearhead marketizer is supported by the data, while that is not the case for road services. Interestingly, for England, we find that the level of use of *in-house providers* is almost equal for park (52%) and road (48%) services (row G), while the differences between the two services are pronounced in all three Scandinavian countries—private provision is much more common in road services than in park services in Scandinavia.

Turning to the upper part of Table 10.1 (rows A–D), the comparative data are organized differently. Here the table shows not averages, but the frequency of four different provision models in the four countries and two policy services. We ask what percentage of the municipalities in each country use a (A) private contractor model, (B) Mixed delivery model, (C) in-house provider model or (D) other provider model?

The comparison of differences in various combinations in the mix of provider types (rows A–E) show that there are several interesting and statistically significant differences between England and each of the three Scandinavian countries.

First, and perhaps most noteworthy, ***mixed delivery*** (row B) is far more common among municipalities in all the three Scandinavian countries than in England for both parks and roads and especially Danish municipalities tend to use this model. In contrast, the majority of municipalities in England rely on one predominant provider type for park and road services: either one ***in-house provider*** (row C) or ***private providers*** (row A). Scandinavian municipalities on the other hand either tend to rely on ***in-house provision*** (row C) or engage in ***mixed delivery*** (row B) in the park sector. In the road sector a clear majority of Scandinavian municipalities relies on ***mixed delivery*** and only to a limited extent on a single provider type (i.e. ***in-house*** or ***private provider***). The reliance on ***mixed delivery*** is most prevalent in Denmark where about four out of five (81%) municipalities has organized their services as ***mixed delivery*** for roads and two out of five (43%) for parks.

*Second*, and contrary to the traditional story of England as a marketization leader, inside-provider models in road services are much more frequently used among English municipalities than among their Scandinavian counterparts (row C in Table 10.1). Instead, the majority of the Scandinavian municipalities rely on the mixed delivery model for road services.

Finally, we turn to other provider types (rows E and H in Table 10.1) than private contractors and in-house provision. Other provider types include organizations such as public-private ventures, community groups and third sector organizations.

*First*, for England, it is a clear finding, in particular for park services, that *other provider types* are important (rows E and H). The statistics indicate that around one-half (47%) of the municipalities in England involve *other provider types* to some degree. However, the share of maintenance budgets allocated to *other provider types* is low (row H). The more detailed data reported in the INOPS survey shows that 7% of the municipalities use collaborative arrangements in terms of ***public-private ventures*** for parks and 4% for roads. ***Public-private ventures*** take up respectively 4% and 5% of overall budgets (unweighted averages). ***Community groups*** and third sector organizations are used by respectively 44% and 20% of all municipalities in England for parks ***Community groups*** and ***third sector organizations*** are virtually non-existing within road services and take up only insignificant shares of overall local road budgets (less than 1%). Similarly, for Sweden *other provider* *types* are involved to some degree. The figures in Table 10.1 for *other provider types* (rows E and H) for Sweden are referring almost equally to *inter-municipal enterprises* and *municipal owned corporations* which provide both park and road services. A few municipalities in Sweden also indicated that *community groups* provide simple maintenance works in local neighborhoods. Overall, the findings show that the additional data for use of *other provider types* indicate a slightly more collaborative approach to the involvement of the private sector (e.g. *public-private ventures*) for service delivery among municipalities in England compared to the three Scandinavian countries. Below, we explore whether this finding is also reflected in how private provisions are organized, focusing on the characteristics of contractual relations with the private sector.

## *Purpose for Using Private Contractors*

Table 10.2 shows results from our comparison of the purposes for involvement of private providers in the delivery of municipal park and road services in England and the three Scandinavian countries. Across

**Table 10.2** Purposes for privatization in delivery of municipal park and road services in England and Scandinavia

| *Purposes*[a] | *Mean scores (standard deviations) and tests of difference with England as reference*[b] | | | |
|---|---|---|---|---|
| | *England (N = 44–47)* | *Sweden (N = 64–65)* | *Denmark (N = 64–67)* | *Norway (N = 68–69)* |
| A. Achieve low costs | 7.8 (2.2) | 7.4 (2.1) | 7.5 (2.0) | 5.8 (3.1)*** |
| B. Test and benchmark prices | 6.3 (2.6) | 6.2 (2.7) | 7.5 (2.3)* | 5.3 (2.8) |
| C. Achieve high quality | 6.3 (2.7) | 5.6 (2.9) | 5.1 (2.7)* | 5.1 (2.8) |
| D. To carry out work the authority cannot do | 5.5 (3.7) | 7.0 (3.0) | 6.7 (3.0) | 8.0 (2.1)*** |
| E. Develop and renew sites and services | 4.4 (3.2) | 4.4 (2.7) | 4.6 (2.3) | 4.2 (2.8) |
| F. Develop internal organization and work methods | 4.2 (3.1) | 4.0 (2.7) | 5.0 (2.3) | 3.9 (3.1) |

*Notes*

[a]Respondents were asked to indicate to what degree a particular purpose was important for the municipality's use of private contractors within park and/or road services. All items measured by an 11-point response-scale with anchors (0 = 'not at all' and 10 = 'Very high degree')

[b]England is used as a reference country for statistical test of differences between the four countries. ANOVA with Games Howell post hoc test. Significance levels *$p < .1$, **$p < .05$, ***$p < .01$

*Source* INOPS survey 2014–2016

rows A–F in Table 10.2 the importance of the purposes appears to be relatively similar across the four countries, but there are some notable differences.

*First*, turning the attention to the relative importance of the different purposes, we find that ***achieving low costs*** receive the highest mean scores across municipalities in England (mean score = 7.8), Sweden (7.4) and Denmark (7.5). Municipalities within each of these three countries are also relatively similar (indicated by the relatively lowest values for standard deviations, ranging from 2.0 to 2.2, across all six purposes) regarding the (high) importance of achieving low costs compared to other purposes for using private providers. The Norwegian municipalities, however, stand out by their substantially lower scoring (mean score = 5.8) and higher disagreement (standard deviation = 3.1) for the importance of achieving low costs. At the other end, the two purposes related to development (rows E and F) receive the lowest scoring in all four countries. All scores for these two purposes equal or are below the mid-point of the measurement scale (5.0).

*Second*, our statistical tests reported in Table 10.2 do not indicate any general pattern which distinguishes municipalities in England from the three Scandinavian countries. Notable, we find no statistically significant differences in the scoring of the importance of the six purposes between England and Sweden. However, the ranking of purposes between the two countries are slightly different, and we find a relatively high, albeit insignificant, difference in the scores for *to carry out work the municipality cannot do* (mean difference = 1.5, $p > .1$). Very high variations in the importance of this purpose among the municipalities within each of the two countries (and particularly for England, standard deviation = 3.7) help explain why the relatively high difference in average scores is insignificant. These statistics furthermore suggest that some within-country differences are likely to be more important than between-country differences.

*Third*, some country differences between respectively England and Denmark, and England versus Norway are found to be statistically significant. The mean differences are larger between England and Norway than they are between England and Denmark. For Denmark, we find that the lower score for *services quality* (mean difference = 1.2, $p < .1$) and the higher score for *test and benchmark of prices* (mean difference = 1.2, $p < .1$) are statistically significant in comparison with England. Interestingly, additional statistical tests (not shown) find that the score for *test and benchmark of prices* in Denmark (mean = 7.5) is statistically significant compared with the relatively lower scores for Sweden (mean difference = 1.3, $p < .05$) and Norway (mean difference = 2.2, $p < .01$). These findings show that Danish municipalities more than municipalities in any of the three other countries involve private contractors for price tests through competitive markets and internal (benchmarking) purposes. For the Norwegian municipalities, *achieving low costs* is less important while *carrying out work the municipalities cannot do* is more important in comparison with the municipalities in England. The mean differences for these two purposes are substantial (respectively 2.0 and 2.5) and statistically significant ($p < .01$). The relatively higher scores for *carrying out work the authority cannot do* in Denmark and Sweden compared to England (mean differences = 1.2 and 1.5) fail to reach statistical significance ($p > .1$). We note that the variation among the municipalities for the importance of this purpose is high within each of the Scandinavian countries (standard deviations around 3.0 or higher).

Additional statistical tests of differences in mean scores for *carrying out work the authority cannot do* find that the difference is statistically significant between Norway and Denmark (mean difference = 1.3, $p < .05$) while statistically insignificant between Norway and Sweden (mean difference = 1.0, $p = .117$). Also, the lower mean score for *achieving low costs* in Norway is statistically significant compared to Sweden (mean difference = 1.6, $p < .01$) and Denmark (mean difference = 1.7, $p < .01$). These findings show that private contractors are involved in service delivery for a substantial different set of key purposes among municipalities in Norway than in the three other countries. Cost concerns are substantially downplayed among Norwegian municipalities who are relatively more dependent on buying in services from private providers due to a lack of in-house operational capacity. The Norwegian and Swedish municipalities are on average found to be similar with regard to the importance of buying in services from private providers. The variation for this purpose (measured by the standard deviation) among Swedish municipalities (SD = 3.0), however, is substantial larger than among Norwegian municipalities (SD = 2.1).

### *Organizing Exchange Relations in Privatized Service Delivery*

Table 10.3 gives an overview of the importance of eight formal contract features used for organizing exchange relations (i.e. contracts) with private providers for park and road maintenance services across municipalities in England and the three Scandinavian countries.

**Table 10.3** Organization of exchange relations in privatized delivery of municipal park and road services in England and Scandinavia

| *Importance of formal contract feature*[a] | *Mean scores (standard deviations) and tests of difference with England as reference*[b] | | | |
|---|---|---|---|---|
| | *England* (N=49–52) | *Sweden* (N=74–80) | *Denmark* (N=65–67) | *Norway* (N=70–74) |
| A. Juridical clauses/agreement (§§) | 8.8 (1.8) | 7.8 (2.8)* | 7.8 (2.3)** | 8.1 (2.6) |
| B. Service specification based on functionality and purpose | 7.6 (2.7) | 6.1 (3.2)** | 6.4 (3.0) | 6.3 (3.2)* |
| C. Service specification based on quantities, instruction and performance measures | 7.4 (2.9) | 6.7 (2.9) | 7.7 (2.3) | 7.0 (2.9) |
| D. Formal collaboration and joint planning | 7.3 (2.7) | 4.3 (3.3)*** | 6.0 (3.0) | 4.8 (3.1)*** |
| E. Competence requirements | 6.9 (2.9) | 6.5 (2.7) | 6.6 (2.4) | 6.4 (2.9) |
| F. Formal sanctions in case of non-compliance | 5.8 (3.3) | 5.7 (3.1) | 6.7 (2.9) | 6.0 (3.1) |
| G. Contractor's involvement/contact with users | 5.6 (3.1) | 3.0 (2.9)*** | 2.9 (2.8)*** | 2.8 (2.9)*** |
| H. Economic incentives for investment, improvements and optimization | 2.8 (3.0) | 2.1 (2.8) | 2.8 (2.7) | 2.5 (2.9) |

*Notes*

[a]All items measured on a scale from 0 to 10 (0='not at all', 10='very high degree') on the question. "On a scale from 0 to 10, Please indicate to which degree the following content is a central part of your department's arrangements with private contractors"

[b]England is used as a reference country for statistical test (ANOVA with Games Howell post hoc test) of differences between the four countries. Significance levels: *$p<.1$, **$p<.05$, ***$p<.01$

*Source* INOPS survey data 2014–2016

*First*, there are substantial differences between the four countries in how they organize exchange relations with private providers. Despite very high variations within each country (indicated by high values for standard deviations) the differences between countries are found to be statistically significant in the comparison between England and the three Scandinavian countries for four of eight formal contract features. These differences relate to the importance of the *juridical framework*, *service specification based on functionality and purpose*, *formal collaboration/joint planning* and *the contractor's involvement/contact with users*. The higher mean scores for England indicate that these features are comparably more important for municipalities in England. We note that three of the four contract features, where the countries differ, are related to typical features in collaborative and more complex approaches to contracting with the private sector (rows B, D, G and H). In comparison, England stands out from the three Scandinavian countries regarding substantial higher scores for the importance of *service specification based on functionality and purpose (row B)*, *formal collaboration and joint planning (row D)* and *contractor's involvement/contact with users (row G)*. Comparing England with Sweden and Norway shows that the mean differences for these three contract features are all statistically significant. However, in the comparison between England and Denmark the mean difference is only significant for the importance of *contractor's involvement/contact with users* (row G). For example, the higher scoring for *formal collaboration and joint planning* among municipalities in England is statistically significant in the comparisons with Sweden (mean difference $= 3.0$, $p < .01$) and Norway (mean difference $= 2.5$, $p < .01$) but insignificant in the comparison with Denmark (mean difference $= 1.3$, $p > .1$).

*Second*, despite some differences among the countries, the importance of a *formal juridical framework* (row A) is found to be very high across all four countries. It is furthermore notable that municipalities in England view most contract features as more important than municipalities in the three Scandinavian countries (except the comparisons with Denmark in rows C and F, but mean differences are statistically insignificant). This finding indicates that the formalization of exchange relations with private contractors is more pervasive in England and does not only concern the juridical parts (row A) but more heavily regulates additional dimensions of the exchange relations including the organization of *collaboration and joint planning* (row D).

Overall, these findings indicate that municipalities in England compared to the three Scandinavian countries use more complex and formalized contracting models in their exchange relations with private providers of park and road services.

### *Contract Duration*

Table 10.4 provides information about the average duration of ordinary contracts and options for extensions used by municipalities in England and Scandinavia in their contracts with private providers of park and road services. Overall, we find that municipalities in England on average use the longest contract durations. For parks, the average ordinary contract duration is 5.8 years and the average option for contract extension is 4.1 years. For roads, the average ordinary contract duration is 7.6 years and the average contract extension is 7.2 years. This indicates that the total contract duration is around 10 years for parks and 15 years for roads in England. In comparison, the total contract duration is about 5–6 years for park and road services among Scandinavian municipalities. The longer contract durations found among municipalities in England compared to municipalities in the three Scandinavia countries are found to be statistically significant for 11 of 12 comparisons made in Table 10.4.

The substantially longer duration of contracts in England can be related to the contract features in England which was found to be more formal and complex than those found in the three Scandinavian countries (Table 10.4). The high variations found within each country for some of the contract features also indicate that within-country differences in contracting practices are important. For example, the inter-municipal variations in contract durations—both ordinary and extensions—are found to be substantially higher among municipalities in Sweden than in the two other Scandinavian countries. Also, the variation in ordinary contract duration for road services among municipalities in England is remarkably high compared to the average length (mean = 7.6 years, standard deviation = 7.2 years).

### *Marketization of Internal Service Delivery*

Table 10.5 presents the frequency of the use of eight formal tools for organizing and managing in-house providers of park and road services

**Table 10.4** Duration (ordinary and extension) of contracts with private providers of municipal park and road services in England and Scandinavia

| *Contract duration (in years)*[a] | *Means (standard deviations) and tests of difference with England as reference*[b] | | | |
|---|---|---|---|---|
| | *England* (N=47/18)[c] | *Sweden* (N=40/56)[c] | *Denmark* (N=40/56)[c] | *Norway* (N=9/55)[c] |
| *Parks* | | | | |
| Ordinary | 5.8 (4.3) | 3.4 (2.5)*** | 3.2 (1.2)*** | 2.2 (.8)*** |
| Extension | 4.1 (3.8) | 2.8 (3.3) | 1.7 (.7)*** | 2.4 (.5)*** |
| *Roads* | | | | |
| Ordinary | 7.6 (7.2) | 3.2 (1.7)** | 4.1(2.9)* | 3.5(1.0)* |
| Extension | 5.3 (4.8) | 1.9 (1.7)** | 1.6 (.8)** | 1.3 (.8)** |

*Notes*

[a]All items measured in years. Respondents were required to indicate the typical duration (ordinary and extension) of their main maintenance contracts for respectively parks and roads

[b]England is used as a reference country for statistical test (ANOVA with Games Howell post hoc test) of differences between the four countries. Significance levels: *$p<.1$, **$p<.05$, ***$p<.01$

[c]Number of cases ($N$) reported for respectively parks and roads

*Source* INOPS survey data 2014–2016

**Table 10.5** Internal organizational tools related to marketization in the delivery of municipal park and road services in England and Scandinavia

| *Formal instruments*[a] | *Proportions and tests of difference (England as reference)*[b] | | | |
|---|---|---|---|---|
| | *England (N=51–55)* | *Sweden (N=61–73)* | *Denmark (N=61–64)* | *Norway (N=65–74)* |
| A. Business planning | 93% | 82%* | 74%*** | 81%* |
| B. Able to offer services for other internal/external clients | 91% | 69%*** | 73%** | 41%*** |
| C. Independent budgeting/financial statement | 71% | 85%* | 87%** | 83% |
| D. In-house provider subject to competitive tendering | 47% | 55% | 75%*** | 64%* |
| E. Independent top management | 45% | 89%*** | 91%*** | 65%** |
| F. Internal purchaser-provider split | 29% | 44% | 54%** | 35% |
| G. Independent monitoring of maintenance operations | 24% | 61%*** | 68%*** | 39%* |
| H. Company ownership structure (100% owned by municipality) | n/a | 12% | 6% | 6% |

*Notes*

[a]The table shows the proportions of positive answers ('yes') for eight key management instruments for the question: "Which of the following management instruments does the municipality uses for managing and organizing the in-house service provision of parks and/or roads maintenance?" The table only count the shares within the group of municipalities that currently has an in-house provider

[b]England is used as a reference country for statistical test ($\chi^2$ tests) of pairwise differences between the four countries. Significance levels: $^{*}p<.1$, $^{**}p<.05$, $^{***}p<.01$

*Source* INOPS survey data 2014–2016

in municipalities across the four countries. Most of the tools are indicators of devolution of responsibilities, and the creation of semiautonomous agencies and purchaser-provider split model which has been at the heart of NPM (see Chapter 2). In this perspective the prevalence of organizational tools like *business planning* (row A), *able to offer services for other internal/external clients* (row B), *independent budgeting/financial statement* (row C), *independent top management* (row E), *independent monitoring of maintenance operations* (row G) and *company ownership structure* (row H) can be considered indicators of the creation of semiautonomous public agencies at the expense of the traditional hierarchical command-and-control regime in public administration (see also Chapter 2 for a more in-depth discussion of these issues). Some of these tools also enhance competition, which is at the heart of marketization. This is the case of *in-house provider subject to competitive tendering* (row D). Also, the use of an *internal purchaser-provider split model* (row F) is often considered an organizational prerequisite for enhancing competition between an in-house and private providers and for the use of a mixed delivery model where both public and private providers are engaged. However, the use of tools like *business planning* without the *internal purchaser-provider* split model or *independent monitoring of maintenance operations* also indicate new models which logic do not rest on the core-NPM regime.

The comparisons of our empirical findings are based on the proportions (percentages) of municipalities within a country with an in-house provider that uses an instrument. Overall, our analysis of responses from municipalities in England and the three Scandinavian countries shows statistically significant differences in the use of all tools where data are available for all four countries (rows A–G).

*First*, the data highlights that municipalities in England differs substantially from municipalities in the three Scandinavian countries in how they organize and manage in-house providers. Overall, we find that municipalities in England have substantially less frequent use of five out of seven formal instruments in the comparisons with the three Scandinavian countries (rows C–G). Only for *business planning* (row A) and for *ability to offer services for other clients* (row B) we find that the proportions are substantially higher in England than in Scandinavia. Particularly, we find that in comparison with the three Scandinavian countries, there is no predominant contemporary use of *internal purchaser-provider split* and use of *separate internal monitoring of in-house provisions in England.* The higher autonomy and specialization of in-house providers among municipalities in Scandinavia compared to England is furthermore evident in the higher proportions of municipalities which use *independent top management* and *independent budgeting and financial statements.* A last important difference is the higher proportions of the use of *business planning* among municipalities in England compared to all three Scandinavian countries.

*Second*, the proportions of *business planning* (row A) and *independent budgeting/financial statement* (row C) are higher than 70% for all four countries. It is also worth noting that proportions for at least two instruments are very high within each of the four countries. For Denmark, for example, the proportions for the use of *independent top management* (row E) and *independent budgeting* (row C) are each higher than 80%. At the other end, the proportions for *internal purchaser-provider split* (row F) are among the lowest for all countries (ranging from 29% for England to 54% for Denmark). For all other instruments the proportions vary in substantial degrees among the four countries. For example, the proportions for use of *independent top management* (row E) range from 45% for England to 91% for Denmark.

*Third*, some country differences are noteworthy for the three Scandinavian countries. For Sweden and Denmark, we find that the proportions for the use of most instruments are similar. All mean differences are found to be statistically insignificant except for *in-house provider subject to competitive tendering* (row D) where the lower proportion in Sweden (55%) is statistically significant ($p < .01$) from the mean score in Denmark (75%). The higher proportion in Denmark is furthermore statistically significant ($p < .1$) in comparison with Norway (64%). Thus, our analysis identifies municipalities in Denmark as the ones that most frequently subject their in-house providers to competitive tendering. The proportion is furthermore relatively high in absolute terms as three out of four (75%) Danish municipalities subject their in-house providers to competitive tendering. It is furthermore a characteristic that the proportions for the use of six out of the eight instruments are higher among municipalities in Denmark than in Sweden and Norway. Municipalities in Norway stand out from municipalities in the two other Scandinavian countries. Compared to municipalities in Denmark five out of eight instruments (rows B, D, E, F and G) are less frequently used among the Norwegian municipalities. For these five instruments the mean differences for the proportions are found to be statistically significant (p-levels between $< .01$ and $< .1$). Similarly, the lower proportions for four out of the eight instruments (rows B, D, E and G) among Norwegian municipalities compared to Swedish municipalities are found to be statistically significant (p-levels between < .01 and < .1).

*Finally*, the proportion of *company ownership structure* (row H) is only measured for the three Scandinavian countries. The data shows that this instrument is relatively rare in all three countries ranging from 6% of the municipalities in Denmark and Norway to 12% in Sweden. The differences between the Scandinavian countries for the proportions using *company ownership structure* are furthermore all found to be statistically insignificant ($p > .1$).

This section clearly indicates that the traditional story line or myth highlighting England as a forerunner in terms of the NPM in general, and marketization in particular, needs substantial amendments. The findings displayed in Table 10.5 indicates that contemporary marketization and agencification, when it comes to the internal municipal organization, is substantially stronger in Scandinavia than in England with Denmark as the country most closely resembling a core-NPM regime

## Discussions

In this chapter we examined to what degree do patterns and variations in contemporary marketization within municipal park and road services differ across England and the three Scandinavian countries. We applied INOPS survey data and statistical tests in our analysis. A key finding is that the key features of marketization varies substantially across the four countries. In the discussed below we interpret these variations further in light of the various marketization models laid out in Chapter 2.

### *External Marketization*

The countries are most similar in terms of the overall level of involvement of private contractors measured by the average budget shares spend on private providers (row F in Table 10.2). Overall, private providers are found to play substantial roles within municipal park and road services across all four countries. Only a lower level of private involvement for park services in Norway was found to be statistically significant in the comparisons. However, when we further explore the ways in which private providers are involved in service delivery across the countries they appear to differ in substantial ways. In Scandinavia, a common feature seems to be the reliance on mixed-service delivery where two or more provider types are involved. In contrast, municipalities in England are found predominantly to rely on one provider type only. However, a broader range of provider types are involved among municipalities in England in comparison with municipalities in Scandinavia.

Despite the substantial role and high-level of involvement of private provision in all four countries, we also find it remarkable that in-house provision is (still) dominating the mix of provider types in all countries after four decades with marketization on the global agenda. In this perspective, we find that in-house provision has been remarkable resilient until the mid-2010s—even for our benchmark country, England.

With regard to the purposes of involving private contractors we find a relatively high degree of similarity among three of our four countries. Cost concerns and benchmarking are dominating the purposes in England, Sweden and Denmark. In Norway, however, we find that the far most important purpose is to involve complementary capabilities when the municipalities do not have the operational capacities to carry out certain tasks themselves. Thus, among the Scandinavian countries we find indications of two different systems for mixed delivery which dominate how service delivery is organized. In Norway, mixed delivery is predominantly embedded within a division of labor, based on the question of operational capacities; while mixed delivery in Denmark is predominantly embedded within a division of labor based on direct competition and benchmarking. Sweden takes up an 'in-between' position.

The comparison of contracting models across the four countries suggest that there are some consistent patterns. Collaborative and long-term contract models are widely adopted in England while conventional and shorter-term contract models are adopted across the three Scandinavian countries. Within Scandinavia, contracts appear slightly more complex and formalized in Denmark and to some degree in Sweden in comparison with Norway. Contracts in Denmark also show some features from the collaborative contracting models.

### *Internal Marketization*

Our findings for organization of in-house provision are somewhat surprising. Notably, we find that features of internal marketization based on core-NPM models are less widespread among municipalities in England than in all three Scandinavian countries. Rather, we find that municipalities in England organize themselves according to features associated with post-NPM models. In particular, internal service delivery in England is primarily coordinated through business plans, separate controls through budgeting and a high degree of flexibility toward customers. The relatively low proportion of English municipalities using features such as the provider-purchaser model also indicates that service providers within municipalities in England are situated within a traditional command-and-control hierarchy of a larger organizational structure to a larger extent in comparison with municipalities in Scandinavia.

Almost ironically, contemporary Scandinavian municipalities are found to rely much more on core-NPM marketization models in their management and organization of in-house provisions than contemporary municipalitie s in England. In particular, we find that municipalities in Denmark adhere most strongly to core-NPM models in how they organize in-house service delivery. The municipalities in Denmark are, for example, subjecting their in-house providers to direct competitive pressures and use private providers for benchmarking purposes more than municipalities in any other country in our comparisons. However, it is also important to note that in-house delivery is widespread in Scandinavia and the proportions which only use private contractors are low compared to England. Thus, marketization appears as a strategy for modernizing service delivery rather than a minimizing strategy for replacing in-house providers with private contractors.

### *Country Variants of Marketization*

In comparison with Scandinavian countries, the UK has a long history of radical and far-reaching reforms promoting different marketization models within public administration. Overall, we find that contemporary marketization among our municipalities in England is strongly characterized by a widespread implementation of post-NPM models while features from core-NPM models are less prominent. Municipalities in England, for example, use relatively complex partnership-based contracts and a greater range of provider types are involved in the overall mix of service providers. These characteristics are in particular notable in the comparisons with the three Scandinavian countries. Some traits from core-NPM models, however, are evident among municipalities in England. Notably, the single-most important purpose for involving private providers was found to be the achievement of low costs.

For Sweden, we find that contemporary marketization within municipal park and road services is predominantly characterized by core-NPM models mixed with some features from pre-NPM and post-NPM models.

For example, in comparison with England relatively conventional and simple formal contracts are used when contracting with the private sector but the emphasis on competition and benchmarking is relatively low in comparison with Denmark.

For Denmark, we find that contemporary marketization within municipal park and road services is strongly characterized by features from core-NPM models mixed with a few features from post-NPM models. Denmark stands out in the comparisons with England and the two other Scandinavian countries as the country where core-NPM models for internal and external marketization have the strongest impact on contemporary marketization. In perspective, Denmark can be argued to represent a new benchmark country in how far core-NPM models for marketization is implemented. In the Danish variant of core-NPM models the provider mix is characterized by mixed public and private delivery and a strong orientation toward direct competition among providers with a focus on low costs and benchmarking.

For Norway, we find that contemporary marketization within municipal park and road services are characterized by a mix of features from pre-NPM and core-NPM models. The impact from core-NPM models on contemporary marketization on internal service delivery is the weakest among the three Scandinavian countries but can to some extent be argued to rival or eclipse the current impact on municipalities in England. Some features of core-NPM models are widely implemented by the municipalities in Norway but still not to the same extent as Sweden and Denmark. Highly surprising, however, is the finding that some features of core-NPM models are more common in Norway—a country historically renowned as a reluctant reformer (see Chapter 8)—than in England. This is in particular evident for the municipalities' organization of internal service delivery. If core-NPM models are the yardstick for evaluating the degree of marketization, then Norway roughly equals, if not surpassing, England (but not the two neighboring countries in Scandinavia). However, as noted, England appears to have moved on toward post-NPM models and Norway shows relatively few features, if none, from these models. In perspective, we find that Norway in our comparisons can still be regarded as a reluctant reformer with regard to implementation of core—and post-NPM models. Overall, marketization in Norway has predominantly taken place internally with adoption of features from core-NPM models in combination with a widespread use of features resembling pre-NPM models for external marketization.

### *The UK Context as Benchmark?*

In perspective, our findings question the overall status of the UK country context as a contemporary 'benchmark' (Barzelay 2001), 'trailblazer' (Christensen and Lægreid 2007) or 'vanguard' (Hood and Dixon 2015) in the implementation (and evaluation) of core-NPM models. These sweeping statements have been made by scholars focusing on national and not local government. Overall, core-NPM models and features for external and in particular internal marketization were more widespread among municipalities in the Scandinavian countries (notably Sweden and Denmark) compared to England. However, within the setting of municipal park and road services we find that England is characterized by higher degrees of post-NPM models and features when compared to Scandinavia. In terms of post-NPM models the English context may be characterized as a leading reform context.

### *Commonalities in Scandinavia?*

The Scandinavian countries are often regarded as a relatively homogeneous country group in terms of the organization of their public sectors and societies more generally. In our analysis, what the three Scandinavian countries have the most in common—and which define them as different from England—is a relatively widespread implementation of features from core-NPM models for internal marketization in the organization and management of in-house provision within two different systems of mixed public-private delivery. Norwegian municipalities appear to implement mixed delivery based on a logic of complementary competencies where Swedish and Danish municipalities appear to approach mixed delivery through a logic of competition.

In perspective, what has emerged among municipalities in Scandinavia after four decades of marketization is a reformed organization of service delivery integrating marketization models in different ways within systems that still emphasize a major role for in-house delivery. The role of the private sector is—through different strategies for involvement and as an ideal for organizing—still critical for the overall system by providing both legitimacy to and spurring efficiency of in-house providers. If the Scandinavian countries are differentiated, Denmark represents the 'purest' core-NPM manifestation of this system in the shape of the most radical competition-based system. Norway, on the other hand, represents a variation with mixed pre-NPM and core-NPM model features where the internal organization is reformed and based on a competence-based division of labor between the public and private sector. Sweden takes up what can be regarded a middle position between Denmark and Norway.

## Conclusion

The analysis in this chapter contributes to understand the cross-national variations in the marketization of local governments with point of departure in park and road services. The findings suggest that models and features of marketization largely differ across the four countries and mostly converge at the level of sub-groups.

Perhaps the most striking and surprising finding is that after four decades of NPM reforms our findings don't lend support to a simple traditional story line of England as the front-runner of core-NPM practices—at least not in the two services included in our study. Furthermore, the comparison shows that a widespread implementation of post-NPM models for internal and external marketization characterize many of the English municipalities. In that sense England, represents a set of new post-NPM practices to be learned from in the future. A mid-range implementation of core-NPM models mixed with some post- and pre-NPM features characterize Sweden. A widespread and strong implementation of core-NPM models for internal and external marketization is typical for Denmark and the country may be regarded as a leading NPM reformer within local park and road services. Norway is characterized by implementation of some features from core-NPM models, particularly for internal marketization, in combination with features from pre-NPM models for external marketization. Sub-variants of some marketization models were also found across the countries; for example two systems for organizing mixed delivery, one based on direct forms for competition (Denmark and partly Sweden) and one based on complementary competencies (Norway and partly Sweden), were evident in Scandinavia. In addition, it is important to note that the implementation of core-NPM models the three Scandinavian countries appears more as a question of modernizing and retaining a key role for local governments in service delivery and less as a question of minimizing local governments' role in service delivery. Thus, the contemporary role of marketization and the organization of service delivery in Scandinavia differ from the ideological orientation and preference for privatization underpinning earlier NPM reforms.

In perspective, the findings raise an interesting discussion about why these variations exist. Do, for example, the four countries' mix of different reform trajectories, political-administrative systems and municipal structures contribute to a better understanding of the observed differences? We provide a more extensive discussion of the 'why' question in Chapter 16. However, before turning to this question we focus on how municipalities have been working with and implemented marketization through four case-studies presented and discussed in the next five chapters (11–15) of the book. In perspective of this chapter, the case-studies add further depth to the understanding of the characteristics of the general patterns and variations we have found across our four countries.

## References

Barzelay, M. (2001). *The New Public Management: Improving Research and Policy Dialogue*. Berkeley: University of California Press.

Christensen, T., & Lægreid, P. (2007). *Transcending New Public Management: The Transformation of Public Sector Reforms*. Burlington: Ashgate.

Fagerland, M. W., & Sandvik, L. (2009). Performance of Five Two-Sample Location Tests for Skewed Distributions with Unequal Variances. *Contemporary Clinical Trials, 30*(5), 490–496.

Hood, C., & Dixon, R. (2015). *A Government That Worked Better and Cost Less? Evaluating Three Decades of Reform and Change in UK Central Government*. Oxford: Oxford University Press.

PART III

# Case Studies

CHAPTER 11

# Long-Term Partnership Contracting in Practice: Queen Elizabeth Olympic Park, London

*Nicola Dempsey, Claudia Leticia Martínez Velarde and Mel Burton*

## Introduction

This chapter will explore one high-profile example of parks management which is governed via a long-term contract-based partnership. Queen Elizabeth Olympic Park (QEOP) is the largest new park to be established in England for over 100 years (Naish and Mason 2014). This is a useful case study for the following reasons: firstly, it was the location of the 2012 London Olympic Games and continues to provide the setting for a number of internationally important sporting venues. Secondly, it forms part of a holistic and integrated social, ecological and economic legacy of the Olympic vision for east London. It will become clear later in the chapter how and why this socio-economically driven mission has a direct impact on the management of the park. And thirdly, it is an

N. Dempsey (✉) · C. L. Martínez Velarde · M. Burton
Department of Landscape Architecture,
University of Sheffield, Sheffield, UK
e-mail: n.dempsey@sheffield.ac.uk



A. C. Lindholst and M. B. Hansen (eds.),
*Marketization in Local Government*,
https://doi.org/10.1007/978-3-030-32478-0_11

example of best practice for the long-term management of a large-scale urban park (Landscape Institute 2015). Its long-term partnership-based contract is distinct from the typical parks management arrangements found in England and Europe, which are traditionally delivered by in-house public sector parks departments or with specific tasks contracted out to a private contractor. The chapter will outline how governance in QEOP involves a more decentralised approach to managing responsibilities through the "thin client model".

Throughout this chapter, we call on data collected through interviews with those practitioners involved in the ongoing park management partnership in QEOP. Our interviews explored how context-specific aspects of the park and the partnership influence, and are influenced by, the management and maintenance processes. We present the data through a discussion of the themes of governance structure, including a focus on community engagement; green space administration; the contract itself and the contractual relationship, ending with some reflections around non-governmental involvement in long-term urban park management and the scope for applying this model to other parks.

## Overview of Queen Elizabeth Olympic Park

It is important to understand the part that the Park plays in terms of the wider political, social, economic and environmental context. According to one of our interviewees, "when we won the Olympics in 2005 it was based primarily on the idea that what would happen after the Olympics would transform this part of London". The underlying mission of this new large-scale park in England's largest, most populated and capital city is to use the opportunity of the London 2012 Games and the creation of QEOP to change the lives of people in east London and drive growth and investment in London and the UK, by developing "an inspiring and innovative place where people want—and can afford—to live, work and visit" (LLDC 2016a).

When housing development is completed, the park and immediate surroundings will be home to over 10,000 households living in five new neighbourhoods in the newly-created E20 postcode. Residents have been moving into the area since 2015. These neighbourhoods are supported by the important transport links which were created for the Olympic Games and connect them with the rest of the city and beyond. This required new and refurbished underground stations and bus routes as well as calling on the high-speed rail connection to Paris and other European cities via the Channel Tunnel Rail Link at Stratford International. In the near future, there will be a new cultural and educational district (as part of the "Olympicopolis Plan") which will include new campuses for University College London and London College of Fashion and new outposts of the Victoria and Albert Museum (Jessel 2018). It is estimated that the "Olympicopolis Plan" will deliver 3000 jobs, 1.5 million additional visitors and generate £2.8 billion of economic value to Stratford and the surrounding area (LLDC 2017).

QEOP covers an area of 560 acres and is located on extensive brownfield land which was heavily contaminated by industrial pollution over many years. Nicholls (2014: 40) describes how the six local rivers were "heavily polluted and virtually inaccessible, choked with silt, invasive species and clogged from fly tipping". The land was remediated which involves the washing and processing of over 2 million tons of soil. The Park today has 6.5 km of waterways, 15 acres of woods, hedgerow and wildlife habitat and over 4300 new trees have been planted (LLDC 2015a; Figs. 1–2). The concept of green infrastructure underpinned the design and planning of the park landscapes. Green infrastructure has been defined as "an interconnected network of protected land and water that supports native species, maintains natural ecological processes, sustains air and water resources and contributes to the health and quality of life for … communities and people" (Williamson 2003: 4; Roe and Mell 2013). Key parts of the Park's green infrastructure include the regenerated river valley, wetlands, tree planting, native and exotic wildflower meadows building on ecologically-based urban vegetation. Issues to be tackled across the site included flooding (because the site lies within the Lee Valley floodplain), extensive land contamination and water pollution.

The Olympic Delivery Authority was responsible for delivering the Olympic Games, after which LLDC took over. LLDC has responsibility for the Olympic Park and the permanent venues including the Aquatics Centre, Copper Box Arena, International Broadcast Centre (IBC), ArcelorMittal Orbit and the Olympic Football Stadium (now the London Stadium) which is home to West Ham United football team which relocated to the ground in 2016. Other venues are owned and operated by other organisations—e.g. Lee Valley Regional Park Authority (LVPRA) manage the Velopark and Hockey and Tennis Centre. The internationally-renowned sports and recreational facilities found in the Park are comparable to those one might find in a major European city.

Post-Olympic Games, the transformation of the Park was focused around three main activities. Firstly, fixtures from the Games were removed (e.g. temporary seating and stadia); secondly, "stitches"—i.e. attractive green connections—were created across the park east to west, north to south to connect the surrounding areas into the park; thirdly, the public parkland was completed (the North Park opened in 2013 and South Park in 2014), which has resulted in a doubling of the size of the Park (Naish and Mason 2014). There are 102 hectares of publicly accessible open space within the Park and immediate surroundings, and 45 hectares of Biodiversity Action Plan (BAP) habitat with links to existing green infrastructure (LLDC 2012). The amount of parkland which is hard-landscaped and urban in character has been attributed to a "creeping urbanism" (Smith 2014: 317) and is outside the scope of this chapter to discuss in detail although it does have implications for the maintenance tasks carried out. The vision was for the Park to be for people and wildlife and of a very high quality in terms of design and management (Landscape Institute 2012). The vision for the management of the park is:

> to take forward the legacy of landscape design and horticultural excellence, beauty and quality, community participation, sustainability and nature conservation created for Games time. (LMS and LLDC 2014: 2)

This vision adheres to the mission statement outlined above. To achieve this, the formal strategy for the Park includes a pledge to "continue the legacy of horticultural excellence…conserve and enhance the biodiversity of the waterways and parklands [and]…ensure that the Park meets the dual needs of a local park for local communities and an iconic national and international destination" (LMS and LLDC 2014: 3). Three Priority Themes "drive the delivery of the Olympic Legacy":

- Promoting convergence and community participation
- Championing equalities and inclusion
- Ensuring high-quality design and environmental sustainability (LMS and LLDC 2014: 26).

Over four million visitors came in the first year that the Park was open, which far exceeded expectations. Based on this, the target of 4.4 million annual visits was set for 2015–2016 (LLDC 2015b) but our interviewees put this at around 5 million annual visitors (on average, up to 13,700 visitors per day). The larger than anticipated number of visitors brings challenges for maintenance and management as the following sections outline.

## The Park's Governance Structure

QEOP has different landowners. The most significant is the London Legacy Development Corporation (LLDC) which is responsible for delivering the physical Olympic legacy to "transform and integrate one of the most challenged areas in the UK into world-class, sustainable and thriving neighbourhoods" (LLDC 2016b). The Greater London Authority (GLA—the administrative body for Greater London, headed by the Mayor of London) funds the LLDC on an annual basis. Other landowners are LVPRA and the London Borough of Hackney (LBH). However, "regardless of land ownership…the LLDC will generally be responsible for the management and maintenance of the parkland" (LMS and LLDC 2014: 25; responsibility for the waterways lies with the Canal & River Trust but they were not consulted as part of this case study). LLDC is a sunset organisation meaning that it will not exist at some (as yet unknown) point in the future. As an LLDC interviewee puts it:

> LLDC "is set up specifically to lead the legacy of the 2012 Olympics… Its boundary…covers four different local authority areas …It has its own planning powers, it writes its own local plan, it owns a lot of the land—not all of it, but a lot of the land…Its remit is to really move forward the legacy of the London 2012 Olympics with regeneration, development, better connectivity, all those sorts of things. It also manages the Olympic Park, so it's responsible for managing the Olympic Park…It's an unusual organisation…and it won't last forever. At some point it will be wound up, and something may or may not replace it. I'm not aware of what that is at the moment".

As the body responsible for the management of the park, LLDC put out to tender the contract for managing the Park based on a 10-year period plus an option of a 5-year renewal. This is much longer than standard parks management contracts—the INOPS survey data suggests that this is, on average, around 5.5 years for parks in England. The QEOP Park management contractor was selected after a year-long process of competitive tendering. The French company ENGIE currently holds the

Estates and Facilities Management (EFM) contract for QEOP Park. The contractor was selected according to criteria relating to quality, the flexibility of the contract, the contractor's experience and track record. There are additional criteria specific to delivering the Olympic legacy which requires the contractor to: invest in the locality, generate employment for local residents and secure volunteers to help manage the park. To achieve these social objectives, a community interest company, Our ParkLife (OPL), was established by the contractor. OPL has the aim of helping deliver the London Legacy through employment, volunteering, training and providing services on the Park. OPL has contractual targets and requirements set by the LLDC for volunteering in the park (which are discussed later). The Landscape Group (TLG) is subcontractor to ENGIE and carries out the grounds maintenance elements of the contract. LLDC instructs the Landscape Group with Management Prescriptions which are underpinned by the Park Management Plan and Biodiversity Action Plan (BAP) which were commissioned by LLDC. BAPs are formal policy instruments derived from the UK's ratification of the 1992 Convention on Biological Diversity (CBD). Underpinned by the UK's BAP, local BAPs are designed to support the recovery of the most threatened species and habitats and to monitor progress towards the UK's CBD target.

Formal monthly meetings are held between LLDC, ENGIE, idVerde (TLG's parent company) and OPL to monitor TLG and OPL's performance according to indicators set out in a Performance Quality Management System. These are recorded via fortnightly inspection reports which are completed by LLDC and TLG on on-site "walk-arounds". A "thin client model" operates here, meaning that the contractor effectively both monitors and delivers the service on a day-to-day level based on an output-based (rather than an input-based) model. In the words of LLDC interviewee (1):

> "With an input specification, which is the old traditional contract, the client would actually write down every single description how they would maintain the park—they would specify how many (grass) cuts a year it would be. You know, what fertiliser, how far you would aerate the ground, you would specify everything. …". With an output specification, "how the contractor delivers the contract technically is down to them. How they actually produce the results and all the day-to-day maintenance operations is up to them how they do that".

In this way, the contractor polices its own performance, and this is subject to regular checks by the client. There are advantages and disadvantages to adopting the output-based model:

> The…downside to that is the output specifications can be expensive. They're pricing for the unknown quantities so where, in terms of grass cutting, you could get a very wet summer and then you're going to increase your mowing regime so there's more resources going into mowing it… [So] there will be times where…they'll lose out because they have to put more [resources] in.… There is an argument that output specifications are good. There is more responsibility on the contractor with an output specification and less client responsibility. (LLDC Interviewee 2).

The regular evaluation meetings focus on the exceptions reports which record where performance needs improving within the contract as a remedial process. If standards are not met by the next monthly meeting—which can include not achieving a quota for employing staff who are local residents (see next section)—this can result in a financial penalty of 5% of the contract for that given period. However, to date, the penalties have not been incurred mostly due to the good working relationship with the contracting team: any issues arising are generally addressed through discussion and negotiation.

## A Focus on Community Engagement

Despite being in England's most densely populated city, because the park was located on industrial land, there was a very limited existing urban population and no real community interest group such as a Friends/Park User Group in the local area. This is unlike most other parks in England. The bulk of the local community did not live there at the time of writing because the housing has not yet been built. As highlighted earlier, OPL was created by the contractor to help deliver the London Legacy objectives around local engagement, education and conservation, and to "connect people to the park through volunteering, training and employment" (OPL interviewee). LLDC has contractual targets and requirements on volunteering which are embedded in the wider EFM contract (held by ENGIE). OPL has therefore acted as subcontractor to ENGIE since autumn 2013 and delivers the conservation and volunteering opportunities as a single point of contact for the 700+volunteers currently on the books, of whom 400–500 are active. Activities have changed significantly since the Games: from mass events to smaller community-based events. The OPL interviewee outlined how OPL also support the managers in the EFM contract to deliver apprenticeships and the Intermediate Labour Market (ILM) programme. This is where local people who have been out of work for some time and need additional support getting back into work are given a 6-month work contract. If everything goes well after that period, they become permanently employed. OPL is a small organisation and describes itself as working in partnership as they are dependent on the skills of private, public charity sectors and social enterprise partners due to the financial, HR procurement and commercial complexities of employing people. The scale and profile of QEOP mean that volunteering can be formally organised through staff who are paid to conduct and manage community engagement. Elsewhere in England, this is something which might be delivered by a small dedicated team of local authority staff across a city but the funding cuts in many local authority budgets since the 1980s mean that the days are long gone when individual parks in the UK had a park-specific park keeper (Layton-Jones 2016).

## Green Space Administration and Grounds Maintenance Contracts in the Park

The QOEP contract is underpinned by specific London Legacy objectives, including:

- Getting local people into work: 80% of the workforce must reside within the local boroughs
- Investment in skills, training and equipment
- Adhering to the Biodiversity Action Plan
- Adhering to the Park Management Plan for the site which includes natural conservation areas
- Creating a high-quality park user experience.

All the interviewees agreed that the QEOP contract is very large compared to other Park contracts, and would not describe it as cost-effective because the contract is not exclusively about achieving cost efficiencies. Unlike standard green space contracts, the foundation of this contract is the London Legacy and its positive social outcomes, which are based on long term and sustainable urban regeneration of the area. For example, employing at least 80% local workforce on the London Living Wage means "that you are providing opportunities to people locally to be employed and giving opportunities for...apprenticeships". However, "these objectives...are different to most contracts within the UK because of this legacy, we've got those other special commitments to meet. And that, in turn, adds a cost to the contract" (Contractor Interviewee). The contractor was also required to invest horticultural skills, training and apprenticeships, given the importance of the BAP which is often not a principle driver of urban park management plans. The much wider range of landscape types in the park than one would find in an average urban park meant that the contractor has had to invest in a diverse range of maintenance equipment. The long-term nature of the contract means that the contractor is able to spend more resources on equipment and skills without adversely affecting profits which would happen on a shorter-term contract. In this way, the contractor has flexibility to take the lead on how contract objectives are achieved. For example, the higher than anticipated numbers of visitors led to the rapid wearing out of footpaths in the Park. The contractor decided to invest significant capital over one year renewing footpath areas with a resin-bound material, which is stronger than the materials originally used and guaranteed for ten years, resulting in minimal costs for the contractor over the next decade. One of the Contractor Interviewees commented: "we decided to put that investment into that with the view that we don't have to come back to it for 10 years to re-do it. With any sort of landscape, you live and learn".

## The Contract and Contractual Relationship in the Park

The QEOP contract is valued at around £2 million p.a. (IdVerde UK 2016). The original contract price is subject to a "change mechanism". As an LLDC interviewee states: the contract "was actually priced for...years back, when it was...pre-built [and] as the park evolved and changed, this change mechanism, this pricing model, would be used to actually adjust the cost". The same interviewee noted that the most difficult part of the contract had been the transition between when it was originally priced and now when the price differences are more apparent. LLDC describe this as very difficult to reconcile because: firstly, there was no green space asset to price up against at the outset as the contract was written before the park landscape was created, and secondly because of the unforeseen issues and challenges that have significant cost implications (e.g. footpaths discussed earlier). LLDC's procurement team seek out efficiencies where they can in the contract over time, particularly given the need to demonstrate value for public money. As noted earlier, the GLA funds the LLDC and as such is subject to the same austerity measures that local authorities are experiencing throughout England.

The outputs which are outlined in the Management Plan and form the basis of the contract are considered to be relatively flexible for both contractor and client. This is well-demonstrated in a worked example. One output is to maintain colourful and species-rich wildflower meadows, and remove invasive species. A number of KPIs (key performance indicators) aid the monitoring of this output, e.g. to provide wildflower meadows which support a specified number of (e.g. insect) species. These species can be counted as part of the client and contractor annual and monthly monitoring. The flexibility in the partnership is attributed to the contract not being overly prescriptive: it is considered a simple and straightforward contract allowing the contractor to use their horticultural skills, which is not necessarily the norm in other parks. For example, the Contractor can retain wildflower meadows until birds, including goldfinches, have stopped foraging, rather than cutting them by a specific date which is often a feature of standard contracts. As TLG interview states: "we're wholly able to make a decision [about] when that can be cut…[The meadows] will be cut, but let's do it when it's right".

The contract length was also described positively, allowing the contractor to invest in equipment and people. There are contractual commitments to employ high proportions of local people (target 80%; actual 85%) from BME (black and minority ethnic) backgrounds (target 45%; actual 65–70%). At the time of writing, the contractor has a workforce of around 40 people who, given the contract flexibility and clear outcomes required (e.g. specified level of litter clearance), can respond quickly to issues, e.g. litter after a football match at the London Stadium. The general perception of the grounds maintenance contract was overwhelmingly positive from all the interviewees. The contract is described as flexible and the working relationships between client, contractor and subcontractors are "very good", "open", "honest" and "sensible". As one interviewee states:

> If you've got a contractor that really knows their subject, and you've got a client that knows their subject, then I think that's the basis for quite a strong partnership.

There were however some concerns (already alluded to) that the contract was not fully fit for purpose raising challenges in the contract for unanticipated glitches and problems, particularly given the "newness" of the Park. The TLG interviewee states: "there is no history…no timeline that says I remember when in 1990 we had rain in June … every day is new". There are significant challenges associated with the unanticipated large numbers of users. The deterioration of footpath materials has already been discussed; the litterbins originally installed in the Park were too small with inadequate capacity, particularly during high-profile events in the Park. The contractors responded quickly to this problem, replacing them with 1100 litre containers. Client and contractor are developing a new bin strategy to address this ongoing issue over the longer term.

LLDC highlighted that improvements could be made to what was described as a "bespoke" contract. This includes enhanced flexibility for LLDC to be a more instructive client (in terms of broad guidance given to the contractor) which LLDC felt would be more beneficial, and making the contract less about prescriptive requirements. It was highlighted that output specifications can be more expensive particularly where a more intensive response might be needed. For LLDC, these issues would be reconciled through the contract renewal process (which would also necessitate a renegotiation of the price of the contract). For the contractor, there were challenges in delivering the experience that Park users want, calling on a range of skills required, not all of them horticultural in nature. For example, the issue of litter is an ongoing one and cleanliness is crucial to maintaining the quality of the Park and the Park experience. To achieve this, the Park must be free of litter by 10 a.m. every morning but achieving that is not a good use of horticulturally-trained staff time. This mismatch between basic grounds maintenance being delivered by highly trained horticulture staff is raised elsewhere in research (Dempsey et al. 2016) and practice (Heritage Lottery Fund 2016).

## Reflections on the Park Contract: Implications for Partnerships in Parks Management

The interviewees we talked to all agreed that managing the QEOP landscape is unlike any other contract they had encountered, largely because the Park is a brand new and changing landscape with many unknowns still to be discovered. The resulting bespoke contract is considered to be a good one, given that it was created before parts of the current and future landscape even existed, and involves strong working relationships between the client, contractor and subcontractors. The length of the contract (at least 15 years) is very positively received as it allows the contractor to invest in skills and equipment to deliver the contract. Having this long-term contract makes achieving the London Legacy objectives which are central to this contract feasible. A standard 5-year parks management contract, on the other hand, would mean that investing in equipment, skills and training is significantly less financially viable. And while the Legacy objectives do not make for a cheap contract in financial terms, they are currently contributing social and ecological benefits of the park to for the wider (human and non-human) community.

While there were different perceptions of how well the contract supports the needs of both client and contractor, all interviewees demonstrated sustained motivation to work together to continuously improve the Park, the working relationships and the Park user experience. Taking an output- rather than an input-based contract approach, as well as the "thin client" model where the contractor polices its own performance and reports to the client, has proved to contribute to a successful approach. The "decentralized" responsibilities of the contractor are further supported by the long-term nature of the contract because it allows the contractor to decide which skills and equipment should be invested in to deliver the contract.

The Park contract highlights the importance of ecological habitats in their management activities, underpinned by the Management Plan and BAP. This brings considerable scope for the contractors to call on horticultural skills and training. However, the underlying focus on litter clearance and general cleanliness in the park does lead to frustration. It was felt that highly trained horticultural staff were spending too much of their time clearing litter. However, to provide a park that is safe, clean and accessible requires the basic grounds maintenance. This is a challenge facing many parks which in the UK has led many parks departments to abandon horticultural skills-based activities to provide the cheaper and more easily delivered grounds maintenance (Dempsey et al. 2016). One does wonder if the rapid response to litter clearance might actually exacerbate the problem, as users know that they can drop litter in the Park which will be picked up by the Contractor. In this way, the penalty for anti-social behaviour is taken away from the park user, passing responsibility for the underlying attitudinal problem to the Contractor who may not necessarily have the requisite skills to deal with it.

The Park management involves OPL, a third sector partner, which reflects an ongoing policy focus shifting responsibility for public sector services to non-public sector stakeholders (Dempsey et al. 2016), also demonstrated in the questionnaire results from English local authorities (reported in Chapter 5). The lack of community group associated with the Park is unique. It is not clear if a Friends Group might develop in QEOP as residents tend to form Friends Groups in England around a collective concern for their local park, e.g. if it is not being maintained to an acceptable standard. Based on current performance, this may not become an issue in QEOP given it is such a high-profile and well-financed park. In light of the significant presence of the Park, future studies could explore the contribution of the Park to what "neighbourhood" means to new residents, their sense of place attachment, and to what extent that manifests itself in community-oriented activities, such as volunteering in the park.

The powers that LLDC has—e.g. autonomous planning authority and primary landowner—are very particular to the Olympic legacy, and go beyond the parks management tasks that are focused on in this chapter. But it does challenge the way that public land is managed and who is accountable for managing parks and green spaces. In light of the austerity measures which continue to apply to English local authorities and their budgets, and the policy shift towards bringing the community and voluntary sector into parks management, how significant will the move away from the public sector delivering parks management become? As Smith (2014: 322) points out, the "new reality of park management" is one where public sector park funding reduces and commercial revenue is expected to make up the shortfall. In this new reality, could the partnership-based contract model in QEOP be adapted to other parks across the country? Recent manifestations of this "new reality" point to the need for governance adaptation in England's parks and green spaces.

For example, Knowsley Council (Merseyside) is selling off seventeen of its parks to 'put £40m from the sale of land into a charitable trust which will run the borough's parks [and]… protect the remainder of its parks from government funding cuts "forever"' (BBC News 2018). Newcastle City Council's response to the 91% fall in their parks budget has been to establish a Charitable Parks Trust. By providing significant funding to the Charitable Parks Trust over the first 10 years of its operation, the Council transfers responsibility for the parks to a non-governmental body which will be able to "establish new income streams not available to the Council" (Newcastle City Council 2017), and e.g. ring-fencing funds which Councils are not easily able to do for non-statutory services. This may lead to changes in parks management beyond the well-established contractor-client relationship in the UK, to perhaps transferring full responsibility away from the public sector client. This raises questions around who will be accountable for England's parks in the future and to what extent they are, and should be, able to provide for "the public good" in the democratic fashion that the public sector historically has.

This chapter has outlined some of the challenges facing one contract-based partnership in park management, and the perceived benefits of working together. The partnership was described as transparent, open, flexible and based on a long-term relationship. Providing a sense of autonomy and meaningful decision-making for the Contractor in the Park was found to contribute to the good working relationship. We therefore conclude that having resources to invest in the workforce, as well as time to develop informal and formal shared working practices around monitoring and evaluation can contribute effectively to achieving the goal of providing a high-quality park user experience. While the length of time and the outcomes-based approach appear to be conducive to a successful contract, ongoing monitoring of the management of the Park is required to examine if this is the case over the very long term. And while this case study clearly sets out the significant time and resources required, it also demonstrates how taking a long-term approach to the funding of parks management is not only feasible but could be indicative of a shift towards less involvement of the public sector, and more involvement of community and voluntary sectors to manage English parks in the future.

## References


BBC News. (2018). *Knowsley Council Parks Sale Plan to Go Ahead After Vote*, online article. Available at http://www.bbc.co.uk/news/uk-england-merseyside-42627492. Accessed 12 January 2018.

Dempsey, N., Burton, M., & Duncan, R. (2016). Evaluating the Effectiveness of a Cross-Sector Partnership for Green Space Management: The Case of Southey Owlerton, Sheffield, UK. *Urban Forestry and Urban Greening, 15*, 155–164.

Heritage Lottery Fund. (2016). *State of UK Public Parks 2016*. London: HLF.

IdVerde UK. (2016). *Queen Elizabeth Olympic Park*. Available at http://www.idverde.co.uk/portfolio/queen-elizabeth-olympic-park/.

Jessel, E. (2018, June 5). Olympicopolis Mark II: Reworked Plans for East London Cultural Hub Revealed. *Architects Journal*, https://www.architectsjournal.co.uk/news/olympicopolis-mark-ii-reworked-plans-for-east-london-cultural-hubrevealed/10031732.article.

Land Management Services (LMS) and London Legacy Development Corporation (LLDC). (2014). *Queen Elizabeth Olympic Park: Park Management Plan 2014 to 2019*. London: London Legacy Development Corporation.

Landscape Institute. (2012). *The Olympic Park: A Landscape Legacy*, film produced by Room60. https://www.youtube.com/watch?v=p9sEccTHlMk.

Landscape Institute. (2015). *LI Awards*. https://www.landscapeinstitute.org/awards/2015-li-awards/. Accessed 12 January 2018.

Layton-Jones, K. (2016). *Uncertain Prospects: Public Parks in the New Age of Austerity*. London: The Gardens Trust.

London Legacy Development Corporation. (2012). *Your Sustainability Guide to Queen Elizabeth Olympic Park 2030*. London: London Legacy Development Corporation.

London Legacy Development Corporation. (2015a). *Overview of the Park*. Internal document (material provided by LLDC).

London Legacy Development Corporation. (2015b). *Corporate Performance Jul–Sep 2015 Q2 2015/16*. London: London Legacy Development Corporation.

London Legacy Development Corporation. (2016a). *Queen Elizabeth Olympic Park and the Surrounding Area Five Year Strategy: 2015–2020 Updated October 2016: Appendix 1*. Available at https://www.london.gov.uk/moderngovlldc/documents/s57393/Item%2012a%20-%20PUBLIC%20-%20LLDC%20Strategy.pdf. Accessed 12 January 2018.

London Legacy Development Corporation. (2016b). *Queen Elizabeth Olympic Park*. Available at http://www.queenelizabetholympicpark.co.uk/. Accessed 12 January 2018.

London Legacy Development Corporation. (2017). *Cultural and Education District*. http://www.queenelizabetholympicpark.co.uk/the-park/attractions/cultural-and-education-district. Accessed 12 January 2018.

Naish, C., & Mason, S. (2014). London 2012 Legacy: Transformation of the Olympic Park. *Civil Engineering, 167*(CE6), 26–32.

Newcastle City Council. (2017). *The Future of Newcastle's Parks Decided*, online article. Available at https://www.newcastle.gov.uk/news/future-newcastles-parks-decided. Accessed 12 January 2018.

Nicholls, A. (2014). London 2012 Legacy: Olympic Park Waterways. *Civil Engineering, 167*(CE6), 40–45.

Roe, M., & Mell, I. C. (2013). Negotiating Value and Priorities: Evaluating the Demands of Green Infrastructure Development. *Journal of Environmental Planning and Management, 56*(5), 650–673.

Smith, A. (2014). From Green Park to Theme Park? Evolving Legacy Visions for London's Olympic Park. *Arq: Architectural Research Quarterly, 18*(4), 315–323.

Williamson, K. S. (2003). *Growing with Green Infrastructure*. Doylestown, PA: Heritage Conservancy.

CHAPTER 12

# Experiences with Public–Private Partnerships in Sweden: Balancing Collaboration and Competition

*Anders Kristoffersson, Andrej Christian Lindholst, Bengt Persson and Thomas Barfoed Randrup*

## Introduction

In this chapter, we present a longitudinal case study of implementation and change of a partnership-style approach to contracting out park maintenance in Täby Municipality, Sweden. The case provides

A. Kristoffersson (✉) · B. Persson · T. B. Randrup
Department of Landscape Architecture, Planning and Management,
Swedish University of Agricultural Sciences, Alnarp, Sweden
e-mail: anders.kristoffersson@slu.se

B. Persson
e-mail: bengt.persson@slu.se

T. B. Randrup
e-mail: thomas.randrup@slu.se

A. C. Lindholst
Department of Politics and Society, Aalborg University, Aalborg, Denmark
e-mail: acl@dps.aau.dk

 
A. C. Lindholst and M. B. Hansen (eds.),
*Marketization in Local Government*,
https://doi.org/10.1007/978-3-030-32478-0_12

unique and informative experiences of implementing a ground-breaking, novel approach to contract management and public–private collaboration within the municipal park and road sectors in Sweden and in a wider Scandinavian context. A range of approaches to contracting out are employed in the park sector, but the Täby case represents an infrequently used approach characterised by formal features such as joint planning and regular inter-organisational collaboration in a single long-term contract for all municipal park and road services, based on visions, strategies and development objectives. Services are specified on the basis of the intended purpose and functionality of areas, with little use of detailed prescriptive specifications on maintenance methods and standards. The Täby case also represents a long history of contracting out dating back to the 1980s. The partnership approach was first implemented through a single all-encompassing contract in the period 2004–2016 and later developed into a set of three contracts in 2016. The developments and experiences had to overcome challenges in balancing and re-balancing complementary requirements for nurturing collaboration and competition at the same time.

Earlier research describes the general features of partnership approaches (Lindholst and Bogetoft 2011) and their potential merits (Dempsey and Burton 2012), but there is a lack of research on experiences with partnership approaches in the context of municipal park management. Moreover, despite the reported advantages of the partnership approach, it is relatively unlikely that municipalities would adopt more elaborate contracting approaches with the park and road sectors. Compared with other municipal services, park and road services are considered relatively well-suited to standard contracting out approaches (see Chapter 4). Against this backdrop, we studied the case of contracting out in Täby Municipality in order to explore in greater detail the reasons for using partnership approaches and the practical outcomes, and thus gauge their potential for park services.

The remainder of this chapter is structured as follows: First, we provide an introduction to Täby Municipality and the park administration organisation. Next, we summarise the municipality's experiences with managing a partnership contract for provision of park maintenance. We then examine development of the latest contract, based on former experiences, followed by an analysis of differences between the original and revised contracts and the intentions behind the changes. Finally, we present some conclusions on strategic development of the contracts. The empirical material used in the case study consisted of various data collected since 2006. Data collection started in 2006 with group interviews with the park and nature management team in Täby Municipality in 2006 and operations managers from the private contractor. The second round of data collection was carried out in 2014 and included four telephone interviews per organisation with staff on different levels, e.g. the head of the technical department in Täby Municipality, the head of division at the private contractor and operations managers in both organisations. The focus in these interviews was on how the formal documents were used. The third round of interviews took place in 2016 with the municipal park and nature management team in Täby Municipality and sought to capture how the revised contract was developed and how it would be implemented. This group interview took place only two months after the revised contract came into force, which meant that many routines were not yet established. Thus the views expressed on the new contract reflected the expectations of the practitioners involved, rather than their practical experiences. We also reviewed formal tender documents from the 2004 and 2016 contracts and official documents, e.g. park policies, green development plans and general information about the municipality (downloaded from www.taby.se), and obtained official statistics on municipal election results collected at www.val.se.

## Täby Municipality

Täby Municipality is located in the outer area of Stockholm County and forms part of the larger and more densely populated metropolitan area of Stockholm. In 2016 Täby had around 64,000 residents (21st most populous of the 290 Swedish municipalities), concentrated within two main built-up areas. Geographically, Täby covers only about 66 km$^2$ (281st largest of the 290 Swedish municipalities), of which 5.4 km$^2$ are occupied by water. The municipality has relatively large recreational 'green' areas, made up of wilderness, nature areas, forests and waters. Public parks, playgrounds, outdoor sports facilities and similar types of recreational green spaces are located in and around the built-up areas and occupy around 1 km$^2$ of all land in the municipality.

Through its geographical location, Täby Municipality offers its residents proximity to the Stockholm metropolitan area and recreational outdoor opportunities 'on their doorstep'. The Stockholm metropolitan area is characterised by strong economic growth and a steady increase in population. The population in Täby has also increased in the past 20 years and is predicted to reach around 80,000 by 2010 (approximately 25% increase from the 2016 population). This expected demographic change will require extensive planning and development. Several large development projects are already underway within Täby Municipality in terms of developing new transport infrastructure, commercial and housing areas and urban green spaces and recreational opportunities. Urban development is deliberatively focused in and around already urbanised areas in the municipality, in order to preserve large and interconnected green areas and ensure sustainable development of urban areas.

Politically, over the years the city council (61 members) has been dominated by the two main right-wing parties in Sweden: 'Moderaterna' and 'Liberalerna', which hold 24 and 16 seats, respectively, in the city council in the current mandate period (2014–2018). Economically, the municipality is relatively well-off, with a good tax base and a balanced economy in good shape. Täby is regarded as one of the flagship municipalities of the Moderaterna party in Sweden, due to its political ambition to contract out many municipal services to private contractors. The average income and education level of Täby citizens are higher than the national averages for Sweden.

Management of green areas is administratively embedded in a long tradition of green planning in Täby and in a planning tradition within the greater Stockholm area to develop new urban infrastructure along several interconnected green wedges (Regionplanekontoret 2010). The history of green planning in Täby dates back to at least 1947, when the first formal green planning documents were drafted, and centres around the importance of large and accessible green spaces offering recreational, biological and historical values within an increasingly densified urban structure. Green planning to this end has developed and has been supported in a series of formal planning documents and in administrative practices in Täby, including a 'Green Plan for Täby Municipality' (Täby Kommun 2007). The plan is viewed within Täby parks unit as a key 'political-strategic' document. The Green Plan defines an overall vision and objectives for the role and development of green spaces in Täby Municipality. Overall, the plan states that 'one half' of Täby should be green space. The vision defines four themes: 'access', 'service & quality', 'management' and 'physical planning'. The plan reflects the fact that, on average, in Swedish municipalities with over 30,000 inhabitants about 50% of the land area is usually categorised as green infrastructure (SCB 2010).

Administrative responsibilities for park and nature areas in Täby Municipality lie with a 'Park and Nature' unit within the technical department. In 2016, the unit had six employees with responsibilities for planning, design and maintenance of all green spaces in Täby municipality, including public parks and nature areas. Nearly all activities relating to park and nature maintenance are contracted out to private firms. The Park and Nature unit is responsible for managing contracts with private providers and for minor in-house maintenance operations.

## Contracting Out in Täby Municipality

### *The Original Contract (2004–2016)*

Täby Municipality has contracted out most park and road maintenance work at least since the mid-1980s. By the mid-1990s, however, the general standard of maintenance of green space services was found to have become unacceptably low. The importance and benefits of green space services were acknowledged by the city council at that time and additional resources were allocated for service improvement.

In June 2004, Täby Municipality implemented an encompassing collaborative approach to contracting out, based on what it called 'The Täby concept' (see Box 12.1). The concept was implemented after public procurement in 2003 of a strongly revised maintenance contract encompassing all park and road maintenance services in the municipality. The two service areas in the contract were envisioned to be managed simultaneously by the parks and roads units within the municipality's technical department.

Two key features in the new contract were a focus on functionality and development of green spaces and a long-term partnership approach. The new contract also bundled virtually all park and road maintenance in Täby Municipality into a single contract for the period 2004–2014, including an option for a two-year extension, giving a total contract period of up to 12 years.

Procurement was organised as an open call to interested bidders, which had to pre-qualify to submit full bids. A total of three contractors pre-qualified and submitted full bids. The main ambition was to find the most economically beneficial contract for the municipality based on an evaluation model including five value factors (maximum points within brackets); partnership model (4), operation plan (3), organisation (3), competence (4) and quality and environmental management (2). A maximum of 16 value points (equal to percentages) was used to adjust the tender price from each bidder in relation to the lowest bidder. The major Swedish contractor NCC, which has an operational basis in all the Scandinavian countries, won the contract as it had the lowest bid after adjustment for value factors.

**Box 12.1. The Täby Concept 2004–2014: Key Features**

- Long contract duration (10 years) plus an optional 2 years extension
- Municipality-wide contract (all maintenance operations for parks and roads in the municipality)
- Task descriptions based on visions, visual materials and development objectives
- Standards for horticultural work based on guidelines rather than detailed specifications of performance requirements and work instructions
- Joint planning and collaboration between purchaser and provider
- Open finances
- Park responsibilities bundled with road responsibilities.

*Formal Contract Management*

The contractual approach in the Täby concept was developed locally, with inspiration from 'partnering' principles found in the construction business and in particular developments in the construction sector in Denmark. Partnering principles were introduced in the Danish construction sector in the 1990s and adopted by national road authorities as a concept for maintenance contracts in the road sector in the early 2000s (Vejdirektoratet 2003). In contrast, national authorities in Sweden did not provide any supportive policy guidance or concepts for partnership approaches to contracting at that time. When developing the Täby concept, the municipality did not know whether other Swedish municipalities had adopted similar ideas and regarded its concept as unique within a Swedish context. Since then, other municipalities often refer to Täby as representing a different or 'interesting' approach to contracting out.

Congruent with key principles in partnering, the 2004 contract was based on a 'partnership' approach, prompting the partners to work in an 'honest', 'fair' and 'open spirit'. The partnership approach was supported at the political level in Täby Municipality and was regarded as a 'political demand' by the park unit. The contract included a range of formal management activities at different organisational levels and with different agendas/purposes. When the contract was initiated, the municipality and the contractor held workshops where common objectives were defined for the upcoming partnership. The workshops focused on three overall objectives, 'budget', 'park services' and 'collaboration', as key themes to guide the day-to-day management. There was also a focus on the personal competences required at different levels in the organisation.

For joint management of day-to-day operations, the contract specified monthly meetings between the parks unit in Täby and the contractor's operations management team. The agenda routinely included items relating to overall progress/performance and finances/use of resources. This joint management of day-to-day operations was complemented with quarterly 'site visit' meetings, which took place at a location chosen by the parks unit. Formally, the day-to-day management organisation consisted of a 'district representative' from the parks unit and an operations manager from the contractor, who managed staff in the field. In addition to meetings focusing on day-to-day operations, a development seminar was held annually, where new common goals for the upcoming season were set. At the level of top management, the contract specified bi-annual steering group meetings for assessment of overall status and progress and addressing any issues not resolved at lower levels. However, while the contract involved shared planning and management by the parks units and the contractor, the contractor was not directly involved in planning and meeting activities related to green space users.

*Budget*

When the original contract was introduced, the annual budget for green space maintenance was approximately SEK 4.7 million (490,000 Euros). The contract had fixed unit prices for individual operations, which could be regulated within the total budget. The municipality had to decide on an overall budget level once a year and allocate a fixed payment for the year. Budgets were index-linked annually. In addition to the maintenance budget, the municipality had a separate investment budget which was not included in the contract. The budget in the contract was organised as 'open books' and all information about costs and resource allocation was shared. The contractor had full discretion about methods for achieving functional requirements and service targets, but the prioritisation of resources was made in consultation with the management team at the monthly meetings. The contract also included an incentive scheme. Savings were shared (50/50) if costs were below budget, while the municipality carried the full burden of any costs above budget.

*Service Specification*

National standards for functional descriptions of park maintenance requirements were used as a key source of inspiration for defining and describing maintenance requirements in the Täby concept (Täby tender documents from 2004 and 2016). Not all municipalities in Sweden use an approach based on functional descriptions for defining their maintenance requirements, but it has been well-known within the park sector over the years and is one of the standard procurement systems in Sweden (the so-called AFF system).

The key document in the contract for managing park maintenance was a 'park policy' that defined a range of functional requirements and development targets for park services. The document also contained a range of advice based on technically defined instruction measures in terms of classification of minimum requirements for all types of green space, e.g. 'superior park' ('*finpark*'). Each green space had to correspond with the vision, with maintenance operations being carried out to ensure that green spaces would meet the functional requirements and service targets. This could also include 'development plans' defining how improvements could be made. No performance- and instruction-based measures were used at the level of individual elements, e.g. shrubs, and the service provider was left with full discretion about maintenance methods. The key documents also had a high degree of visual content in terms of photos and illustrations, as key guidance for maintenance operations. A database sharing all information on all green spaces was implemented to support the collaborative approach.

*Performance*

The general perception by the management team interviewees of implementation of the Täby concept was that it was not 'fixed and final', but 'developed' in the course of implementation. The contract and day-to-day collaboration were seen as more than a written agreement, e.g. as 'ongoing' in terms of a 'practice for working together', while the partnership with the provider involved 'give and take'.

The municipal management team leader and the provider's contract manager both reported that they found it challenging to implement the vision, service targets and functional descriptions in day-to-day operations. Both admitted that it was always a question of 'interpretation' and thus a basis for discussions, rather than a clear measurement against pre-defined standards. In practice, common interpretations were developed through site visits, park meetings and continued dialogue.

Implementation of the contract also sometimes involved a mix of prioritisations and changes in ongoing maintenance routines and new (smaller) additional investments funded by the municipality.

Responsibility for overall contract performance was perceived as shared by both parties. If problems with day-to-day performance were identified, they were handled in immediate dialogue and ad hoc joint site visits. Site visits included horticultural discussions, e.g. on whether a particular element was adequately maintained or whether it was in poor condition (e.g. older shrubs). Thus, direct dialogue in the field between the management team and the operations staff was welcomed. The management team also discussed challenges and ideas with the operations staff at an annual workshop for managers and field staff (the '*park träff*'). Topics included e.g. whether older flower beds should be refurbished (defined as a maintenance operation and not an investment in the contract) or simply maintained.

Overall, the management team expressed general satisfaction with the contract and the performance of the contractor. However, various issues emerged in the course of the contract and had to be handled. When the contractor took over maintenance operations, newly planted areas in particular were not maintained as necessary or forgotten, and weed control quickly became an issue. The issue was addressed by the management team and the contractor had to perform more costly weed control operations exceeding the specified payments in the contract. However, no economic penalties were imposed on the contractor and the issue was solved by dialogue. Another challenge was to reach a uniform standard of service across the municipality. The management team was aware that the contractor did not always achieve this, despite its intention to do so. The final level of quality was in general found to depend on the motivation among the field staff carrying out maintenance work in a specific part of the municipality. However, the management team took the view that it was important to acknowledge and work with positive motivation (e.g. personal engagement) rather than embarking on a more adversarial approach.

### *Revised Contract 2016–2021*

After the original contract ended in 2014, Täby Municipality decided to carry on with the functional partnering approach. Overall, Täby Municipality was reported to be satisfied with the outcome of the first

10-year contract, in which only one provider had maintained practically all public green spaces in the municipality. However, experiences at all levels in the organisation were evaluated and included in the decision on how a new contract should be designed.

First, both the management team and the provider found that formal documents were gradually being used less and less, especially among the contractor's field staff. The documents were referred to when the parties had differences of opinion on performance, and in such situations the functional descriptions were often reviewed for guidance on expected performance. The functional descriptions were preferred over the more detailed descriptions prescribing specific frequencies of maintenance and e.g. grass height in centimetres, simply because they allowed all parties at all levels to take on more responsibility and thus to be more engaged, without compromising the overall quality of the maintenance performed.

In 2015, a working group with politicians representing all parties in Täby was established to discuss the overall principles for the new contract. Important political aspects concerned how to increase competition and include more contractors. The discussion was very open-minded regarding new ways of organising the contract and in the beginning the working group even discussed splitting the contract in very small pieces across the municipality, in order to attract small companies.

The process of preparing the new contract lasted one and a half years and included an open hearing with potential contractors. At an early stage, it was agreed to continue using the 2004 contract's award criteria based on the economically most beneficial tender, rather than seeking the lowest price. It was also agreed to continue the partnership approach. However, there was also an ambition to increase competition, attract more bidders than previously and potentially lower contract costs. Based on these considerations and ambitions, the contract length was reduced from 10 to 5 years (but with an option for a three-year extension) and services were organised into four smaller contracts for: (a) streets and green space management, (b) paving, (c) bridges and structures, and (d) removing graffiti.

The new approach resulted in reduced bid prices for all services in comparison with the earlier contract. The total estimated annual budget for the new contract for streets and green space management was within the range 25–35 million SEK (depending on the municipal budget), with an estimated budget for complementary work comprising 15–25 million SEK and adjustment with fixed unit prices.

A new service provider won the main contract for maintenance of streets and parks. The change of service provider meant that existing working relations and the outgoing provider's experience were lost. In addition, almost all key personnel in the management team for Täby's parks unit changed jobs in the same period. This was acknowledged as a possibility for a fresh start, but also as a severe loss of local knowledge and experience built-up during the first contract period.

*Formal Contract Management*

The basic principles of the original contract, such as adherence to a fair and honest spirit and meeting structures, were upheld in the revised contract. Meetings for steering the revised contract were required on two levels (a) the monthly 'construction meeting' and (b) the quarterly 'cooperation meeting'. Weekly meetings were also specified, to discuss specific questions about maintenance operations and daily performance.

A novel component in the revised contract was a change in the incentive scheme to a new model with a yearly sum of 1 million SEK, a limited amount compared with the total annual value of the contract. The incentive scheme was regarded as both innovative and relatively complex by the interviewees, as it consisted of 10 focus areas with 15 different demands (e.g. time and delivery performance, quality and cost). Each of the 15 demands was to be graded on a five-point scale The required performance had to be achieved four times a year, but the incentive level would be set annually. At the time of interview (2016), the managers had not yet decided how to apply the model in detail, but they expressed concern about how to manage all the judgments and evaluations, which would increase the level of control significantly compared with the original contract. An electronic platform for a reporting diary, changes in the contract and similar has been implemented, but is expected to be further extended during the contract period. A yearly conference between the parties was not included in the revised contract.

*Budget*

The same principles were applied in the revised contract regarding open books (accounting), yearly adjustments of the total contract sum due to the municipal budget and annual index-linking. As mentioned, the incentive model was new. In their tenders, contractors had to indicate the economic value of the incentive model in a range between 1 and 3 million SEK and the value they proposed was included in the evaluation of tenders. All contractors indicated 1 million SEK. Another innovative part when calculating the 'comparative sum' was the intention to reward presentation of detailed cost estimations for management. Compared with the original contract, the revised contract had more focus on rewarding intentions to cooperate during the contract.

*Service Specification*

The service specification was based on the same principles for functional descriptions as in the original contract. In comparison with more prescriptive approaches, it was regarded as less demanding and included a better approach for contract monitoring. It was supplemented with a few new functions and updated pictures better representing the different functions in the municipality's different types of green spaces. The database with classifications of the different areas was updated, as was the park policy, including the overall goals and intentions for different parks and recreation areas. In interviews, the management team emphasised that the policy was only a help to understand the intentions (including among green space users) and that only the functional descriptions were part of the formal and binding contract requirements. Despite the effort to improve the functional descriptions, it was emphasised that it would still be important to make adjustment on a day-to-day basis when the parties meet on-site.

*Performance*

There was a start-up meeting with both parties in order to establish a common perception on what cooperation means, the core reason for doing the job (expressed as 'serving the citizens') and how to make the communication work.

Planning and monitoring in the revised contract was similar to that in the original contract, involving much communication on-site on a daily basis between managers from both parties. A new incentive model was added to the revised contract, which included performance measures related to quality, inspections and risk management. Earlier issues with newly planted areas established by sub-contractors and not maintained by the main provider during a critical period were taken into account by adding new categories related to 'under establishment' with a higher price to compensate for any extra resources needed.

## Motives for Change and Expected Effects

The main principles in both contracts were very much the same, but the revised contract incorporated a range of adjustments based on past experiences and new strategic objectives (Table 12.1).

In general, Täby Municipality was satisfied with the original contract, but after 10 + 2 years politicians were eager to increase competition and potentially to engage with new local contractors. After one and a half years of preparations, the municipality ended up with a revised, but in many aspects similar, form of contract. An analysis of potential providers in the local market, including an open hearing with interested contractors, concluded that increased competition could be achieved by splitting the contract into one major (parks and streets) and three smaller contracts (street paving, bridges and structures, graffiti removal). The change resulted in new contractors for all contracts. From the perspective of competition the strategy was successful, as all contracts had more than three qualified bidders and in general prices decreased compared with the original contract.

## Discussion and Conclusions

In Sweden, managerial and organisational reforms of municipal park and road departments were initiated systematically in the 1980s (Dahlin 1987; Hansson 1990). In the course of these reforms, different organisational designs were introduced and tested, including different designs for organising purchaser and provider functions and private sector involvement. At an early stage, the approach mainly involved internal organisational changes with less emphasis on market testing and contracting out to the private sector. Swedish municipalities have always bought a substantial part of their materials and maintenance services from external suppliers, ranging from local farmers to professional private contractors, but market testing and contracting out have only become regular practices at a later reform stage. Nowadays there are two main approaches to private sector involvement: (i) buying in specialist services such as tree care or other complementary services on behalf of an in-house service department and (ii) abolishing in-house service departments and contracting out all services to the private sector. Täby Municipality represents a unique case of the latter approach to private sector involvement.

**Table 12.1** Main characteristics of the original contract (2014) and the revised contract (2016)

| | *Original contract* | *Revised contract* |
|---|---|---|
| Provider selection criteria | Most favourable price based on the bid adjusted for five value factors | Most favourable price based on the bid adjusted for selection points, degree of open operation cost calculations and chosen size of incentive |
| Number of providers | One | Three |
| Contract length | Ten + two years | Five + three years |
| Number of contracts | One contract for operation and maintenance costs including parks, streets and paving | One contract for operation and maintenance costs including parks and streets. Other contracts for paving, bridges and structures and removing graffiti |
| Formal contract | Partnership approach. Formal meetings on two levels, one monthly and one quarterly<br>Specified reports<br>Communication among operations managers on a daily basis<br>Yearly conference | Similar approach but with omission of the annual joint planning conference. No specified reports in the contract |
| Budget | Fixed unit prices, varying budget for maintenance and complements. Separate investment budget outside contract.<br>Incentive split 50/50 if below budget | Similar, but no incentive split. Instead a qualitative incentive scheme of SEK 1 million/year |
| Service specification | Park policy based on strategic descriptions on long-term goals on park level and specification of functional goals on individual element level (shrubs, lawns, etc.) | Similar approach, but updated |
| Perception | The Täby concept is not fixed and final, but under constant development, challenging at times and always requires both parties to 'give and take' | Similar perception, underlined by new providers and new managers |
| Performance | Responsibility perceived as shared. Followed up on daily basis, via formal meetings and the annual park meeting. In general OK, no formal penalty fees paid | Similar, but the incentive scheme is believed to add value to the contract |

*Note* Based on analysis of research interviews and documents

Based on changes between the original and revised contracts, some general conclusions can be drawn. From a Swedish perspective, the original Täby contract was unique in: (i) using partnering as the basic concept, (ii) using an overall strategic park policy as a performance-setting mechanism, (iii) using functional descriptions for specifying performance, and (iv) applying a long contract duration of 10 + 2 years. The overall principles were retained in the revised contract which, despite some changes, must still be regarded as unique in contracting out contemporary green space management in Sweden. The experiences from the original contract resulted in some new initiatives when procurement of the revised contract started. Based on strategic thinking and reflections on the historical perspective, the overall goal to add value to Täby Municipality by delivering an attractive outdoor environment is still crucial. However, overall green space quality was improved during the first contract period, so that issue was not as important for the revised contract. Important concerns were keeping up quality and increasing competition, to which end the contract was split into four parts, the contract period was shortened and a more comprehensive incentive scheme was created.

The original contract model in Täby (the Täby concept) implemented in 2004 relied heavily on partnering principles prevalent in the road sector in Denmark at that time. The contract also adopted the Swedish tradition of visual and functional description of requirements for green space maintenance. As this case study showed, adoption of partnering principles for the contract was initiated and supported at the political level in Täby. The contractor who won the original contract also had operations within construction, road maintenance and public works in both Sweden and Denmark. Overall, the contract model seemed unique in terms of combining ideas found in Denmark with ideas found in Sweden.

The partnership and embedding the contract in a park policy were also part of a larger strategy to make Täby Municipality an attractive place in which to live within the overall metropolitan area in Stockholm. This strategy was supported by allocation of additional municipal investment funds for green space development. The overall strategy, together with the Täby concept, resulted in a significant improvement in green space standards in the municipality from the 1990s until the mid-2000s. The initial intention with the contract was not to achieve cost savings, but to provide an arrangement for service delivery capable of helping to realise the overall municipal strategy in Täby. The contract still involved concerns about overall economic performance in terms of technical and in particular allocative efficiency. Concerns about economic performance were ensured in the initial competitive tendering for the contract (which involved three qualified bidders), continuous prioritisation of resource use within an open contract budget and contractual incentives for seeking efficiency gains in maintenance operations.

However, with the revised contract it was decided at political level to change the ordinary contract duration from 10 to 5 years and to divide the services into one major and three smaller contracts in order to attract more local bids and to serve the local community. Thus, relying on a large single service provider was not perceived as being the optimal solution on local level. This perception may be strictly political, but may also be grounded in inconsistencies and too many challenges between the parties during the first contract period. In order to resolve these problems, a shorter contract period and smaller contracts were chosen.

Another major change was the introduction of the incentive scheme, which is intended to strengthen the engagement of the provider even more in the process of delivering park and road services. However, the significantly increased amount of control routines related to the scheme must be regarded as contradicting the original incentives in the partnering contract and the functional descriptions. Moreover, the amount of resources allocated to such controls may prove to be beyond the scope and benefit of the incentive scheme, while the increased controls may actually establish a new platform for discussions of non-performance, which is also counter-productive to the original incentive of the partnering contract.

The revised contract involved new personnel on both sides (Täby management staff, new contractors). Lack of knowledge transfer between the two contracts created challenges with re-establishing effective collaboration and managerial routines and reaching a common understanding on acceptable performance levels. Experiences from the original contract showed that reaching collaboration and agreement on service standards and performance required active and continued efforts by both parties. Thus the decision to remove the annual planning meetings in the revised contract may prove to be costly in several dimensions.

The Täby case reflects a strategic and collaborative approach to contracting out recurrently called upon in the literature (Dempsey and Burton 2012; Jones 2000). The case illuminates practical experiences with such approaches, but also represents a particular approach to collaboration focusing only on the relationship between purchaser and service provider and excluding any active involvement of users and citizens. Users and citizens were only represented indirectly through the municipality and through more passive approaches such as user surveys and access to reported complaints on the municipal website.

Analysis of the differences between the two contracts also illustrated the relevance of viewing particular contracting arrangements through the lens of different contracting models (Dehoog 1990). In the Täby case, contract design was found to incorporate objectives and design features related to requirements for ensuring service development and long-term functionality of parks and green spaces, and was only partly driven by cost considerations. For example, politicians and managers in Täby Municipality made trade-offs in the procurement processes between objectives related to service development and cost considerations. Furthermore, the case highlights the important role in practice of local knowledge, the relational embeddedness of maintenance operations and intrinsic motivational perspectives, as indicated by earlier research (Lindholst and Bogetoft 2011). The change of staff that came with the revised contract required the municipality and the new main contractor to devote extra resources (e.g. time) to familiarising themselves with service provision in Täby's parks and green spaces and establishing effective management routines within a collaborative arrangement. The original and revised contracts also relied on motivational drivers based on professional expertise and personal engagement, rather than on (threats of) sanctions for non-compliance with pre-defined service standards.

## References


Dahlin, A. (1987). *Grönyteförvaltningens organisation* [Greenspace Management Organization]. Uppsala: Swedish University of Agricultural sciences, Stad & Land, Issue 60 (in Swedish).

Dehoog, R. (1990). Competition, Negotiation, or Cooperation: Three Models for Service Contracting. *Administration and Society, 22*(3), 317–340.

Dempsey, N., & Burton, M. (2012). Defining Place-Keeping: The Long-Term Management of Public Spaces. *Urban Forestry & Urban Greening, 11*(1), 11–20.

Hansson, L. (1990). Grönsektorns organisation – en spekulativ analys av olika utvecklingsinriktningar. Alnarp: Stad & Land nr. 82 (in Swedish).

Jones, R. (2000). Managing the Green Spaces: Problems of Maintaining Quality in a Local Government Service Department. *Managing Service Quality, 10*(1), 19–31.

Lindholst, A. C., & Bogetoft, P. (2011). Managerial Challenges in Public Service Contracting: Lessons in Green-Space Management. *Public Administration, 89*(3), 1036–1062.

Regionplanekontoret. (2010). *Regional utvecklingsplan för Stockholmsregionen, RUFS 2010* (Rapport nr: 2010:5). Stockholm: Stockholms Läns Landsting, Regionplanekontoret (in Swedish).

Vejdirektoratet. (2003). *Partnering ved vejdrift og beplantningspleje - Udbud, partnering og kontrahering*. København: Vejdirektoratet (in Danish).

CHAPTER 13

# When Rust Never Sleeps: Marketization as Continuous Organizational Change

*Andrej Christian Lindholst, Thomas Haase Jensen and Troels Høgfeldt Kjems*

## Introduction

The implementation of contracting out in public service delivery where internal (in-house) provision is displaced by external (private) provision is often portrayed as an outcome from rational and episodic change processes, i.e. make or buy decisions, driven by cost-focused rationales and strategies (Bel et al. 2018). In this portrait, the efficacy of contracting out is typically seen as dependent upon the inherent characteristics of a particular public service and its context, such as the ease of specification and monitoring and the level of available competition (Dehoog 1990).

A. C. Lindholst (✉) · T. H. Jensen · T. H. Kjems
Department of Politics and Society, Aalborg University, Aalborg, Denmark
e-mail: acl@dps.aau.dk

T. H. Jensen
VIVE, the Danish Center for Social Science Research, Copenhagen, Denmark

T. H. Kjems
Epinion, Aarhus, Denmark



A. C. Lindholst and M. B. Hansen (eds.),
*Marketization in Local Government*,
https://doi.org/10.1007/978-3-030-32478-0_13

With inspiration from the organizational change literature (Weick and Quinn 1999), this chapter offers an alternative portrait theorizing the implementation and efficacy of contracting out as a path of dynamic and continuous organizational change driven by relational embeddedness, organizational learning, fluctuating circumstances and shifting strategic objectives. The two portraits are partly complementary and can be viewed as organizational changes of respectively a first and second order. First-order changes refer to the fundamental replacement of an organizational arrangement where operational capacities are located internally (in-house) with an organizational arrangement where operational capacities are located externally (contracting out). Second-order changes refer to the degree organizational arrangements based on externalization of operational capacities are altered and refined over time. In other words, first-order changes involve more radical and disruptive changes in formal and informal organizational structures within a short time span, while second-order changes involve a series of less radical and incremental changes. Continuous second-order changes may, however, over prolonged time spans sum up to substantial changes rivalling those associated with first-order changes such as strategic shifts between outsourcing and insourcing (Warner and Hefetz 2012) and provide an alternative to organizational reform strategies, such as inter-municipal cooperation or mixed delivery (Bel et al. 2018). With this point of departure this chapter contributes to the marketization literature by highlighting the importance of accounting for second-order changes in order to understand the dynamic changes and efficacy of organizational arrangements based on externalization of operational capacities.

The chapter calls upon a longitudinal single case study (Yin 2003) of contracting out park and road services in a Danish mid-sized municipality (Holstebro) renowned within professional networks for being a 'first-mover' in this service context in Denmark. The study's historical context represents a timeline from a point in time where large-scale contracting with the private sector was only starting to emerge as a viable arrangement for service delivery and towards its maturation and widespread use within the municipal park and road sectors in Denmark (Lindholst, Hansen and Petersen 2016). The case study is arranged as a chronological and rich narrative, elucidating changes in the organization of the contracting model in the time period 2000–2017. Following a temporal bracketing strategy (Langley 1999), the changes are decomposed into a series of sequential contracting phases, each delineated by major events such as the choice to contract out and contract renewals. This decomposition enables the examination of how actions in one phase affect subsequent actions and theorization of the processes driving organizational change over time.

Several types of material and data sources were used in the case study, including research interviews with key personnel in the municipality and the private contractor (representing an 'organizational memory' of the period under study), and documents such as procurement and contract material, meeting minutes from city council meetings, press notes and municipal webpages. A rich descriptive case report (available in Danish) was subsequently produced, including sections on context and background, organization, content of formal contracts, contract management and collaboration, and results and experiences (Lindholst et al. 2017). The content of the report was validated by key personnel within the municipality and the private contractor.

The remainder of the chapter is organized in the following parts. *First*, key features of the case study context are presented. *Second*, a chronological narrative provides insights into the key dimensions of change and stability in the organization of service delivery by contract in the focal municipality. *Third*, and finally, key insights on change processes are discussed and summarized.

## Context of the Case Study

### *Marketization of Municipal Park and Road Services in Denmark*

The overall policy approach to marketization in Denmark has roughly been characterized as being more pragmatic rather than ideological, with a greater emphasis on (internal) modernization than (external) marketization (see Chapter 7). In the 1980s, a reform agenda promoting a range of well-known new public management doctrines was introduced and became centre stage in ideological and political disputes and demarcations. In the park sector most services were at that time organized in-house and only a very low level of services was purchased from the private sector (around 10%). In the road sector, however, a widespread use of private purchases (around 40%) already took place for services requiring a substantial level of specialized investments (e.g. asphalt production). In the 1990s, a consensus emerged, and municipalities engaged themselves in experiments with reform doctrines on smaller scales within different service sectors. Road services were among the first services in the 1990s where new standards and practices for competitive tendering had an impact on a larger scale (roughly by replacing informal and restricted use of competition with formalized and more open approaches), while reform doctrines found their way and had their impact in the late 1990s within park services. In the 2000s and onward, more refined standards and models for marketization were further promoted in the municipal sector, including the park and road sector. A stronger policy push including compulsory policy instruments was also introduced in the 2000s and implemented either directly by law or by negotiated agreements between the central and local government level. By the mid-2010s, the share of maintenance budgets spent on private purchases in the municipal road sector reached about 50%, while the share in the municipal park sector reached about 30% (see also Chapter 10).

## *Contracting Out Park and Road Services in Holstebro Municipality*

### *Holstebro Municipality*

The current Holstebro Municipality was established in 2007 as a consequence of a structural reform restructuring the number and service portfolio of municipalities, including a reduction of municipalities from 271 to 98. Holstebro Municipality was established by the merger of the former Holstebro Municipality with two smaller municipalities (Ulfborg-Vemb and Vinderup), which were established in an earlier municipal reform implemented in 1970. By 2016, about 58,000 inhabitants lived in Holstebro Municipality of whom most (about 36,000) lived in Holstebro City. Thus, the number of inhabitants is very close to the national average size for Danish municipalities. Geographically, the municipality is located in a sparsely populated region and outside the main urban centres in Denmark. The municipality covers a total area of around 800 $km^2$, of which most parts are classified as rural zones, including land uses for forestry and agriculture. The transport infrastructure includes an approximately 1100 km long road grid. Common area types in the green infrastructure include roadsides and grass surfaces, municipal-owned parks, forests and city trees and outdoor areas for municipal institutions (e.g. kindergartens and homes for the elderly), playgrounds and sport fields.

Politically, the city council has been led by shifting left- and right-wing mayors. The political administration of the municipality is organized through eight permanent committees made up of members of the city council, while responsibilities for municipal services are organized into four major administrative areas. In the administrative organization, all responsibilities for park and road services are organized within the technical and environmental administration. All park and road responsibilities are further organized in a 'traffic and park' department, which by 2016 had a management team of 16 employees in total. Their responsibilities included implementation of political objectives, planning (e.g. city planning), administration (e.g. law-related issues), management (e.g. monitoring maintenance contracts or setting service levels), budgets and development (e.g. establishment of new infrastructure). The department is finally mainly responsible for competitive tendering and management of maintenance contracts with external service providers (contractors). The municipality has contracted out all park and road maintenance since 2000 and until the present day (2017) with a temporary return to mixed delivery in 2007–2009 as a consequence of the structural reform implemented in 2007.

Table 13.1 provides a chronological overview decomposed into five main phases through which contracting out within park and road services in Holstebro Municipality developed in the period from 2000 to 2017. The time period covers a total of four consecutive contract periods demarcated by four rounds of competitive tendering. The trajectories are detailed further in the following sections.

### *2000–2005: The First Contract*

After years of preparations and planning, Holstebro Municipality decided in 2000 to contract out most of their park and road maintenance services. The final decision to contract out all services was made on the basis of a competitive tender of a single five-year contract with the 'economically most advantageous offer', weighting both price and quality in incoming bids, as the main evaluative criterion. The contract included responsibilities for all park and most road maintenance services except major repair works (contracted out separately in one-year contracts), staff transfer of all operational personnel and the option of buying machinery and renting locations and housing in the municipality. The municipality participated in the tender by submitting a bid for a potential continued in-house production.

**Table 13.1** Trajectories of contracting out park and road services in Holstebro Municipality

| 2000 | 2005 | 2007 | 2010 | 2015 |
|---|---|---|---|---|
| *Event* | | | | |
| Market test including an internal bid resulting in contracting out of all services in one 5-year contract, transfer of all (70) staff and sales of assets. One winning contractor | Re-tender without internal bidding of all services in one 5-year partnering-based contract with strongly revised service specifications. Incumbent contractor wins/continues | Municipal merger and takeover of two in-house organizations. Reintroduction of mixed delivery | Re-tender without internal bidding of all maintenance services in two 5-year partnering-based contracts. Incumbent local contractor and national contractor win the contracts | Re-tender without internal bidding of all services in one 5-year partnering-based contract. Incumbent local contractor wins/continues |
| *Strategic focus* | | | | |
| Competition, maintenance costs, staff management and informal collaboration | Normalizing maintenance operations. Formalizing collaborative processes | Evaluation of alternatives for reorganization | Involvement of local markets, ensuring even service levels across contracts and geographical areas | Incentives, multiple objectives, innovation, collaboration and service development |
| *External assistance* | | | | |
| Extensive use of external consultancy | Some use of external consultancy | – | Limited use of external consultancy | No use of external consultancy |
| *Economic outcome* | | | | |
| An 8% cost reduction in maintenance costs and substantial one-off profits from asset sales | A minor increase in maintenance costs (the 'market price') | – | No change in maintenance costs (the 'market price') | No change in maintenance costs (the 'market price') |

*Note* The table is based on information from municipal documents and research interviews

The decision to contract out was a result of a wish in the city council to benchmark the performance of the in-house organization in an open market test. The market test came on top of a deliberate agenda in the 1990s, aimed at establishing a professional and cost-effective in-house organization, and the decision to contract out was based on pragmatic concerns about cost-efficiency rather than ideological preferences. However, the idea of an open market test was initially promoted by a right-wing majority in the early 1990s. Later the political support for contracting out park and road services found a broad consensus across political parties in the city council. The consensus has been recurrently expressed in statements from later left-wing mayors, such as the city council's obligation to make the 'best uses of the citizens' money' or 'contracting out is not about political orientation or ideology—it is about common sense'.

The preparation of the first tender and the design of the contract and service specification relied heavily on external expertise with the involvement of the state authority for national transport infrastructure and a leading private consultancy. The state authority and the consultancy were at that time representing leading national expertise on road contracts and service specifications for maintenance. Additionally, the municipality considered how competition for the contract could be maximized, how the burdens for subsequent contract administration could be minimized, how operational expertise and local knowledge could be retained if services were contracted out, and which set-up of (a) contract(s) could provide the most cost-efficient organization. The municipality concluded that the best organization of the contract was a single contract including all park and road services and a potential complete transfer of the operational part of the in-house organization.

The winning bid submitted by a local contractor was evaluated to result in an approximately eight per cent reduction in budgeted maintenance costs per year and provided substantial one-off profits from the sale of assets (e.g. machinery). The reduction in maintenance costs was estimated to be around two millions DKK per year. In addition, the one-off profits from the sale were around 6.5 million DKK. However, the total expenditures for consultancy, planning and internal administration of the tender process were estimated to be around 2.9 million DKK.

All staff (a total of 70 employees) were transferred to and integrated in the contractor's organization. The municipality had already established a relatively well-performing and professional organization in the 1990s and took great care to involve and prepare the in-house organization in planning processes. The staff were particularly interested in continuing to work within a single organization keeping all collegial relations intact. This preference was met in the organization of the new contract. Furthermore, the conditions in the winning bid and the identity of the winning contractor were also received positively by staff. As an outcome the staff transfer went smoothly.

Shortly after initiating the new contract, the parties realized that managing maintenance operations was severely challenged by what was regarded as poorly adopted service specifications and incorrect register-based information on areas and elements. Overall, the formal framework provided little guidance for managing maintenance operations and the parties found it necessary to adapt the contract into a workable framework within the contract duration. The challenge partly reflected the overall (early) stage of the development of contract and technical standards in the park and road sector in the 1990s. In particular, the parties found that an extremely detailed system for service specification and pricing used by state authorities in their large-scale maintenance contracts since the 1980s did not make much sense for guiding maintenance operations at the municipal level. The parties found ad hoc solutions within the contract period by engaging in informal collaborative behaviours and partly by relying on former maintenance routines among staff in order to make the contract workable. The parties reported that the relationship was very much about working jointly together in a collaborative spirit, accepting the contract as a 'give and take' and being flexible in particular situations, while keeping an eye on the overall balance in favour for both parties in the longer run.

*2005–2010: The Second Contract*

Experiences from the first contract formed a basis for redesigning the contract framework. A new consultancy was called upon for assistance with the redesign. The new consultancy was chosen due to recent and sector-leading experiences with the design of contracts and service specifications for use in the municipal park and road sectors. The new contract included completely revised service specifications and a so-called 'partnering' agreement. The revised service specification was based on a mix of (less detailed) performance and instruction measures for a range of tasks defined at a higher level than in the former contract (e.g. specifying the job of repairing a certain length of paved surface rather than decomposing the task into a detailed set of subtasks). The partnering agreement provided an open-ended formal framework and process for setting up strategic joint objectives and a collaborative approach to contract management and monitoring. A formalization of a collaborative framework was prioritized after good experiences with informal collaboration with the contractor in the first contract. Inclusion of a formalized collaborative framework in the contract would also signal the intended approach to other potential contractors and ensure a continued focus on collaboration if a new contractor should win the contract. The contract period included a five-year ordinary period and an option for an extension of up to three additional years.

In tight competition with several other contractors, the incumbent contractor won the new contract in an evaluation based on the economically most advantageous offer as the award criterion. The winning bid was evaluated to offer the best organization of the service delivery, but also offered the lowest price. Still, the bid was evaluated to result in a minor increase in maintenance costs. Given the competition, the winning bid was found to provide the 'market price' for services included in the contract. Additional expenditures for consultancy, planning and administration were estimated to be around 750,000 DKK. Although the new service specification as a generally workable system was found to be a significant improvement over the specifications in the first contract, it was still a main challenge for the parties to readjust service specifications to the needs and preferences of particular types of areas and elements and adjust and reclassify information provided in the geographical information systems (GIS) and maps to the actual content of areas (or vice versa). The focus on adjusting and updating service specifications and information on areas and elements was particularly dominant in the first half of the contract's five-year period. Overall, a familiarity and corresponding working routines in compliance with the contract's formal systems were established for managing maintenance operations through the second-contract period. The familiarity and the routines enabled the formal systems to be used more effectively.

*2007: Municipal Merger and New Strategic Options*

The municipality was left with no in-house operational capacity for park and road services whatsoever after contracting out all maintenance responsibilities in 2000. A municipal merger in 2007, however, gave an opportunity to reconsider the overall strategy. The merger included two in-house organizations with operational capacities (a total of 26 employees) that carried out maintenance in the two smaller municipalities of Ulfborg-Vemb and Vinderup, which merged with Holstebro Municipality. Several options were considered, including different strategies for mixed delivery and full internalization with the re-establishment of in-house operational capacity for all maintenance services. Cost calculations indicated that integrating and continuing the two smaller in-house organizations within a mixed-delivery strategy would be relatively expensive and lack opportunities to exploit scale economies from, for example, investments in machinery and buildings. Similarly, it was found costly to establish a new in-house capacity for all road and park services in the new municipality. Politically, it was decided to continue the two in-house organizations on a temporary basis and later include these in the next tender of the main contract.

*2010–2015: The Third Contract*

It was decided to re-tender services when the main contract ended after the normal contract duration without the use of an option for extending the contract with an additional three years. It was prioritized to reorganize services by including the services provided in-house in the two former and now merged municipalities. The administration expected that the advantages of contracting out all maintenance in one contract compared to dividing services into several smaller contracts would include better-scale economies, easier administration, less need for monitoring, preservation of local knowledge and an even service level across the whole municipality. Furthermore, the municipality prioritized a strategy with full outsourcing of all services and no internal bid was submitted. However, the new city council in the merged and politically reoriented Holstebro Municipality raised voices for organizing park and road services through a more diverse set of contracts. In particular it was the politicians from the smaller municipalities in the merger who raised the voices. Arguments sounded in the city council were focused on enabling smaller and locally based businesses to submit bids and possibilities for trying out long-term contracts based on functional descriptions for some parts of the road network. These political voices in the planning stage ran counter to the arguments of the administration that preferred all services to be organized in one single contract. After internal discussions, a compromise between political ideas and administrative preferences was found. The city council decided to split services geographically into a smaller contract for rural zones and a larger contract for urban zones. The contracts also included staff being transferred from the two earlier in-house organizations.

Similarly to the two first tenders, an external consultant, the same as in the previous tender, was involved in the planning and administration of the tender for the new contract. However, the required role was now limited to basic support for writing up and organizing the tender and contract material, juridical advice and the evaluation of incoming bids. The tender was based on the same award criterion as the two former tenders.

The tender resulted in two different contractors winning the contracts. The former local contractor won the urban zone contract while a nationally operating contractor won the rural zone contract. Both contracts included a five-year ordinary period and an option of up to three additional years. The overall effect on cost levels was evaluated to be neutral while the expenditure on consultancy was further reduced and limited to 300,000 DKK.

A key challenge for the two new contracts was to establish an even service level across the geographical borders of the three old municipalities, which were merged in 2007. The challenge in the merged municipality areas where services had been provided in-house was similar to the challenge in the foregoing contracts, with adjusting service specifications and the reclassification of areas in the geographical information system. Furthermore, the administration of the two contracts was found to result in an increased administrative burden compared to the earlier administration of a single contract with one contractor. This lesson was used as an argument for reorganizing services into a single contract anew.

*2015–2020: The Fourth Contract*

A new contract including all municipal park and road services, approximately 800 ha of green space and 800 km of roads in urban and rural zones, was tendered for the years 2015–2020 with an option of a three-year extension. The contract was won anew by the incumbent local contractor. Similarly to earlier tenders the main award criterion was the economically most advantageous offer. The winning bid did not offer the overall lowest price but was evaluated to deliver an overall more advantageous offer in particular terms of an outline for organizing and managing the contract and for handling environmental concerns. The administration further evaluated the winning bid to have no immediate cost effects and as a whole representing the 'market price'.

In contrast to earlier, no external consultancies were involved in the tender for the new contract. The administration came to the realization that they had accumulated the necessary expertise to carry out a full tender process including the readjustment and fine-tuning of service specifications. Legal expertise was provided in the process by the municipal's internal unit for external purchases. The process of preparing and adjusting service specifications was based on a participatory approach where all employees in the management team were involved. This was in contrast to the earlier approach, which mainly took point of departure in deliveries from the external consultancy or reuse of earlier specifications. The approach was slightly time-consuming but improved internal knowledge and understanding of the importance of even small adjustments for service standards and the need to readjust service specifications for various areas and elements. One result was that the internal familiarity with and ownership of the formal documents forming the core of the contractual relationship and contract management were enhanced.

The model for collaboration was further refined and now included five main types of formal coordination activities between the parties located at different organizational levels and held with different frequencies. A revised incentive scheme with a sum (1 million DKK) roughly corresponding to 2–3% of total annual payments for the contract was included. The incentive scheme focused on the provision of an overall satisfactory maintenance service, a well-working collaborative relationship and the achievement of jointly agreed objectives and good performance of social responsibilities.

Within the first months of the new contract the parties found that the earlier re-emerging needs for adjustment of service specifications and reclassification of areas in the information systems did not appear in the new contract. Apparently—and after 15 years of contracting—service specifications and register-based information had reached an adequate level corresponding to the actual state of the municipality's parks and roads and the service preferences in the municipality as managed by the administration.

Beyond the focus on core services, the new contract included several new strategic focal areas. Firstly, the parties engaged in the joint design and development of a new management platform based on a new ICT system, with the purpose of providing an effective platform for reporting and information sharing across key stakeholders to the contract. The ICT system was designed to provide easy and instant access to reporting and information for management and operational staff in the organizations of respectively the municipality and the contractor, and furthermore provide similar access for users and citizens.

Secondly, the contract included a strategy for citizen involvement based on a municipal concept for 'citizenship'. The strategy aimed at involving the contractor in local deliberation and planning processes or projects with citizens alongside city planners and managers from the municipality. For example, some citizen initiatives would require a change of work specified in the maintenance contract with economic consequences. In such cases, involvement of the contractor opens for input to reorganization of work and alternative uses of the economic resources. The strategy also emphasizes contact between the contractor and citizens without the direct involvement of the management team in the municipality.

Social responsibility was a third and recurrent strategic focus theme in the new contract. Earlier contracts had also emphasized social responsibility as part of the contract terms. Across the different contracts, social responsibilities included requirements for education and training and protected jobs for people with reduced employability. For each contract the level of social responsibilities was adjusted according to the length and size of the contract. The municipality did, furthermore, consider the impact on price with the aim of avoiding any too costly requirements. In the new contract, the work with social responsibilities was further supported by the incentive system. The contractor, however, had over the years developed internal activities related to social responsibilities in collaboration with other parts of the municipality (e.g. department for employment services) beyond those required by the formal contract. These activities included, for example, an internal contact centre where the unemployed could receive job training under supervision of a mentor (managers within the contractor's organization). In perspective, these activities were also seen by the contractor as internally beneficial as a source for recruitment of new personnel and a way to develop the mentors' personal and management skills.

## Discussions

### *Development of the Formal Contract*

The narrative shows that the formal contract, including service specification and contract type, were changed over time according to previous experiences and emerging strategic challenges. The core of the contract, the service specification, was deliberately adjusted throughout the whole period under study. Initially, working with a service specification represented a radical break with work routines used in the former in-house organization. The first service specification, based on an imported template with very detailed work descriptions, was found inapt as a tool for organizing contract management and guiding maintenance operations. In consequence, the parties had to rely on (informal) routines and engage in the development of a system for service specification more fit for local purposes. Both external consultancy and internal resources were engaged in developing the service specification. Through the observed time period, the ongoing development shifted away from more radical changes and reliance on external consultancy towards more incremental changes and reliance on internal expertise. The development was also found to make the services specification and areal registrations better adapted to professional preferences of the municipality and to correspond better with the actual state of parks and roads in the municipality.

In the development, the type of contract and in particular the formal framework for contract management, was altered from a standard approach based on centralized and unilateral decision rights allocated to the management team towards a collaborative approach based on a more decentralized and bilateral organization of decision rights. A major shift was initiated from the first to the second contract, but the collaborative approach was developed and extended in all the subsequent contracts. The need for further formalization of a collaborative approach was accentuated with the involvement of a new contractor in the contract for 2010–2015. The accumulated tacit knowledge and taken-for-granted routines were challenged by the involvement of a new contractor unfamiliar with the established collaborative routines and daily interactions.

### *Development in Strategic Focus and Collaboration*

Collaboration between the contracting parties was ongoing throughout all four contracts. Initially, collaboration was organized informally and based on a collaborative spirit. Later, collaboration was supported by an increasingly complex and formalized framework for collaboration specified in contract documents.

The development of a formal collaborative framework supported shifts in the strategic objectives behind the contract. The strategic focus for the parties in the first contract was centred upon the establishment of basic operational routines and making as much sense as possible of the formal framework. Later, the strategic focus in the contract shifted from maintenance operations towards multiple objectives, including development of services and management. The formal criteria for performance evaluation and management were developed from a system based on deduction in payments for non-compliance with prespecified technical and horticultural standards to include a comprehensive incentive scheme rewarding high performance within the three focal areas: maintenance operations (minimizing quality issues), joint development projects and social performance. The strategic objectives in the contract for 2015–2020 also included an additional focus on greater and more direct dialogue between the contractor and citizens/users based on a general municipal concept for citizen involvement.

The economic objectives for contracting were also found to change after the first contract. The point of departure for shifting from in-house provisions to contracting out was the economic benefit in terms of a substantial cost saving. The initial tender had its primary focus on harvesting potential cost gains from a market test (although the economically most advantageous offer was applied as an award criterion). Later, the economic objectives became focused on accountability in terms of ensuring that services were provided at 'market prices'. Cost savings were still an objective but were now handled within the contract period by using the established formal framework for identifying and prioritizing potential cost savings from adjusting maintenance levels. The development of an effective contract management system provided transparency on cost and service levels, which could be used for identifying and prioritizing potential savings. The expertise of the contractor was also involved for these purposes. For example, the municipal management team and the contractor produced 'cost savings catalogues' ('sparekatalog'), which were used as a basis for making decisions on maintenance levels.

### *Change Drivers*

From the case study, the drivers or mechanisms facilitating the observed second-order changes in the contracting model can be argued to be constituted around a mix of factors, including (a) relational embeddedness of the client–contractor relations, (b) organizational learning processes where past experiences are used to shape future choices, (c) a shift in strategic objectives and (d) risks and unforeseen change in circumstances.

The case study highlighted the importance of the characteristics of the client–contractor relations for the development of the approach to contracting out. The recurrently winning contractor was locally based in the Holstebro area and was reported to display a sustained sense of ownership of and pride in delivering maintenance services within the local community. The relational embeddedness in the local community provided a dedication and flexibility going beyond the requirements of day-to-day operations. The relational embeddedness was furthermore sustained by staff transfers, where familiarity and technical know-how with local service requirements and physical areas were established and maintained within the contractor's organization. The embeddedness of the client–contractor relationship also facilitated continuous organizational learning processes under shifting strategic purposes. In the first phases of the contracting out, learning was focused on developing effective work routines and formalized service standards. Later, learning also focused upon development of the formal collaborative framework in the contract and adjustment of service specifications. Finally, fluctuating circumstances for service delivery, such as the municipal merger in 2007, required the client to reconsider how service delivery could be organized most effectively. The need to recurrently tender the contract to the market also required the client to consider the event of a new contractor replacing the incumbent contractor. The formal contract was deliberately developed with this possibility in mind and the positive experiences with a collaborative approach were observed reflected in the incremental development of a more refined and extended formal collaborative model in the contract.

## Summary

The case study reported in this chapter offers a portrait of contracting with the private sector as a path of continuous organizational change. The case study is idiosyncratic in its details but reveals and also illustrates insights of wider interest. In particular, the case study suggests that the organization of contracting models in a longitudinal perspective cannot adequately be captured and understood as an episodic change related to 'make or buy decisions'—a choice based on cost concerns between internalization and externalization of operational capacities—as much of the contracting literature implicitly or explicitly tend to do. The question of how to organize the externalization of operational capacities was ever-present and was deliberately dealt with in an ongoing change process in concordance with internal and external dynamics within the particular context of the case study. In particular, the strategic aims with contracting were observed to shift from cost concerns in the early stage to service development and ongoing improvements of management in later stages. The observed organizational and contractual changes driven by shifting strategic considerations suggest that the optimal organization of the 'buy' option is not given once and for all but shifts overtime—or more metaphorically: when 'rust never sleeps' one has to be imaginative and inventive. Addressing the challenges emerging from this fundamental condition allows public clients to reap a fuller set of benefits—and avoid the tendency to 'go rusty' (Bel and Costas 2006)—from the involvement of private contractors in service delivery.

## References

Bel, G., & Costas, A. (2006) Do Public Sector Reforms Get Rusty? Local Privatization in Spain. *Journal of Policy Reform, 9*(1), 1–24.

Bel, G., Hebdon, R., & Warner, M. (2018). Beyond Privatisation and Cost Savings: Alternatives for Local Government Reform. *Local Government Studies, 44*(2), 173–182.

Dehoog, R. (1990). Competition, Negotiation, or Cooperation: Three Models for Service Contracting. *Administration and Society, 22*(3), 317–340.

Langley, A. (1999). Strategies for Theorizing from Process Data. *Academy of Management Review, 24*(4), 691–710.

Lindholst, A. C., Hansen, M. B., & Petersen, O. H. (2016). Marketization Trajectories in the Danish Road and Park Sectors: A Story of Incremental Institutional Change. *International Journal of Public Sector Management, 29*(5), 457–473.

Lindholst, A. C., Jensen, T. H., & Kjems, T. H. (2017). *Fem danske casestudier: En undersøgelse af udlicitering af park- og vejdrift i fem danske kommuner.* Aalborg: Aalborg University (in Danish).

Warner, M. E., & Hefetz, A. (2012). Insourcing and Outsourcing. *Journal of the American Planning Association, 78*(3), 313–327.

Weick, K. E., & Quinn, R. E. (1999). Organizational Change and Development. *Annual Review of Psychology, 50*(1), 361–386.

Yin, R. K. (2003). *Case Study Research: Design and Methods* (3rd ed.). London: Sage.

CHAPTER 14

# Municipal Enterprise as a Pretext for Marketization of Park Services: Insights from Oslo

*Ingjerd Solfjeld and Merethe Dotterud Leiren*

## Introduction

With the aim to acquire a deeper understanding of how and why municipalities organize local technical services the way they do, we provide insights into the development of marketization of park services in one large Norwegian municipality. Within local park and local road maintenance, most Norwegian municipalities have organized their maintenance service as a 'mixed model' (see Chapter 8). This means that only a few municipalities are one-tracked, i.e. either carry out all such tasks in-house (i.e. the public authorities provide the services themselves) or contract out all service provision to private entrepreneurs. It is far more common

I. Solfjeld (✉)
Faculty of Landscape and Society, Norwegian University of Life Sciences, Ås, Norway
e-mail: ingjerd.solfjeld@nmbu.no

M. D. Leiren
CICERO—Center for International Climate Research, Oslo, Norway
e-mail: merethe.leiren@cicero.oslo.no

 
A. C. Lindholst and M. B. Hansen (eds.),
*Marketization in Local Government*,
https://doi.org/10.1007/978-3-030-32478-0_14

to do both: provide some services in-house, while contracting out other services. Leiren et al. (2016) find that a key reason why Norwegian municipalities contract out parts of their park and road services to private entrepreneurs is that municipalities lack the capacity (staff or equipment or both) to perform specific services themselves. It is therefore of interest here to study the largest municipality in Norway, Oslo. Because of its size (666,759 inhabitants in January 2017), Oslo is expected to have the capacity to carry out its services in-house. However, after years of internal reorganizations aimed at reforming in-house provision, Oslo ended up contracting out all maintenance services in the park and road sectors to private entrepreneurs.

Focusing on the park sector, we explore the development of marketization in Oslo. It is a story that includes a move from in-house service provision to the establishment of a municipal enterprise, which failed and was closed down after only four years of operation; the city council eventually decided to contract out all park services to private entrepreneurs. We ask the questions: What factors have driven the process of marketization of park maintenance services? Why did Oslo create a municipal enterprise in the marketization process, and why did it fail?

The questions are interesting because the conclusions found in the literature concerning why municipalities choose different organizational forms are ambiguous. Literature about government restructuring (e.g. Bel et al. 2018; Hefetz and Warner 2004; Warner and Hebdon 2001) understands public government as active and pragmatic in its search for efficient production strategies. Local governments search for the best way to organize themselves so as to be able to serve political and public interests as well as manage the market. In Norway, there are several examples of municipalities that have tried or wanted to establish municipal enterprises but that have failed in doing so—for example, the failure to reintegrate local public transport services (Leiren 2015), or cases where semi-autonomous agencies at the local level have been reintegrated into the public administration (Krogstad and Leiren 2016). There is also the example of Stavanger Municipality (see Chapter 8), which established a municipal enterprise in the park sector. However, Voorn et al. (2017) finds a lack of contributions addressing the development that some municipalities choose in the marketization process, by establishing municipal enterprises that are expected to compete in the market alongside private entrepreneurs. Municipally owned provider units can be structured in several ways. Municipal enterprises as they have been practised in Norway are semi-autonomous organizations owned by the municipality and staffed by municipal employees The organization has its own board of directors and a managing director. The municipal enterprise is governed by the City Council and deficits are covered by the municipality. As a single case study, the organization of the park sector in Oslo can provide useful insights into the issues related to such organizational models in a large municipality. Based on document studies (municipal policy papers, annual reports, minutes of political meetings and reports from consultants) as well as on interviews with three civil servants in the park and road management in Oslo and phone contact with one former member of the enterprise's board of directors, we describe how operation and maintenance of park services in Oslo have evolved over the past twenty years.

The chapter proceeds as follows; The first section provides an overview of marketization, including the tale of the rise and fall of the municipal enterprise. In the next section, we point to key factors explaining these organizational changes. We then present our conclusion.

## Marketization of Park Services in Oslo

Oslo Municipality has traditionally ensured its park services in-house via different internal departments with responsibilities for different services. The first clear sign of marketization in this sector occurred when the politicians decided, in 2004, to establish a municipal enterprise. In the course of the next few years, the municipality gradually put all park maintenance tasks out to tender. During the first year, the municipal enterprise was awarded "contracts" from the municipality without any competition; thereafter, competition operated on market terms. However, four years later the politicians decided to abolish the municipal enterprise and instead merged the park responsibilities with road responsibilities and contracted out all park and road services to external entrepreneurs. In this section, we describe this motley development, including the perceptions, thoughts and information about why the development occurred the way it did.

### *Introduction of Competitive Tendering*

In the late 1990s, Oslo municipality elaborated a set of main principles and guidelines for competitive tendering "City council announcement"

1/1998. The politicians wanted all service production evaluated for competitive tendering. Technical tasks such as park operations were considered suitable for contracting out. However, the implementation of marketization of park services was not straightforward. In 1997, the Parks and Sports Department administered the parks management, operation and maintenance as an in-house provider. In 1999, The City Council decided to merge the Parks and Sports Department with the Forests and Recreations Department in a new unit named Agency for Outdoor Recreation and Nature Management. At the same time, local politicians suggested that management and operation be split into two separate units (Oslo City Council, case 426/1999). In June 2000, an organizational model comprising two units: one responsible for purchasing (the Division of Management) and one for provision (the Division of Operations and Maintenance) was created (see Table 14.1).

In 2003, the City Government decided to gradually implement marketization over a period of three years. An important first step was to turn the Division of Operations and Maintenance into a municipal enterprise, Park and Sports Oslo KF[1] (City government case 265/03) which would operate on market terms. This entity consisted of parks operation and maintenance, nursery production (of plants) and a construction unit. The unions questioned the reorganization. The trade union ("*Norsk kommuneforbund*" and its local unit), were against separating the management into one unit within the municipal administration and operation and maintenance into a municipal enterprise. One union (*Nafo*) was concerned about the repeating organizational reforms. Another union (*NITO*) agreed that a municipal enterprise was a good organizational solution, given the political goals and guiding principles. However, they questioned if there were economic and professional gains connected to the rise of a municipal enterprise and the marketization processes. The unions were comforted by the fact that the legal positions of the employees would not change, as it meant that the existing employees' rights would remain. The fact that the employees would remain "municipal employees' reduced the trade unions" opposition against the reorganization, but made the new organization dependent on a constant flow

[1] KF means that this is a municipal enterprise. KFs offer no limited liability for the owner but have a separate board of directors and a managing director. If more than one municipality and/or county is owner, the company is an intermunicipal company.

**Table 14.1** The organizational development of parks management, operation and maintenance in Oslo

| *Year* | *Event* |
|---|---|
| 1997 | The Parks and Sports Department performed the management, operations and maintenance in-house |
| 1999 | The Agency for Outdoor Recreation and Nature Management arose ("*Friluftsetaten*"), which was a merger of the Parks and Sports Department and the Forests and Recreations Department |
| 2002 | The Agency for Outdoor Recreation and Nature Management developed a "purchaser-provider" model with two divisions:<br>(1) the Division of Management including: the Sports Department, the Forests and Recreations Department, the Parks Department; and<br>(2) the Division of Operations and Maintenance<br>Oslo's public baths were separated into a separate entity with its own budget |
| 2004 | The Division of Operations and Maintenance created a municipal enterprise named Oslo Green and Sports, later renamed Park and Sports Oslo KF, operational as of 1 January 2005<br>The operation of the "Maritime" area and "The Forest" remained in-house |
| 2004 | The "reform of the City districts" resulted in a transfer of 250 parks and outdoor facilities from the Agency for Outdoor Recreation and Nature Management to the City Districts of Oslo<br>The City Districts of Oslo were responsible for their own parks management<br>The Agency for Outdoor Recreation and Nature Management continued to manage six districts<br>Management of city trees remained in the Agency for Outdoor Recreation and Nature Management |
| 2005 | Park and Sports Oslo KF started to operate in the market with the municipality as the most important customer |
| 2006 | The Agency for Outdoor Recreation and Nature Management (Division of Management) initiated competitive tendering in two areas for the first time. Park and Sports Oslo KF won both tenders |
| 2007 | The Agency for Outdoor Recreation and Nature Management (Division of Management) signed four new contracts. Park and Sports Oslo KF got two contracts and a private entrepreneur got two contracts |
| January 2009 | Park and Sport Oslo KF was decommissioned and a "Department under liquidation" (Oslo Park and Sports) arose |
| 2011 | "Oslo Park and Sports" the administration's operation and maintenance unit was dissolved and the employees transferred to other municipal units |
| May 2011 | The management and procurer unit Department of Environment and Transport arose as a merger between the Roads Department, the Agency for Outdoor Recreation and Nature Management, the Traffic Department the Culture and Sports Department and the Energy Department |

of tasks, including the tasks handed over without competition, and this made the municipal enterprise vulnerable to a full market entrance.

As a next step, the Agency for Outdoor Recreation and Nature Management put the first park maintenance contract out for tender in 2005, and by 2006 all park maintenance was subject to competitive bidding. A consultancy was hired to evaluate the initial period of tendering, including the years 2006, 2007 and 2008. They evaluated the period as compared to 2005 (Lyche et al. 2010). The consultant concluded that it had been economically beneficial for the municipality to expose the services to competitive tendering, despite having to increase the management staff by three persons. However, the consultant questioned the level of pricing in this early stage of contracting out. "The cost-reduction could be an effect of efficiency processes in front of introducing the tending process or it could be an effect of the first years tactical prizing" (Lyche et al. 2010).

### *The Rise of the Municipal Enterprise*

The municipal enterprise Park and Sports Oslo KF started up operations 1 January 2005. During the period 2005–2008, the enterprise took part in Oslo's bidding processes in the parks sector. The municipal enterprise was expected to "build, operate and maintain sports and recreation spaces, parks, and outdoors facilities" and to operate in line with business principles and to generate a surplus based on its operations (i.e. without being favoured by the owner). Its primary service areas were Oslo and the surrounding county, Akershus. The most important customer during the first year of operation was Oslo municipality (e.g. the Agency for Outdoor Recreation and Nature Management, the Culture and Sports Department and the Districts of Oslo). The municipal enterprise got several assignments with the municipality without having to compete to get the contracts. This possibility of favouring its own municipal enterprise was agreed upon under the understanding that the enterprise "knows the tasks and areas" and would therefore be able to "step in" on short notice. In fact, the main income (over 60%) in 2005 came from internal agreements with the municipality (without competition). The ratio in customers during 2005 were: 72% Oslo municipality, 14% private, 7% other municipalities, and 7% governmental customers (*Kommunerevisjonen* 2006).

In 2006, Oslo Municipality was still Park and Sports Oslo KF's most important customer; however, the municipal enterprise won an increasing share of its contracts in competition with private actors. All park responsibilities managed by the Agency for Outdoor Recreation and Nature Management by the end of 2006 were subject to competitive tendering. The municipal enterprise won the first two tenders (starting in 2006) and *two of the four* subsequent tenders (starting in 2007) that the Agency put out for tender. The loss of two tenders meant that the municipal enterprise lost tasks it traditionally had performed (i.e. prior to the establishment of the municipal enterprise).

In 2007, Park and Sports Oslo KF got a new board of directors after the old board refused to take responsibility for the annual account in 2006. The enterprise launched measures to increase income as well as reduce costs. By this time, approximately 70% of the municipal enterprise's income came from contracts won via competitive tendering.

Oslo established the municipal enterprise at a time when the market situation was prosperous, in 2004. However, issues related to economy emerged already after one year and negative economic results followed year after year. After four years, the politicians decided to discontinue the municipal enterprise.

### *The Downfall of the Municipal Enterprise*

During the four years of operation,Park and Sports Oslo KF delivered services to Oslo Municipality (about 85%) and private actors (about 15%) (The City government case 1092.1/09). However, its economic results were poor, as the operating profit during the four years in operation was negative.

- 2005: negative result under the Accounting Act: −5 million NOK;
- 2006: negative result under the Accounting Act: −7.7 million NOK;
- 2007: real negative operation profit: −14 million NOK;
- 2008: real negative operation profit: −25 million NOK.

The negative results meant that the municipal enterprise was dependent on considerable transfers of money from the owner (the City of Oslo) to be able to continue.

The City Council found that the municipal enterprise did not achieve the necessary economic performance for being able to compete—and therefore to survive in a market situation. When preparing the budget for 2009, the City Council decided to dissolve Park and Sports Oslo KF by 2009 (The City government case 1092.1/09). This would affect 172 employees. As a result of this decision, the City Council established a provider unit internally in its administration and named it Park and Sports Oslo. This unit was expected to manage and deliver already signed contracts during the decommissioning period—this was not intended to be a permanent solution.

### *The Situation After the Decommissioning of the Municipal Enterprise*

After the municipal enterprise was decommissioned, the Park and Sports Oslo, an in-house "organization under liquidation", continued to operate until 2011 when the employees were relocated in new jobs within the municipality. The same year, the Agency for Outdoor Recreation and Nature Management merged with the Roads Department, the Traffic Department, the Sports Department and the Energy Department into the Department of Environment and Transport. This new department eventually contracted out the majority of parks and all roads maintenance to private entrepreneurs.

The decision to discontinue the internal provider unit Park and Sports Oslo in 2011 was not clear-cut, as it was still believed that there would be advantages in keeping responsibility for operations and maintenance in public hands. The organization's knowledge as an operator and, hence, market competence, as well as experience with providing local public services represented important competence for being able to professionally evaluate calls for tender, bids and contracts. *Flexibility* was emphasized as another advantage of keeping a "provider"—division in-house (i.e. the operation and maintenance within the municipality). The municipality had the opportunity to use their own employees without competition in some areas and perform some tasks. Another advantage that was mentioned in the discussions was the possibility to "flex" the workforce during the seasons. Staff from different units could help each other out in certain situations, for example, large arrangements or unexpected situations caused by weather. This could be done without any administrative difficulties.

The political left wing argued in favour of stopping the process of abolishing the internal provider unit Park and Sports Oslo, because of concerns about the loss of competence and issues related to employees' working conditions. The Socialist Left party suggested that in-house production be continued, a proposal supported by Labour and the Red Party. However, the right-wing majority turned down this suggestion (The City council case 11/00177-6).

Considerable criticism, especially from former employees, was levelled at the municipality for the decision to dissolve the municipal provider unit, Park and Sports Oslo and outsource all operations in the parks and outdoor facilities (Fantoft 2014). The national interest organization for parks (*Bad, park og idrett*) (Bugge 2011), scholars in the "Green Space Management" sector (Thoren and Bergaust 2011 and the unions (Guldbrandsen 2011) also criticized the decision. The main concerns were the loss of qualified staff and the practice of "lowest price wins the bid" and the consequences this could have for the quality of park maintenance.

## Explaining the Reorganizations of the Park Services

The evidence shows that there are several reasons why Oslo Municipality has reorganized its park services. In this section, we highlight the key factors that explain why Oslo created a municipal enterprise on the way to marketization of the park services and why it failed and was discontinued.

The operation and maintenance of parks is a municipal responsibility. As long as the municipality adheres to laws and regulations, it is free to organize its public services in whatever way it deems best. The local municipalities tend to organize themselves in a pragmatic way (Leiren et al. 2016; Warner and Hebdon 2001). The politicians in Oslo Municipality were inspired by organizational reform trends in Norway (see Chapter 8), and the belief that marketcompetition is the most efficient and cost saving way of delivering services when opting to contract out park services. In 1998, the politicians launched a key document "City Council Announcement" 1/1998, which stated that the municipality *should* take part in competitions and submit bids. This aim is important for understanding why the municipality chose to initiate the processes of dividing the Agency for Outdoor Recreation and Nature Management into a "procurer-provider model" and create two divisions (the Division of Management and the Division of Operations and Maintenance), which forced the organization to go out to the market and make the provider compete for bids. This process led to increased pressure to enhance cost efficiency and promote budget discipline. The City Government's "guiding star" during this period was to the ideal of becoming ever more efficient (i.e. to increase the service quality and get "more value for money"). Politicians expected marketizing to improve service delivery according to prevalent theories, even though contemporary analyses (e.g. Hefetz and Warner 2004; Warner and Hebdon 2001) questioned the outcomes of exaggerated competition. Recent analyses confirm that organizational reforms in park and road services only partly result in improvements (e.g. Lindholst 2017) and that improvements in public service delivery must be looked upon in a more nuanced way as, for example, public opinion and the local labour market are important to the municipalities (Bel et al. 2018).

The establishment of the municipal enterprise was one stage in the politically launched marketization process. The enterprise had considerable (operational) competence, given its extensive experience in providing park services, although as a different organization. The fact that the municipal enterprise had experience with and therefore also knowledge and insights into the municipality as an organization and how political processes work was considered advantageous intellectual capital. The municipal enterprise, with its 172 employees, was also a large organization. The politicians expected that a relatively large organization would be fit to compete with other companies in the market. Therefore, it was expected that a large organization would be better at preventing a "monopoly situation", where only one or very few private entrepreneurs would compete in the initial phase of marketization.

However, because of the enterprise's continuous series of negative economic results, the politicians decided to dissolve the enterprise after only four years, despite a foreseen period of adjustment and calibration. Failure in the initial phase is not uncommon (Voorn et al. 2017) but according to Warner and Hebdon (2001), the adjustment to fiscal reality and moving towards the most beneficial alternatives (economically) are typical for local municipalities. The key rationale behind decommissioning the municipal enterprise was the expectation that private companies would be more innovative and provide "more and better services for the money", because they would be affected by fewer regulations than the municipal organization.

There were also concerns related to whether municipal enterprises and private companies can compete on equal terms. Other sectors in Norway are affected by a rule that restricts the possibilities for in-house enterprises to compete. For example, the European law that regulates public service obligations in the local public transport sector does not allow in-house operators who have acquired their contract via direct award and not competition to compete for contracts in other jurisdictions (Leiren 2015).

Several reasons why the municipal enterprise was unsuccessful can be emphasized. The municipal enterprise Park and Sports Oslo KF faced *capacity challenges.* One informant mentioned that the company tried to fulfil tasks without possessing the capacity to fulfil them; for example, the company intended to carry out line clearance for the electricity cable company Hafslund. This was a demanding task that they were unable to do on time and had to hire a subcontractor to fulfil the contractual obligations (Leiren and Solfjeld 2016). This might also be explained by a drawback embedded disadvantage that the municipal enterprise struggled with, namely a lack of confidence among its employees because of the frequent reorganizations of the park services and failure to give them enough time for the organization to "settle". Key persons left the organization, and the municipal enterprise did not perform in line with political expectations. Capacity and staff qualifications are obviously important criteria for being considered successful (Boyne 2003).

Informants also mention that because the enterprise primarily had permanent employees, it was not always able to get the workers it needed. A more flexible organization would be in a better position to ensure staffing. This is also related to the fact, as mentioned in a "strategic document" from 2008, that the staff was (more than) fully engaged during the growing season. In contrast, during the winter months there was an overcapacity of 50 man-years (110 workers during 4 months). Whereas the company in some periods was unable to deliver on time and was fined for delays, it had too many employees during other periods. One informant mentions that during the last year that the municipal enterprise was operational, the enterprise was fined "daily penalties" amounting to more than one million NOK in total. This money was never paid back to the City, as the City was the owner of the company (Leiren and Solfjeld 2016). Another concern was related to *professionality.* The municipal enterprise operated largely in the same manner as before tendering and was not as efficient as it could have been, thereby struggling to adjust to the new market situation. Employees sometimes found it unnecessary to have to wait through an ordering process and to leave tasks undone in the meantime, rather than simply getting the job done right away. However, the ordering process was necessary because the Division of Management had to make priorities between tasks and requests, as there were several actors and several contracts to manage.

The two main reasons for the *economically* poor result were, the following: firstly, the administration lacked resources and the calculation of contracts came out with a price that won the tender but led to negative results in the accounting. Secondly, there was an issue related to *social aspects*. One challenge the municipal enterprise faced was that some of the staff in the parks service unit had got their job through special agreements, such as work training programmes, which were eventually turned into permanent employment positions. Some of the staff therefore had conditions such as reduced working capacity. Site managers who had to supervise staff in their daily work might experience this as challenging. The Park and Sports Oslo KF was compensated for employees on special terms, i.e. the municipality provided extra support for the KF for having a share of employees, who were less efficient because of special needs (e.g. disabilities, age). However, our informants question whether the compensation that the company received was sufficient.

Moreover, the municipal enterprise faced criticism due to the recurrent economic transfers from the city. Such transfers were considered *anti-competitive* and in conflict with EU law,[2] as they favoured one specific operator.

Having decommissioned the municipal enterprise, Oslo Municipality decided to introduce full-scale contracting out and competitive tendering to external entrepreneurs. The key reason was the expectation that this would make the services more efficient and that this would be an improvement. In the first years of contracting out, one private entrepreneur and the municipally owned Park and Sports Oslo KF were the providers for the municipality. According to an independent consultant, there was no clear difference in the quality of services between the two contracts (Lyche et al. 2010). Beliefs in the economic benefits of marketization that do not entail a decrease in quality prompted the political decision to introduce full-scale contracting out and competitive

[2]Norway belongs to the European Economic Area (EEA), which means that EU law related to the internal market is also transposed into Norwegian law.

tendering to private entrepreneurs. This seems to be a rather simplified view of improvement in the public sector, but it is symptomatic of the time. Norway may appear to be rather reluctant and to lag behind in municipal organization of its park services (see Chapter 8).

## Conclusion

The marketization process in Oslo Municipality was initiated by principles and guidelines of competitive tendering in the document "City council announcement" 1/1998. The municipal enterprise Park and Sports Oslo KF started to operate in 2005 as an internal bidder in the municipality. This was the first large structural change related to marketization of park services in Oslo. The key motivation was to get a more professional park service with competence in the professional market, while at the same time keeping competence in-house. The new municipally owned enterprise, after the initial start-up period when it relied heavily on contracts given to the enterprise without competition, was intended to operate on market terms. However, the economic performance was poor and the enterprise accumulated substantial annual deficits. Reasons for the poor economic performance were not evident, but underestimation of costs and miscalculation were major issues. When unbundling took place, the new procurement agency was assigned new tasks to develop calls for tender. Given lack of judicial competence in developing tendering documents and evaluating bids, this new role proved challenging. Similarly, there was a lack of experience in the municipal enterprise in making bids and ensuring correct calculations (e.g. including administrative costs in the bids). The chief administrator of the enterprise had an exaggerated confidence in in-house competence and in combination with deficient knowledge of the scope of the tasks, the result was daily penalties and additional costs for hiring external entrepreneurs to fulfil obligations. Also, lack of flexibility in terms of staff exchanges, over-capacity issues during winter periods, combined with municipal social responsibilities for the workforce (many employees with reduced working capacities) made it difficult for this new enterprise to compete on par with other market participants. After four years in operation, the politicians decided to dissolve this municipal enterprise and reinforce the entity as an "agency under liquidation". This was the second change, which was initially made based on the negative economic results in the municipal enterprise. However, the municipality still had the responsibilities for the staff and for the remaining ongoing contracts. The staff continued during the next two years with park maintenance until the third reform occurred two years later, in 2011, when the municipality decided to merge the management of local park and road responsibilities into one management and procurement body, the Department of Environment and Transport. All park operations were eventually contracted out to external providers and the remaining staff relocated within the municipality. Building an organization robust enough to compete on market terms had not been successful during a four-year period. The creation of municipally owned enterprises may be looked upon as an expensive detour if the administrative goal is to contract out technical services like park and road services to external entrepreneurs.

## References

Bel, G., Hebdon, R., & Warner, M. (2018). Beyond Privatisation and Cost Savings: Alternatives for Local Government Reform. *Local Government Studies,* Online First, 1–10.

Boyne, G. A. (2003). Sources of Public Service Improvement: A Critical Review and Research Agenda. *Journal of Public Administration Research and Theory, 13*(3), 367–394.

Bugge, H. (2011). *Noen har sovet i timen. Oslodebatt*, Aftenposten aften, 31. May, p. 30. (In Norwegian).

Fantoft, S. (2014). *Privat parkdrift, et trist syn. Konkurranseutsetting.* Temahefte nr. 34, 8–10. Fagbladet. Available at: www.fagbladet.no. Received April 2018. (In Norwegian).

Guldbrandsen, S. (2011). *Park-Oslo anno 2014: Søppelflyt og ødelagte trær.* Fagforbundet. Fagbladet nr. 4, 38. Available at: www.fagbladet.no. Received April 2018. (In Norwegian).

Hefetz, A., & Warner, M. (2004). Privatization and Its Reverse: Explaining the Dynamics of the Government Contracting Process. *Journal of Public Administration Research and Theory, 14*(2), 171–190.

*Kommunerevisjonen.* (2006). Økonomistyring i Friluftsetaten, Kultur- og idrettsetaten og Park- og idrett Oslo. 2006 (8) Oslo Municipality. 55pp. Available at: www.oslo.kommune.no. Received April 2018. (In Norwegian).

Krogstad, J. R., & Leiren, M. D. (2016). Gradual Change Towards Re-Integration. Insights from Local Public Transport in Norway. *Public Policy and Administration, 31*(4), 324–341.

Leiren, M. D. (2015). Re-Integration Failure and Outsourcing Upside: Organisation of Public Transport in Norway. *Local Government Studies, 41*(2), 240–259.

Leiren, M. D., Lindholst, A. C., Solfjeld, I., & Randrup, T. B. (2016). Capability Versus Efficiency: Contracting Out Park and Road Services in Norway. *International Journal of Public Sector Management, 29*(5), 474–487.

Leiren, M. D., & Solfjeld, I. (2016). *Utsetting av locale park og veitjenester til private i stor skala: En norsk case-studie.* TØI-rapporter nr 1521. Institute of Transport Economics Norwegian Centre for Transport Research. (In Norwegian).

Lindholst, A. C. (2017). A Review of the Outcomes from Contracting Out Urban Green Space Maintenance: What We Know, Don't Know and Should Know. *Urban Forestry and Urban Greening, 27*, 50–58.

Lyche, C., Råd, O. G., & Tollefsen, I. W. (2010). *Evaluering av effektene av konkurranseutsetting av friluftsetatens drift av parker og friområder. Del 5.: Resultatevaluering av sentrum, Frognerparken, Indre by og Nordvest/Bygdøy for 2008.* Evaluation Report. Asplan Viak AS. (In Norwegian).

Thoren, A. K. H., & Bergaust, T. E. (2011). *Ofrer grønt miljø. Fagmiljøet i friluftsetaten pulveriseres. Oslodebatt,* Aftenposten aften, 16. February, p. 32. (In Norwegian).

Voorn, B., Van Genugten, M. L., & van Thiel, S. (2017). The Efficiency and Effectiveness of Municipally Owned Corporations: A Systematic Review. *Local Government Studies, 43*(5), 820–841.

Warner, M., & Hebdon, R. (2001). Local Government Restructuring: Privatization and Its Alternatives. *Journal of Policy Analysis and Management, 20*(2), 315–336.

CHAPTER 15

# Lessons from Case Studies: Working with Marketization

*Andrej Christian Lindholst, Nicola Dempsey, Thomas Barfoed Randrup and Ingjerd Solfjeld*

## Introduction

Chapters 11–14 provided four single-case studies—one from each of our four country contexts. The four cases were all selected to illustrate and explore leading national examples of innovative practices involving marketization and private contractors in park and road services at the municipal level. The four case studies also provided a level of richness and contextual detail essential for comprehending the organizational and managerial realities and practicalities

A. C. Lindholst (✉)
Department of Politics and Society, Aalborg University, Aalborg, Denmark
e-mail: acl@dps.aau.dk

N. Dempsey
Department of Landscape Architecture, University of Sheffield, Sheffield, UK
e-mail: n.dempsey@sheffield.ac.uk

T. B. Randrup
Department of Landscape Architecture, Planning and Management, Swedish University of Agricultural Sciences, Alnarp, Sweden
e-mail: thomas.randrup@slu.se



A. C. Lindholst and M. B. Hansen (eds.),
*Marketization in Local Government*,
https://doi.org/10.1007/978-3-030-32478-0_15

of marketization at the municipal level. In particular, the case studies offered insights into how municipalities are working with marketization within the particular national contexts, as outlined earlier in the book.

In this chapter the four case studies are used as starting points for illustrating and discussing more general lessons on (a) organizational learning and changes, (b) the challenge of balancing competition and collaboration, (c) the inherent difficulties in establishing municipal owned corporations/enterprises within competitive environments, (d) the widespread use of 'corporate-like' in-house organizations, and (e) the future scope for developing contracting models within local park and road services. These discussions connect to and address key research themes raised in Part I of this book.

## The Importance of Incremental Change

It is worth highlighting some of the differences in the distinct but overlapping bodies of literature around organizational change and public service delivery. Much of the literature around the organization of public service delivery and contracting out considers organizational change as an episodic choice between a set of alternative organizational forms such as (a) in-house provision, (b) contracting with for-profit (or non-profit) service providers, (c) concurrent contracting (or 'mixed delivery'), or (d) municipal or inter-municipal owned corporations/enterprises and other government providers (e.g. Bel et al. 2007; Hefetz and Warner 2004). In this approach, which is sometimes portrayed as a 'make or buy' (or a 'make and buy') choice, organizational change is mainly understood as shifts between discrete organizational forms or modes of service delivery.

The (vast) literature on organizational change, however, offers a range of complementary perspectives on organizational change and development in the public sector (Kuipers et al. 2014). First of all, the organizational change literature does not confine organizational change to choices between discrete organizational alternatives but includes a broader range of organizational variables open for change, including formal and informal structures and processes. Secondly, change may not be as radical, path-breaking and episodic as those caused by shifts between alternative discrete organizational forms. Organizational change

I. Solfjeld
Faculty of Landscape and Society,
Norwegian University of Life Sciences, Ås, Norway
e-mail: ingjerd.solfjeld@nmbu.no

can be incremental and continuous in its characteristics and guided by attempts to readjust or improve parts of existing structures and processes rather than displacing these with new structures and processes. From a wider perspective, continuous change can be viewed as an inherent and desirable characteristic in any organizational arrangement (Weick and Quinn 1999)—which we here extend to any contractual arrangement.

In Chapter 13, the case study in Holstebro Municipality, Denmark explored the historical development of contracting out from a continuous change perspective. The case study covered the initial shift from in-house to private provision in 2000 and subsequent developments through four contract periods, including three rounds of contract renewals, the latest of which was in 2015. The case study portrayed the development of the contracting model as driven by relational embeddedness, organizational learning, fluctuating circumstances and shifting strategic objectives. One particular finding is that the shift from in-house to external provision did not imply that a final organizational and managerial approach to contracting was settled. Changing circumstances, practical experiences and shifts in strategic objectives required Holstebro Municipality to learn and adapt their contracting model. In this specific case, the adaptations took the shape of a gradual development of a more complex and formalized collaborative contracting approach replacing a conventional contracting model. It was shown that the municipality had to stay innovative in order to avoid contracting failures or misalignment of their contracting model with changing strategic objectives and fluctuating circumstances over the years. In the case study, this was interpreted metaphorically with a reference to a reality where 'rust never sleeps'—an ambiguous metaphor denoting the irreversible tendency for decay and entropy in natural processes combined with a reminder of the need for humans to stay ahead and remain vital by moving forward and being innovative.

The case studies of the reorganization of park and road services in Oslo Municipality, Norway (Chapter 14) and adjustments of the contracting model in Täby Municipality, Sweden (Chapter 12) also illuminated organizational change stories. The case study in Täby Municipality is similar to that of Holstebro in terms of the process of incremental change of the contracting model (by rebalancing competition and collaboration) in the contract renewal. The case study in Oslo municipality, however, observed more radical path-breaking changes through subsequent shifts between discrete alternatives rather than incremental developments of one particular contracting or organizational model.

Nevertheless, learning from experience and an incremental change process, although at a grander scale measured by municipal size, were also key characteristics in the case study in Oslo Municipality, where service delivery was contracted out in response to poor experiences with establishing a municipal owned corporation (also see section below).

From the findings in the Holstebro case study, one could also argue that the development of contracting out at the local level to some degree follows a path resembling a 'lifecycle' or a 'stage' model, where additional layers of skills and managerial dimensions are incorporated and refined within the overall contracting model. In the first stage, we can observe challenges related to learning the fundamentals of managing through a traditional contracting model in terms of a 'transactional' contract framework (information systems, area registrations, service standards, monitoring routines, etc.). These fundamentals are very similar to the capabilities highlighted in Kettl's 'smart buyer' theorem for contract management, pointing out the needs for developing the skills to know what to buy, who to buy from and what has been bought (1993). In the second stage, we can observe challenges related to a more collaboratively and 'transformational' approach (Entwistle and Martin 2005), where delegation of responsibilities, improvement of managerial systems and service development became important. In the third stage, we can observe challenges related to the introduction of a fuller 'relational' or 'responsive' governance approach (Vincent-Jones 2007), focusing on integrating users and citizens more actively into the management of services. In the Holstebro case study, the development of skills indicated that contract management capabilities were developed over time. Learning the skills for managing contracts has recurrently been highlighted in the literature as an important challenge and precondition for successful adoption of marketization and involvement of the private sector (Andrews and Entwistle 2015; Brown and Potoski 2003; Kettl 1993). The Holstebro case study indicates that these skills not only take time to learn but also that the required skills change over time. Put into perspective, harvesting the fuller benefit from marketization may not come at once but comes in smaller portions when and if a municipality learns and refines its art of contract management.

## Strengthening Competition for Collaboration

Parts of the literature on public sector reform have long highlighted a shift away from the reliance on markets and competition towards greater reliance on networks and collaboration in public service delivery.

This shift encompasses new forms of involving the private sector in public service delivery based on ideas of partnerships and collaboration within long-term relationships (Donahue and Zeckhauser 2011; Entwistle and Martin 2005; Hodge et al. 2012; Sullivan and Skelcher 2002; Walker and Davis 1999). In a reform perspective (Chapter 2), the shift reflects the general move away from core new public management (NPM) models for organizing service delivery towards post-NPM models (Christensen and Lægreid 2007).

Theoretically speaking, competition and collaboration can be seen as two different and partly opposing mechanisms for coordinating and organizing public service delivery (Dehoog 1990; Walker and Davis 1999). Emphasis on competition as a coordination mechanism in public service delivery typically involves the establishment and use of markets where services to be delivered (at a later stage) are bought and sold based on price, quality and quantities. There is then the subsequent organization of service delivery with arm-length relations between seller(s) and buyer(s) based on clear rights and obligations engraved in legally binding contracts—typically on a short-term basis in order to enhance and invoke the competition mechanism more frequently. In contrast, emphasis on collaboration typically involves long-term and trust-based relations, open and direct dialogue about services to be produced and flexibility towards the roles of those involved and the services to be provided. However, an examination of the case study in Täby Municipality shows that competition was not found to be replaced by collaboration. Rather, a focus on *ex ante* competition was retained while a collaborative logic was replacing the conventional contractual logic inherited from the core-NPM models. One may formulate the reorganization of competition, contracts and collaboration as a (metaphorical) difference between a situation where potential providers are 'competing for contracts' and a situation where providers are 'competing for collaboration'. Ideally, *ex ante* competition in the former case is focused on choosing the provider who will deliver a number of predefined services specified by the purchaser at the lowest possible cost (i.e. the conventional contracting model), while *ex ante* competition in the latter case is (also) focused upon choosing a competent partner who can successfully be engaged in a more open-ended collaboration (or partnership) for delivering services. The case study in Täby Municipality detailed the experiences with the use of a partnership-based approach to contracting and compared the development of the overall approach to contracting across two contract periods. The first contract reviewed in the case study was in place for 12 years between 2004 and 2016. In the contract renewal in 2016 the former contract was split into three smaller contracts, each implemented with expected contract durations of up to eight years. In the case study, it was found that the municipality in the planning phase of the contract renewal decided to reorganize its approach with the intent of obtaining more *ex ante* competition while reorganizing the role of *ex post* collaboration. The case study illustrated the balance between competition and collaboration as dynamic, and driven by changing strategic objectives set by the purchasing authority. The former collaborative approach where the provision of all park and road services was bundled in one 10-year partnership-based contract (plus an option for extension) was evaluated as a limiting factor for exploiting the benefits of competition more fully. In consequence, the municipality concluded that it would be beneficial to reorganize the collaborative approach within three smaller contracts in order to enhance *ex ante* competition.

At first glance, this case challenges the promises highlighted in the literature of the benefits of collaborative approaches and the pitfalls of competitive approaches (e.g. Entwistle and Martin 2005). However, at a second glance, we find that a dominant strategic emphasis on a collaborative approach utilized in the first partnership contract in Täby Municipality was complemented—not substituted—by a stronger strategic focus on *ex ante* competition in the second set of partnership-based contracts. In other words, Täby Municipality sought to strike other levels of competition and collaboration in its contractual approach. Briefly summarized, the case illuminates a situation where the strategy aimed to rebalance *ex ante* competition and *ex post* collaboration by strengthening *competition* for collaboration within a set of smaller contracts. A wider lesson from the case study in Täby Municipality is that collaboration and competition is shown to work in conjunction as two complementary mechanisms rather than as two opposing—or alternative—mechanisms.

## Stories of Failing Municipal Enterprises/Corporations

The literature on the organization of public service delivery has highlighted the prospects of municipal and inter-municipal corporations/enterprises as an alternative to contracting out or in-house provision (Voorn et al. 2017). Municipal owned corporations (MOCs) are autonomous organizations owned by municipalities used to produce or deliver local public services outside the local bureaucracy. Their use and importance have been steadily growing since the beginning of the twenty-first century across different countries and different municipal service sectors (Wollmann and Marcou 2010). MOCs are alternatives to conventional bureaucratic forms of in-house provision within the public sector and are likely to perform differently due to greater legal and managerial autonomy and more indirect relations to local politics. There is some indication that MOCs are relatively more efficient than bureaucratic modes of service provision for some services (utilities), but also that MOCs have a relatively high initial failure rate. Overall, however, relatively little is known about the comparative performance of MOCs in the public sector (Voorn et al. 2017).

The case study from Oslo Municipality, Norway brings a detailed story of the rise and downfall of a municipal enterprise. The case study traced efforts with the internal restructuring of park and road services from the early 2000s and until the early 2010s, when all services were finally decided to be contracted out. Oslo Municipality is the Norwegian capital and with more than 650,000 inhabitants the largest city in the country. Due to the municipality's size and available operational capacity, one would expect the municipality to provide the service in-house, as the majority of Norwegian Municipalities state that the reason for contracting out is to address capacity challenges rather than seek cost reductions and/or benchmark prices in the marketplace (Leiren et al. 2016). The politicians in Oslo Municipality, however, decided to proceed towards marketization and thereby break away from the dominant logic for contracting out among Norwegian municipalities. It was expected that the establishment of a municipal enterprise—embodying promises of both flexibility (through a municipal ownership structure) and efficiency (through scale economies)—would be an important factor in the new and emerging market of entrepreneurs capable of handling large maintenance contracts. The enterprise was expected to work on market conditions and make bids for contracts from the municipality and other private and governmental customers. However, after only four years of operation the municipal enterprise was liquidated due to a failing financial performance. Based on this experience, the municipalities took steps towards contracting out all services to private providers.

The story of the downfall of the municipality enterprise in Oslo echoes similar experiences from the 2000s in Denmark (briefly reported in Chapter 7). In the early 2000s, the two municipalities of Vejle and

Odense (representing about 235,000 inhabitants) established a jointly owned enterprise—Infraservice I/S—with the purpose of providing park and road services to clients within their own municipalities (e.g. the park and road administrations) as well as to other clients such as neighbouring municipalities and private customers. Similarly to the enterprise in Oslo Municipality, the inter-municipal enterprise had to operate on market-like conditions and win their contracts in open competition with private bidders. However, the inter-municipal enterprise was liquidated after only a few years of operation due to continued poor financial performance. The cases point to some of the potential problems and issues arising with the set-up of municipal and inter-municipal enterprises when these are supposed to work in an environment with direct and market-based competition from private enterprises. In both cases, the enterprises were supposed to reorganize themselves and their service delivery from operating within a non-competitive environment towards operating and surviving under market-like terms within competitive environments. However, the business set-up was based on the existing staff, their labour agreements and an expectation that the contracts offered by the owner (the municipality) would be won. In both cases the enterprises failed to meet the challenge and were liquidated. Financial losses had to be covered by the municipalities involved. Services were subsequently contracted out in Oslo and Odense Municipalities while Vejle Municipality chose to restore operational capacity within an in-house arrangement.

Put into perspective, while confirming the risk for initial failure, these cases moderate some of the hopes raised in the public administration literature for MOCs as efficient alternatives for organizing service delivery within the public sector (Voorn et al. 2017). It is worth noting that both cases took place in settings where the MOCs, in principle, should be able to exploit increasing returns from scale economics. The two cases discussed above bring evidence of MOCs being economically less viable and ineffective alternatives for organizing public service delivery when market competition is available and these are fully exposed to market competition. Thus, our findings are in line with Vining and Weimar's (1990) argument regarding the decreasing economic viability in terms of technical and allocative efficiency of government production in situations with increasing degrees of market contestability for supply and/or ownership. One salient discussion, however, is whether the performance of MOCs and in-house providers should be judged and contested by 'narrow' economic criteria only (see also discussions in Lindholst 2017).

Provision by the public sector may, for example, provide flexibility, versatility and robustness into a service delivery system This also raises arguments supporting the importance of ensuring broader social values such as responsibilities of the public sector to provide oportunities for vocational training and promote an 'inclusive work life' in the community. In support of the importance of evaluating performance against a broader set of criteria, the INOPS survey data presented for Denmark (Chapter 7) and Norway (Chapter 8) indicated that in-house providers tend to be used with a wider range of purposes in mind than private providers.

Returning to the argument of the limited economic viability of MOCs and/or high risk of initial failures, the INOPS survey data showed that fully MOCs are used only to a very limited extent for organizing the provision of park and road services across Scandinavia (no data are available for England). The use of MOCs was most prevalent in Sweden where around 12% of the municipalities in the survey reported using MOCs to deliver park and road services to some degree. Interestingly, the analysis of data on the organization of in-house provision in Chapter 10 (see Table 10.5) found that in-house providers to varying degrees have been organized as 'corporate-like' entities, which depart in their organizational features from the classical public 'bureau' receiving a lump-sum budget for producing a service without contestability. Top-management and annual budget statements for park and road services, for example, were found to be arranged separately (but still internally) from the remaining municipal organization in a majority of the municipalities in Scandinavia and partly in England. 'Business planning' was also found to dominate the management and organization of in-house provisions. Thus, similarly to the discussions on the development of contracting models as a result of organizational learning, it can be said that corporatization is not only a discrete organizational choice (i.e. the formal establishment of a municipal owned corporation) but also a continuum made up of multiple dimensions where corporate-like structures are incorporated (see also discussions in Chapter 10). On reflection, the organization and functioning of contemporary in-house provision cannot be understood adequately with reference to the theoretical modelling of these as classic bureaucratic organizations riddled with assumed inefficiencies and malaises of public ownership, as typically found in arguments based on public choice thinking (Boyne 1998). This finding recalls Vining and Weimar's (1990) argument that the introduction of market contestability for supply and/or ownership will spur organizational arrangements and behaviours in government production to become more like those of the (sometimes 'idealized') competitive and privately owned firm.

## The Future Scope for Contracting

What is the future scope for marketization and contracting with the private sector within hard services such as park and road services? One well-established suggestion from the literature is that the contracting model for park and road services—similar to many other 'hard' services—should resemble the characteristics of conventional contracting models (Davis and Walker 1998; Dehoog 1990). Among the key assumptions underpinning the conventional contracting model are beliefs that most hard services provided by the municipal level can be sensibly specified *ex ante* within a legally binding contract, competition for contracts can be raised, and subsequent contract management should be focused on monitoring and contract compliance. The idea is that alignment of the provision of hard services with a conventional contracting model (rather than in-house or more complex contracting alternatives) should be able to ensure cost-effective service delivery with no or only few detrimental effects.

Our analysis of cost effects from contracting out in Scandinavia in Chapter 9 only brought limited evidence in support of the assumptions in the conventional contracting model. While strong support was found for Denmark, only weaker or no support was found for Sweden and Norway, respectively. These findings support discussions in the literature which have emphasized the need to address broader contracting failures with conventional and cost-focused contracting approaches applied within park management (Dempsey et al. 2014; Jones 2000; Lindholst 2008). Neither does the suggestion that conventional contracting models should be the optimal way for contracting within hard services, fits neatly with the variations found implemented in the formal contract designs for park and road services (see Chapter 10) or the contracting models and developments highlighted by the case studies (Chapters 11–14). A further exploration of the INOPS survey data on the importance of various contract features indicates that features related to more complex or alternative contract designs are relatively important for a notable number of municipalities within each country. Table 15.1 provides an analysis of the

**Table 15.1** Percentile distribution of importance of selected contract features among municipalities in England and Scandinavia

| *Contract feature*[a] | *Percentile distributions* | | | | | | | | | | | |
|---|---|---|---|---|---|---|---|---|---|---|---|---|
| | *England* | | | *Sweden* | | | *Denmark* | | | *Norway* | | |
| | $P_{25}$ | $P_{50}$ | $P_{75}$ | $P_{25}$ | $P_{50}$ | $P_{75}$ | $P_{25}$ | $P_{50}$ | $P_{75}$ | $P_{25}$ | $P_{50}$ | $P_{75}$ |
| Service specification based on functionality and purpose | 5.5 | 8.0 | 10.0 | 3.5 | 6.0 | 9.0 | 4.0 | 7.0 | 9.0 | 4.0 | 7.0 | 9.0 |
| Formal collaboration and joint planning | 5.0 | 8.0 | 10.0 | 2.0 | 4.0 | 7.0 | 4.75 | 6.5 | 9.0 | 2.0 | 5.0 | 7.0 |
| Contractor's involvement/ contact with users | 3.0 | 6.0 | 8.0 | 0.75 | 2.0 | 5.0 | 0.5 | 2.0 | 5.0 | 0.0 | 2.0 | 5.0 |
| Economic incentives for investment, improvements and optimization | 0.0 | 2.0 | 5.0 | 0.0 | 1.0 | 4.0 | 1.0 | 2.0 | 5.0 | 0.0 | 2.0 | 4.25 |
| Competence requirements | 5.0 | 7.0 | 9.0 | 6.0 | 8.0 | 9.0 | 5.0 | 7.0 | 8.0 | 5.0 | 7.0 | 9.0 |

*Source* INOPS survey data

[a]All items measured on a scale from 0 to 10 (0 = 'not at all', 10 = 'very high degree') on the question 'On a scale from 0 to 10, please indicate to what degree the following content is a central part of your department's arrangements with private contractors'

relative importance of formal contract features associated with more complex or alternative contract designs in each of the studied four countries based on the distribution of scores across percentiles. For example, from the table it is found that for England the municipalities in the 50th and 75th percentiles for 'service specification based on functionality and purpose' scored the importance of this feature with 8 or higher. At the other end, the 25th percentile scored the importance lower than 5. Recalling that the scale ranges from 0 indicating 'no or a very low importance' to 10 indicating 'a very high importance', it is clear that this feature is of substantial importance for a majority of the municipalities in England. Overall, the findings from Table 15.1 indicate that contract features associated with more complex contract designs are relatively important for a minority, but still a considerable number of municipalities in each country. For all countries, almost all features in Table 15.1 are scored with 5 or higher for the 75th percentiles. Reflecting the earlier analysis based on mean scores for various contract features (see Chapter 10) it is further confirmed that more complex contracts involving several relatively more important contract features are used by municipalities in England compared to municipalities in the three Scandinavian countries. The most striking difference between England and all three Scandinavian countries is the importance of 'contractor's involvement/contact with users'. This feature appears far more important for far more municipalities in England compared to Scandinavia.

The scope and extent of alternatives to the traditional contracting model were perhaps most vividly illuminated in the case study of Queen Elizabeth Olympic Park, London, England (Chapter 11). This study of an atypical case explored the structure of and experience with a partnership approach between an independent single-purpose local authority and a private contractor for managing and maintaining a newly constructed and high-profile park located in the metropolitan area of London. The case study detailed how responsibilities for maintenance operations, management of volunteers and the achievement of strategic objectives, including social, economic and service objectives, to a large part can be delegated and shared with a private contractor. The espoused contracting model deliberately incorporated the idea that a contract needs to be open, flexible and adaptive in order to be effective and responsive towards service needs. This is contrary to the conventional contracting model where adaptions are predominantly decided either unilaterally by one side of the contract, i.e. by the authority/purchaser, or organized as part of recurrent contract renewals. Overall, key features of the approach to contracting in Queen Elizabeth Olympic Park has more resemblance with models for collaborative governance than conventional models for contracting (Donahue and Zeckhauser 2011; Entwistle and Martin 2005).

The case study of Queen Elizabeth Olympic Park also illustrated practical details of key differences between a high-profile collaborative contracting approach in England and the more conventional approaches found in the three Scandinavian countries. The comparison of the survey data for formal contract features in the four countries (Table 15.1) showed that municipalities in England emphasize formal aspects related to specification of functionality and purpose, contractor's involvement with users/citizens and collaboration/joint planning to a greater extent than municipalities in the three Scandinavian countries. The differences in terms of average scores were more accentuated for Sweden and Norway than for Denmark. The case study of Queen Elizabeth Olympic Park helps us comprehend some of the special characteristics of the approach to organizing private sector involvement in England in comparison with Scandinavia. Even the case study of partnership contracting in Täby Municipality, Sweden (Chapter 12), highlighting this as a unique and progressive approach to contracting out within the context of Scandinavia, does not reveal the same extent or level of collaborative practices as did the case study of Queen Elizabeth Olympic Park. The same can be said when making comparisons with the case study of the development towards a collaborative contracting model in Holstebro Municipality, Denmark. Put into perspective, our findings on the approaches to private sector involvement in England, drawing upon logics of collaborative governance rather than conventional contracting models, provide park and road management elsewhere with a beacon for future developments of service delivery systems in shifts from core-NPM towards post-NPM models for marketization- and governance-based models involving a broader range of options (e.g. Buijs et al. 2018). From this perspective, the case study illuminates the future scope for how to contract with the private sector.

However, the future in a post-NPM era is open and other scenarios and different management models are emerging to potentially define other paths. Recent austerity policies in the UK have resulted in a range of examples of different ways of organizing, if not shedding, local services away from local authority responsibility. Interestingly, these examples are not necessarily new, but date back to before the Second World War, when the welfare state was established. However, they are still novel given their low levels of implementation. They range from local community groups raising their own revenue funds through subscriptions for individual parks (e.g. Heeley People's Park in Sheffield, England), developing partnerships and philanthropy between businesses and local community groups (e.g. Darlington, England) to city-scale transfers of parks management. This last example is being implemented in Newcastle-upon-Tyne, England where the city council has cut funding for parks by 90% and is now transferring the management of the city's parks to a charitable trust. This is contingent on the provision of an endowment, the value of which is currently not known but has been estimated to cost the council £9.5m as revenue contribution to cover the first 10 years of operation (Abbott 2017).

Knowsley Council in Merseyside, England had planned a similar transfer of public space management, funded by the sale of up to 10% of its green spaces for development, but backed down in June 2018 in the face of public opposition after a change in political leadership.[1] This perception of the council 'selling off the family silver' was felt in Sheffield when the possibility of transferring the city's parks to an independent trust was rejected outright.

As parks provision is not a statutory duty in the UK, significant capital funding for parks has been provided by the National Lottery (through the sale of lottery tickets and weekly draws). The National Lottery raises an average £30m per week, with over £950m spent on parks since 1996 (HLF 2018), which we estimate at about 3% of the overall revenue. Their most recent investment in parks is the £10m fund 'Future Parks Accelerator (FPA)', which is aimed at helping the parks services of up to eight local authorities to become self-sufficient (Cosgrove 2018). It is interesting to note that the underlying 'inspiration for the FPA came out of a conference which launched a toolkit for establishing a parks trust as well as Newcastle City Council's move to create a parks trust' (Cosgrove 2018). This indicates strong support for the parks trust model, which we may see more of in the UK going forward as a model of good practice.

[1] http://knowsleynews.co.uk/parks-not-for-sale/.

## Summary and Perspectives

The discussions of our case studies against theory and survey data in this chapter have highlighted a handful of key insights helpful for understanding the diffusion and evolution of marketization. We summarize these as follows:

*First*, obtaining the requisite skills and familiarity with contracting takes time and involves learning processes within the municipal administration. Skills for proper contract management are likely to be developed and incorporated little by little over time within the municipal administration. The development of contracting out at the local level was argued to follow paths resembling a 'lifecycle' or a 'stage' model, through which the model of contracting is changed through incremental steps. Changing circumstances and new strategic objectives within the context of contracting may also render earlier skills redundant (e.g. dealing with personnel transfers), which will require new skills (e.g. working collaboratively) to be developed within the municipal administration.

*Second*, the discussions touched upon the relationship between competition and collaboration as two major coordination mechanisms in public service delivery (Sullivan and Skelcher 2002). In particular, the discussions highlighted the two mechanisms as complementary rather than substitutes. *Ex ante* competition can be combined with either a conventional contracting approach or an approach that, to various degrees, incorporates a collaborative approach. In the first case, competition is about winning a contract for delivering services ('competing for contracts'), while in the latter competition is about winning an engagement in a collaborative arrangement for service delivery ('competing for collaboration'). The challenge, as shown in the case studies, is to adopt and (re-)balance the level of collaboration within the contractual relationship. In some cases (Holstebro Municipality), this implies a movement towards decentralization and a gradual development of more extensive collaborative models, and in other cases (Täby Municipality) this implies a movement towards recentralization and a reduction in the level of collaboration by strengthening the role of the client vis-à-vis service providers.

*Third*, the discussions touched upon the viability of MOCs, and in particular their viability within contexts where private competition is readily at hand. Our case-based evidence showed that MOCs appear vulnerable and financially unsustainable if they are organized to work in competitive environments, including direct competition from private providers. Interestingly, the INOPS survey data showed that in-house provision to different degrees has been 'internally corporatized' in all four countries (Chapter 10). In comparison, internal corporatization appeared to be substantially more widespread than externalization of service delivery by the creation of MOCs. The Scandinavian countries appeared to be dominated by features of core-NPM models for internal corporatization, while England appeared to be dominated by features of post-NPM models. Put into perspective, our findings and discussions highlight internal corporatization within the municipal bureaucracy as an important organizational variable, which represent a continuum made up of multiple dimensions rather than a discrete either/or choice. This finding adds to discussions on the shifting balance between public and private provision and the attractiveness and effectiveness of different alternatives (Voorn et al. 2017; Wollmann and Marcou 2010).

*Fourth*, our findings and discussions highlight the importance of focusing on the strategic aims of contracting in order to understand the choice and development of models for service delivery. Collaborative approaches to contracting appear, in particular, to be associated with development and a broader range of strategic aims. This finding also questions the relevance of applying similar or a limited range of criteria for evaluating the performance of different forms of organizing service delivery. In particular, salient outcomes for involved stakeholders in collaborative approaches (e.g. service development) are likely to differ from salient outcomes in more conventional approaches (e.g. cost savings).

*Fifth*, our findings and discussions suggest that the leading edge in contracting practices in England has evolved into a set of post-NPM models, which are still developing. Findings from our survey showed that features from post-NPM models are relatively more common in England than in Scandinavia. The case studies also highlighted the country differences between leading-edge experiences with contracting, showing the English case as far more radical and wide-ranging in how a collaborative logic can be implemented. In perspective, the status of the UK context as a vanguard (Hood and Dixon 2015) or benchmark (Barzelay 2001) for public management reforms is indicated to be less about conventional forms of marketization associated with the features of core-NPM models of marketization, than it is about understanding and evaluating features and outcomes from the implementation of post-NPM models. In relation to the longer experiences and the different policy arrangements in England and the broader context of the UK compared to Scandinavia, it may be relevant to discuss to what degree the three Scandinavian countries can all learn from the experiences derived in England. Blurring these discussions, however, are the policy responses to severe austerity, which has hit the public sector, and in particular local governments in England, in the 2010s. Austerity has in some cases changed the policy agenda from seeking improvements of public service delivery in terms of costs and quality to far more radical measures such as down-sizing and outright service shedding. On reflection, these developments are also indicative of the limitations and ineffectiveness of the core-NPM models as a means to political and administrative ends for local governments facing more drastic circumstances, such as those emerging in times of severe austerity.

## References


Abbott, J. (2017, November 29). How Will Newcastle Benefit by Establishing a Parks Trust? *Horticulture Week*. www.hortweek.com/will-newcastle-benefit-establishing-parks-trust/parks-and-gardens/article/1451608. Accessed November 2018.

Andrews, R., & Entwistle, T. (2015). Public-Private Partnerships, Management Capacity and Public Service Efficiency. *Policy and Politics, 43*(2), 273–290.

Barzelay, M. (2001). *The New Public Management: Improving Research and Policy Dialogue*. Berkeley: University of California Press.

Bel, G., Hebdon, R., & Warner, M. (2007). Local Government Reform: Privatisation and Its Alternatives. *Local Government Studies, 33*(4), 507–515.

Boyne, G. A. (1998). *Public Choice and Local Government: A Comparative Analysis of the UK and the USA*. Basingstoke: Macmillan.

Brown, T. L., & Potoski, M. (2003). Contract-Management Capacity in Municipal and County Governments. *Public Administration Review, 63*(2), 153–164.

Buijs, A., Hansen, R., Van der Jagt, S., Ambrose-Oji, B., Elands, B., Lorance Rall, E., et al. (2018). Mosaic Governance for Urban Green Infrastructure: Upscaling Active Citizenship from a Local Government Perspective. *Urban Forestry and Urban Greening, 40,* 53–62.

Christensen, T., & Lægreid, P. (2007). *Transcending New Public Management: The Transformation of Public Sector Reforms*. Burlington: Ashgate.

Cosgrove, S. (2018). Heritage Lottery Fund and National Trust Launch £10m Parks Innovation Fund. *Horticulture Week, 22*(October).

Davis, H., & Walker, B. (1998). Trust and Competition: Blue-Collar Services in Local Government. In A. Coulson (Ed.), *Trust and Contracts: Relationships in Local Government, Health and Public Services* (pp. 159–182). Bristol: Policy Press.

Dehoog, R. (1990). Competition, Negotiation, or Cooperation: Three Models for Service Contracting. *Administration and Society, 22*(3), 317–340.

Dempsey, N., Smith, H., & Burton, M. (2014). *Place-Keeping: Open Space Management in Practice.* London: Routledge.

Donahue, J. D., & Zeckhauser, R. J. (2011). *Collaborative Governance Private Roles for Public Goals in Turbulent Times.* Princeton: Princeton University Press.

Entwistle, T., & Martin, S. (2005). From Competition to Collaboration in Public Service Delivery: A New Agenda for Research. *Public Administration, 83*(1), 233–242.

Hefetz, A., & Warner, M. E. (2004). Privatization and Its Reverse: Explaining the Dynamics of the Government Contracting Process. *Journal of Public Administration Research and Theory, 14*(2), 171–190.

HLF. (2018, July 19). *National Lottery Cash Revives Run-Down UK Parks* (Press release). Heritage Lottery Fund. www.hlf.org.uk/about-us/media-centre/press-releases/national-lottery-cash-revives-run-down-uk-parks. Accessed November 2018.

Hodge, G. A., Greve, C., & Boardman, A. E. (2012). *International Handbook on Public-Private Partnerships.* Cheltenham: Edward Edgar.

Hood, C., & Dixon, R. (2015). *A Government That Worked Better and Cost Less? Evaluating Three Decades of Reform and Change in UK Central Government.* Oxford: Oxford University Press.

Jones, R. (2000). Managing the Green Spaces: Problems of Maintaining Quality in a Local Government Service Department. *Managing Service Quality, 10*(1), 19–31.

Kettl, D. F. (1993). *Sharing Power: Public Governance and Private Markets.* Washington, DC: Brookings Institution.

Kuipers, B. S., Higgs, M., Kickert, W., Tummers, L., Grandia, J., & Van, D. V. (2014). The Management of Change in Public Organizations: A Literature Review. *Public Administration, 92*(1), 1–20.

Leiren, M. D., Lindholst, A. C., Ingjerd, S., & Randrup, T. B. (2016). Capability versus Efficiency: Contracting Out Park and Road Services in Norway. *International Journal of Public Sector Management, 29*(5), 474–487.

Lindholst, A. C. (2008). Improving Contract Design and Management for Urban Green-Space Maintenance Through Action Research. *Urban Forestry and Urban Greening, 7*(2), 77–91.

Lindholst, A. C. (2017). A Review of the Outcomes from Contracting Out Urban Green Space Maintenance: What We Know, Don't Know and Should Know. *Urban Forestry and Urban Greening, 27*(October), 50–58.

Sullivan, H., & Skelcher, C. (2002). *Working Across Boundaries: Collaboration in Public Services.* Basingstoke: Palgrave.

Vincent-Jones, P. (2007). The New Public Contracting: Public Versus Private Ordering? *Indiana Journal of Global Legal Studies, 14*(2), 259–278.

Vining, A. R., & Weimer, D. L. (1990). Government Supply and Government Production Failure: A Framework Based on Contestability. *Journal of Public Policy, 10*(1), 1–22.

Voorn, B., van Genugten, M. L., & van Thiel, S. (2017). The Efficiency and Effectiveness of Municipally Owned Corporations: A Systematic Review. *Local Government Studies, 43*(5), 820–841.

Walker, B., & Davis, H. (1999). Perspectives on Contractual Relationships and the Move to Best Value in Local Authorities. In G. A. Boyne (Ed.), *Managing Local Services: From CCT to Best Value* (pp. 16–37). London: Frank Cass.

Weick, K. E., & Quinn, R. E. (1999). Organizational Change and Development. *Annual Review of Psychology, 50*(1), 361–386.

Wollmann, H., & Marcou, G. (Eds.). (2010). *The Provision of Public Services in Europe Between State, Local Government and Market*. Cheltenham: Edward Elgar.

# PART IV

# Conclusions and Outlook

CHAPTER 16

# Histories and Futures of Marketization

*Morten Balle Hansen,*
*Andrej Christian Lindholst and Carsten Greve*

## Introduction

> *... there is ample evidence from many studies of public administration, that context can make a huge difference ... Conceptually identical, or at least similar, reforms develop differently in one national (or sectoral or local) context as compared with another.* (Pollitt and Bouckaert 2017: 46)

Marketization—the use of competition and free choice in public service delivery—has been a predominant element in public management reforms since the 1980s. Its significance and meaning has however varied between countries (Hansen and Lauridsen 2004; Pollitt and Bouckaert

M. B. Hansen (✉) · A. C. Lindholst
Department of Politics and Society, Aalborg University, Aalborg, Denmark
e-mail: mbh@dps.aau.dk

A. C. Lindholst
e-mail: acl@dps.aau.dk

C. Greve
Department of Organization, Copenhagen Business School, Frederiksberg, Denmark
e-mail: cagr.ioa@cbs.dk



A. C. Lindholst and M. B. Hansen (eds.),
*Marketization in Local Government*,
https://doi.org/10.1007/978-3-030-32478-0_16

2017) as well as between different sectors and local governments within a country (Boyne 1998; Hansen 2011). Marketization was an important part of the New Public Management (NPM) movement (Hood 1991), and was—especially in Anglo-Saxon versions—associated with privatization and the downsizing of the state. But marketization was also seen as a way to modernize the public sector and make the delivery of public services more efficient. This 'Neo-Weberian State' approach (Pollitt and Bouckaert 2017—see Chapter 2) has been the predominant interpretation of marketization in the Scandinavian context where the downsizing of public sector activities never had the same scope as in England.

In this book, we have analyzed the theory and practice of marketization from the late 1970s to the late 2010s of public services as it has evolved in two local services—park and road maintenance—in England and in the three Scandinavian countries: Denmark, Sweden and Norway. Our approach has been comparative and historical. While England, along with other Anglo-Saxon countries, has been described as a front-runner of NPM practices (Christensen and Lægreid 2007; Dunleavy et al. 2006; Hood and Peters 2004), the three Scandinavian countries in our comparative study tend to be portrayed as reluctant reformers less prone to NPM (Christensen and Lægreid 2001; Greve et al. 2016; Olsen 1996; Olsen and Peters 1996). Thus, we expected England to show different reform trajectories than the three Scandinavian countries.

Empirically, our focus has been on two local public services—park and road services—but theoretically, we used these two services as cases to analyze marketization more broadly as one of the most influential reform strategies in Public Administration (PA) in recent decades.

One of the basic notions of our book, as outlined in Chapters 1 and 2, has been that the phenomena of marketization and privatization is likely to have changed substantially since the first wave of NPM reforms in the 1980s and 1990s. We envisioned that more or less pragmatic processes of problem-solving and evolutionary learning in many countries gradually had resulted in revised and perhaps improved models of marketization and privatization (Ansell 2011). One of our aims has been to examine how far and in what ways newer reform developments and adaptations in local contexts have replaced, altered or supplemented the now classical marketization models from the early NPM era (Knudsen and Rothstein 1994; Pollitt and Bouckaert 2011; Premfors 1998).

The book questioned whether we could rely on conventional ideas and models of marketization established in the heydays of NPM reforms in the 1980s and 1990s or whether we should revise these ideas and models in concordance with more recent developments in reform and practice. In Chapter 1, we suggested that the key principles of the NPM version of marketization consist of a combined move toward respectively (1) a strategic focus on economic objectives, (2) structural devolution and specialization of responsibilities, and (3) market-based coordination of activities. We furthermore highlighted a range of newer developments in reform and practice, which increasingly have challenged marketization.

In Chapter 2 we elaborated a Public Administration perspective in which the rationale for marketization is about using competition and choice to enhance performance[1] in the delivery of public services (see Chapter 2). Marketization often involves privatization—the transfer of activities from the public to the private sector—but competition mechanisms can also be enhanced within the public sector through various organizational arrangements such as contracting, vouchers and free choice and benchmarking (Hansen and Lindholst 2016—see also Chapter 2). The classical argument (or intervention theory—see Chapter 2) supporting marketization was that all organizations, in order to encourage progress, avoid deterioration and enhance learning and innovation, need one type of signals when they improve performance and another type of signals when they worsen performance and that marketization can deliver such signals. Previous research indicates that some types of marketization especially in the first decades did deliver cheaper services—at least to some extent in some contexts (Hodge 2000; Savas 2000)—but also that a number of other unanticipated consequences—positive or negative—evolved (Christensen and Lægreid 2002; Dunleavy et al. 2006; Froud et al. 2017; Hood and Peters 2004; Lindholst et al. 2018).

In the public sector in a liberal democracy, the traditional way to provide signals from citizens concerning good and bad performance is through free debate and elections—the voice mechanism in Hirschman's conceptualization (Hirschman 1970—see Chapter 2). If people are dissatisfied with public services they can raise criticism and through free elections vote for another local or national government. Marketization

[1]We use the performance concept as an abstraction that in practice may refer to various types of performance measures (e.g. lower costs and/or higher quality, quantity or productivity in the delivery of public services) (Boyne 2003; Hansen 2017; Lindholst et al. 2018). What counts as performance can sometimes be complex, paradoxical and subject to political conflict.

provides competition as another mechanism to enhance signals of improving or deteriorating performance. Various organizational arrangements can enhance competition (see Chapter 2) and in the public services analyzed here—local park and road services—the predominant model, especially in the 1980s and 1990s, has been to organize competition through contracting out and benchmark between in-house and private providers as shown in previous chapters.

In Chapter 1, we formulated two research questions—one descriptive and one interpretive:

*RQ1*: Are contemporary models of marketization in local service delivery in the 2010s (a) similar or dissimilar to earlier models found in the NPM reform wave from the 1980s and 1990s, and (b) are marketization in local service delivery converging or diverging across national contexts?

*RQ2*: How can we understand the observed patterns of divergence and/or convergence in the historical development of marketization in local service delivery across different national contexts?

In this final chapter, we first briefly review the basic research design of the book and thus the basis of our knowledge claims. Second, we review our main findings in relation to the two research questions presented above. Third, we discuss the future of marketization and provide a brief conclusion.

## Characteristics of the Research Project and the Generated Knowledge

This book is one outcome from the INOPS project—an international co-financed research project carried out in a collaboration between researchers from four countries with expertise within respectively local park and road services and public management reforms. In Chapter 3, we described the project background and the overall mixed methods research design (Feilzer 2010; Hendren et al. 2018; Small 2011), methods and data sources underpinning the book.

The book's empirical foundation which consists of primary data, collected through national surveys (2015–2016), research interviews and document analysis (2015–2016), and secondary data originating from earlier studies and register-based sources from the UK, Denmark, Sweden,

Norway and OECD. These data have been analyzed in Chapters 4–15. In Chapter 4, we used register-based sources from primarily OECD to outline basic similarities and differences relevant to marketization between our four countries. In Part II of the book, Chapters 5–8 presented analyses of marketization and its implementation in local park and road services since the 1980s in each of our four countries. These analyses where based on survey data from each country as well as secondary data and previous published research. Chapters 9 and 10 provided direct country comparisons on the organization and performance of marketization based on statistical analysis of cross-sectional data.

In the book's Part III, Chapters 11–14 provided four detailed case studies—one case study from each country—on how local governments have implemented and developed marketization. The case studies also added an interpretive layer to the statistical analysis by exemplifying unique characteristics of the marketization within local park and road services in each country. In Chapter 15, we summarized and discussed the case studies main findings and wider theoretical importance.

In the sections below, we provide a review of our main findings as they relate to our two major research questions.

## Review of the Main Findings

We organize our review of the book's main findings in relation to the two research questions from Chapter 1 and presented in the introduction to this chapter. Throughout this section we use our ideal-typical stage-model distinction between pre-NPM, core-NPM and post-NPM models of marketization (see Table 2.2 from Chapter 2) as a reference point to compare to our findings.

*Pre-NPM* was the predominant model before the 1980s. In the internal organization of public service provision it was characterized by Weberian style rule-based hierarchical command and control procedures and professional expertise. The contracting models if private providers was present was rather informal and the purpose of private provider involvement was primarily to complement public service provision by delivering highly specialized services/equipment and/or to ensure provision of services that the public sector was not able to deliver.

*Core-NPM* was the most trendsetting and predominant model in the 1980s and 1990s. In the internal organization of public service provision it was characterized by highly formalized purchaser-provider split models and devolution of responsibilities. The contracting model was formal often compulsory competitive tendering regimes with a predominant performance focus on simple conventional short-term cost-savings, exposure to price competition and 'corporate-like' features of public providers. In this model, the role of private providers is to compete on price and quality (and in mixed delivery systems competition between public and private providers) to enhance more cost-efficient solutions.

*Post-NPM* has since the 2000s been the most trendsetting model in the international discourse on public management reforms (Reiter and Klenk 2019). In marketization Post-NPM the internal organization of public service production is also characterized by formalized structures and but has a broader and more long term performance orientation. The contracting model is more focused on the longterm and competition concerns long-term collaboration rather than short-term cost-savings. As in pre-NPM the predominant function of private providers is to complement the competences of the public sector.

### *RQ1: Models of Marketization in England and the Scandinavian Countries*

Before comparing the countries three overall findings from Chapter 10 should be emphasized.

First, marketization has certainly increased substantially in all four countries, but despite four decades with marketization on the global agenda in-house provision has been remarkably resilient and is (still) dominating the mix of provider types in all four countries—even in England.

Second, important differences in marketization exist between our two public services and especially in the Scandinavian context we find a substantially stronger marketization in road maintenance than in park maintenance.

Third, we found significant variations in marketization between the four countries on most dimensions indicating the significance of national context and below we examine the most important country differences.

Contemporary marketization of local park and road services in *England* is characterized by the widespread implementation of post-NPM models while features from core-NPM models are less prominent. Municipalities in England, for example, use relatively complex partnership-based contracts and a more diverse mix of provider types is involved.

These characteristics are particularly notable in comparisons with the three Scandinavian countries who are much less prone to post-NPM practices. The case study in Chapter 11 told us about what the content and purpose in these post-NPM models can be. Thus, practitioners and researchers interested in post-NPM models for organizing park and road services should go to England. Some traits from core-NPM models, however, are still evident among municipalities in England. Notably, the single-most important purpose for involving private providers in England was found to be the achievement of low costs.

For *Sweden*, we learned that contemporary marketization within municipal park and road services is predominantly characterized by core-NPM models mixed with some features from pre-NPM and post-NPM models. This heterogeneity is related to the huge demographic and geographical differences between the Swedish municipalities (see Chapter 4). Core-NPM and a few post-NPM practices has been influential in the densely populated municipalities, while pre-NPM practices tend to be more influential in sparsely populated localities. In comparison with England relatively conventional and simple formal contracts are used when contracting with the private sector but the emphasis on competition and benchmarking is relatively low in comparison with Denmark.

For *Denmark*, we learned that contemporary marketization within municipal park and road services is strongly characterized by features from core-NPM models mixed with a few features from post-NPM models. Denmark stands out in the comparisons with England and the two other Scandinavian countries as the country where core-NPM models for internal and external marketization have the strongest impact on contemporary marketization. In perspective, Denmark can be argued to represent a contemporary benchmark country in how far core-NPM models for marketization is implemented. In the Danish variant of core-NPM models, provision is characterized by mixed public–private delivery and a strong orientation toward direct competition among providers with emphasis on low costs and benchmarking. Still, we also learned that some post-NPM features such as a more collaborative approach, are gaining ground in the contracting models used for provision of local park and road services. Contracts are in some cases getting somewhat more longterm and with a performance focus broader than simple cost-savings. The case study in Chapter 13 indicated how this approach has evolved in Denmark.

For *Norway*, we learned that contemporary marketization within municipal park and road services are characterized by a mix of features from pre-NPM and core-NPM models. The impact from core-NPM models on contemporary marketization on internal service delivery is the weakest in Scandinavia. A few features however of core-NPM models are widely implemented by the municipalities in Norway but still not to the same extent as Sweden and Denmark. Highly surprising, however, was that some features of core-NPM models are more common in Norway than in England. This is in particular evident for the internal municipal organization of service delivery. If core-NPM models are the yardstick for evaluating the degree of marketization, then Norway roughly equals, if not surpassing, England (but not the two neighboring countries in Scandinavia). However, as noted, England appears to have moved on toward post-NPM models and Norway shows relatively few features, if any, from these models. In perspective, we find that Norway in our comparisons can still be regarded as a reluctant reformer with regard to implementation of core- and post-NPM models. Overall, marketization in Norway has predominantly taken place internally with adoption of features from core-NPM models in combination with a widespread use of features resembling pre-NPM models for external marketization. As in Sweden, pre-NPM practices tend to be most influential in the more sparsely populated localities.

*Commonalities in Scandinavia?*

The Scandinavian countries are often regarded as a relatively homogeneous country group in terms of the organization of their public sectors and societies more generally. The findings in Chapter 10 show us that what Scandinavian countries have the most in common—and which define them as different from England—is a relatively widespread implementation of features from core-NPM models for internal marketization of in-house provision within two different systems of mixed public–private delivery. Norwegian municipalities appear to implement mixed delivery based on a logic of complementary competencies where Danish and to a lesser extent Swedish municipalities approach mixed delivery through a logic of competition.

A mid-range implementation of core-NPM models mixed with some post- and pre-NPM features characterize Sweden. A widespread and strong implementation of core-NPM models for internal and external marketization is typical for Denmark and the country may be regarded as a leading NPM reformer within local park and road services. Norway is characterized by implementation of some features from core-NPM models, particularly for internal marketization, in combination with features from pre-NPM models for external marketization. Sub-variants of some marketization models were also found across the countries; for example two systems for organizing mixed delivery, one based on direct forms for competition (Denmark and partly Sweden) and one based on complementary competencies (Norway and partly Sweden), were evident in Scandinavia.

In perspective, what has emerged among municipalities in Scandinavia after four decades of marketization is a reformed organization of service delivery integrating marketization models in different ways. The role of the private sector is—through different strategies for involvement and as an ideal for organizing—still critical for the overall system by providing both legitimacy to and spurring efficiency of in-house providers. If the Scandinavian countries are differentiated, Denmark represents the 'purest' core-NPM manifestation of this system in the shape of the most radical competition-based system. In this sense, Denmark represents the core-NPM-model. Norway, on the other hand, represents a variation with mixed pre-NPM and core-NPM model features where the internal organization is reformed and based on a competence-based division of labor between the public and private sector. Sweden takes up what can be regarded a middle position between Denmark and Norway.

### *Summing up Main Findings*

The findings discussed above may be summarized as follows:

- *Resilience of in-house provision*: While marketization has increased substantially in all four countries in-house provision has been remarkably resilient
- *Importance of public service*: Marketization varies significantly between the public services of park- and road maintenance and especially in the Scandinavian context road maintenance is significantly more marketized
- *Country comparisons*: Marketization varies significantly between the four countries and the main differences may be summarized through the distinction between pre-, core- and post-NPM practices

- *England as the frontrunner of Post-NPM practices*: Perhaps the most striking and surprising finding is that after four decades of NPM reforms our findings no more lend support to a story-line of *England* as a frontrunner of core-NPM practices—at least not in the two local services analyzed here. Widespread implementation of post-NPM models for internal and external marketization characterize many of the English municipalities. In that sense England may represent a new vanguard position in terms of various types of post-NPM practices to be learned from.
- *Denmark as frontrunner of Core-NPM practices*: In the park and road services analyzed here core-NPM practices tend to be strongest in the Danish context, but also in a number of Swedish municipalities. The majority of Danish municipalities has gradually expanded the core-NPM model, while pre- and post-NPM practices are rare. Especially the model with competition between both public and private providers has been influential in Denmark. Within this model a trend towards less focus on short term cost savings and more focus on long term strategic development may be evolving as indicated by the Danish case study (see Chapter 13).
- *Norway as frontrunner of Pre-NPM practices*: In the park and road services pre-NPM practices tend to be strongest in Norwegian local government, but also in a number of Swedish municipalities—especially in municipalities characterized by vast areas and a sparse population. Here private providers complement public provision and competition is low. Elements of NPM has however entered in the internal organization of public services.

The distinction between pre- core- and post-NPM should not necessarily be understood as suggestive of progress or higher performance as indicated in Chapter 9. It is perfectly possible that the modernized pre-NPM practices we found in many Norwegian municipalities provides a better organizational solution to public service provision in that context as we discuss below.

### *RQ2: Possible Reasons for Variations in Marketization—A Discussion*

The differences in marketization trajectories and contemporary practices found in previous chapters and briefly reviewed above sustains the relevance of discussions about how to understand and explain these differences. We will pursue that discussion briefly through different theoretical perspectives. Our analytical approach to these perspectives are complementary and contrasting rather than prioritizing (Roness 2009). We treat them as perspectives that adds nuances to our understanding of the observed variations.

*Institutional interpretations*: Institutional perspectives deliver a useful conceptual framework for understanding the broad trends we have observed through conceptual lenses like cognitive frames and path-dependency. In both economic, sociological and historical versions of institutional theory (Hall and Taylor 1996; Peters 2019), marketization represent a new governance system enhancing various types of rule-systems to support the use of market-type mechanisms in the public sector. Sociological institutionalism emphasize how marketization has been theorized as a highly legitimate governance structure in the global world culture (Meyer et al. 1997; Scott 2014). This helps understand the trend toward marketization in most countries including those analyzed here. Economic institutionalism and the economic theories introduced in Chapter 2 suggest that marketization often will enhance more efficient delivery of public services and helps understand some of the difficulties in accomplishing that. While sociological institutionalism emphasizes global processes enhancing the diffusion of marketization, historical institutionalism emphasizes the importance of national and local traditions and path-dependencies (Mahoney and Thelen 2010). Thus, due to processes of national and local adaptation and translation, we expected the different versions of public sector marketization that we found in the four countries we analyzed in this book.

*Pragmatism, problem solving and learning*: In a problem solving pragmatic learning perspective which has been the primary perspective of this book (Ansell 2011; Levinthal and March 1993; Levitt and March 1988) marketization is seen as an attempt to solve problems of public service provision and as processes of learning derived from often paradoxical and ambiguous experience with marketization solutions (Hood and Peters 2004). The perspective suggest a story by and large in concordance with our four case studies (see Chapter 11–15) as well as the four national trajectories analyzed in Chapter 5–8. Attempts to practice contracting out versions of marketization has been practiced in all four countries and has faced various kinds of difficulties. Especially in England many municipalities have moved on to post-NPM models after decades of core-NPM practice, which may be interpreted as an outcome of learning processes supported by changed national reform approaches. Interestingly reforms supporting marketization in England have developed from highly compulsory regimes based on core-NPM models toward more pragmatic reforms based on higher degrees of local adaption and autonomy in the implementation. Thus, the exact forms for contemporary marketization at the local level are not the requirement of national policies and regulations. In comparison, national reforms in Scandinavia have not boosted post-NPM models for marketization to the same degree as found in England. In Denmark core-NPM marketization was slowly introduced and has gradually been strengthened and according to the findings of Chapter 9 tend to covary with higher performance in terms of better cost-efficiency in the Danish context. In Norway and to some extent Sweden core-NPM practices has been tried out but have been somewhat less successful than in Denmark (see Chapter 9). Thus modernized pre-NPM practices tend to be the preferred solution in many especially small rural municipalities.

*Leaders, laggards and the meaning of marketization*: Historically the public administration literature has often told the marketization story as a version of the hare and the turtle tale (Dunleavy et al. 2006; Hood 1991) and our observations by and large confirm that story. England has been described as historically belonging to a country group of early adopting and leading NPM reform countries emphasizing 'minimization' and 'marketization' rather than 'modernization' strategies. In comparison to England, the Scandinavian countries have historically belonged to a group of later-adopting or 'reluctant' reform countries which have emphasized 'modernization' rather than 'marketization' or 'minimization' strategies for reform of the state apparatus (Pollitt and Bouckaert 2017). Overall, we learned from Chapter 4 that England and the three Scandinavian countries exhibits fundamental differences in ideological outlook, policy orientation toward the welfare state, national political systems, economic history (e.g. timing of financial crisis) and the possibilities for national governments to pursue reform in local governments. Thus, our findings indicate that marketization tend to be given different meanings in the English and the Scandinavian context. For example, we learned in Chapter 10 that different mix of purposes drives contracting out across our four countries. Research needs to take these variations in context and approach into account. 'Contracting out is not just contracting out' (such as private and public production)—several models are in play and comparing performance would require us to pay attention to the characteristics of the different models. In a Scandinavian reform-to-preserve approach (Hirschman 1991) marketization tend to be seen in a Neo-Weberian state perspective as a means to strengthen the public sector by making it more efficient. In an English neoliberal reform-to-downsize approach marketization tends to be seen as a means to roll the state back. Thus marketization serves different strategies for public management reform (Pollitt and Bouckaert 2017: 28).

*Formal structure, geography and demography*: One plausible interpretation of the observed variations is to take context serious and elaborate on some structural characteristics of the four countries that may be understood as path-dependencies influencing the usefulness of marketization. While the three Scandinavian countries are similar on a number of dimensions and in contrast to Englands liberal market economy may be characterized as coordinated market economies (Hall and Soskice 2001; Hall 2015) with a neo-weberian type of state administration (Pollitt and Bouckaert 2017) they are very different on dimensions that seems crucial to marketization in local government. On average Danish municipalities are economically larger and more densely populated than Norwegian and Swedish municipalities while they have a smaller geographical area to serve (see Chapter 4). Perhaps especially for the types of services analyzed here, this seems important to the usefulness of marketization and part of the reason why core-NPM practices tend to work better in Denmark than in Norway and parts of Sweden (see Chapter 9). In order to make contracting out work well you need several competitors willing to compete for a contract. In the geographically vast and thinly populated municipalities of Norway and parts of Sweden the main problem to solve often is to find a contractor willing to do the job—not to make competition work. A more general version of our argument is the hypothesis that marketization tend to work better in densely populated metropolitan areas than in sparsely populated rural areas.

*Task characteristics*: Taking context serious also means to reflect on differences between public services. Park and road maintenance has historically had some characteristics crucial to their marketization potential. Comparing to a classical economic typology, as discussed in Chapter 2, they have characteristics closer to a public good than to a private good. Thus competition between providers can relatively easy be organized through contracting out, while competition through free choice for users is difficult if not impossible to organize. Due to these characteristics various versions of contracting out has been the basic marketization model in all our four countries, while the quasi-market model has been absent (see Chapter 2 for an elaboration of these models). They are also physical services using space and land which indicate that factors such as distance and land characteristics are important contextual factors. Thus, our argument that marketization tend to work better in densely populated metropolitan areas than in sparsely populated rural areas may be especially relevant to this type of services.

*Alternative theoretical lenses—policy bubles and power*: Our primary theoretical lense on marketization has been a pragmatic organizational learning perspective combined with institutional perspectives and we believe it has worked well. But there are of course other perspectives on marketization that may enrich our understanding. Marketization reorganize and change social relations within and around the public sector and these changes are likely to have a number of anticipated and unanticipated consequences. Forinstance the concept of policy bubles suggest a different interpretation of marketization (Jones et al. 2014) somewhat resembling the fashion perspective (Abrahamson 1996) of sociological institutionalism (Meyer et al. 1997). In this perspective declining performance as a consequence of marketization is more likely. The power perspective has also been largely absent from our analysis but marketization has many consequences and one of them is to redistribute the relative power of different groups of actors (Froud et al. 2017; Hansen 2010). Future research should also pursue such alternative perspectives on marketization in order to enhance understanding of the many possible outcomes of marketization (Lindholst et al. 2018).

## Conclusion and Reflections on the Future of Marketization

The evolution and contemporary practice of marketization from the early 1980s to the late 2010s was analyzed for local park and road services in England and three Scandinavian countries. Contracting out has been the predominant model of marketization for these two public services, but has changed substantially with important variations in how it is practiced. While privatization through increased use of private contractors has increased significantly, in-house provision has been remarkably resilient in all four countries. Significant differences in marketization between the two services where found indicating the importance of task characteristics and policy area to the scope and content of marketization. In terms of country comparisons England was the front-runner of core-NPM in the early decades, but many English municipalities have moved on to post-NPM practices in the late 2010s. Contemporary core-NPM practices with a mixed delivery system of competition between public and private providers was found to most predominant in Denmark. Pre-NPM practices where strongest in Norway, while Sweden represent the most within country variation with both pre-, core- and post-NPM practices in use. As a broad interpretive frame for understanding main trends, the theoretical lenses of institutionalism and pragmatic learning has been useful, but other approaches should also be considered in future research. The contextual variables of formal structure, geography and demography seems especially useful for understanding within country variation. For the public services analyzed here marketization tend to work better in densely populated metropolitan areas than in sparsely populated rural areas.

*The future of marketization*: Our analysis begs reflections concerning the future of marketization. Such questions can be approached by means of the three concepts of ***extrapolation, anticipation*** and/or ***imagination*** (Klausen 2014), but we delimit our discussion to a few reflections based on the former two: (a) If we extrapolate the trends we have documented in the analyses of this book, how would the most likely future of public sector marketization look like? (b) If we anticipate the future through the lenses of institutionalism and pragmatic learning how would the most likely futures of public sector marketization look like? If one basically see Anglo-Saxon countries as front-runners of a global world culture one may extrapolate the English trend toward post-NPM practices through public–private partnerships and various other types of partnership arrangements (Greve and Hodge 2013). In such a perspective competition is transformed from simple price competition to a competition for long-term partnerships. If England is a front-runner we would expect such post-NPM trends to be strengthened also in the Scandinavian countries. From a path-dependency and pracmatic learning perspective however, we would expect more variation due to different contextual preconditions. We would expect to see a mix of modernized pre-, core- and post-NPM practices and in that perspective, the huge within country variation of Sweden may represent the most likely future. Briefly including imagination and taking a long-term perspective we may envision a different future with technology and climate changes requiring entirely different models of organizing than marketization. So far however, marketization has been remarkably resilient and has become institutionalized as a basic part of the organizing toolbox of public administration.

## References


Abrahamson, E. (1996). Management Fashion. *Academy of Management Review, 21*(1), 254–285.

Ansell, C. (2011). *Pragmatist Democracy: Evolutionary Learning as Public Philosophy*. New York: Oxford University Press.

Boyne, G. A. (1998). *Public Choice Theory and Local Government: A Comparative Analysis of the UK and the USA*. Basingstoke: Macmillan.

Boyne, G. A. (2003). What Is Public Service Improvement? *Public Administration, 81*(2), 211–227.

Christensen, T., & Lægreid, P. (Eds.). (2001). *New Public Management: The Transformation of Ideas and Practice*. Aldershot: Ashgate.

Christensen, T., & Lægreid, P. (2002). New Public Management: Puzzles of Democracy and the Influence of Citizens. *Journal of Political Philosophy, 10*(3), 267–295.

Christensen, T., & Lægreid, P. (Eds.). (2007). *Transcending New Public Management: The Transformation of Public Sector Reforms*. Aldershot: Ashgate.

Dunleavy, P., Margetts, H., Bastow, S., & Tinkler, J. (2006). New Public Management Is Dead—Long Live Digital-Era Governance. *Journal of Public Administration Research and Theory, 16*(3), 467–494.

Feilzer, M. Y. (2010). Doing Mixed Methods Research Pragmatically: Implications for the Rediscovery of Pragmatism as a Research Paradigm. *Journal of Mixed Methods Research, 4*(1), 6–16. https://doi.org/10.1177/1558689809349691.

Froud, J., Johal, S., Moran, M., & Williams, K. (2017). Outsourcing the State: New Sources of Elite Power. *Theory, Culture & Society, 34*(5–6), 77–101.

Greve, C., & Hodge, G. (2013). *Rethinking Public-Private Partnerships: Strategies for Turbulent Times*. London: Routledge.

Greve, C., Lægreid, P., & Rykkja, L. H. (2016). The Nordic Model Revisited: Active Reformers and High Performing Public Administrations. In C. Greve, P. Lægreid, & L. H. Rykkja (Eds.), *Nordic Administrative Reforms: Lessons for Public Management* (pp. 189–212). London: Palgrave Macmillan.

Hall, P. A. (2015). Varieties of Capitalism. In *Emerging Trends in the Social and Behavioral Sciences: An Interdisciplinary, Searchable, and Linkable Resource*. Hoboken, NJ: Wiley.

Hall, P. A., & Soskice, D. (2001). An Introduction to Varieties of Capitalism. In P. A. Hall & D. Soskice (Eds.), *Varieties of Capitalism* (pp. 1–68). Oxford: Oxford University Press.

Hall, P. A., & Taylor, R. C. R. (1996). Political Science and the Three New Institutionalisms. *Political Studies, 44*(5), 936–957.

Hansen, M. B. (2010). Privatisering, Demokrati Og Magt I De Danske Kommuner. *Politica, 42*(2), 183–201.

Hansen, M. B. (2011). Antecedents of Organizational Innovation: The Diffusion of New Public Management into Danish Local Government. *Public Administration, 89*(2), 285–306. https://doi.org/10.1111/j.1467-9299.2010.01855.x.

Hansen, M. B. (2017). Performance Management and Evaluation. In B. Greve (Ed.), *Handbook of Social Policy Evaluation*. London: Edward Elgar.

Hansen, M. B., & Lauridsen, J. (2004). The Institutional Context of Market Ideology: A Comparative Analysis of the Values and Perceptions of Local Government CEOs in 14 OECD Countries. *Public Administration, 82*(2), 491–524.

Hansen, M. B., & Lindholst, A. C. (2016). Marketization Revisited. *International Journal of Public Sector Management, 29*(5), 398–408.

Hendren, K., Luo, Q. E., & Pandey, S. K. (2018). The State of Mixed Methods Research in Public Administration and Public Policy. *Public Administration Review, 78*(6), 904–916. https://doi.org/10.1111/puar.12981.

Hirschman, A. O. (1970). *Exit, Voice, and Loyalty: Responses to Decline in Firms, Organizations, and States*. Cambridge, MA: Harvard University Press.

Hirschman, A. O. (1991). *The Rhetoric of Reaction: Perversity, Futitlity, Jeopardy*. Cambridge: The Belknap Press of Harvard Press.

Hodge, G. (2000). *Privatization: An International Review of Performance*. Boulder: Westview Press.

Hood, C. (1991). A Public Management for All Seasons. *Public Administration, 69*(1), 3–19.

Hood, C., & Peters, B. G. (2004). The Middle Aging of New Public Management: Into the Age of Paradox? *Journal of Public Administration Research and Theory, 14*(3), 267–282.

Jones, B. D., Thomas, H. F., III, & Wolfe, M. (2014). Policy Bubbles. *Policy Studies Journal, 42*(1), 146–171.

Klausen, K. K. (2014). *Strategisk Ledelse I Det Offentlige: Fremskrive, Forudse, Forestille*. København: Gyldendal.

Knudsen, T., & Rothstein, B. (1994). State-Building in Scandinavia. *Comparative Politics, 26*(2), 203–220.

Levinthal, D. A., & March, J. G. (1993). The Myopia of Learning. *Strategic Management Journal, 14*, 95–112.

Levitt, B., & March, J. G. (1988). Organizational Learning. *Annual Review of Sociology, 14*, 319–340.

Lindholst, A. C., Hansen, M. B., Randrup, T. B., Persson, B., & Kristoffersson, A. (2018). The Many Outcomes from Contracting Out: The Voice of Public Managers. *Environment and Planning C-Politics and Space, 36*(6), 1046–1067. https://doi.org/10.1177/2399654417733992.

Mahoney, J., & Thelen, K. (2010). A Theory of Gradual Institutional Change. In J. Mahoney & K. Thelen (Eds.), *Explaining Institutional Change: Ambiguity, Agency, and Power* (pp. 1–37). Cambridge: Cambridge University Press.
Meyer, J. W., Boli, J., Thomas, G. M., & Ramirez, F. O. (1997). World Society and the Nation-State. *American Journal of Sociology, 103*(1), 144–181.
Olsen, J. P. (1996). Norway: Slow Learner or Another Triumpf of the Tortoise? In J. P. Olsen & B. G. Peters (Eds.), *Lessons from Experience: Experimental Reforms in Eight Democracies.* Oslo: Scandinavian University Press.
Olsen, J. P., & Peters, B. G. (1996). *Lessons from Experience: Experimental Reforms in Eight Democracies.* Oslo: Scandinavian University Press.
Peters, B. G. (2019). *Institutional Theory in Political Science: The New Institutionalism.* Cheltenham, UK: Edward Elgar.
Pollitt, C., & Bouckaert, G. (2011). *Public Management Reform: Comparative Analysis of New Public Management, Governance and the Neo-Weberian State.* Oxford: Oxford University Press.
Pollitt, C., & Bouckaert, G. (2017). *Public Management Reform: A Comparative Analysis—Into the Age of Austerity.* Oxford: Oxford University Press.
Premfors, R. (1998). Reshaping the Democratic State: Swedish Experience in a Comparative Perspective. *Public Administration, 76*(1), 141–159.
Reiter, R., & Klenk, T. (2019). The Manifold Meanings of 'Post-New Public Management'—A Systematic Literature Review. *International Review of Administrative Sciences, 85*(1), 11–27.
Roness, P. G. (2009). Handling Theoretical Diversity on Agency Autonomy. In *Change and Continuity in Public Sector Organizations: Essays in Honour of Per Lægreid* (pp. 45–62). Bergen: Fagbokforlaget.
Savas, E. S. (2000). *Privatization and Public-Private Partnerships.* New York: Chatham House.
Scott, W. R. (2014). *Institutions and Organizations: Ideas, Interests, and Identities.* Los Angeles: Sage.
Small, M. L. (2011). How to Conduct a Mixed Methods Study: Recent Trends in a Rapidly Growing Literature. *Annual Review of Sociology, 37,* 57–86.

# Appendix

This appendix reports a set of statistical tests on the representativeness of the INOPS survey data for England, Sweden, Denmark and Norway. Results from the tests are summarized in a non-technical language in Chapter 4. Tests for representativeness according to municipal size in terms of population size and area size are included for all four countries. Tests for representativeness according to regional distribution are included for the three Scandinavian countries. In Denmark, a test for representativeness according to differences in the share of budgets spend on private provisions is also included. Finally, the proportions of the national populations represented by municipalities with survey data are also calculated. Two main statistical tests are applied. A more restrictive Welch's *t*-test, where statistics for groups with survey data are compared to groups without survey data, and a less restrictive one sample *t*-test, where statistics for groups with survey data are compared to statistics for all cases in the sample frame. In addition, chi-test is applied for categorial data. Results from the *t*-tests with a $p$-level $\leq .1$ are used as ultimate criterion for evaluating whether the samples are representative for the sample frames.



A. C. Lindholst and M. B. Hansen (eds.),
*Marketization in Local Government*,
https://doi.org/10.1007/978-3-030-32478-0

## England

The final dataset for England included data for organization of parks and/or roads services for altogether 103 out of a total of 326—equal to 31.6% of—lower-tier local authorities in England. Fifty-nine local authorities provided specific data for the organisation of road maintenance and all 103 local authorities provided specific data for the organisation of park maintenance. The local authorities in the dataset represent approximately 41% of the English population equal to 21,478,000 out of 53,013,000 inhabitants (2011 figures).

The statistical test (one sample *t*-test) for differences between identifiable local authorities included cases in the dataset and all English local authorities (the sample frame) revealed a significant statistical difference for population size ($p = .03$). The average population of English local authorities included in the dataset is 213,000 where the average population for all English local authorities is 166,615 (2014 figures).

The average area size for those in the sample is 493 $km^2$ while the average size for all 326 local authorities is 400 $km^2$. The statistical test (one sample *t*-test) shows that the difference in average size between English local authorities in the sample and all local authorities is statistically insignificant ($p = .392$).

Overall, the results indicate that the dataset is fairly representative for English local authorities in terms of area but tends to represent local authorities with slightly larger population sizes.

## Sweden

For Sweden, the final dataset included data for organization of parks and/or roads services in altogether 115 out of a total of 290 Swedish municipalities—a number equal to approximately 40% of all Swedish municipalities. One hundred and five municipalities provided specific data for the organisation of road maintenance and 98 municipalities provided specific data for the organisation of park maintenance. The 115 municipalities in the dataset furthermore represent approximately 53% of the Swedish population equal to 5,195,000 out of 9,730,000 inhabitants (2014 figures).

A statistical test (Welch's *t*-test) of the difference in average municipal population for Swedish cases with survey data ($M = 45{,}176$, $SD = 99{,}802$) and without survey ($M = 25{,}913$, $SD = 35{,}982$)

found the mean difference (=19,263) to be statistical significant, $t(133.668)=3.947$, $p=.049$. The less restrictive one-sample $t$-test comparing the mean population for cases with available survey data with the average population for all Swedish municipalities ($N=290$, $M=33{,}552$, $SD=69{,}265$) found the difference to be insignificant, $t(114)=1.249$, $p=.214$.

The statistical test of the difference in average municipal areal ($km^2$) for Swedish cases with survey data ($M=1580$, $SD=2044$) and without survey data ($M=1981$, $SD=3230$) found the mean difference (=401) to be statistical insignificant, Welch's $t$-test, $t(287.650)=1.678$, $p=.169$.

The statistical test (chi-test) for differences between the included cases in the dataset and all cases in the target revealed no significant statistical differences regarding geographical distribution across the Northern, Southern and Eastern regions in Sweden ($\chi^2=1.709$, $p=.425$).

Given the acceptable representation of municipalities in the final dataset (39.7%) and the computed non-bias toward municipal population, areal and geographical distribution, our dataset should provide a fairly representative dataset for Swedish municipalities.

## Denmark

The final dataset for Denmark included data for organization of parks and/or roads services in altogether 75 out of a total of 98 Danish municipalities—a number equal to 76.5% of all Danish municipalities. Seventy-three municipalities provided specific data for the organisation of road maintenance and 73 municipalities provided specific data for the organisation of park maintenance. Approximately 4,605,000 inhabitants out of a total population of 5,640,000 equal to approximately 82% (2014 figures) live in the 75 municipalities represented in the survey.

A chi-test testing bias in geographical distribution across the five major geographic and administrative regions in Denmark (North Jutland, South Denmark, Mid Jutland, Zealand and The Capital) showed no significant statistical difference between observed and expected number of cases within each category ($\chi^2=2.133$, $p=.711$). The statistical test (Welch's) of the difference in average municipal population for Danish cases with survey data ($M=61{,}400$, $SD=73{,}683$) and without survey data ($M=44{,}984$, $SD=40{,}321$) found the mean difference (=16,416) to be statistical insignificant, $t(68.709)=1.883$, $p=.174$). The statistical test (Welch's) of the difference in average municipal area ($km^2$) for cases with survey data (*M*=458, SD=369) and without survey data (*M*=371, SD=383) found the mean difference to be statistical insignificant, *t*(35.451)=.919, *p*=.344).

Additional and country specific *t*-tests (Welch's) based on available register data (2014 figures) for differences between the average share of maintenance budgets spend on private purchases within parks and roads found the difference between municipalities with and without survey data to be insignificant for parks (*t*=2.048, *p*=.161) and significant for roads (*t*=3.533, *p*=.065). A less restrictive one-sample *t*-test for roads comparing the group of municipalities with survey data (*N*=75, *M*=48%) with all Danish municipalities (*N*=98, *M*=46%) found that this difference was insignificant (*t*=.666, *p*=.508).

Given the acceptable representation of municipalities in the final dataset (76.5%) and the estimated non-biases for municipal population, area, geographical distribution and average use of private contractors the survey data is found to provide a representative dataset for all Danish municipalities.

## Norway

The final dataset included data for organization of parks and/or roads services in altogether 96 out of a total of 428 Norwegian municipalities equal to 22.4% of all Norwegian municipalities. Eighty-two municipalities provided specific data for road maintenance and 74 municipalities provided specific data for park maintenance. Approximately 2,590,000 inhabitants out of a total population of 5,170,000 equal to approximately 50% of all Norwegians (2014 figures) live in the 96 municipalities represented in the survey.

A statistical test of the difference in average municipal population for cases with survey data (*M*=26,992, SD=72,752) and without survey data (*M*=7735, SD=14,218) found the mean difference (=19,257) to be statistical significant, Welch's *t*-test, *t*(97.100)=6653, *p*=.011. A less restrictive one-sample *t*-test comparing the mean population for cases with available survey data with the average population for all Norwegian municipalities (*M*=12,044) also found a significant difference, *t*(95)=2013, *p*=.045. A subsequent *t*-test (Welch's) for the difference in the group of 114 Norwegian municipalities with populations larger than 10,000 between the subset of 51 cases with survey data ($M$=46,503, SD=96,031) and the 63 cases without survey data ($M$=26,093, SD=25,249) found the difference (=20 410) to be statistically insignificant, $t(55.612)=2.182$, $p=.145$.

A statistical test (chi-test) for differences in the representation in the dataset of municipalities across geographical distribution across the five main administrative regions in Norway found statistically significant differences. Statistics for chi-test of difference between expected and observed cases in the regional distribution were $\chi^2=20.144$, $p=.001$. In particular the Eastern and Southern regions were found to be represented to a higher degree than Western and Northern regions. An alternative test based on Norwegian municipalities with populations larger than 10,000 ($N$=114) found no statistical differences ($\chi^2=3.063$, $p=.547$) in the regional distribution between municipalities with and without survey data.

Finally, a $t$-test (Welch's) for differences in the municipal areal (km$^2$) between municipalities with survey data ($M$=609, SD=723) and without survey data ($M$=797, SD=939) found the mean difference (=188) to be significant, $t(196.722)=4.349$, $p=.038$. By limiting the test to municipalities with populations larger than 10,000 inhabitants the difference in areal between municipalities with survey data ($M$=501, SD=675) and without survey data (M=618, SD=808) was found to be insignificant, $t(111.883)=.705$, $p=.403$.

Overall, the dataset tend to represents Norwegian municipalities with larger populations but smaller areas located in Eastern Norway (Østlandet) and Southern Norway (Sørlandet) rather than Northern and Western Norway. When limited to municipalities with more than 10,000 inhabitants the differences in representation are found to become statistically insignificant. The dataset furthermore represents municipal park and road services for approximately 50% of the Norwegian population. Overall, statistical findings for Norway based on the survey data need to be qualified against the relatively low overall response rate and the statistically significant biases in representativeness for population, area and regional distribution.

# Index





A. C. Lindholst and M. B. Hansen (eds.), *Marketization in Local Government*, https://doi.org/10.1007/978-3-030-32478-0